BEYOND CONQUEST

AMY E. DEN OUDEN

# Beyond Conquest

## *Native Peoples and the Struggle for History in New England*

University of Nebraska Press

Lincoln and London

 Manufactured in the United States of America ♾
Set in Quadraat types by Bob Reitz.
Book designed by Richard Eckersley.

Portions of chapter four previously appeared as "Recovering Gendered Political Histories: Local Struggles and Native Women's Resistance in Colonial Southern New England" by Trudie Lamb Richmond and Amy E. Den Ouden, in *Reinterpreting New England Indians and the Colonial Experience*, ed. Colin G. Calloway and Neal Salisbury (Boston: Colonial Society of Massachusetts, 2003).

*Library of Congress Cataloging-in-Publication Data*
Den Ouden, Amy E.
Beyond conquest: Native peoples and the struggle for history in New England / Amy E. Den Ouden. p. cm. – (Fourth world rising)
Includes bibliographical references and index.
ISBN-13: 978-0-8032-1725-6 (cloth: alk. paper)
ISBN-10: 0-8032-1725-0 (cloth: alk. paper)
ISBN-13: 978-0-8032-6658-2 (pbk.: alk. paper)
ISBN-10: 0-8032-6658-8 (pbk.: alk. paper) [etc.]
1. Indians of North America – Connecticut – Historiography. 2. Indians, Treatment of – Connecticut – History. 3. Indians of North America – Land tenure – Connecticut. 4. Local history – Connecticut. 5. Connecticut – Historiography. 6. Connecticut – Politics and government. I. Title. II. Series.
E78.C7D46 2005 974.6'01 – dc22 2005014567

For Alton Smith Sr., *who had wisdom and shared it, and all the other elders and ancestors of* the Native nations of Connecticut;

For my *great-grandmother,* Eugenie Bourgeois, born in Memramcook, New Brunswick, in 1870; *and*

For my son, Liam, *who is all about* possibility

# CONTENTS

# ILLUSTRATIONS

# Series Editors' Introduction

*Beyond Conquest* is the fifth volume in Fourth World Rising, a series of contemporary ethnographies from the University of Nebraska Press. The series focuses on contemporary issues, including class, gender, religion, and politics: in sum, it addresses social and cultural differentiation among and between Native peoples as they confront those around them and each other in struggles for better lives, better futures, and better visions of their own pasts. This focus thus represents a departure from many of the monographs produced by anthropologists about Native peoples, which often have sought to reproduce either visions of ways of life now long past or else pasts refracted through current idealization. In the process, traditional anthropology has helped enshrine a backward-looking focus to Native culture that has, at times, been influential in the way laws are framed and even in how Native peoples come to see their own identity.

Ideas, especially when enshrined in law and lent the authority of governments, have power. And the idea that Native cultures and societies are historical artifacts rather than ongoing projects has served to narrow the politics of Native identity or indigenism worldwide. One purpose of this series is to change this focus and broaden the conception of Native struggle to match its current complexity.

This is especially important now, for the last two decades have provided prominent examples of Native peoples seeking to recast the public – and, ultimately, political – basis of their Native identity in ways other than the reproduction of often fanciful, even fictional, pasts. Our hope is that by offering a variety of texts focused on these and other contemporary issues, structured for classroom use and a general audience, we can help change the public perception of Native struggle – allowing people to see that Native cultures and societies are very much ongoing (and, to a surprising extent, on their own terms) and that the issues they confront carry important practical and theoretical implications for a more general understanding of cultural and political processes.

The primary geographical and topical emphasis of the Fourth World Rising series is the Native peoples of the Americas, but the series also includes comparative cases from Australia, Africa, Asia, the circumpolar Arctic and sub-Arctic, and the Pacific Islands. Yet beyond its unique topical and contemporary focus, four critical theoretical and political features distinguish the series as well:

1. A focus on the struggles Native peoples must fight, with the dominant society and with each other, whether they wish to or not, in order to survive as peoples, as communities, and as individuals, as well as the struggles they choose to fight.

2. A consideration of how the intensifying inequalities within and between Native communities – emerging from social, cultural, and economic differences among Native peoples – create unavoidable antagonisms, so that there cannot be any simple lines of cleavage between a dominant, oppressive, and exploitative state on the one side and its long-suffering victims on the other. Thus the series pays particular attention to gender, identity, religion, age, and class divisions among Native peoples, along with differences in the goals and strategies that emerge from these struggles.

An emphasis on internal differences and tensions among Native peoples is not at all intended to let the dominant states and societies off the hook for their policies and practices. Rather, this perspective calls to the foreground how internal complexities and divisions among Native peoples and communities shape their struggles within and against the larger societies in which they find themselves. Indeed, it is precisely these internal differences among and between Native peoples (and how these differences unfold over time and through Native peoples' complex relations to one another) that give Native people their own history and their own social processes that are, ultimately, partly separate from the history imposed upon them by the dominant society.

3. An emphasis on the praxis of Native struggles: what works, and why, and with what intended and unintended effects; who benefits within Native communities and who loses what, and why. The series monographs are thus not advocacy tracts in the conventional sense of that term, though they are undeniably political constructs. Rather, the emphasis on contemporary social processes and the political praxis of participants, advocates, and anthropologists serves as a stimulus for dialogue and debate about the changing pressures and possibilities for

particular Native societies and the political situations confronting Native peoples more generally.

4. An attempt to clarify the situation facing those whose concerns and fundamentally decent impulses lead them to want to help the victims of domination and exploitation. Such honorable commitments need to be developed in the midst of realizing that the radiant innocence of an earlier applied anthropology, and of many aid programs, along with the social world that sustained this innocence, has crumbled. It is no longer possible to say or to think "*we* will help *them*." Now we must ask who is helped and who is hurt both by the success and by the frequent failure of aid programs, and why, and how.

The primary audience for this series is students in college courses in anthropology, political science, Native and ethnic studies, economics, and sociology. Yet the series achieves its importance among a college and popular audience by being developed for a second audience as well. One of the major purposes of this series is to present case studies of Native peoples' current struggles that have broader strategic relevance to those engaged in similar or complementary struggles and to advocates whose concerns lie more directly along the lines of what has worked in the past or in other areas, what has not, and with what consequences.

Hence this volume becomes part of a new way of both doing and teaching anthropology and Native studies. On one level the case studies seek to bring together activists, Native peoples, and academics, not simply by dramatizing the immediacy of Native struggles but also by dispelling the notion that Native societies derive their Nativeness from being internally homogeneous and externally timeless. On a second level the series as a whole helps those currently teaching Native studies to pursue an engaged, contemporary perspective and a broad geographic approach – allowing for and in fact encouraging a global, contemporary Native studies that is deeply rooted both in a fundamental caring for Native peoples' well-being and in the realities of internal differentiation among Native peoples.

*Kirk Dombrowski    Gerald Sider*

# Acknowledgments

For their patience, generosity, and wisdom, I would like to thank the elders who have been important mentors and most gracious friends to me since this project began, especially Alton Smith Sr., Chief Hockeo, Trudie Lamb Richmond, Mary Sebastian, Betty Jackson Fletcher, and Chief Big Eagle. It is in their honor, and with deep respect and gratitude for what they have fought for, that I devote the proceeds from this book to the Native American Rights Fund.

Initial research for this book was funded by a 1996 Smithsonian Predoctoral Fellowship Award and by a grant from the Philips Native American Fund of the American Philosophical Society. As a part of my work for the Golden Hill Paugussett and Eastern Pequot federal acknowledgment projects throughout the 1990s, I conducted ethnographic and documentary research as well as oral history interviews. I was always welcomed with warmth and honesty by the members of these Native nations, and through both informal and formal discussions with Eastern Pequot and Paugussett people over the past decade, and more recently with members of the Mashpee Wampanoag nation, I have learned a great deal more about the twentieth-century history of southern New England's Native peoples and the complexity of their struggles for justice than I can properly convey. Through their tireless generosity, and in the stories and anecdotes of their own and their ancestors' lives that they have candidly shared, I have learned something of the depth of the tolerance and wisdom that lies at the core of their shared historical experience. I am forever in their debt, and wish especially to thank Kathy Sebastian, Darlene Hamlin, Mark Sebastian, Marcia Flowers, Lillian Sebastian and Idabelle Sebastian Jordan, Anne Foxx, John Peters, Jr., Dr. Louis Randall, Burne Stanley Peters, Bobby Sebastian, and Ron Wolf Jackson. A graduate assistantship in the Institute for African American Studies at the University of Connecticut was immensely helpful to me as I conducted research in the early stages of this project. For their support and friendship, I wish to thank Professor Ronald Taylor, then the institute's director, and Rose

Lovelace, the institute's administrator. As I began my research and writing for this book, I was fortunate to have been encouraged and guided by scholars for whom I have long held great respect, especially Professors James Faris, Bernard Magubane, Hugh Hamill, Irene Silverblatt, Francoise Dussart, and Robert Bee. I wish also to extend special thanks to Professor Kevin McBride, who may remember that it is now over a dozen years ago that we sat with Chief Hockeo of the Eastern Pequot Nation in the aging trailer – then the Tribal Office – on the Eastern Pequot reservation in North Stonington, Connecticut, to discuss research for the Eastern Pequot federal acknowledgment project. It was at that moment that I was first struck with the historical power of reservation land, and thus it is that moment that most accurately marks the launching of this project. I also extend my most sincere thanks to Paul Grant-Costa, a longtime friend and co-researcher. His transcriptions of documents from the Connecticut Archives collection known as the "Indian Papers" were an invaluable resource.

Professor Gerald Sider, whose *Lumbee Indian Histories* remains a crucial source of inspiration for my own work, was generous enough to read – on the spot – the manuscript I sent to him several years ago. In fact, no more than three days after I sent it to him, the phone in my kitchen rang. While I had hoped for but never expected such a response, Gerald was on the other end of the line, telling me how much he liked the project and how well he though it would fit into the *Fourth World Rising* series that he and Kirk Dombrowski edit. I am unable to adequately thank them both for believing in this book, for their invaluable advice as editors, and for offering many timely words of encouragement as I worked to complete it. Their close reading of my manuscript and their willingness to share their breadth of knowledge on the subject of colonialism and its impact on indigenous peoples helped me to refine my analyses significantly. Any shortcomings readers may discern here are of course my own.

As I completed the final revisions of this manuscript, I had the support of many wonderful colleagues and friends whose keen intellectual insights, many kindnesses, and abiding sense of humor sustained me. So I wish then to extend my most heartfelt gratitude to Rogaia Abu Sharaf, Ana Aparicio, Tracy Brown, Penny DeFrino, Anne Foxx, Sherry Horton, Steve Silliman, Heather Trigg, and Darlene Hull.

I cannot fully express my love and appreciation for my parents, Irene and Timothy Driscoll, and for my brothers, George and Tim. Finally, my deepest love and dedication goes to my most precious son Liam, who, from the time he was barely a two-year-old, took a genuine and persistent interest in his mother's work as he sat and played on the floor of what he called my "work-done-room." Even then, he began to ask thoughtful questions about the copies of historical documents strewn about us, and about the lives of the people into which those documents offer glimpses. Thank you, Liam, for your love, but also for always revealing the importance of listening and openness to understanding.

# 1

# Dilemmas of Conquest

## *Recovering Histories of Struggle*

In September of 1736 Mohegans held a ceremony on their reserved land to name a new leader. This land, where perhaps three hundred or more Mohegans were known to "dwell and plant" (Connecticut Archives, "Indians" [hereafter IND], 1st ser., vol. 1:122), was engulfed by the town of New London and was the remaining fragment of what had been a much larger reservation, long known to Connecticut officials as the "sequestered lands" (1:89) or the "Mohegan fields" (1:122).[1] Three decades prior to this leadership ceremony, Mohegans initiated what became a lengthy and complex legal dispute with the colony of Connecticut in an effort to protect their reserved planting and hunting lands. In 1704 Mohegan sachem Owaneco petitioned the English Crown to complain against dispossession at the hands of the Connecticut government; by 1705 an imperial commission determined that the lands in question had been unjustly appropriated and should be restored to Mohegans. In setting this order before the colony, the decision described Mohegans as "*a considerable tribe or people* . . . [who] cannot subsist without their lands" (*Governor and Company of Connecticut, and Mohegan Indians, by their Guardians: Certified Copy of Book of Proceedings before Commissioners of Review*, 1769 [hereafter *Proc.*] 1769:29, emphasis in original).

This notion that the presumably conquered Indians in their midst existed as distinct political entities – as *peoples* who possessed an inherent and enduring right to their reserved lands – was to become a gnarly bone of contention for the Connecticut government.[2] Indeed, in eighteenth-century Connecticut disputes over Native rights to reservation land, and reservation communities' tenacious struggles to preserve these lands, posed a challenge to colonial authority and called into question colonial notions about conquest itself.[3] As Native women and men resisted colonial encroachment on their reserved lands, so too did they argue for the future of their communities and their collective rights to their remaining lands. Their efforts to resist dispossession in the era following the devastation wrought by European disease, the major "Indian Wars" of southern New England, and the extensive expropriation of indigenous lands during the seventeenth century were in no sense a flight of fancy.[4] The eighteenth-century struggles of reservation communities were grounded in and produced by their own knowledge of the past and of the colonial world in which they were enmeshed. This book examines these histories of struggle and the cultural and political facets of colonial relations of domination beyond the period of military conquest.

Native women and men defending their reservations against encroachers and colonial pillaging of their ever-diminishing economic resources well understood the tenuousness of colonial justice. This they made clear in their protests, some of which were articulated in petitions to the Connecticut government requesting its intervention or protection in land disputes. In much rarer instances, Native communities opposing both dispossession and government intrusion into their own political affairs overtly defied colonial authority, as was the case with Mohegan resisters who brought their complaints to the Crown and mounted a public protest in September 1736. The colonial government did not take such defiance lightly, and its responses to Native resistance in this period offer important insight into the cultural and legal machinations of colonial power in the context of nonmilitary (but not necessarily nonviolent) confrontations with indigenous people.

I have begun with the Mohegan leadership ceremony to suggest that Native resistance to conquest – conquest, that is, as an ongoing, multiform process extending beyond the seventeenth-century period of "contact" and "pacification" – was central to the production of local Native histories in the eighteenth century. Moreover, the 1736 ceremony is elicited to begin to demonstrate that the locus of this challenge to colonial domination was reservation land: land that was "set apart" or "sequestered" for a particular Native people or community, and that was acknowledged and ostensibly protected by colonial law. In profound and persistent ways these lands proved not to be wholly conquered terrain. Bound up in eighteenth-century disputes over reservation lands were questions about legal ownership and Native land use, intertwined with competing interpretations of history, Indian identity, and the possible future of Native communities. These disputes embroiled members of reservation communities, encroachers, government officials, colonial "guardians" of reservation land, and missionaries in debates that produced and contested notions of Indianness, conquest, and cultural legitimacy that were to have lasting consequences.

A brief introduction to the legally and culturally contentious matters of the Mohegan case elucidates this point. Connecticut refused to comply with the 1705 decision and did not let pass the suggestion that the Mohegan people constituted something akin to an autonomous or sovereign political entity: in its appeal to the Crown, Connecticut's representative Sir Henry Ashurst asserted that Mohegans were instead "*inconsiderable Indians*" (*Proc.* 1769:153–55). As the eighteenth century and reservation communities' opposition to dispossession wore on, such disparagements came to be no minor point in Native-Anglo disputes over rights to reservation land, and in fact, Connecticut's characterization of Mohegan people in its response to the 1705 decision hinted at the emergence of a colonial Indian policy that would divert attention from the problem of illegal encroachment on reservation lands and focus instead on the presumed cultural and political illegitimacy of reservation communities and particular Native identities.

Indian policy and colonial laws directed at Native populations in eighteenth-century Connecticut recycled and sustained European ideas about Indian "savagery" that had infused colonial relations of domination in the seventeenth century, such as the notion that Indians did not "improve" the land and thus did not have property rights comparable to that of their "civilized" European conquerors. But colonial debates over the legal status of reservations reflected shifting and competing colonial notions about the nature of indigenous land rights, and about Indianness as well. Colonists who sought to claim reserved lands for themselves, and the government officials from whom reservation communities sought redress for encroachment, occasionally asserted conflicting views about the nature of Native rights to reserved lands. In one rather telling instance, town leaders in Groton petitioned the Connecticut General Assembly in an effort to bring an end to the "long controversy" over who held the right to "improve" Mashantucket Pequot reservation land (IND 2nd, 2:109), which was encompassed by the town of Groton at the time. This controversy, they argued, "appears likely to continue and the matter somewhat doubtful, how far said Proprietors [those who controlled the town's "undivided" or "common" lands] have a right in said lands or whether said Indians have any more than a right to the use and improvement of s[ai]d lands according to their ancient manners of improvement of lands and not the absolute fee thereof [i.e., the legal title to the land] – and the courts have judged variously relating thereto" (2:109). Colonial assessments of Natives' agricultural practices and of the value of their labor were thus infused into the legal debate over rights to reservation land. And if colonial legislators did not definitively establish the nature of Natives' land rights or the validity of their "ancient manners," encroachers sometimes resorted to more aggressive means of appropriating reservation land: targeting Indian labor and laying waste to a reservation community's crops – by employing such tactics, for instance, as "cut[ting] our Stoaks [cornstalks]" before the corn was ready for harvesting – was not an uncommon practice among encroachers (IND 1st, 1:227, 1:231; see chapter 5 for further discussion). Mashantucket Pequots reported in 1735 that "wee Shold be Glad if thare Cold be a Stop Put to it the Stoake being our own Labbour wee Shold be Glad to have them for our own use" (1:227).

Although encroachers and colonial officials alike obscured or ignored it in the eighteenth century, the fact remained that the colony of Connecticut had set down a precise definition of Native rights to reservation land in a 1680 law, which stipulated the following: "what land is allotted or set apart for any parcels of Indians within the bownds of any plantation, it shall be recorded to them and the same shall remayn to them and their heirs for ever; and it shall not be in the power of any such Indian or Indians to make any alienation thereof; and whatsoever Englishmen shall purchases any such lands layd out or allotted to the sayd Indians, he shall forfeit treble the value of what he so purchases to the publique treasure, and the bargain shall be voyd and null" (*Public Records of the Colony of Connecticut* [hereafter CR], 3:56–57). The phrase in the 1680 reservation law that was to become most problematic for the Connecticut government in the eighteenth century – "*shall remayn to them and their heirs for ever*" – not only acknowledged Natives' collective rights to their reserved lands but also acknowledged the land rights of the future generations of those "parcells of Indians" possessing reservation lands. This notion that a Native people or community held rights to their reserved land as a *collectivity, in perpetuity* (a notion encoded in this colonial law *after* English military supremacy had been finally established over the Native peoples of southern New England with the culmination of "King Philip's War" in 1676) embodied a key dilemma for colonial authority in the eighteenth century: that the claim of conquest – as the historical and "legal" grounding of colonial legitimacy – was to be mitigated not only by the persistence of indigenous identities in the colonial world but by Natives' own assertions of historical continuity and political autonomy. If military conquest was to have initiated the inevitable disappearance of Indians from the landscape and was thus to have paved the way for ever-expanding, unobstructed colonial "settlement," reservations and the Native communities that continued to live upon and defend them were an historically evocative and legally unsettling presence in the eighteenth-century colonial world.

The documents that recount disputes over reservation land in eighteenth-century New London County indicate that this presence, especially as it was manifested in sometimes overt expressions of Native resistance to colonial authority, was keenly felt by colonial officials and encroachers alike, eliciting, not surprisingly, affirmations of conquest as well as derogations of Indianness and Indian land use. And in the eighteenth century, new tactics of surveillance and control emerged as those who sought to circumvent the 1680 reservation law determined that it was not colonial encroachment that required monitoring, but reservation communities themselves: their size and the numbers of adult men among them, their use of reservation land, and indeed their Indian identity.[5]

During the course of the legal disputes over both the Mohegan and Mashantucket Pequot reservations in eighteenth-century New London County, examined at length in chapters 4 and 5, the 1680 law was evoked by Native complainants and obfuscated by their opponents. In the Mohegan case, for instance, the 1680 law was submitted to confirm the illegality of the colony's appropriation of reserved Mohegan land, and thus it offered a legal counterpoint to Connecticut's claim that all Mohegan lands were ultimately "conquest lands" won via the massacre of Pequots in 1637. The very idea of military conquest, and the presumption that it had erased indigenous land rights as well as indigenous histories, weighed heavily upon reservation communities in eighteenth-century Connecticut. Yet, as Mohegans made clear in September 1736, Native women and men continued to view themselves as agents in, and interpreters of, their own histories.

It was perhaps the audacious claim to both political autonomy and historical relevance that most vexed Connecticut officials contending with Mohegan resisters in 1736. Squelching Mohegan resistance to dispossession during the three decades following the 1705 decision turned out to be a difficult endeavor, and as chapter 4 illustrates, colonial officials and usurpers of reservation land deployed both legal chicanery and conventional colonial strategies of cultural domination (i.e., "civilizing" and "Christianizing") in an effort to "quiet" Mohegans' complaints, as officials would phrase it in that era. The interweaving of these tactics, and the Connecticut government's efforts to undermine and control Mohegan sachems, served to mask the illegality of dispossession. As I explain in chapters 3 through 6, such legal and cultural manipulations were not necessarily subtle discursive maneuvers, nor were they wholly detached from threats of force. Indeed, it was ultimately raw exertions of colonial power, buttressed and legitimized by the language of colonial law and the mission to "civilize," that silenced Native resistance and trampled reservation communities' rights to their lands. In colonial situations power is both veiled and conveyed by discourse; and in the context of Native-Anglo disputes over reservation land in eighteenth-century Connecticut, *colonial* claims to legal and cultural legitimacy continued to depend upon the production and dissemination of politically expedient notions of Indianness.

Tracing the machinations of colonial power during the course of the Mohegan case thus becomes important to our understanding of how new or refined tactics of subjugation – particularly those infused with such malleable cultural meanings – were produced and sustained after colonial military supremacy was established. But eighteenth-century contests over rights to reservation land are also immensely important because they reveal connections between relations of power in the past and those that shape Native struggles in the present, particularly in southern New England, where the practice of interrogating and denying the authenticity of Native identities has been a popular Euro-American response to Native communities' efforts to assert their sovereignty and land rights or narrate their own histories. In Connecticut, Euro-American scrutiny and disparagement of particular Indian identities – commonly expressed in distinctly racialized and racist terms – has been the prevailing response to federal acknowledgment petitions over the last decade and has been an effective means of silencing local Native histories.

The surveillance of Native identities, and the production of specific notions of Indian "illegitimacy," became strategic means of eliding the legal question of Native land rights in eighteenth-century Connecticut. In the 1730s, Connecticut's governor Joseph Talcott sought to control political leadership within the Mohegan reservation community in order to thwart Mohegans' legal case against the colony. Ben Uncas II was to have been the Mohegan sachem of compliance for the colony; but Mohegans themselves had embraced another as their rightful representative: Mahomet II, who had journeyed to England in 1736 with Mohegans' second complaint against Connecticut in hand. Talcott, seeking to undermine Mahomet's leadership, claimed that he was an "impostor," neither a legitimate sachem *nor* a legitimate Mohegan. In an effort to prove this, Talcott dispatched an official to the Mohegan reservation with orders to interrogate Mohegans and extract from them "Evidences of their Discarding of Mahamit the 2" (*Talcott Papers* [hereafter TP], 1:337, 350). The operative, however, informed Talcott in February 1736 that he could gain no such evidence against the rebellious sachem (1:350). Mahomet II, whose mission to England had threatened colonial authority enough that his own identity – as both a sachem *and* a Mohegan – was subjected to what we might refer to today as a smear campaign, died of smallpox in August of that year while still in England.

The testimony of the two colonists present at the September 1736 ceremony indicates that word of Mahomet's death had not yet reached the reservation community. Nonetheless, the account of the event reveals that it was not only their sachem but the broader population of Mohegan people who had become defiant, refusing to yield to the will of the Connecticut government. These were the people who had been described by Talcott's investigator just months before as unworthy of the Crown's attention since they were, he claimed, "not only few but miserable pore [poor]" (TP 1:350). The ceremony's colonial observers, however, offered a contrasting view of Mohegans on September 10, 1736, when, as they reported, "a very great number of Moheagan Indians" gathered "on the Indian land at Moheagan," the "general seat and rendezvous of the said Indians," and announced that "the principal cause of their meeting or dance" was to "establish Anne the daughter of [deceased sachem] Cesar . . . to be their ruler until Mahomet [II] returned" (*Proc.* 1769:235–36). During the ceremony Mohegans also declared their support for Mahomet's endeavor in England and their rejection of Ben Uncas II, who had, it seemed, crumpled to the will of colonial officials and encroachers alike.[6]

As chapter 4 explains in further detail, the September 1736 ceremony was a significant act of political protest, one that chafed at the presumptions of colonial authority. It marks an important moment not only in Mohegan history but in the history of colonial debates over Native land rights in the region. For one thing, both the Mohegan land case and the broader question of Native land rights had become a rather troublesome legal matter for Connecticut. Mohegans had raised the possibility that yet another imperial commission would be assigned to investigate the legality of colonial claims to Mohegan land. Moreover, in eighteenth-century Connecticut there were other struggles over reservation land running concurrently with that waged by Mohegans and posing multiple legal dilemmas for the colony. New London County – which encompassed Connecticut's largest combined population of indigenous peoples as well as the four largest reservations in the colony – was a critical site of Native resistance in the period beyond military conquest.

During the first half of the eighteenth century, Mohegans as well as their neighboring reservation communities in New London County – Mashantucket Pequots at their reservation in Groton, Eastern Pequots in Stonington, and Niantics in Lyme – had submitted petitions to the Connecticut General Assembly that detailed the acts of encroachers, invoked colonial laws established to protect reservation land, and called upon the Connecticut government for justice. In September 1736 these struggles against dispossession converged when Mohegans were joined by Pequot and Niantic supporters "at a general meeting" during which "the whole body of them did renounce Ben Uncas [II]" (*Proc.* 1769:218). Coinciding, then, with the Mohegan leadership ceremony, this concerted act of protest was compelling evidence of the formation of a political alliance among these reservation communities, communities that colonial reservation boundaries were to have rigidly demarcated and contained, but that were nonetheless connected by ties of kinship, as well as a common history of struggle against ongoing processes of conquest.[7] In this instance Mohegans, Pequots, and Niantics openly proclaimed their consciousness of that shared historical experience, and their willingness to act upon it.

In recounting these histories of struggle, I have sought to identify and examine the moments and expressions of dissent that suggest that

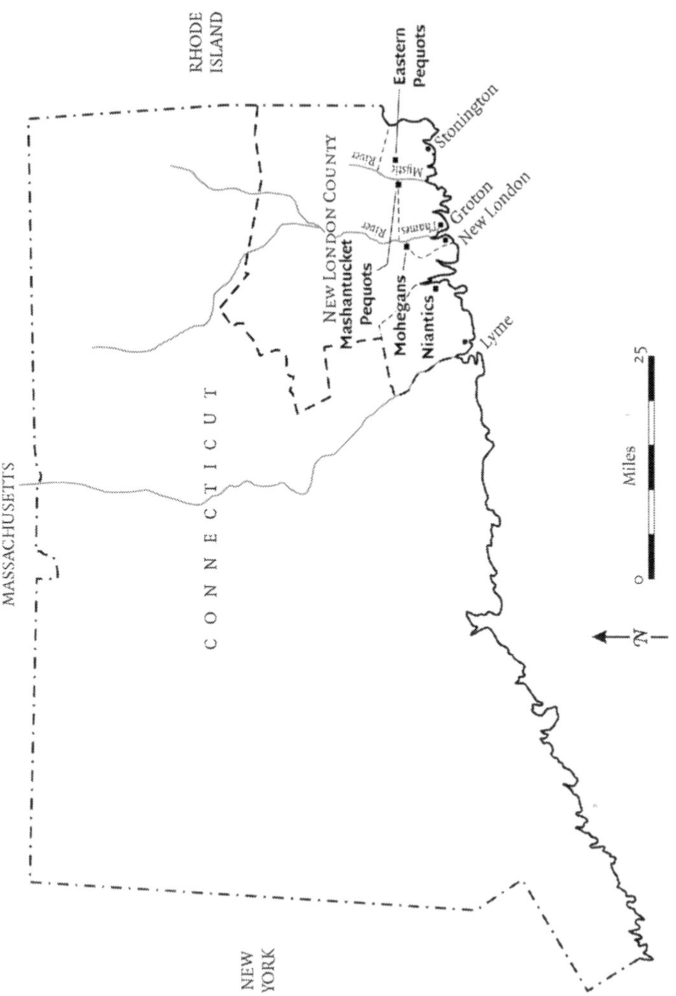


Reservation Communities in New London County, Connecticut, ca. 1700

reservation communities envisioned a past, and a future, that challenged the history dictated by their presumed conquerors. Thus I begin to trace the course of disputes over reservation land and articulations of Native resistance to dispossession in the early eighteenth century, after the fundamental institutions of colonial power – that is, military force and an imposed "rule of law" – were to have precluded the possibility for politically effective or historically significant opposition to colonial domination.

As I argue in chapter 2, colonial discourse played an extremely important role in producing ideas about Indianness that underpinned colonial claims to land and justified dispossession and domination of indigenous peoples long after colonial military supremacy was established in southern New England. In the context of eighteenth-century struggles over reservation land, the evocation of certain constructions of Indianness, particularly those that were forged in colonial narrations of Connecticut's foundational moment of military conquest – the so-called Pequot War – infused colonial assessments of Native land rights. And as chapters 4 and 5 illustrate, "Pequot conquest" was invoked and referenced at crucial junctures during the disputes over both Mohegan and Mashantucket Pequot reservation land. Indeed the idea of "Pequot conquest" took on a renewed significance for colonial authority in the early eighteenth century, serving to justify encroachment on reservation lands and obfuscate Native histories.

## *Narrations of Power and the Cultural Claims of Conquest*

Legitimacy is the central dilemma of conquest, one not to be resolved by military "victories" over indigenous peoples. How it is to be manufactured and normalized is a cultural problem that is intertwined with the material, inherently violent project of imposing and enforcing a system of domination. Conquest must be understood, then, as entailing varied, imbricated material and discursive processes. The process of dispossession that lies at the core of the European and Euro-American geographic conquest of North America has not only entailed physical acts of expropriation. It has also required the construction and naturalization of particular cultural concepts and representations: the concept of land, for instance, as a commodity or as "property"; representations of indigenous peoples as "savages" and obstacles to "civilization" who must be transformed or annihilated; and, no less important, representations of colonial political legitimacy and legality. Colonial ideas about both Indianness and the "right" of conquest (that is, the claimed right to control both the land and its indigenous people) had to be enshrined in law, and by such means these claims were to be elevated to an unimpeachable historical (and cultural) status.[8] Colonial law, like history, is a narration of power, and thus it becomes important to examine how and when constructions of legality, and the cultural forms upon which they depend, were articulated and disseminated in local contexts, where their implementation was of immediate and continuing concern.[9]

Peter Hulme has said that "the particular difficulty associated with the establishment of the European colonies [in America] concerned what might be called the planting of a narrative, the hacking away of enough surrounding 'weeds' to let flourish a narrative field in which the colonists could settle themselves" (1985:23).[10] And as Edward Said has so aptly observed, "the power to narrate, or to block other narratives from forming and emerging, is very important to culture and imperialism, and constitutes one of the main connections between them" (Said 1993:xii–xiii; see also Trouillot 1995:108–40). Narrations of Pequot conquest, the rhetorical power of which relied upon the objectification of Pequots as the supreme nemesis of "civilization," were crucial to the naturalization of colonial domination in seventeenth- and eighteenth-century Connecticut. The conspicuous publication in 1736 of Maj. John Mason's account of the Pequot massacre – announced as a "new book" and used as evidence in the Mohegan land dispute – points to the relationship between narrations of conquest and assertions of colonial legitimacy in the eighteenth century.[11] Moreover, it suggests the peculiar way in which violence could be simultaneously extolled and *distanced* from ongoing processes of conquest. As Mason's account insists, it is the intensity of the violence that was inflicted upon Pequots that reveals their conquest to be not only absolute and final, but also quite out of the hands, so to speak, of English colonists. For in 1637,

> such a dreadful Terror did the ALMIGHTY let fall upon their Spirits, that they would fly from us and run into the very flames, where many of them perished. . . . Thus were [Pequots] now at their Wits End, who not many Hours before exalted themselves in their great Pride,

> threatening and resolving the utter Ruin and Destruction of all the *English*, Exulting and Rejoycing with Songs and Dances: But God was above them . . . making them as a fiery Oven. . . . Thus did the Lord judge among the Heathen, filling the Place with dead Bodies! . . . And thus in *little more than one Hour's space* was their impregnable Fort with themselves utterly destroyed, to the Number of *six* or *seven Hundred*, as some of themselves confessed (cited in *Proc.* 1769:268–69, emphasis in original).[12]

The quintessential claims of Pequot conquest were articulated first in the 1638 Treaty of Hartford, which was not only to have marked the establishment of "peace" in the colony but also to have emblazoned in colonial law the "extinguishment" of Pequots' "national existence" (De-Forest 1852:160). That is, the treaty proclaimed that the Pequot survivors of the 1637 massacre "shall no more be called Pequots," nor were they to "live in the country that was formerly theirs, but now is the English by conquest."[13] The treaty thus made it quite explicit that the official, "legal" erasure of Pequot identity was as important to the process of imposing and securing colonial territory as was the attempt at ridding the landscape of Pequot bodies.

The great irony, of course, is that the subsequent evocation of Pequot identity, as the colonial epitome of savagery, was absolutely essential to the production of a colonial history in which the brute violence of conquest might be transformed into the guileless act of "settlers," whose smiting of the Pequots was, in effect, a good deed.[14] Roger Wolcott's eighteenth-century rendering of conquest is a case in point:

> Posterity will hardly believe this thing, scarcely paralleled in any place or aye upon the globe, that a few men coming into a wilderness full of barbarous Indians, rather as pilgrims than men of power, without the least pretense of right to the land or legal power over their neighbors, should assume to themselves this authority and maintain it and so much good within so long a time. (Wolcott 1895:327)

For Wolcott and his readers, the early colonizers of Connecticut were not to be remembered as "men of power," but only as "pilgrims" who lacked "*the least pretense of right* to the land" (Wolcott 1895:327, emphasis added). This is shrewd phrasing, for it suggests that the assumption of colonial authority (which includes, of course, the construction and implementation of laws that facilitated Native dispossession) is not propelled by, or imposed in the service of, colonial hunger for land and resources. What Wolcott's language suggests is not that these unpretentious pilgrims lack a right to the land they have conquered, but rather that they *lack colonial desires*. There is a distinct political and cultural salience to such a construction of colonial identity – the conqueror who is not a colonizer – in that it both assumes and denies relations of domination. This duality is not a contradiction for colonial narrators of Pequot conquest, but rather an essential condition for colonial legitimacy, since the conquest of Pequots was to be cast as the obligatory (and precedent-setting) pacification of savagery.

The idea that the 1637 massacre of Pequots achieved the pacification of Native people in Connecticut in toto, and thus secured colonial territory and the sanctity of colonial society, remained important to legitimizations of colonial authority in Connecticut long after 1637. And as colonial narrations of Pequot conquest suggest, it was an act that laid the foundation for colonial Indian policy as well as colonial history itself. Just as the Treaty of Hartford enshrined a colonial version of history in a document of law, so too did subsequent narrations of Pequot conquest enmesh claims of legality (the "rights" of conquest) with the construction of historical events.

As the following accounts indicate, Pequot conquest was the crucial initiation of colonial authority in southern New England, a historical "first" that set the cultural and legal precedents allowing for the flourishing of colonial society. When Connecticut faced the possibility that it would lose control over its own militia to the English Crown during the early period of the Anglo-French border wars, the 1693 "Narrative of the Service of Connecticut in the Indian Wars" offered imperial authority an argument that emphasized the historical implications of Connecticut's auspicious conquest of Pequots.[15] The narrative boasts that the "first action between the English & natives in New England that deserves the name of warr was performed by this Colony": this was an action which demonstrated colonial military might as well as Puritan beneficence, for while colonial soldiers "tooke those Nimrods by the throat [and] destroy[ed] them utterly," they had allowed for the survival of "some few as objects of pitty to evidence that clemency had its place in protestants hearts as well as justice" (Hoadly 1932:65). Here, then, is the birth of the colony's Indian policy recounted, its "justice" embedded in simultaneous violence and "clemency" toward the Indian nemesis. The effect of this act of destruction on *other* Native peoples in the region is summarized thus: "This [Pequot] nation was very numerous & the head kingdom so that their vanquishing was in effect the subdueing of the whole. . . . The terror of this action so seized all the natives that for near forty years after [i.e., until King Philip's War in 1675] all New England was in peace" (Hoadly 1932:66).

In the eighteenth century, Connecticut's treatise "Reasons Why the British Colonies in America Should Not Be Charged with Internal Taxes" included a dramatic narration of Pequot conquest and "the Settlement" of Connecticut, which proclaimed that the "first settlers of the colony"

> were forced, for the Defence of their Lives and [their] Settlements, which in a fair and equitable Manner they had made, to enter into a War with the principal Tribe of *Indians* . . . who rose with all their barbarous, insidious, crafty Force and Cruelty to rout these new Settlers out of the Country, as the first Effort of their set and declared Design to break up and prevent the Settlement of *New England*. Against this numerous and powerful Tribe, enraged with jealousy at the *English*, these Planters . . . overthrew, conquered and effectually subdued these their crafty, bloody and inveterate Enemies. And as this was the first *Indian War* in *New England*, and issued so successfully on the Part of the *English*, whose Courage, Force and Conduct in War now became the Dread and Terror of the Natives throughout the Land, it Laid a Foundation for Tranquility in general for almost forty Years after, which gave a most favourable Opportunity for the Settlements in the Country to multiply and increase in Strength and Vigour. (CR 12:663–664, emphasis in original)

This narration repeats the key refrain of the earlier account: that the conquest of Pequots was an act of Indian pacification that extended beyond the realm of the Pequot nation and across four decades. And, as in Wolcott's commemoration of the colony's first "pilgrims," the above rendering of Pequot conquest pits "barbarous, insidious, crafty" Pequots – who alone possess a "declared Design" of destruction – against "these Planters," who, *without* design, "Laid a Foundation for Tranquility in general" and thus allowed "the Settlements in the Country" to prosper. Thus do narrations of Pequot conquest work to transform colonial violence – even in its most extreme expressions – into "pacification," the ultimate duty of those who are divinely destined to convey "civilization."

Such narrations of conquest are meant to render legitimate Native resistance unthinkable and to obscure, or render irrelevant, indigenous accounts of history. Yet, as colonial officials always knew, military conquest obliterated neither Pequots' connection to their ancestral land or the local, kin- and land-based roots of Pequot identity.[16] By April of 1638, less than a year after the massacre, Roger Williams would write to John Winthrop that "the Pequts are gathered into one, and plant their old fields" (Williams 1988:150). By 1675 the colony of Connecticut imposed a specific code of laws upon Pequots and approved Pequot "governors" for the two Pequot communities it now acknowledged (CR 2:256–57; 574–76). More important, however, was the creation of Pequot reservations within their ancestral territory. In 1651 the Connecticut government reserved land at Noank, an area of about five hundred acres on the coast of southeastern Connecticut, for Pequots who are today known as the Mashantucket Pequot Tribal Nation. In 1683 a reservation was created in Stonington for Pequots who are known today as the Eastern Pequot Tribal Nation. The creation of these Pequot reservations was, on the one hand, an important counterpoint to the claims of military conquest, for here was Pequot identity and the existence of Pequot communities, not only acknowledged by colonial authority but inscribed in the colonized landscape. Nevertheless, Pequots' rights to their reserved lands were threatened throughout the eighteenth century, and like other reservation communities, Pequots continued to assert their land rights. In so doing they articulated their own historical knowledge and revealed their understanding of the duplicity of colonial claims to legitimacy.

## Reservations and Resistance

Reservation lands – their local meanings as well as their broader historical significance for analyses of conquest and Native resistance in North America – are a main subject of this book. In eighteenth-century Connecticut, reservation lands were not simply geographical spaces that marked the historical and political reality of conquest. They were the locus of community life for Native peoples, as well as sites of ancestral and ongoing struggle. In a very real sense, then, they were homelands.[17]

Alfonso Ortiz has said that anthropologists have often underestimated "the role a well-established sense of place, of belonging to a space, can play in a people's will to endure" (Ortiz 1994:298).[18] Likewise, archaeologist Russell Handsman and Schaghticoke elder Trudie Lamb Richmond have pointed out that Euro-American assessments of the histories of the Native peoples of New England have tended to overlook the fact that indigenous men and women "consciously decided to continue living in their ancestral homelands" (Handsman and Richmond 1995:103). Members of reservation communities in eighteenth-century Connecticut not only consciously decided to remain on their reservations, as their petitions against dispossession attest, but they also argued for the right of future generations to live on reservation land. This is not to suggest that reservations were sanctuaries, insulating Native communities from an "outside" colonial world.[19] Indeed, reservations were not treated as sanctuaries by colonial legislators or encroachers; nor do reservation communities' protests against dispossession indicate that they envisioned their reservations as sanctuaries any more than they actually experienced them as such. As revealed in both Mohegans' and Mashantucket Pequots' resistance to dispossession throughout the first half of the eighteenth century (see chapters 3, 4, 5), members of reservation communities were realistic rather than romantic in their own assessments of reservation life.

A passage from Sherman Alexie's remarkable novel *Reservation Blues* points to the profound contradictions and complexities of reservation land as cultural, political, and historical space.[20] "The word *gone* echoed all over the reservation. The reservation was gone itself, just a shell of its former self, just a fragment of the whole. But the reservation still possessed power and rage, magic and loss, joys and jealousy. The reservation tugged at the lives of its Indians, stole from them in the middle of the night, watched impassively as the horses and salmon disappeared. But the reservation forgave, too" (Alexie 1995:96). Alexie's words, like the petitions of eighteenth-century reservation communities, urge us to dispense with the notion that the existence of reservations reflects a gesture of "fairness" on the part of colonizing powers or, more preposterously, that they reflect an effort to "protect" Native peoples and their land rights. The fundamental colonial precept of the reservation system was "complete submission and obedience" (Warner 1935:256); and as historian Lion Miles has observed, colonial officials were "fully aware that by concentrating the Indians in one location it could control them more effectively and free more land for English settlement" (Miles 1994:48).[21]

Historian Gary Nash has argued that the 1646 treaty between English colonists in Virginia and members of the Powhatan Confederacy – penned after militarily outmatched Native men mounted an "all out attack" and showed colonizers that "Indians could rarely be cowed into submissiveness" – was significant in that it "drew a line between red and white territory and promised Indians safety in their areas" (Nash 1992:63). Nash contends that this "was the beginning of the modern reservation system, for it recognized that assimilation of the two peoples was unlikely and guaranteed to the indigenous people a sanctuary from white land hunger and aggression" (63). This characterization implies that inherent or "natural" cultural boundaries were "recognized" by colonizers, who thus inevitably transposed those boundaries onto the landscape itself to create such Indian "sanctuaries." But there is nothing inevitable or natural about the creation of the reservation system, and to view it in such a way is to miss the point that the reservation system – as a form of governmental control that was created in the context of colonial struggles – not only demanded continuous policing but also reflected a colonial notion of *historical inevitability* that cast Indianness as "vanishing." Indeed the creation of the reservation system is directly linked to the colonial construction of racial hierarchy, ultimately inscribing it upon the landscape.[22] The "promises" of colonial and Euro-American law worked to legitimize and naturalize notions like "red and white territory": "white territory" being necessarily an ever-expanding, unlimited living space required by a flourishing "civilization," while "red territory" was thus "naturally" constricted and diminishing.

Not incidentally, then, ideas about the naturalness of cultural boundaries or the inevitability of what has been called "culture clash" have served to mask raw colonial power and to obscure the fact that its multiple cultural expressions – such as the reservation system and colonial law itself – sustained relations of domination and justified processes of dispossession. As Vine Deloria Jr. has suggested, the notion that the history of Native-Euro-American relations can be reduced to an inevitable "conflict of cultures" may cloud the history of, and possibilities for, resistance as well: "The white is after Indian lands and resources. He always has been and always will be. For Indians to continue to think of their basic conflict with the white man as cultural is the height of folly. The problem is and always has been the adjustment of the legal relationship between the Indian tribes and the federal government, between the true owners of the land and the usurpers" (Deloria 1969:174).

The relevance of Deloria's statement is not to be underestimated. As I demonstrate in subsequent chapters, in the context of Native-Anglo land disputes in eighteenth-century Connecticut the legal "adjustments" that undermined Native land rights – such as strategic circumventions of previously established laws protecting reservation land – played upon and asserted notions of cultural difference and Indian cultural "illegitimacy." In an important sense, then, culture – and more precisely, an idea of irrevocable cultural otherness and inferiority – serves to obfuscate histories of struggle and deny the validity of resistance.

As historian Colin Calloway has observed, Euro-American historiography has tended to depict English military conquest as marking the end of Native histories (and their political relevance to Euro-American history) and as initiating the cultural degeneration of Indianness: "In American history as a whole, it seems that Indians figure in the story only when they offer violent resistance. Indians are 'the frontier'; once their armed resistance is overcome, once the 'frontier' has passed them by, they no longer seem to count. Many historians and most members of the general public seem to share the not-so-sneaking suspicion that 'real Indians' steadfastly resist European expansion and oppose cultural change. Indians who stop fighting stop being Indians, so why bother with Indian history after King Philip's War?" (Calloway 1996:4).

As Calloway's commentary suggests, there is an important connection between Euro-American notions of Indianness and the obfuscation of Native resistance after the period of military conquest. Euro-American scholars have cast King Philip's War (1675–76) as "the last great stand of the Indians" (Bradshaw 1935:52) and "the last Indian challenge" (Selesky 1990:16) in southern New England. Ethnohistorian Laurie Weinstein has argued that colonists' crushing of this resistance movement, led by the Wampanoag sachem Metacom, resulted in "New England Indians [being] defeated in their efforts to protect their lands from further colonial encroachment"; hence she concludes that "there were no more barriers to colonial settlement of New England" after 1675 (Weinstein 1983:v). Such assessments elide the historical specificity and precise localities of the struggles ensuing within a broad arena of colonial power relations that military conquest served to demarcate and initiate. The historical, political, and cultural implications of military conquest were complex and enduring, as Native-Anglo struggles over rights to reservation land in the eighteenth-century illustrate. The popular Euro-American idea of the military "defeat" of the rhetorically convenient category "the Indian" offers little historical insight but nonetheless has effectively conveyed the notion that conquest obliterated "the Indian's" historical agency.[23]

Nor is Native resistance to colonial domination deemed possible, credible, or politically and historically relevant when colonialism is cast as a "conflict of cultures" that resulted in an ineluctable process of "Indian acculturation." The post-seventeenth-century histories of the Native peoples of southern New England have often been inserted into the timeworn "acculturation model," resulting, for example, in the conclusion that "the years of 1700–1900" can be reduced to a period "of slow and painful acculturation" (Conkey, Boissevain, and Goddard 1978:184). Concerned with identifying what are deemed original cultural "traits" and practices, and with assessing the extent to which Native societies have been able to "adapt" to the presence of purportedly more complex, dynamic European cultures, the idea of acculturation assumes the existence of a pristine "Indian culture" (and a "pure" Indian identity) prior to colonization.[24] The acculturation model thus seeks ultimately to distinguish what it deems authentic cultural forms or traditions from those that have been introduced by Europeans.[25] Such conceptualizations of culture, however, extract it from its actual context of social relations and fail to recognize that cultural practices, and the sociopolitical entities that are called cultures, are always *in process* (see, for instance, Roseberry 1982; Sider 1994; Wolf 1982).[26] As James Clifford has succinctly put it, cultures are always "contested, temporal, and emergent" (Clifford 1986:19).

Cultural forms, like the struggles within which they may be enmeshed at any given moment, have histories. Moreover, in contexts of domination cultural beliefs and practices are politically charged, infused into and shaped by contests over rights and resources. And those who are subjected to colonial power are not merely receptacles of or reactors to colonial cultural forms. As anthropologist Bernard Cohn has explained, systems of colonial control have depended upon the construction and dissemination of knowledge about colonized populations (Cohn 1987: 44–56; see also Cohn 1996:2–15); but those populations that colonizers sought to categorize, objectify, and control became crucial sources of information themselves and as such were "caught up in a complex dialectic" in which they acted "not merely as informants, but frequently as shapers and interpreters" of culture (Cohn 1987:63). Indigenous peoples have sometimes turned colonially imposed ideas against their colonial rulers, as did seventeenth-century Andean men and women, for example, who appropriated the category "Indian" as a means of challenging the gender and class divisions of colonial society in Peru (Silverblatt 1995:279–94). And as attested to in the enduring history of the Maya people of Guatemala, who have been subjected to the most brutal forms of oppression and genocide, local knowledge and historically rooted cultural meanings may be reproduced and sustained under the most abysmal conditions. Indeed, Mayas of Guatemala have responded to devastatingly violent assaults on their land rights and on community solidarity by asserting, sometimes at great risk, that ties to community and locality continue to sustain their cultural identity (Lovell 1988; Sanford 2003). In evoking, manipulating, and contesting cultural categories and meanings – those that are imposed as well as those that are rooted in local histories – peoples subjected to colonial domination produce their own knowledges and struggle to make their own histories "both within and against" the strictures of power (Sider 1994:114–17; see also Sider 1993).[27]

In eighteenth-century Connecticut, Native women and men drew upon the history in which they were immersed, and they evoked and asserted cultural meanings of local significance to argue for their rights to land. Military conquest had not rendered them devoid of historical consciousness or political will. Colonial accounts of the "rumored Indian Plot" of 1669 suggest that historical memory and the lived experience of domination fueled Natives' opposition to dispossession and shaped their relationships to land in an increasingly restrictive colonial world. The rumor held that the "plott on foote" involved "the French and almost all the Indians in the country [i.e., southern New England]" (CR 2:548). Colonists suspected that an attack had been planned "att the last dance at Robin Casynemons" – that is, at Mashantucket Pequots' reservation at Noank, in New London (IND 1st, 1:17) – and that Ninigret, an Eastern Niantic sachem, had initiated this conspiracy and rallied the support of Narragansetts, Pequots, Mohegans, Nipmucks, and Montauks of Long Island (1:17, 23). According to a colonist's testimony in July 1669, the "plot was to bee fully concluded when Ninecrafts [Ninigret's] greate dance was to bee," at the time of harvest "when greene indian corne was ripe anufe to make their breade of" (1:17). Thomas Stanton, a well-known interpreter of local Native languages, warned that Pequots were "verie hie [i.e., haughty] of late and slite all authorietie of the English" (CR 2:549). Testimony regarding one key figure in this supposed "plot" – Mawsamp, who was described as a "man of note" among Pequots (2:549; see also IND 1st, 1:10) – appears to support Stanton's claim about Pequots' defiance: "The boy hee came to Mawsamp in his ffield a weeding & asked him wheather hee woulde plant againe [on] the land[.] hee sayd no: thay now hated the place but when itt was thayers thay loved it as Thayer lives: but they woulde have the land againe and if there was a war the Indians woulde run downe oute of the woods and woulde first knock them [on] the heade with Thayer tumheags and that because they hated them for living on [C]ausattuck Land" (CR 2:549; see also IND 1st, 1:10).[28] What Mawsamp was actually doing at the moment he was questioned is curious, given the colonial rumor about an impending military assault by local Indians. He was brandishing no weapons, but rather was weeding a field that lay within Pequot ancestral territory that had been violently claimed by colonists as conquest lands. Mawsamp's alleged utterance at this moment is equally curious and compelling: if he did indeed declare that he was not preparing the field for planting because Pequots "now hated the place but when itt was thayers they loved it as Thayer lives," the ostensibly mundane act of weeding that field seems to suggest a way of both engaging the past and laying a claim on a possible future. What this testimony appears to have captured is a rare moment during which a "hidden transcript" of resistance (see Scott 1990:4–15) is openly expressed by a member of an oppressed group. As James Scott has explained, such hidden transcripts – or critiques of domination – are "specific to a given social site and to a particular set of actors" (Scott 1990:14). Locally generated, then, and typically expressed only within and among the subordinated group, these hidden critiques may erupt "in the face of power" with potentially disastrous consequences (Scott 1990:4–7). In this instance, however, Mawsamp – whose physical pose at that moment was far from menacing – has articulated an objection to dispossession and a threat of vengeance not in the presence of official representatives of colonial power, but to an Anglo boy, who Mawsamp apparently knew and had likely spoken to before, and to whom he may have sought to convey something of a history lesson. Might Mawsamp have believed that the boy was more likely to hear him out, and to accurately recount his words (to colonial officials) without injecting his own interpretation or cultivated hostilities toward Pequots?

If Mawsamp's behavior was deemed "verie hie" by colonists, problematic as well was the possibility that certain Native leaders who were assumed by colonial officials to regard each other as enemies – primarily Ninigret and Uncas (the Mohegan sachem that the Connecticut government had claimed as an important Indian ally since the time of the Pequot massacre) – were apparently engaged in collaborative anti-colonial strategizing. Thomas Stanton expressed his own astonishment thus: "Ninagrets and Unckas beeing together at the dans at [Pequot leader] Robins town is and was a matter of wonderment to mee [that] thaaye who durst not Looke Each uppon [the] other this 20 yeeres but at the mussell of a Gunn or at the pille of an arrow should now bee so great [friends]" (IND 1st, 1:10; see also CR 2:549).

Stanton's comment suggests that seventeenth-century makers of Indian policy probably understood little of local Native experiences of and responses to the ongoing processes of conquest, or of the nature of the political relationships that were sustained and created between Native communities in Connecticut after English military supremacy had been established in 1637. Seventeenth-century colonial officials may have sought, as one historian put it, to treat "the Indians of Connecticut . . . like so many dogs, [who] were to be set at the throats of each other" (Sylvester 1910:343), but kin ties, which had intertwined members of distinct Native nations in southern New England long before the European invasion, may well have superseded Native leaders' alliances with colonial governments in many matters of local concern to Native communities.[29]

By the time of the 1669 "conspiracy" a shared experience of struggle against dispossession and cultural domination bound members of distinct indigenous communities in ways that seventeenth-century colonists, and twentieth-century researchers, may never grasp. That colonial officials reported only conspiracy in the "great dance" is no surprise: not all forms of resistance, or their significance to those who engage in them, will be visible or meaningful to those in power. As Barry O'Connell has pointed out, the histories of Native people in southern New England "are not only insufficiently or entirely unrecorded – for those in power partly legitimate themselves by not valuing or even noticing those on whose necks their feet rest – but also the modes of cultural survival and invention favored by the powerless are disguised or maintained almost like habit or reflex" (O'Connell 1991:91).

If the "great dance" that Ninigret was to hold in 1669 was to coincide with the ceremony of green corn harvesting, which was generally held in late August or early September (Richmond 1991:13, 1989:24–25; see also Merchant 1989:72–73), then the local meaning of the event would have been grounded in social relations and historical processes that preceded colonial intrusions. For the Native peoples of southern New England, corn had long been the primary crop and a sustainer of life.[30] As Schaghticoke elder and educator Trudie Lamb Richmond has explained, the Green Corn Ceremony marked "the high point of the summer cycle, epitomizing native people's relationship to all living and growing things" (Richmond 1989:25). During the ceremony "prayers were given, special games played, songs and dances performed" (Richmond 1991:13). Ninigret's "great dance," then, was sure to have had far broader significance for the members of the Native communities involved than colonial authorities conceived.[31] For such contexts in which kin and community ties are made apparent and reaffirmed, and in which common experiences are articulated, become sites of cultural production, "contained" or limited as they may be by the conditions of colonial power.[32] The extent to which the "great dance" was politicized – its planning was "conspiracy" for colonial authority but likely an assertion of political autonomy and a gesture of self-determination for the Native participants – emphasizes its historical significance all the more. Thus while Mawsamp's reported vow to "have the land againe" is an overt challenge to colonial power, his laboring upon the land at Caussatuck at that moment, and his simultaneous admission that Pequots "now hate the place" they had once "loved as their lives," point to the importance of locality, and indeed of the continuation of the most routine practices (such as the weeding of planting fields), to resistance and the perpetuation of community life. Moreover, it suggests an understanding, and a forging, of historical continuity that accommodates the disruptions and fractures wrought by conquest.

We can glean from the account of the 1669 "plot" that although struggles over land occurred in a context of knowledge production that was dominated by colonizers, there were articulations of and motivations for resistance that did not readily lend themselves to monitoring and manipulation by colonial officials. In important instances reservation lands provided a space and an impetus for acts of political dissent and critiques of colonial power that directly engaged, and demanded a response from, colonial law.

A case in point is the May 1680 confrontation between local Native leaders and Connecticut officials that resulted in the creation of the colony's first law defining Native rights to reservation land (CR 3:56–57). This event marks the initiation of the prolonged disputes over legal rights to reservation land that ensued in the eighteenth century. At the 1680 meeting, the committee appointed by the General Assembly "for composing differences between the English and Indians" regarding "boundaries of their [i.e., Natives'] lands," heard complaints from Pequot, Niantic, Paugussett, and Mohegan leaders who sought to defend the collective land rights of their respective constituents.[33] The committee's report indicates that Momoho, an Eastern Pequot, reminded the officials that the General Assembly had promised to reserve land "for him and for his people to live and plant on, and say he hath had promiss at Court Twic but it [has] not [been] done" (IND 1st ser., 1:39). The Niantic sachem, as well, asked "that a piece of land may be assigned for him selfe and people" (1:39). In addition, Paugussett sachem Ackenack and Mohegan sachem Uncas requested protection for the lands previously reserved for their communities. Stipulating that reserved lands were to be "recorded to" a "parcel of Indians" and "remayn to them and their heirs forever" (CR 3:56–57), the 1680 law reflects the sachems' concern that collective land rights be preserved. The pronouncements of colonial law and Indian policy are not mirrors of colonial practice, however, and the 1680 law did not ensure governmental protection of reservation lands or the livelihood of reservation communities.

Some might argue that impoverishment and desperation – a sense, perhaps, that there was nothing to lose – propelled reservation communities' resistance to dispossession. For indeed, as attested in both Natives' petitions to the Connecticut General Assembly and colonial officials' reports on disputes over reservation land, life within reservation boundaries during the eighteenth century was arduous and embattled. Corn crops were often destroyed by the wandering livestock of Anglo neighbors; for people who had long depended on harvesting the ocean's resources, being deprived of access to the coast by threat of arrest for trespassing on colonial property, as Mashantucket Pequots noted in a 1713 petition, would have a significant impact on subsistence practices; and colonial encroachers not only disregarded reservation boundaries but also destroyed fences built by reservation communities, helped themselves to the timber on reserved lands, and in some instances subjected the Native proprietors of those lands to threats and acts of violence. In 1749, for instance, colonial officials investigating Eastern Pequots' complaints against encroachers found "that there had been Considerable Timber Cutt" on the Stonington reservation and that the "unruly horses Cattle and Sheep" from Anglo farms bordering the reservation "have Eat up & Destroyed good part of their Corn & beens" (IND lst, 2:44). The officials were also informed that Eastern Pequots had "attempted to fence in some of their land for pasture, but have been beaten off from it and their fence thrown down" (2:44). Such conditions of life induced despair. As a 1728 Niantic petition reports, residents of the town of Lyme had "from time to Time for the space of Twenty Years" allowed their "Cows horsese Swine Sheep & c" to run loose on the reservation, so that Niantics' crops were "wholly destroyed" (1:132). Lamenting that they had "not for the space of tenn years had one Crop of Corn," Niantics had become "discouraged from planting any more since [our] Labour hath proved lost" (1:132).

Mashantucket Pequots' eighteenth-century petitions suggest that the agricultural labor that was invested in their diminishing lands but frequently lost to the scavenging of colonial encroachers and their livestock had a distinct historical and cultural significance. Agricultural labor entailed an engagement between a living community and the landscape that drew upon local knowledge, and evoked the presence of ancestors. Thus Mashantucket Pequot sachem Robin Cassacinamon II proclaimed in a May 1721 petition that the land at Mashantucket is "where our Predicessors anciently dwelt, And Improved, by Planting both Corn & orchards; & our orchards are of great worth & value to us by reason our Grandfathers & fathers Planted them & the Apples are a great relief to us" (IND 1st, 1:95). The labor expended by Native communities on reservation land sustained life, meager though that sustenance often was because of the ravages of encroachment; but their labor also sustained a sense of historical continuity – a direct, tangible connection with the past and with one's ancestors. Both Natives' labor and the reservation land it imbued with historical meaning were central to the reproduction of community life at a time when the possibilities for creating a viable future were drastically limited.

While the rhetorical style of Natives' petitions to the Connecticut General Assembly is often deferential, their message was not. Petitioning was a practice imposed with the English colonial legal system, but it nonetheless became a vehicle or protest, providing a colonially sanctioned legal space in which reservation communities' critiques of colonial authority, and its injustices, might be articulated.[34] While in their petitions Native leaders questioned the legality of dispossession and asserted their rights to reserved lands, these documents also attest to the ways in which colonial power permeated the daily lives of Native women and men living on reservation land. They saw this power in their trampled corn fields and broken fences, but they also experienced it in face-to-face encounters with missionaries, government officials, encroachers, and the reservation "guardians" or overseers who leased out reservation lands for their own profit or, as in the Mohegan case, relinquished plots of reservation land to encroachers (see chapter 4). When, in their petitions, Native leaders and other members of reservation communities invoked colonial laws that were intended to protect reservation land, or when they cited prior agreements between Native leaders and colonial officials that were to have preserved reservation boundaries, they asserted legal arguments that demanded a response from the colonial government. If the petitions submitted to the Connecticut government during the first half of the eighteenth century by Mohegans, Eastern Pequots, Mashantucket Pequots, and Niantics articulate common statements, they are, in the simplest terms, the following: these are the damages and threats we have borne on our reservation because of encroachment and pillaging; we, and our children – or our "posterity," as it was sometimes put – have a shared right to this land, which we have tilled and harvested; and we know something of your laws and of your obligation to protect our rights; will you do it?

Natives' assertions of their land rights and queries into the meaning of – or possibility for – justice *for Indians* in the colonial world struck a chord with some colonial legislators, reservation overseers, and missionaries. In 1735, for instance, the Reverend Benjamin Colman of Boston, a commissioner of the Society for the Propagation of the Gospel in New England, admonished the Connecticut government for "the Injury done" to Mohegans, who had conveyed their complaints against the colony to the society. Writing to the Reverend Eliphalet Adams of New London, Colman asked the pressing question of the moment, "What would it be for Your Province to do the Indians Right[?]" (TP 1:327–28).

If Native resistance to dispossession had posed unanticipated and potentially subversive legal questions to the colony, it also revealed a historical consciousness that shaped acts of dissent and refusal, like the 1736 leadership ceremony at Mohegan. It might be argued, then, that in their overt statements of protest, as well as in their appeal to colonial laws and covenants regarding reserved lands, reservation communities in early eighteenth-century Connecticut announced that they had not succumbed to a history of conquest. Moreover, their protests against encroachment suggest that local histories and identities were embedded in those colonially circumscribed, shrinking lands upon which they labored – fuelled, as Cassacinamon's 1721 petition reveals, by the kin and community ties that rendered defense of reservation land a means of preserving part of the past and carving out a collective future.

But the documents that lend insight into Natives' land struggles do not suggest a simple history of communities that were consistently politically cohesive or uniformly driven toward a common goal of opposing or accommodating colonial domination: the conditions of daily life for Native people in the early eighteenth century greatly limited the possibilities for unanimous and overt resistance to dispossession and colonial authority. As Mashantucket Pequots' overseer James Avery explained to the General Assembly in 1722, Anglo encroachers' tactics of dispossession not only posed a threat to reservation communities' livelihood but could also undermine social relations within those communities. Detailing the continuing efforts by Groton residents to appropriate the Mashantucket reservation, Avery stated that Pequots

> have been much disturbed again by some of ye people of said Groton by their driving said Indians from their improvement and taking away their fields and fruit trees which for a long time they have planted and improved on said Mashuntuxet lands, now some of the people of said Groton have seemingly stopt the mouths of some of the said Pequet Indians by such means as they have seen cause to use and brought them to sign something, but some of them say to me they did not know to what[,] which has made a great division amongst the said Indians that they are become as it were two parties . . . these things

> have much disturbed some of those Indians that they should be forced from off the land which they and their Predecessors have so long a time possess'd that they have been some times apt to say it would be better for them to march off from out of the hearing of those things. (IND 1st, 1:101; see chapter 5)

Such manipulations of reservation communities' internal affairs reflect, to borrow Gerald Sider's phrase, the "peculiar intimacy" of colonial domination (Sider 1987:11). For it was, ultimately, the dismantling and destruction of reservation communities themselves (what came to be referred to as *detribalization*) that was required to make reservation land fully "accessible" to colonists. The ties to kin and locality that held reservation communities together and lent authority to their leaders (as the 1736 Mohegan leadership ceremony so explicitly announced) were a source of power, creating possibilities for resistance that were not necessarily a trifling matter for the Connecticut government. Thus it was just such internal bonds of community that were targeted by those who sought to silence Native resisters.[35] And in an equally important and complementary maneuver of governmental control, Natives' bodies were objectified by what was one of the most quotidian, but ultimately insidious, forms of colonial surveillance: the practice of *counting Indians* living within the bounds of reservation land as a means of evaluating that community's social viability (according to colonial standards), and hence of assessing, or undermining, their rights to land. As I explain in subsequent chapters, this was a practice shaped by colonists' patriarchal conception of land rights (it was the presence, or absence, of adult men in reservation communities that colonial officials and encroachers alike were concerned to evaluate), and it was a colonial response to the presence, and authority, of Native women on reservation land. The male-focused reservation head count might suggest that adult Native men were "disappearing" from reservation land (and the colonial demand for their service in colonial wars, as well as the need to leave the reservation to find wage labor or to hunt were certainly factors affecting the life chances as well as the residence of Native men in reservation communities in the early eighteenth century); but it could not be said that reservation communities were disintegrating, or that reservation lands were being "deserted," if Native women's roles in reservation communities and their deeply rooted connections to reservation lands were acknowledged. This, of course, is another point expressed by the Mohegans' 1736 leadership ceremony, at which they named a woman, Anne, as their sachem or *sunksquaw*.[36]

An Eastern Pequot leader, Mary Momoho, protested encroachment on the Stonington reservation during the first half of the eighteenth century, informing colonial legislators in one of her petitions that "we suppose there will be some pleas made that wee are almost all dead & indeed so we be but yet wee have Thirty three men yet alive . . . besides woemen & Children" (IND 1st, 1:73). Having understood, it appears, the necessity for emphasizing the presence of men in the reservation community, Mary Momoho argued that the Eastern Pequot reservation community continued to exist, and that their rights to land required the "prudent care" of the "Honoured Courtt [the General Assembly]" (1:73). The response of colonial legislators in this instance was ineffectual, and subsequently an investigatory committee abetted encroachers by determining that "a Small Quantity of Land would Suffice" for Eastern Pequots and their "Posterity to plant upon" (IND 2nd, 2:22). Mary Momoho, along with eight other Eastern Pequots, petitioned again in 1723, objecting to a report that their reservation population included only "three men & four Squaws, & of Male Children twenty four"; in this case, the petitioners maintained that the reservation community included "above one hundred and thirty," both "Male and Female" (2:22). Eastern Pequots were compelled to prove their existence and argue for the legitimacy of their communities to a colonial government that, in 1721, had reduced the Mohegan reservation to one-fourth its original size and declared that what remained of the reservation would be turned over to the town of New London when "*the stock of s[ai]d [Mohegan] Indians are extinct*" (*Proc.* 1769:194, emphasis added).

The doctrine of anticipated "Indian extinction" was thus introduced into colonial legal prescriptions regarding Natives' rights to reservation land. And the monitoring of Native existence (and concomitantly the "adjusting" of Native land rights) would come to require more than simply counting Indians: the policing of Native identities and the imposition of boundaries on those identities were tactics of rule that emerged out of struggles over reservation land in the eighteenth century. But this, too, was challenged by Native communities, and like the struggle for land rights, the struggle over identity continues today.

## "Race" and the Conquest of History

*They presented the usual spectacle of a savage and vagrant race living among a civilized community, subject to all the diseases and vices of civilization without the defence of its virtues and its thrift. Their later history has little that is interesting.*
— Maj. Bela Peck Learned, "The Distribution of the Pequot Lands"

One of the main tenets of the contemporary racial discourse on Indianness in southern New England is that there are no longer any "real Indians" in the region.[37] This assumption is firmly grounded in the Euro-American notion of "the Indian" as a "race" that is distinguishable by physical features that have been designated by Euro-Americans, and that must be readily "recognizable" to them.[38] That is, "real Indians" must have a particular physical appearance (namely that of the Euro-American image of "the Plains Indian" as emblazoned on the "Indian head" nickel), which in turn serves as the definitive marker of "Indian blood."[39]

Among the Native nations and communities of southern New England, there are many individuals of mixed ancestry – that is, individuals of combined Native American ancestries as well as Native and African American or Native and Euro-American ancestry. Virtually all nations and communities throughout the Americas are constituted of mixed-ancestry populations, of course (including those that identify as "white"); but popular Euro-American assessments of Indian identity have long been shaped by a racial mythos that adheres to and promotes the notion that the only truly "authentic" Native Americans – and thus the only Indians considered to be endowed with indigenous rights – are those who display presumed (that is, Euro-American- and government-sanctioned) characteristics of "pure-bloodedness." In southern New England, Native Americans who also have African American ancestry have been subjected to intensely racist scrutiny, and disparagements of their identity are informed by the "one-drop rule," a tenet of the white supremacist ideology that construes what is perniciously termed "black blood" as a contaminant that negates Indian identity. In the final section of chapter 6 I examine a 1993 *Hartford Courant* cartoon which relies upon a virulent caricature of imagined "black features" to depict Golden Hill Paugussetts as frauds. Disparaging the kin ties and the experiences of oppression that sometimes bound Native American and African American peoples and their histories, such racist characterizations thereby deny the complexity of contemporary Native identities and the struggles for survival that both threatened and sustained them. Moreover, as I argue in the conclusion, such depictions of mixed-ancestry Native identities bring into relief connections between the colonial past and the present-day relations of power that structure Native people's historical possibilities. As I argue in chapter 6, the monitoring and disparaging of specific Native identities and communities in distinctly *racialized* terms emerged as a governmental tactic of control in the late eighteenth century.

It should also be emphasized that the notions of "racial purity" that have been imposed on Native communities and deployed to undermine or divert attention from the matter of Natives' rights (to land, livelihood, and a future) are interwoven with and bolstered by a discourse of conquest that continues to influence popular Euro-American understandings of history and thus to have an impact on Natives' efforts to achieve federal acknowledgement, for instance, or pursue land claims. There is a prevailing Euro-American assumption, which has been conveyed by the historiography of the colonial period, that although there may have been some unpleasantness that occurred during the "settlement" period, it happened hundreds of years ago and could not be helped. As it was put by an exasperated Euro-American man in the early 1990s, during an interview with a local news station regarding Golden Hill Paugussetts' land claims, "We fought the Indians three hundred years ago. Do we have to fight them again?" Statements like these speak volumes not just about the persistence of the racist stereotype of "the Indian" as a "problem" to be eliminated but indicate that late twentieth-century Euro-American assumptions about a "natural" social hierarchy are rooted in an enduring myth of conquest. Like bad weather, "the Indians" were obstacles that "we" had to fight off to fulfill a grand destiny. Conquest, then, tends to be envisioned first as a single moment in a remote past and second as essential to the predetermined progress of an "advanced" (i.e., white) "civilization." Thus the "vanishing" of Indians, while sometimes regarded as unfortunate, is generally considered to be "as natural, inevitable, and free of human responsibility, as glaciation," as Ward Churchill has put it (Churchill 1994:123).

Native peoples of southern New England who are engaged in the process of petitioning for federal acknowledgment as "Indian tribes" have been confronted with government officials' blindness to the violence and enduring legacy of conquest.[40] Consider, for instance, the following comment from a member of the staff of the Bureau of Indian Affairs' (BIA) Branch of Acknowledgement and Research (BAR), quoted in a major Connecticut newspaper. With regard to the eighteenth- and nineteenth-century histories of the "unrecognized tribes" of southern New England, she stated: "We don't see them . . . Something happened. We didn't see what it was. Did they go out some exit we don't see? Did they die inside the tunnel?" (*Hartford Courant Sunday Magazine*, February 20, 1994).

Unwittingly, the BIA official conjures an apt colonial metaphor in "the tunnel," which serves to obscure the forms of domination endured by New England's Native people, casting their struggles as the nebulous "something" that "we" (the BAR staff and perhaps most Euro-Americans) "don't see." From the perspective of such a "comfortable fiction," to borrow Vine Deloria's term (1992), Native peoples in New England petitioning for federal acknowledgment have emerged *ex nihilo* in the twentieth century.[41]

The reservation lands that continue to exist in Connecticut stand as one point of entry into those indigenous histories that aren't "seen" or, more accurately, that have been silenced or ignored. Indeed, reservations situate the colonial past squarely in the present: the rigid demarcation of populations as well as geographic and cultural territories, which characterizes the reservation system, is a reminder of the exertion of raw colonial power. As I have already noted, struggles over reservation land were crucial to the emergence of the colonial practice of monitoring the legitimacy of Indianness. In the nineteenth and twentieth centuries reservations were to become sites of racial surveillance in Connecticut.[42] As I learned from an Eastern Pequot elder, Euro-American assertions of authority over reservation land could entail threats of violence, as when more than a dozen carloads of Ku Klux Klan members erected and burned a cross at the summit of Lantern Hill, overlooking the Eastern Pequot reservation in North Stonington, Connecticut, in the mid-1920s.[43] This, of course, occurred long before there was any purported fear of Indian casinos among Euro-Americans or any notion of federal acknowledgment for Native peoples in New England. I mentioned the Klan's assault on the Eastern Pequot reservation in a paper I presented at an academic conference, and a member of the audience commented that the Klan members "must have thought that the Eastern

Pequots were *black*." But the idea that the cross burning on Lantern Hill represented a case of "mistaken identity" misses the point. Irrespective of what the individual Klansmen who perpetrated the cross burnings may have believed about Eastern Pequot identity, this event cannot be reduced to a random act of racist violence; rather, it is one tied to a colonial history of interwoven practices of social and geographic control, which, upon close inspection, reveal the precise ways in which Euro-American notions of "race" have shaped and masked histories of struggle.

By the late eighteenth century, government officials in Connecticut would begin to evaluate the identity and legitimacy of reservation communities in terms of the emergent racial notion of "Indian blood," reflecting Anglo-American fears that reservation populations, which were to have been in the process of disappearing, might instead be replenished by intermarriages between Native Americans and African Americans.[44] In 1804 an Anglo-American overseer of the Mashantucket Pequot reservation remarked, "Some of them [Pequots] Match & propagate with Negroes which makes us some trouble" (IND 2nd, 2:33). As this overseer's report to the Connecticut governor subsequently indicated, the "trouble" was articulated by Anglo residents of Groton as concern about the financial "burden" the town might incur as a result of an increase in the reservation population, and the presumed concomitant increase in potential indigents: "we hear it is Suggested that the Indian Land is an Inlet to Negroes which brings Burdens on the Town of Groton, to this it is Sufficient to say, that the Authority of Groton have the same right to prevent burdens there [on the reservation], as in other parts of the Town" (IND 2nd, 2:34). The overseer added, however, that "the Indians are not a Burden to that Town if they Sicken & die or break their Limbs [since] the Town take no Care about them" (2:34). It was the reservation overseers who were to attend to Pequots who were elderly, sick, or dying, and they alone were to see that "the Expense of Coffins & c" was covered – expenses, as this report indicates, that were covered by the sale of parcels of reservation land.

But it was not simply the Anglo townspeople's fear of having too many paupers on their hands that was at issue here. Explaining that "there never was a Negro moved into that place by our Consent," the overseer's report implies that there were aspects of community life on the reservation that were beyond his control. Such discourse about the potential "trouble" posed by unmonitored social relations within this Pequot community captures a moment during which government officials grappled with the possibility that the reservation community, and indeed Pequot identity as well, were being regenerated. Certainly the presence of mixed-ancestry individuals in the Pequot reservation community would challenge colonially imposed "racial" boundaries;[45] likewise it called into question the extent to which the geographic boundaries of reservation land could be effectively policed to seal off – and allow for the "extinction" of – reservation populations. The reservation overseers were not simply contending with the insidious administrative task of "racial classification" for *individual* members of the reservation community (that is, of assessing their identity in terms of the mutually exclusive Euro-American categories "Indian" and "Negro"). Indeed, what was to be done with this collectivity – the Pequot reservation community that was reconstituting itself? As these reports suggest, what was troublesome for government officials was that Pequots – impoverished and desperate as their circumstances were throughout the eighteenth century – had *produced and sustained kin and community ties on their own terms*, and in the face of a history that had demanded their annihilation. In so doing, did they not also perpetuate their collective rights to their reservation land?

In the nineteenth and twentieth centuries European and Euro-American ideas of "racial degeneration" and the government-imposed notion of "blood quantum" would become the quintessential means by which Native identities and Native land rights would be assessed, and undermined, by external authorities (see Jaimes 1992, 1994; Churchill 1998; Strong and Van Winkle 1996; Herndon and Sekatau 1997). Through broad application of racial categories, such as "mulatto" or "colored," government officials and record keepers in nineteenth-century southern New England would obscure Native identities altogether, thus denying their land rights as well.[46] Nineteenth-century federal census reports in the United States reflected as much in their categorization of many Native people as "colored."[47] In officially asserting the "disappearance" of indigenous peoples, such fallacies of racial classification have served to obfuscate ongoing processes of dispossession and to legitimize the Euro-American claim to unimpeachable authority over the continent.

Like the Klan's cross burning on the Eastern Pequot reservation in the 1920s, such government-enacted strategies of historical erasure are linked to forms of domination and dispossession that emerged in the context of disputes over Natives' rights to reservation land in the eighteenth century – disputes into which the newly forming category of "white" identity was ultimately inserted. It is, perhaps, that category more than any other that has demanded vigilant historical and political legitimization, and has been most effectively accomplished by diversionary tactics and through the consummately diversionary discourse of "race," with its relentless scrutiny and management of the presumed illegitimacy of "other" identities. Indeed, the Klan's cross burning on the Eastern Pequot reservation was surely an assertion of "white" authority over the reservation land below, as well as over the identity and history of Eastern Pequot people.

As suggested in anthropologist Frank Speck's description of Pequot identity in the early twentieth century, the importance of reservation land to evocations of conquest and to the production of a "natural" racial hierarchy should not be overlooked. Speck explains that Lantern Hill, which "rises several hundred feet above the horizon," is "a widely known landmark of Indian days" in Connecticut: "From its almost bare summit is an extensive view across the birch swamps renowned in the Pequot war of 163[7], where the natives sought refuge from the vengeance of the Pilgrims. Now, almost under the shadow of Lantern Hill, lies their diminutive reservation, where the several families of Pequot mixed bloods reside" (Speck 1928:254).

Here Lantern Hill itself, looming now over "Pequot mixed bloods," affirms the conquest. Speck's description thus points to the historical processes, symbolic and violent, by which hierarchies of race have been inscribed into the landscape of southern New England, transforming indigenous homelands into sites of conquest that have been as meaningful for Euro-Americans in the twentieth century as they were for colonists in the eighteenth.[48]

So, too, is Euro-American historiography of conquest is implicated in the historical processes by which colonial geographies and Native identities that have been reconfigured into a "natural" hierarchy. In the vision of nineteenth-century New England historian William Weeden: "that great awakening of the human mind, the new birth of man, which no term fully embodies, which no single movement, not even the Reformation, could contain, swept over the Aryan races, impelling them to new explorations, new conquests of their mother earth" (Weeden 1963:2–3). For Weeden, *mother earth* – the cultural conception and lived reality of indigenous peoples of North America – is transformed into the domain of an "Aryanness" that represents the "great awakening of the human mind." Weeden's conquerors are not simply white and finally American; they are *the* representation of humanity – more "native" to colonized terrain than indigenous people. In another essay Weeden defines conquest as the ineluctable consequence of a "conflict of race" (1884:33). "If the barbarian could have ignored the vices of his Puritan neighbor," Weeden explains, "and could have adopted his virtues only, all might have gone well, and the blood of the American might have commingled with the Aryan stream"; however, he continues, "when the narrowing land contracted so much that the rude hoe could not keep pace with the incoming plow of the agriculturalist, the end came. . . . There was an absolute and actual conflict, not of good and bad men, not of will and the conduct of government, but of race, social structure, and of hereditary civilization" (34).

Here, again, colonial domination is transformed into an inevitability of nature, part of an evolutionary process driven by the inherent supremacy of an "Aryan civilization." This notion found renewed significance in the twentieth-century historiography of colonial New England. Historian Samuel Eliot Morison, in his introduction to Douglas Leach's popular history of King Philip's War, *Flintlock and Tomahawk* (1958), also cast conquest in the same terms of "race conflict," though in this passage the depiction of the seventeenth-century colonial struggle is a justification for twentieth-century imperialism and Western domination of "backward peoples" in other locales:

> Most historians, including myself, believe that [King Philips War] was the most severe of all the colonial Indian wars, subsequent to the 1622 massacre in Virginia. In view of our recent experiences of warfare, and of the many instances today of backward peoples getting enlarged notions of nationalism and turning ferociously on Europeans who have attempted to civilize them, this early conflict of the same nature cannot help but be of interest. It was an intensely dramatic struggle, decisive for the survival of the English race in New England, and the eventual disappearance of the Algonkian Indians. . . . The New England colonists tried hard to be fair and just to the natives; but their best was not good enough to absorb them without a conflict. (Morison 1958:ix)

The idea of the "naturalness" of conquest – and of the inevitable dispossession and erasure of indigenous peoples from the North American landscape – lives on in Euro-American scholarship. Though far more subtle than Morison's rhetoric, this introductory statement in a 1995 geography text, *Dividing the Land: Early American Beginnings of Our Private Property Mosaic*, is a relevant example: "Colonial settlement advanced in waves over the pristine American land, greatly varied in its nature, but little divided or improved by its aboriginal inhabitants" (Price 1995:3). It is startling to consider that seventeenth- and eighteenth-century colonial notions (i.e., that indigenous peoples failed to "improve" the land) continue to be so casually and insidiously reaffirmed, sustaining Euro-American notions of racial supremacy, and indeed implying (as does the collective pronoun "our" in the book's title) the necessity of Euro-American control over the continent. Conquest, then, is not just the appropriation of territories and resources and the destruction of indigenous populations; it is also the consumption of other histories and other ancestries via a conquering discourse – in this case, the discourse of race masquerading as history.[49]

The racial discourse on Indianness that persists in southern New England today, and that continues to be deployed to deny both history and authenticity to some Native peoples, is, in effect, a still-burning cross, rooted in colonial contests over Native rights to land and political autonomy – contests in which both the past and the future were at stake for reservation communities. By examining their struggles for land and the forms of domination that infused but did not wholly determine Native people's lives in eighteenth-century Connecticut, we may come to better understand how history fuels resistance and how resistance, in turn, has articulated knowledges and identities that continue to challenge the claims of conquest.

# 2

# Manufacturing Colonial Legitimacy

## *Constructing Indianness, Claiming Land*

English claims to Native lands entailed the production of a discourse of conquest that conjoined ideas about colonial cultural legitimacy, property rights, and "Indian savagery." [1] It is by now a truism to say that colonial discourse – and particularly the ideas about "others" that it has conveyed – is itself a crucial mechanism of power. [2] Colonial discourse "longs for mastery," as Gyan Prakash has so aptly put it, and assumes "a panoptic position" of surveillance (Prakash 1992:170). [3] But the assumptions about and constructions of otherness that such discourse seeks to render as unimpeachable truths are neither stable nor mechanically self-sustaining. Within the context of Native-Anglo struggles over reservation land in eighteenth-century Connecticut, colonial notions about Indianness, and concomitantly ideas about the right and legitimacy of conquest, were called into question. While these struggles were sites of both the production and contestation of colonial discourse on Indianness and conquest, it must be emphasized that the potency of such discourse lies as much in what it denies or obscures as in what it claims or seeks to affirm and legitimize. Colonial discourse is expressed not only in diffuse cultural forms but also in specific administrative and juridical forums to which colonized people have limited access and over which they have no control. Indeed, if colonial discourse is the speaking of power, then that speaking is always also a silencing; and what is silenced must be investigated.

It is not only oppositional voices and other histories that colonial discourse seeks to overwrite: it also works to mask the tenuousness of colonial authority. Discourse on Indianness and conquest in colonial southern New England reflects the connection between ideas about the nature of Indian identity and the manufacturing of a "legal" and cultural grounding for the domination of indigenous peoples and their lands. The cultural matters of conquest – that is, the precise forms through which its legitimacy is fabricated and proclaimed – required monitoring and regulation, recycling and reaffirmation, precisely because they were produced in the presence of alternative knowledges and against the "others" who asserted their own claims to legitimacy.[4]

Appropriating land and subjugating its indigenous inhabitants by force is a task that may be achieved rather swiftly, as was the case with the Pequot massacre in 1637; but the legitimacy of this founding moment of conquest was reconstructed and reaffirmed for specific political reasons well after the massacre took place. As I have noted in the previous chapter, strategic narrations of Pequot conquest in the seventeenth and eighteenth centuries offered versions of the past that justified the ongoing domination and dispossession of indigenous peoples. Thus the colonial story of the "Pequot War" is not really a story about Pequots; nor is it solely a story about colonial "bravery" in the face of "evil," or of "civilization" over "savagery": it is, perhaps most importantly, a story that is meant to render the colonizers a natural presence in the landscape. It is Pequots who are cast as aliens, and their "hostile" presence is swept from the terrain by the will of the English god.[5] But this myth was contested in the eighteenth century not just by Pequots but by other Native people who dared to assert their land rights and to question colonial justice.

If, as I am arguing, the central dilemma of colonialism in eighteenth-century Connecticut was legitimacy (i.e., the problem of normalizing and obscuring the forms of domination by which colonizers claimed both land and political authority over indigenous populations), then the "Indian problem" is, likewise, a problem of knowledge control. The scrutiny of, and production of information about, Indianness was surely a part of "the quotidian processes of hegemony," to borrow Edward Said's phrase (Said 1993:109). But colonial surveillance and the dissemination of authoritative knowledge about specific Native peoples demanded a certain expertise, of the sort that could be claimed by missionaries, for instance, who had had sustained interactions and confrontations with Native women and men. Understanding the nature of colonial power relations in the period after military conquest requires that we interrogate the discourse on Indianness produced by colonial "experts" – missionaries, for instance, as well as government officials and those who were appointed as "guardians" or overseers of reservation communities.[6]

## The Cultural Production of Racial Hierarchy

In the case of a text such as Daniel Gookin's 1674 *Historical Collections of the Indians in New England*, the introduction to which is examined below, the exegesis of "Indian origins" reveals that the colonial construction of a hierarchy of cultures and cultural practices (practices that, ostensibly, were to be "transformed" or "improved" by the Christianizing mission) also embodied a fomenting racialized notion of Indianness, casting the presumed cultural inadequacy or degeneracy of Indianness as innate and indelible. Thus colonial assessments of the "essence" of Indianness and disparagements of Indian cultural practices not only conveyed a message about the necessity, and the right, of conquest but also proffered a racialized formulation of historical processes as well, in the context of which Indianness was ineluctably doomed not because of conquest and colonization, but because of its inherent, "original" deficiencies. Indeed, Gookin's theorizing on "Indian origins" demonstrates that colonizers who had "planted" themselves in New England, and who claimed authoritative knowledge of Indianness, deployed an interesting twist on Robert Johnson's early-seventeenth-century assertion that the English had journeyed to Indian lands "not to supplant and root them out but to bring them from their base condition to a far better" (R. Johnson 1968:29). The stated goals of the Christianizing mission were surely grand to think upon – and to announce – for they lay at the heart of early claims to colonial legitimacy; but the saving grace of colonialism beyond the seventeenth century was to be the production of a discourse that, alongside of if not embedded in the politically and culturally expedient proclamations of the colonial "civilizing" project, elaborated upon and "proved" the *impossibility* of "bring[ing Indians] from their base condition to a far better."[7] The racialization of Indianness was thus firmly linked to constructions of colonial cultural legitimacy and ultimately buttressed the "legality" of colonial claims to Native lands.

If colonial discourse on Indianness in southern New England can be said to have a strategy, it is a strategy of diversion and deflection as well as one of silencing. And as a diversionary tactic of control, it reveals itself to be most productive, having spun out stories of Indian illegitimacy and alienness that posed the Native presence as a cultural problem and, simultaneously, an emergent "racial" problem that colonial authority was obliged to address and rectify. And as seventeenth- and eighteenth-century colonial discourse expounded upon Indian cultural degeneracy and, concomitantly, constructed the cultural boundaries that were to mark and delimit Indianness, it honed a racialized notion of "the Indian" that was to become a most effective means of denying the histories and land rights of local Native peoples.

This discourse has a history, and some of its foundational expressions should be reviewed in order to illuminate the precise ways in which it was manipulated, affirmed, or countered in the context of eighteenth-century disputes over reservation land. Seventeenth-century English "propaganda for colonization" (Wright and Fowler 1968:27) offered the theologically based premise that the English empire existed in North America before the fact of colonization, laying a foundation for subsequent colonial notions of Indianness as culturally "alien" to the continent. In his 1624 essay "Encouragement to Colonies," Sir William Alexander is explicit on this point: "I have never remembered any thing with more admiration than America, considering how it hath pleased the Lord to locke it up so long amidst the depths, concealing it from the curiosities of the Ancients, that it might be discovered in a fit time for their posteritie" (1873:40). Since the English god had "reserved" North America for Englishmen, any inhabitants of that domain prior to English colonization would have no permanent claim to the land – no valid cultural grounding there – and hence colonization would not displace them.[8] In America, Alexander asserted, Englishmen "*may possesse themselves without dispossessing of others*, the Land either wanting Inhabitants, or having none that doe appropriate to themselves any peculiar ground, but (in a straggling company) runne like beasts after beasts, seeking no soile, but only their prey" (Alexander 1873:37, emphasis added).

Classifying New England as a *vacuum domicilium* required the notion of Indians as "unbridled beasts," as Robert Johnson referred to indigenous people in his 1609 *Nova Britannia* (cited in Wright and Fowler 1968:29), who failed to "subdue" and "improve" the land as the English god demanded (see also Neuwirth 1982:6–8; Seed 1995:31–40).[9] The notion that the soil of North America was uncultivated was, of course, an English imperial fantasy: the Native peoples of southern New England, as some seventeenth-century English colonists noted, were highly efficient agriculturalists, as well as hunters and harvesters of the sea's resources.[10]

As Alexander's rhetoric suggests, the acquisition of Native lands was a matter of manufacturing both the legality and the cultural legitimacy of the English presence.[11] Colonial authorities claimed a legal appropriation of Native lands via military conquest or purchase; but such processes of dispossession entailed routine cultural affirmations. Historian Patricia Seed has explained that through the most "ordinary" of activities – such as the fixing of boundaries with fences and hedges, constructing English style houses, and planting gardens – English colonists both "took possession" of Native lands and demonstrated the presumed cultural deficiencies of Indianness (Seed 1995:37–39).[12] The "absence" of fences, for instance, or of domesticated livestock and other tangible connections to the land deemed valid by colonists, became the ubiquitous evidence of Indians' lack of "property" rights (Seed 1995:39).[13] Defining indigenous cultural practices as "an accumulation of negatives" (Seed 1995:39), seventeenth-century colonizers affirmed the legality of colonial titles and asserted their own cultural claim to a homeland in the "New World."[14]

However, just as military conquest and the ravages of European disease had not managed to fully annihilate Native populations in the seventeenth century, neither did colonial cultural processes of "settlement" serve to extinguish the indigenous presence in southern New England. Sustaining the claim to a homeland on colonized terrain, in the presence of the vanquished, is a silencing mission, as well as a project of constructing and policing cultural, racial, and geographic boundaries. Indians' own cultural relationship to the landscape had to be pondered and theorized, and indeed indigenous knowledges had to be overwritten, obscured, and invalidated. Gookin's *Historical Collections* (1972) offers an important example of how colonial cultural legitimacy was constructed vis-à-vis a construing of Indian "savagery" that worked to recycle and refine, in racialized terms, the foundational cultural and legal claim of English colonialism: that colonists in North America "may possesse themselves without dispossessing others" (Alexander 1873:37).

Gookin opens his *Historical Collections* with an account of "Indian origins," entitled "Several Conjectures of their Original," which elaborates the "divers opinions" held by Europeans on the subject (1972:4).[15] As Gookin explains it, there are three major positions: 1) that "this people are of the race of the ten tribes of Israel"; 2) "that the original of these Americans is from the Tartars, or Scythians, that live in the northeast parts of Asia"; or 3) that they are descendents of "the tawny Moors of Africa" (4–6). Gookin's deployment of these "racial" categories underpins his theorizing about the alienness of the Indian presence in the New England landscape. The essence of Indianness – that is, its own cultural (and as suggested by such classifications, ultimately "biological") roots, are "foreign." This alienness is further detailed in his discussion of the circumstances under which Indians are to have departed from their supposed territory of origin. In the case of the first theory, Gookin writes that it was "God . . . by some means or other, not yet discovered, [who] brought them into America," which

> fulfilled his just threatening against them, of which we may read, II. Kings, xvii. from 6 to the 19 verse; and hath reduced them into such woeful blindness and barbarism, as all those Americans are in. . . . A reason given for this is taken from the practice of sundry Americans, especially of those inhabiting Peru and Mexico, who were most populous, and had great cities and wealth; and hence are probably apprehended to be the first possessors of America. Now of these the historians write, that they used circumcision and sacrifices, though oftentimes of human flesh; so did the Israelites sacrifice their sons unto Moloch. (4–5)

If Indians, in this case, were ultimately a product of a divine act of dispossession, this is evidenced in the "barbarism" of some of the presumed cultural practices of those Indians who are identified as "the first possessors of America." But even they had "great cities and wealth" and were also "most populous." Gookin goes on to note that the Indians of northeastern North America demonstrate none of those features (which are cast as positive or productive here), and thus he suggests that the historical process of Indian geographic movement or migration in the Americas is one of *degeneration*.

Gookin's explanation of the second theory of Indian origins (that Indians are derived from "Tartars, or Scythians") points to the mundane way in which assessments of Indian physical appearance were interwoven with cultural classifications. This second theory "gained more credit than the former," he contends, "because the people of America are not altogether unlike in *colour, shape, and manners*, unto the Scythian people, and in regard that such a land travel is more feasible and probable, than a voyage by sea . . . from other inhabited places, either in Europe, Asia, or Africa" (4–5, emphasis added). Gookin's racial theorizing, though in embryonic form, reveals itself to be conspicuously connected to a colonial hierarchy of cultural practices and capabilities.[16] And the importance of particular forms of cultural evidence to Gookin's construction of Indianness as disconnected from the New England landscape should not be underestimated. He questions why,

> if this people be sprung from the Tartarian or Scythian people . . . they did not attend the known practice of that people; who, in all their removes and plantations, take with them their kine, sheep, horses, and camels, and the like tame beasts; which that people keep in great numbers and drive with them in all their removes. But of these sorts and kinds of beasts used by the Tartars, none were found in America among the Indians. This question of objection is answered by some thus. First, possibly the first people were banished for some notorious offences; and so not permitted to take with them of these tame beasts. Or, secondly, possibly the gulf, or passage, between Asia and America, though narrow, comparatively, is yet too broad to waft over any of those creatures; and yet possibly men and women might pass over it in canoes made of hollow trees, or with barks of trees, wherein, it is known, the Indians will transport themselves, wives, and children, over lakes and gulfs very considerable for breadth. (5)

Such tediously detailed ruminations convey an urgency to establish expert (or "scientific") authority on Indianness that, here, depends upon the command and articulation of a fomenting cultural-racial lexicon, one that renders Indians an inherently dispossessed, wandering people – wholly alien in the claimed territory of the English empire.

Gookin ultimately conjoins the first and second of the main propositions regarding Indian origins and further refines his assessment of the inherent cultural deficiencies of Indianness, linking it to a notion of the *reproductive inadequacy* and presumed *insularity* of Indian populations. His argument proceeds thus: that if "the origination of the Americans came from Asia, by the northwest of America, where the continents are conceived to meet very near, which is indeed very probable . . . this doth not hinder the truth of the first conjecture [that Indians are derived from the "ten tribes of Israel"]":

> for the king of Assyria who led [the Israelites] captive . . . transported them into Asia, and placed them in several provinces and cities. . . . Now possibly, in process of time, this people, or at least some considerable number of them, whose custom and manner it was to keep themselves distinct from the other nations they lived amongst; and did commonly intermarry only with their own people; and also their religion being so different from the heathen, unto whom they were generally an abomination as they were to the Egyptians; and also partly from God's judgement following them for their sins: I say, it is not impossible but a considerable number of them might withdraw themselves; and so pass gradually into the extreme parts of the continent of Asia; and wherever they came, being disrelished by the heathen, might for their own security, pass further and further, till they found America; which being unpeopled, there they found some rest; and so, in many hundred years, *spread themselves in American in that thin manner, as they were found there, especially in the northern parts of it; which country is able to contain and accommodate millions of mankind more than were found in it.* And for their speech, which is not only different among themselves, but from the Hebrew, that might easily be lost by their often removes or God's judgement. (Gookin 1972:6, emphasis added)

Laden with allusions that could be applied to Puritans' own cultural dilemma of separation from their "kinsfolk" in England, Gookin's theory nevertheless labors to silence the question of *English* alienness in New England, weaving instead a tale of "disrelished" and *infertile* Indians, nomadic and isolationist. Having "found rest" – *not a homeland* – in America, Gookin's Indians are not regenerated but dispersed and "thinned" further, "especially in the northern parts" of America (1972:6). Here again, then, Gookin's rhetoric intertwines racial and cultural notions to construct Indianness as innately, irrevocably detached from the landscape: this detachment is as evident in their presumed inability to adequately propagate themselves and thus "plant" themselves into a "country [that] is able to contain and accommodate millions of mankind more," as it is in the absence of livestock, "great cities," and copious material wealth.[17] Gookin's Indians of "the northern parts" are rendered not simply as "children of wrath; and hence . . . objects of all Christians' pity and compassion" (7), but as cultural and "racial" castaways.

Gookin's theorizing is, to be sure, a silencing maneuver par excellence. And it is first and foremost the historical facts of conquest that are so artfully diverted and obscured in the strategic introduction to his *Historical Collections*. The only possible points of Indian origination acknowledged by Europeans, as Gookin relates them, all render Indians a homeless, degenerate lot *before* the fact of colonization. But Gookin's subsequent "ethnographic" description of the Native peoples in his midst reveals the great irony of his text, contradicting some of the key assumptions of his theorizing about Native origins. Gookin knew, of course, that New England was not a *vacuum domicilium* at the time of English colonizers' arrival in 1620, and that it was not "thinly" populated. In fact, in his description of "the principal Indians" of New England, in the following chapter, he refers to Pequots as a "potent" people, who "could in former times, raise four thousand men, fit for war," but who "now . . . are few . . . being made subject unto the English, who conquered and destroyed most of them" (1972:7). Narragansetts of Rhode Island and the Native nations of Massachusetts are all described by Gookin as having been "a great people heretofore." Moreover, he acknowledges the existence of Natives' own distinct geographic territories, along with what he interprets as the "chief seats" of their respective sachems (7–9).

Here, then, in his recounting of recent, local Native history, Gookin acknowledges both indigenous relationships to the land and the impact of English conquest on Native populations. This rather conspicuous break from some of the crucial claims made in his discussion of Indian origins is not simply an instance of rhetorical inconsistency; nor does it mean that Gookin offered up the origins theorizing merely for entertainment value. His account of Indian origins makes, of course, an essential political argument: that regardless of which theory one upholds as the final "truth," they all reinforce the notion that the colonial presence in New England is benevolent, preordained, and necessary. But again, such claims to colonial legitimacy required affirmation as colonizers confronted the social realities of the colonial world; and Gookin's text points to the complex and curious ways in which colonial discourse was mediated by confrontations with Native peoples and their local histories.

Gookin's narrative suggests an emergent Euro-American cultural dilemma, and perhaps psychological schism, produced by the colonial experience of alienness, a condition that requires strategic and perpetual denial. Colonial alienness was not to be resolved by the exertion of military power and the inscription of English cultural forms on the landscape. The "civilizing" mission – and its particular assaults on indigenous minds and social relations – may be seen as a classic colonial strategy of diversion, of obscuring colonial foreignness by obsessing upon and elaborating the characteristics and detriments of imagined "savagery," casting it as the thing that must be "converted" (or eradicated). But in southern New England the endeavor of "Indian conversion" was fraught with difficulties and failures and was challenged, as I discuss later in the chapter, by Native people who critiqued English claims to both land and cultural superiority.

If the colonial dilemma of sustaining claims to legitimacy in the enduring presence of indigenous communities is reflected in Gookin's incongruous assessments of the viability of Indian populations in the northeast, it is most evident in the overt denial of indigenous knowledge that brings his theorizing about Indian origins to a close. Here Gookin asserts his ethnographic authority by proclaiming that he has "discoursed and questioned about this matter [of their origins] with some of the most judicious of the Indians, but their answers are divers and fabulous" (Gookin 1972:6–7). He then offers a fragment of what those accounts conveyed, which, he concluded, "suffice to give a taste of their great ignorance touching their origin[s]":

> Some of the inland Indians say, that they came from such as inhabit the sea coasts. Others say, that there were two young squaws, or women, being at first either swimming or wading in the water: The froth or foam of the water touched their bodies, from whence they became with child; and one of them brought forth a male; and the other, a female child; and then the two women died and left the earth: So their son and daughter were their first progenitors. Other fables and figments are among them touching this thing, which are not worthy to be inserted. (6–7])

Indigenous knowledge is thus evoked only so that it may be invalidated and silenced. Indeed Gookin insists that Natives' accounts and understandings of their own pasts and of their own historical embedment in the local landscape do not qualify as knowledge at all: because Indians are "ignorant of letters and records of antiquity," Gookin contends, "any true knowledge of their ancestors is utterly lost among them" (1972:6). Absent documentary evidence, the account of the wading women is necessarily a "fable and figment"; but for English colonists, such an indigenous origins story might also be upheld as evidence of Indian cultural and reproductive, or sexual, chaos – an outrageous defiance of preordained Euro-Christian prescriptions of gender and sexuality that the English presence is deigned to subdue and overwrite. That may well explain Gookin's inclusion of this particular account: in light of the idea of Indian alienness laboriously conveyed in his discussion of Indian origins, this representation of a local, indigenous origins story crystallizes Indian otherness and compels Gookin's readers to reject Indianness altogether. For here are indigenous women, sensuously intermingling with and enveloped by the very forces of nature (*not* god, or at least not the Christian god), and without impregnation by a clearly distinguishable masculine presence (divine or human) they *create* the "first progenitors" of the local Indian people. Imbued with deific power, and intimately conjoined with the elements of the natural world (including the land under English colonists' feet), it is Native women, in this local account, who embody the histories and identities of their people and bind them to their homeland. I would suggest, then, that Gookin offers up this sampling of indigenous knowledge to depict "Indian culture" – and Native understandings of history – as having run disastrously afoul. From the perspective of Christian patriarchal authority, the story of the wading women would be an intolerable affront to the masculine Christian god and his seventeenth-century colonial adherents, for whom the "planting" of the earth (with crops, colonies, and Christian souls) – and thus the production and proliferation of culture – was deemed the proper work of *men*. In Gookin's rendering, indigenous knowledge is prima facie false on cultural grounds; and their alienness is presented as a condition reflected even in Natives' understanding of their relationships to each other and the world around them. European theories of Indian origins may bolster colonial claims to legitimacy, but colonial "ethnographic" authority – its claim to firsthand knowledge of Indianness – could pose indigenous knowledge as an immediate "Indian problem" that demanded eradication.[18]

Lest we forget that colonial power is not to be equated with or reduced to discourse, but is rather interwoven with and sustained by it, it is important to emphasize that the silencing of indigenous knowledges (even as perpetrated by missionaries) was enmeshed with the material and military processes of dispossession. As historian John Frederick Martin explains, Gookin, like other "Indian experts," was invaluable to the process of colonial land acquisition and town founding (Martin 1991:18). Martin identifies "two kinds of Indian experts" in seventeenth-century New England: "those who knew the Indians as traders and neighbors and were valuable in founding towns because they spoke the Indians' language and could negotiate with Indians for the purchase of land, and those who were military experts and were valuable in town-founding because, often without provocation, they attacked and exterminated Native Americans and then led the efforts to form new towns on the conquered lands" (18).

As Martin observes, Gookin was a politically and economically ambitious colonist (Martin 1991:23–28). He served as superintendent of the "Praying Indians" in Massachusetts Bay Colony and subsequently as superintendent of all Native people in the colony until his death in 1687. In addition to holding political offices in the colony throughout much of his lifetime, he served as head of the Cambridge militia and commander in chief of Massachusetts Bay's military as well. In 1677 he was "one of three commanders of an expedition against the Indians in Maine" (23).

Gookin's authority as Indian expert, then, was in no sense confined solely to matters of religion and the compulsion to "convert": colonial endeavors of social control and land acquisition put his expertise to use. His "mission" to Nipmucks in 1674, for instance, included a meeting with Nipmuck sachems who "executed to Gookin and his committee the deed for the tract of Worcester [Massachusetts]" (Martin 1991:27–28). Subsequently, during King Philips War in 1675, the Nipmuck population was devastated at the hands of military leaders who were also Worcester town proprietors and members of the committee that oversaw the founding of the town. Gookin's activities as an Indian expert directly contributed to his having "accumulated a sizable estate, much of it in wilderness lands," as Martin explains (23). His estate included 500 acres in Pequot ancestral territory (in what would become Stonington, Connecticut), which were granted to him by the Massachusetts General Court in 1657 (23–24). Thus Gookin became a town proprietor in the very core of military conquest – and, it might be argued, of Indian-hating – in southern New England.

And so Gookin's discourse on Indianness, like that of other missionaries, lay at the heart of the dilemma of colonial legitimacy: the problem of simultaneously masking and perpetuating violent processes of conquest. John Eliot's *New England's First Fruits* (1643), for example, posits a colonial scenario in which Puritans are engaged in a neighborly effort to both "civilize" Indians and "compound with them" in the use of land. In the opening of the passage in *First Fruits* entitled "In respect of the Indians, &c," Eliot commends his colonial brethren for their "dealings and carriages . . . towards [the Indians]," for

> 1. At our entrance upon the Land, it was not with violence and intrusion, but free and faire, with their consents and allowance the chief Sagamores of all that part of the Country, entertaining us heartily, and professed we were all much welcome.
>
> 2. When any of them had possession of, or right unto any Land we were to plant upon, none were suffered, (to our knowledge) to take one acre from them, but do use to *compound with them to content . . . Yet (mistake us not) we are wont to keep them at such a distance,* knowing they serve the Devill and are led by him) as not to imbolden them too much or trust them too farre; though we do them what good we can. (Eliot 1643:9, emphasis added)

Eliot's depiction of seventeenth-century colonists as "compounding with" indigenous people (implying a cultural "mixing" or intermingling), while also making sure to "keep them at a distance," belies the ideological underpinnings of the emergent reservation system, which served as a means of segregating, controlling, and classifying indigenous populations while also "legalizing" their dispossession. [19] But Eliot's account of a successful Indian "conversion" – the quintessential evidence of colonially orchestrated cultural compounding – reveals that such cultural processes of control were underpinned by military power and the threat of violence, albeit violence represented as the expression of Puritan righteousness:

> The last instance [of a successful conversion] we will give shall be of that famous Indian *Wequash* who was a Captaine, a proper man of person, and a very grave and sober spirit; the Story of which comming to our hands very lately, was indeed the occasion of writing all the rest: This man a few yeares since, seeing and beholding the might power of God in our English Forces, how they fell upon the Pequots, where

> divers hundreds of them were slaine in an houre: The Lord, as a God of glory in great terrour did appeare unto the Soule and Conscience of this poore Wretch, in that very act; and though before that time he had low apprehensions of our God, having conceived him to be (as he said) but a *Muskette* God . . . and as meane thoughts of the English that served this God, that they were silly weak men; yet from that time he was convinced and persuaded that our God was a most dreadfull God; and that one *English* man by the help of his God was able to slay and put to flight an hundred *Indians*. This conviction did pursue and follow him night and day, so that he Could have no rest or quiet because hee was ignorant of the *English mans God*: he went up and down bemoaning his condition, and filling every place where he came with sighes and groanes. (Eliot 1643:6, emphasis in original)

The "Muskette God," in whose service Wequash was engaged when he assisted English soldiers in the 1637 massacre of Pequots, had not won Pequot lands or Wequash's conversion by consent or mutual cultural compounding, but by terror. Yet, as Eliot suggests, the daily struggles of conversion were not simply those that ensued as missionaries sought to convey "the might power of God" to their indigenous subjects, but also entailed debates among Native people themselves: for as Wequash "grew greatly in the knowledge of Christ, and in the Principles of Religion," he faced "many trials . . . from the Indians" (Eliot 1643:6), many of whom surely understood that the English god had been no protector of indigenous land rights.

Though Eliot's discourse silences the knowledge of the Native resisters who made Wequash face these "many trials," by the eighteenth century the common practice of selling or leasing Native lands to cover the costs of the missionary project in southern New England could have only fueled indigenous resistance to Christianity.[20] Cotton Mather made clear in a November 1711 entry in his diary that there was an urgent need for proposals that would begin to revitalize the missionary endeavor in Connecticut: "One is, to send a couple of Missionaries unto the Mohegan Indians, and their neighbors [presumably Pequots and Niantics], in the Colony of Connecticut, which unto the shame of us all, continue still in Paganism" (Mather 1912:199). As an enticement to "certain Indians, who are uncommon Examples of Temperance," Mather suggests that a gift of a hat, "for each of them . . . may be an Encouragement unto others to follow the pattern." He adds to these proposals, finally, that he would support the "letting out," or leasing, of Native lands to Anglos in order to fund the Christianization effort.

In telling instances, however, missionaries critiqued the economic opportunism that drove colonial "compounding" with local indigenous people. In 1723 the Reverend Solomon Stoddard of Northampton, Massachusetts, exhorted his brethren for disregarding the supposed "principal design" of colonization. His tract, called "Question: Whether GOD is not Angry with the Country for doing so little towards the Conversion of the Indians?" asserts:

> *The Profession of those that Adventured into this Country was, that it was their principal design, to bring the Indians to the knowledge of the true God and Saviour of Mankind, and the Christian Faith*; as the King declares in the Charter: The like is expressed in the Charter for *Connecticut*. And it would have been the Honour of the Country, if they had answered that Profession. Indeed we gave the Heathen an Example; and if they had not been miserably besotted, they would have taken more notice of it. But we have done very little to Answer our Profession. Some few pious persons, of their own accord, have taken some Pains, and had some Success. And some Money that has been contributed in *England* for the furtherance of that Design, has been faithfully expended that way: But the Country has been at very little Cost for the Conversion of the Heathen. Many Men have been more careful to make a booty of them, than to gain them to the practice of Religion. (Stoddard [1723]:8–9, emphasis in original)

At the close of the tract, Stoddard's final argument in favor of a more concerted effort toward Indian conversion is that it "*will be much better, than to Destroy them.*" "Some men in their Rage," Stoddard states, "mediate nothing but their utter Destruction; They *throw Fire-brands, Arrows* and *Death*: They are like *Edom*, and the *Ishmaelites* that said, *Let us cut them off from being a Nation, that the Name of Israel may be no more in Remembrance*, Psalm. 83.4. These men sh[o]w a Bloody Spirit: 'Tis much better to Convert them: Then they will do good, they will serve and glorify God, they will help to enlarge his Kingdom, and be a benefit to their Neighbors" (Stoddard 1723:12, emphasis in original).

The depth of Anglo hostility toward Native people that Stoddard describes here, at a time long after colonial military supremacy had been established and the indigenous populations of southern New England had been drastically diminished, suggests not only the extent to which colonial land hunger – or the desire to "make a booty" from Native lands – continued to structure Native-Anglo relations, but that the indigenous cultural presence within Anglos' claimed homeland continued to be construed as a threat to colonial society. Despite his critique of Indian-hating, however, Stoddard does not go so far as to suggest that Native people's own religious beliefs had legitimacy, or that the failure of the colonial "design" to "convert the heathen" in southern New England may have been attributable to more than the greed, hostility, or lack of interest in soul saving that colonists had stirred among the indigenous peoples in their midst. Indeed, for those Anglos who were intent upon invigorating the "civilizing mission" in the period beyond military conquest, what was to be made of the persistence of local indigenous beliefs and practices, and of overt resistance to Christian conversion?

Nearly a century after Gookin's *Historical Collections* was penned, missionary Eleazar Wheelock's *Plain and Faithful Narrative . . . of the Indian Charity-School at Lebanon, in Connecticut* (1763) identifies the reproduction of indigenous beliefs and practices as a distinct problem for the Christianization effort. Wheelock does not entertain the possibility that these beliefs and practices have an inherent validity, and thus he acknowledges no legitimate Native resistance to conversion. Concerned with the immediate problem of rooting out "Indian savagery," Wheelock's argument relies, on the one hand, on an evocation of hackneyed European notions about the essential attributes of a "savage" lifestyle (e.g., that it is "nomadic," that it entails too much hunting and not enough "improvement" of the land via agriculture). As he explains: "that great, and hitherto insuperable Difficulty, so constantly complained of by all our Missionaries among them as the great Impediment in the Way to the Success of their Mission, viz., their [the Indians'] continual rambling about; which they can't avoid so long as they depend so much upon Fishing, Fowling, and Hunting for their Support" (Wheelock 1763:15).

Wheelock's plan for the domestication of Indianness entailed the extraction of boys and girls from their Native communities, putting the boys into service as missionaries "in Conjunction with the English," and seeing that girls "be instructed in whatever should be necessary to render them fit, to perform the Female Part, as House-wives, School-mistresses, Tayloresses, &c" (Wheelock 1763:15). This project of transforming Native gender roles and inculcating patriarchal Christian doctrine was to require a more fervent and concerted effort than previously exhibited by colonists, particularly those he characterizes as "partaking in the public Guilt of our Land and Nation in such a Neglect of them [the Indians]" (14). But Wheelock also argues that Native people's reluctance to accept "civilization" had been incited by colonial land hunger and the concomitant appropriation of Native resources. He casts Native resistance to colonial domination as a "deep rooted Prejudice" that Native women and men "have so generally imbibed against the English": namely, that the English

> are selfish, and have secret Designs to incroach upon their Lands, or otherwise wrong them in their Interests. This Jealousy seems to have been occasioned, nourished, and confirmed by some of their Neighbors, who have got large Tracts of their Lands for a very inconsiderable Part of their true Value, and it is commonly said, by taking Advantage of them when they were intoxicated with Liquor. And also, by unrighteous Dealers, who have taken such Advantage to buy their Skins and Furrs at less than half Price, & c. And perhaps these Jealousies may be, not a little, increased by a Consciousness of their own Perfidy and Inhumanity towards the English. (15–16)

In contrast to his seventeenth-century predecessor John Eliot's *New England's First Fruits*, Wheelock's narrative did not claim a general beneficence on the part of colonists in their relations with indigenous people, particularly with regard to land acquisitions. Having confronted the failures of the missionary endeavor through the testimony of Native people, Wheelock is compelled to acknowledge that indigenous men and women had *consciously and actively opposed* "civilization." Yet while he does not wholly deny the validity of Natives' mistrust of colonists, neither does he consider the legitimacy, indeed the *humanity*, of their own ways of life: Indianness is profoundly "savage" to Wheelock and more than just *culturally* "other." As unscrupulous as "some of their [Anglo] Neighbors" may be, it is their own "Perfidy and Inhumanity" that the Indians themselves must be made to contemplate. Despite his eagerness to gather broad support for his plan, Wheelock expounded upon the difficulties of overcoming what he deemed the *innateness* of savagery: "I am fully perswaded for the Acquiantance I have had with them, it will be found, whenever the Trial shall be made, to be very difficult if not impossible, unless the Arm of the Lord should be revealed in an eminent Manner, to cure them of such savage and sordid Practices, *as they have been inured to from their Mother's Womb*, and form their Minds and Manners to proper Rules of Virtue, Decency and Humanity, while they are daily under the pernicious Influence of their Parents Example, and their many Vices made familiar thereby" (Wheelock 1763:25, emphasis added).

Situating Indian savagery in "*their Mother's Womb*," Wheelock's narrative is a telling expression of eighteenth-century notions of race and of the virulently racist and devastating program for Indian "conversion" that it ultimately demanded. In Wheelock's plan, civilizing Indianness requires the outright destruction of indigenous familial relations: "the Children taken quite away from their Parents, and the pernicious Influence of Indian Examples," as he put it (Wheelock 1763:25). Wheelock's proposed removal of Native children from their families and their communities required, of course, their removal from their homelands and from the local histories those lands embodied.

Like Gookin, Wheelock disparages Indian origins; but his racial theorizing is concerned with the present, and he suggests that the existence of Indianness and its "savage" lifestyle is a contemporary problem of *reproductive relations* within Native communities. For Wheelock, the potency of Indian "savagery" is exhibited in the persistence of indigenous subsistence practices, for instance, which are sustained by familial ties. Through routine social and economic activities (childrearing as well as hunting and fishing), Native women and men reproduce their own way of life. Thus "savagery," Wheelock's narrative suggests, is conveyed through the intimate enmeshing of cultural practices and inherited "racial" identity. And while Gookin denied the existence of a valid indigenous knowledge, Wheelock does indeed recognize indigenous familial relations as sites of knowledge production and suggests that this knowledge – emanating ultimately from the womb, and as such being innate or "racially" charged – does indeed have a power that demands vigilant surveillance and drastic measures of eradication.

For Wheelock, then, "savagery" was not to be naturally overcome by proximity to "civilization," nor was it to be transformed by a haphazardly practiced and carefully distanced "compounding" with Indians. At once inherently genocidal and violence-effacing, Wheelock's plan points to the formation of a Euro-American Indian policy driven by both the cultural exigencies of the colonial civilizing mission and emergent notions of race. Wheelock thus emphasizes the necessity of *removals* that would not only displace Native girls and boys geographically but that would be intended to culturally extricate them from their "racial" origin (i.e., the womb).[21] The desired outcome was to be the annihilation of indigenous knowledge and identities *and* of the means by which they were reproduced: indigenous familial and community relations.

## *Native Communities on Their Own Ground*

If indigenous knowledge had a potency that might challenge colonial claims to legitimacy well after military conquest, it directed colonial attention not only to the reproduction of Native kin and community ties but also to the connection between Native communities and those lands that were not wholly controlled by colonial authorities. In early-eighteenth-century Connecticut Native women and men who rejected or avoided "conversion" were also embroiled in struggles to protect their reserved lands. Missionaries, like Experience Mayhew, were confronted with strategies of resistance that asserted the power of indigenous knowledge, the locus of which was kin and community relations as well as ties to land. In 1713 and 1714 Mayhew made "visitations" to Narragansetts, whose reservation was located in southwestern Rhode Island, and to Mashantucket Pequots and Mohegans, whose reserved lands were in Groton and New London, respectively.[22] Mayhew's account implies that he was ignorant of the threats to land and livelihood that these Native communities faced, yet all were engaged in heated land disputes with colonists at the time of his visits. Narragansett leader Ninigret II, having been "pressed to concentrate his people's settlements in one place" by the colony of Rhode Island (Grumet 1995:137), made an agreement in 1709 by which the entirety of Narragansetts' " 'vacant' lands (that is, lands not yet possessed by colonists)" were deeded to Rhode Island, "except for a reservation in the southwestern part of the colony" (Herndon and Sekatau 1997:454n3). However, as Grumet explains, "nearby colonists soon compelled Narragansett people to sell or lease even this land," which encompassed sixty-four square miles in the area of Charlestown (Herndon and Sekatau 1995:137). During the eighteenth century "the reserved area shrank as non-Narragansett people acquired tracts through sale, theft, and gifts" (Herndon and Sekatau 1997:434). Likewise, Mashantucket Pequots' reserved land at Noank had been besieged by colonists, the impact of which was detailed in their 1712 petition to the Connecticut General Assembly (IND 1st, 1:75). Contradicting a 1709 ruling that had affirmed Pequots' rights to the Noank reservation and ordered Anglo-American encroachers to "remove themselves" (CR 15:566–67), the Connecticut General Assembly ignored Pequots' argument for Noank's continuing importance to their community's livelihood and turned over control of the land to the town of Groton in 1714 (IND 1st, 1:83; see chapter 5). Mohegans' early-eighteenth-century struggle to preserve their land rights was no less discouraging: although Mohegan sachem Owaneco's 1704 petition to the English Crown had led to the establishment of an imperial commission to investigate the colony's appropriation of Mohegans' reserved lands, the commission's 1705 decision in favor of Mohegans was disregarded by Connecticut officials, and Mohegans' legal dispute with the colony was to endure throughout most of the century (see chapter 4).

This was the context of struggle, ostensibly unknown to Mayhew, into which this particular conversion effort was interjected in 1713; and Mayhew's description of Natives' responses to his visits offers important insight into the significance of reservation land to the reproduction of community life and to Native resistance to the colonial "civilizing" project. By his own admission, Mayhew's attempt to rouse Native interest in the gospel met with little enthusiasm. His account of a meeting with Ninigret attests to the degree of opposition to "English ways" that endured even among Native leaders who had had long-standing relationships with colonists. For when Mayhew told Ninigret that he "desired him to consent that his people should hear me open the mysteries of Religion to them," Ninigret

> did not seem at all inclineable to what I proposed: He demanded of me why I did not make the English good in the first place: for he said many of them were still bad: He also told me that he had seen Martha's Vinyard Indians [the Christianized Wampanoags who had been the focus of almost a century of missionary work by Mayhew, his father, and grandfather] at Rode Island, that would steal, and these he said I should first reform before I came to them. He further objected that the English there at Narragansett were divided, some keeping Saturday, others Sunday, and others not keeping any day; so that ye Indians could

> not tell what religion to be of, if they had a mind to be Christians. He also added that his people were many of them indebted to the English, & lived much amongst them and so did not care for him, nor would hear me preach, tho he should bid them: *and said he*, If they should go to meeting, their English masters would send constables for them, and take them away. (Mayhew 1896:110, emphasis in original)

If Mayhew learned anything from Ninigret's remonstrance, it would be that opposing the Christianizing mission was something to which Narragansetts had devoted considerable thought and discussion. Ninigret may well have sought to quickly deflect Mayhew with this litany of objections, but it appears that he was also conveying to Mayhew that he and his community were savvy, that they knew what was happening in the lives of their Indian neighbors and that they shared information with each other about the matters that directly affected all their lives. Ninigret was apparently determined not to endure any more of Mayhew than he had to, for he subsequently "upbraided" him, saying "that [Mayhew] had hindered him of his business that day, by discoursing w[i]th him" (1896:111). When Mayhew responded that Ninigret should at least do "honour to the Queen, and the Gentlemen that sent [him]," Ninigret commented "that he did not despise the Queen, nor God: but I had best to try first what I could do with the Pequots, and Mohegins, and if they would submit to Religion, it may be he and his people might do so too: but he was not willing to be the first. I would discourse more w[i]th him; but he would stay no longer" (111).

Here again, Ninigret's invoking of the presence of his neighbors, Pequots and Mohegans, and his relationship to them, should not be overlooked as a mere attempt at deflection. What he proposes to Mayhew – that if Pequots and Mohegans were to "submit" (and of course we cannot know if that was indeed the term Ninigret employed), Narragansetts might consider conversion as well – is also an assertion of a particularly significant connection between these neighboring reservation communities. As other colonial accounts attest (see chapters 4 and 5), there is evidence that intercommunity relations were forged and sustained not only by kin ties and an imperative of knowledge sharing but by a concerted effort at political strategizing focused on the common problem of contending with dispossession and the intrusions of colonial authority. It is likely that Ninigret knew that Pequots and Mohegans, like Narragansetts, had been struggling to protect their reserved lands from colonial encroachment, and that they too would be wary or resentful of Mayhew's intentions.

When Mayhew first attempted to preach to Mashantucket Pequots at Groton in October 1713, he had little success in assembling them to a meeting and was unable to secure an audience with "Skuttaub," whom Mayhew identified as "the chief of pequot Sachims," since he was "gone a hunting"(1896:100). [23] Among the Pequots he did meet with, however, he recruited an interpreter, Joseph, whom he identified as a man who "speakes English very well," and who was the son of a former sachem (100). [24] Mayhew describes the sermon he gave to Pequots at this first meeting in detail, and though he required an interpreter, he explains Pequots' reactions thus: "To these things & many others [that] I then spake, the Indians seemed to give a very good attention and at the end of almost every sentence some of [the] chief of them would still say something, and as to many things they shewed some approbation" (101).

Although Mayhew notes that Pequots "showed themselves pleased" with "the proposal of learning to read & write" (1896:101), he indicates that he received no definitive response from Pequots at the conclusion of his sermon, most of whom were apparently women, who, when they "expressed their thankfulness," added that "when their men returned from hunting, they would have a meeting to consider of the things proposed to them" (102).

He had less success in his next attempt to convert Mohegans. Mayhew sent a message requesting a meeting through his Pequot interpreter, "who returning next day with one old [Mohegan] man with him said that the Mohegins were so universally gone out a hunting that it was not possible to obtain a meeting"(1896:104). Commenting on this failed effort, Mayhew reveals something of the way in which colonial power was marshaled to further the missionary endeavor:

> Now considering that the Governor [of Connecticut, Gurdon Saltonstall] had sent them [Mohegans] word that he himself would come with me to their meeting; and also Mr. Adams [the] minister of the place, and yet we could not obtain a meeting, I was much discouraged, and knew not well [what] to do further in the affair; but there his

> Hon[o]r [the governor] advised me to draw up in writing some of the principal things I desired to say to them; and he was pleased to say that when they returned from their hunting, *he would cause them to assemble together, and would go up to them, and would cause my Letter to be interpreted.* (104, emphasis added)

Mayhew does not indicate by what precise methods the Connecticut governor would "cause" these things to happen, and it appears that Mayhew was utterly ignorant of the fact that Mohegans were also in the midst of an intense land dispute with the Connecticut government, which was surely at least part of the reason they refused the meeting. By the time Mayhew made his second visit to Connecticut, however, in September and October of 1714, he had learned something about the encroachment on Mashantucket Pequots' Noank reservation, probably initially through the Pequot interpreter Joseph, with whom he had by then "discoursed largely . . . concerning the state of the Indians thereabouts" (112). Having sent Joseph "away to the [Mashantucket Pequot] Indian Sachims Skuttaub, and Robert" (presumably Robin Cassacinamon II) to request another meeting, Mayhew was told by Joseph that Mashantucket Pequots were "so out of frame with the trouble they had lately met with, and were still under that he could by no means prevail with them":

> I was informed that the English Inhabitants of Groton had lately divided among themselves a neck of Land lying by the Sea side [Mashantucket Pequots' Noank reservation], which the Indians claim as belonging of Right unto them; and that the Indians haveing pulled up and removed some fence that the English had made there, were sued for it, & damages and charges recovered of them to the value of seven or eight pounds; that for this, executions had been lately brought upon the Estate of the two Sachims, and that one of the Sachims [Skuttaub] being something of a Dealer in Smithery had by the officers, his Anvill and some other of his tools taken from him & c – These things hap'ning Just before I came there, proved a very unhappie obstruction in my way, and produced in the Indians a greater aversion to the English and their Religion than otherwise they would have had. (113–14)

When Mayhew finally had his opportunity, in the following month, to deliver his sermon to Skuttaub and other Mashantucket Pequots, he reported that they thanked him "but objected as a great discouragement to them, the Injuries which they supposed were done them by the English, with relation to the Lands before mentioned" (1896:116). Apparently determined to pave the way for Pequots' conversion, Mayhew met with Governor Saltonstall soon after to discuss "the dissatisfaction of the Indians at Groton about [Noank]" (119). Saltonstall dismissed the matter, telling Mayhew that he did not believe that Mashantucket Pequots "had any real wrong in the matter they complained of, but rather that certain Englishmen had . . . encouraged them [Pequots] in their discontent, and so promoted their offence at religion" (117). As noted above, the notion that there could be no legitimate Indian resistance to Christianization was proffered in missionaries' discourse, but it also became a particularly significant silencing tactic for government officials who sought to mask the illegality of encroachment on reservation lands in early-eighteenth-century Connecticut. Indeed, the idea that Indians who complained about infringement on their land rights had been incited to do so by "outside agitators" was a powerful theme in the Connecticut government's response to Mohegans' resistance to dispossession (see chapter 4).

Mayhew was to hear more about the mistrust that colonial practices of land acquisition had engendered among Native communities in Connecticut. When he preached to Mohegans for "about an hour & a halfe" in October of 1714, he was thanked, once again, but told by Mohegans who were present that, "as several nations had their distinct way of worship, so they had theirs; and that they Thought their way was Good, and that they had no reason to alter it" (1896:118–19). Some Mohegans, Mayhew wrote, also told him that "they could not see That men were ever the better for being Christians, for the English that were Christians would cheat the Indians of their Land and otherwise wrong them, and that their knowledge of books made them the more Cunning to Cheat others & so did more hurt than good" (120).

Rather than the ready compliance of presumably pacified Indians, Mayhew had thus confronted an overtly articulated resistance to "civilization." Although he had been politely received by the members of the Native communities he sought out, his call to Christianity was for the most part diverted and rejected. Perhaps this was due as much to his failure to comprehend the struggles that shaped the lives of these Native women and men as it was to the general arrogance and oppressiveness of the Christianizing mission itself. Nor did Mayhew acknowledge, it appears, the relationship between his particular actions as a missionary and government officials' efforts to confine and control Native populations and their lands. Indeed, Mayhew elicited the authority of the Connecticut governor to attempt to convert Mohegans and Pequots, and thus he caused the forces of both colonial government and the missionary endeavor to converge upon the reservation communities whose souls he sought to win.

Mayhew's account, then, reveals something of the machinations of colonial power as it was deployed in the context of the nonmilitary, but nonetheless inherently violent, "civilizing" project. But it also suggests that in the period beyond military conquest, reservation communities in southern New England were not fully contained – geographically or culturally – by colonially imposed boundaries, and that even the ostensibly mundane activities of Native people's daily lives did not readily lend themselves to colonial scrutiny and control. Apparently engaged in subsistence hunting, Native men in the reservation communities Mayhew sought to convert, and perhaps some women as well (as suggested in the Pequot interpreter's report that Mohegans could not be summoned for a meeting with Mayhew because they were "universally gone out a hunting"),[25] transgressed reservation boundaries as well as colonial cultural prescriptions in their search for wild game.[26] Hunting, undoubtedly an important supplement to early-eighteenth-century reservation economies ravaged by colonial encroachment on planting lands (see chapter 3), also asserted a Native community's rights to lands and resources that extended beyond the realm of the colonially designated reservation.[27] And since hunting had been the leisure activity of elites in Europe (see Jennings 1975:169n70; Calloway 1997:55), indigenous men's subsistence hunting was viewed by seventeenth-century colonists as evidence that Indian men were "lazy savages" who, having "forced" their wives to do the agricultural work, failed to "improve" the land (Cronon 1983:52–53). Hence, as historian William Cronon has explained, such a colonial construction of illegitimate male behavior was employed by colonists "to deny that Indians had a rightful claim to the land they hunted" (53).[28] In revealing the link between hunting and Natives' resistance to Christianization, Mayhew's narrative suggests that, for reservation communities, the routines of daily life were locally determined in spite of multiple external pressures and intrusions. But Native women and men in early-eighteenth-century southern New England undoubtedly knew that their hunting was perceived negatively by Anglos, and thus they, too, might view it as a means of maintaining cultural distance between Anglos and themselves. One can imagine that Native people would recognize moments when it might be useful to take advantage of imposed ideas about the "otherness" of indigenous ways of life to try to keep missionaries at bay. Indeed, we should not forget the rather brilliant cultural and political argument Ninigret offered in response to Mayhew's pestering; or that Mashantucket Pequot women, while agreeing to listen to Mayhew, told him that they could give him no response until "their men returned from hunting," and only then would they "have a meeting to consider" Mayhew's proposal (Mayhew 1896:102). Likewise, when Mayhew could not summon Mohegans because they were "universally gone out a hunting," they may well have been hunting, but Mohegans also may have been happy to have that particular message announced, with a deliberate cultural and political message (i.e., *keep your distance*).

Over twenty years after Mayhew's visitations, Mohegans, who had openly protested the Connecticut government's appropriation of their planting and hunting lands, were under the close scrutiny of colonial officials who sought to deny the legitimacy of their sachem, Mahomet II. An investigator, sent to the Mohegan reservation by the Connecticut governor to solicit evidence that could be used against Mahomet II, reported that Mohegans told him "that they did not care to Declare or say anything about it, without the People were all together" (TP 1:350–51). Such refusals and strategic silences on the part of reservation communities were also transgressions that, however briefly, subverted government authority. In rebuffing missionaries and government officials in this way, Native women and men insisted that some aspects of their lives were to be conducted beyond the realm of colonial supervision and manipulation. Thus, in early-eighteenth-century Connecticut, the demands of reservation life and the locally renewed and, to some extent, transformed significance of indigenous knowledges and ways of life – as they were expressed even in the most routine of practices, such as subsistence activities – hampered the colonial "civilizing" mission just as they proclaimed Natives' enduring connection to their homelands.

# 3

# Colonial Law and Native Lives

Colonial law cannot be understood as a consistent protector of reservation lands or of the indigenous communities that labored to make a life upon them in eighteenth-century Connecticut. Native women and men could petition the General Assembly to protest encroachment and argue for their rights to land, but colonial legislators were by no means objective arbiters in matters concerning indigenous land rights. Historians have observed that the colonial courts in southern New England were "most self-serving" in their treatment of Indian people (Koehler 1979:20), and as G. E. Thomas has explained with regard to "Puritans' approach to land acquisition," colonists failed "to treat Indians on an equal basis even when the Indians were willing to deal on the Puritans' own terms" (Thomas 1975:10). English law, Thomas maintains, "actually worked against the Indians' interests on a massive scale" (11). Offering a broader critique of colonial as well as U.S. federal Indian law, legal scholar Robert Clinton debunks the notion of fair treatment, arguing that "white law," as he refers to it, has "played a powerful role in justifying and rationalizing, first, the colonial expropriation of Indian land and resources and, later, the colonial subjugation of Indian peoples to governance" by "their invader" (Clinton 1993:77).

Colonial laws directed at Native communities in eighteenth-century Connecticut – such as those meant to confine the geographic movements of indigenous populations (discussed later in the chapter) – threatened what remained of the subsistence economies of local Native communities. Moreover, eighteenth-century colonial law perpetuated and normalized the objectification and dehumanization of indigenous people, as it did with African Americans. As eighteenth-century laws regarding treatment of slaves make clear, long after colonial military supremacy was established, indigenous peoples in southern New England were cast as irredeemable savages who posed a persistent threat to colonial society. As such, Native people, and Native polities, were objects of colonial scrutiny. Ideas about "Indian savagery" propounded in such laws cannot be separated from the juridical processes engaged by Native leaders who opposed dispossession via colonially legitimated means, such as petitioning the General Assembly. While it cannot be said that colonial law always directly reflected or determined colonial social practice with regard to treatment of Native people, it was nonetheless a crucial vehicle of cultural and political domination. An assessment of the general conditions of life for Native communities in early-eighteenth-century Connecticut, and of the ways in which law was implicated in everyday forms of colonial domination, makes that clear.

Historians have pointed out that the eighteenth century was a period of rapidly increasing economic prosperity in British North America, which was "widely shared by the colonists – with the obvious and crucial exceptions of black slaves and native Americans, groups whose members paid a frightful price for white society's well-being" (McCusker and Menard 1985:51). In eighteenth-century Connecticut colonial land hunger was augmented as economic prosperity increased. Historian Richard Bushman notes that the most important factors driving colonial land acquisitions in early-eighteenth-century Connecticut were dramatic population growth among colonists, their increasing need for cattle pasture, "the exhaustion of old lands," and the general desire among Anglo-American fathers that their "sons would prosper at least to the degree [they] had" (Bushman 1967:42). According to Bushman, the "intensified search for new farms" in Connecticut's "wilderness" resulted in the establishment of "nearly twice as many towns . . . in the thirty years after 1690 as in the thirty years before" (83). In addition, by the eighteenth century the colonial practice of making "pitches," or "taking up a piece of land wherever desired in the unoccupied land of a town" (Ford 1976:12), became the popular way of "settling" what were called the "common" or "undivided" lands of Connecticut towns.[1] The General Assembly began to encourage this practice in the late seventeenth century, when it allowed soldiers to make pitches at any location they chose within "conquered" lands (13). Reservations in some cases encompassed part of, or existed within, areas designated as common lands, as was the case with the Mashantucket Pequot reservation in Groton. As I demonstrate in this and subsequent chapters, town residents and town proprietors – those who assigned a town's lands to its inhabitants – often failed to acknowledge Native land rights or respect reservation boundaries.

Heightened colonial land hunger directly impacted reservation communities, including those that existed in the more remote region of the colony. In the town of Kent, in northwestern Connecticut, colonial land speculation increased during the first half of the eighteenth century, when even "the humblest pioneers were apparently speculating their heads off" (Grant 1967:302). Grant explains that the land that was "traded most frequently among local pioneers" in Kent was not land that had any unusual asset, but "merely good farming lots" (304). Grant's discussion of colonial land acquisition in mid-eighteenth-century Kent does not address the presence of Schaghticoke people, however, who at that time had two reservations within the town. In his *History of the Indians of Connecticut*, DeForest observes that while land in Kent "was sold to the original settlers by the colony . . . no records or papers remain to show whether the land was usurped from the Indians, or was obtained from them by purchase" (DeForest 1852:413). The existing Schaghticoke reservation, established in 1752, initially included 2,200 acres, but continual encroachment throughout the eighteenth century and government-imposed liquidation in the nineteenth reduced it to 400 acres of land "too rough and woody . . . to be cultivated" (420).

Colonial expansion posed an immediate threat not just to existing reservation lands but to the livelihood of reservation communities. Petitioning the Connecticut General Assembly in October 1703, Mohegan leaders Owaneco, Ben Uncas I, and Mahomet I made it clear that Anglo-American land hunger had destructive consequences for Mohegans' lives. As is common in Natives' petitions against encroachment in the eighteenth century, Mohegans recount the history of agreements made between their own leaders and the colonial government that were to have preserved their land rights. "As to our Boundaries," they remind colonial legislators, "they have been established by youre fathers & ours. Your records declare the same and what was by them Done we acknowledged and the articles made by them we own . . . [but] you have Suffered your people to Doe us wrong in setleing upon our Lands notwithstanding our complaints from time to time" (IND 1st, 1:52). The petitioners go on to explain that Mohegans had been threatened "to be Killed" by townspeople of Colchester

> whoe are setled upon our Land without our consent . . . and they have burnt our Hunting house that we Dare not goe to hunting upon our own Land for feare of being Killed by them and we forced to defend

> ourselves. The Governr. Did in a time of snow Last winter turne our women & children of[f] our planting fields Claiming it for his own and the people of N. London did take away great part of our planting Land far above theire bounds which have been known between them & us for many years and Last May your courte granted to New London & Coulchester all the Rest of our Lands s[o] that we have noe Land eithere to plant or hunt upon. we have [claimed] nothing but what your own Records Declare and now we heare by the scouts that are out that the English up Conecticot River threten to take our Scalps and the pequots and make money of them acording to boston Law. (1:52)[2]

Here Mohegan leaders have summarized the general conditions of reservation life in early-eighteenth-century Connecticut. Those Native women and men who sought to continue to live upon and protect what they could of their ancestral lands were quite literally under siege. Colonial encroachment upon reservation lands was a common practice, which sometimes entailed the destruction of Native crops and fences, the cutting of trees and theft of timber, and threats and acts of physical violence against reservation communities.[3] The notion that Native peoples failed to "improve" the land served as a justification for encroachment and plundering. Timber, for instance, was an important export product for New England in the early eighteenth century (CR 7:583). And as colonial chronicler Daniel Neal's "History of New England" reveals, English colonists deemed that Indians had not made adequate use of this resource: "their Country is stock'd with the best Timber for Shipping in the World, yet they never made any Improvement of it, beyond their canoes wrought out of the Trunks of Trees made hollow by Fire" (Neal 1720:25–26).

Petitions to the Connecticut General Assembly from Niantics, Paugussetts, Pequots, and Mohegans attest to the devastating effects that continual encroachment had on reservation communities. Although the colonial government in Connecticut generally appointed committees, comprised of Anglos only, to look into reservation communities' complaints, this practice offered no guarantee of fair treatment for Native petitioners but rather imparted an "aura of fairness," to borrow Neal Salisbury's phrase (Salisbury 1972:61), to legislative decisions regarding Native rights to reservation land. As one historian has explained, even government-appointed reservation "guardians" or overseers were often "unfaithful and negligent" in their duties to reservation communities (Bradshaw 1935:53). During the course of the Mohegan land dispute, Bradshaw notes, the Connecticut government "deliberately named overseers who were favorable to the English cause and thus took the Mohegan lands piece by piece" (53). This legislatively sanctioned assault on reservation communities' land rights happened in other cases as well. Paugussetts of the Golden Hill reservation in Fairfield charged in a 1763 petition that townspeople of Stratford and Fairfield had not only illegally occupied their land but had physically forced Paugussetts from the reservation and torn down one of their wigwams (IND 1st, 2:147, 149). The committee appointed by the General Assembly to investigate, however, argued on behalf of the encroachers, whom they presented as good tenants of the land who had "improved" it, while Paugussetts, as they deemed it, had not (2:149). Subsequently, two of the colonists that Paugussetts identified as having "unjustly and unlawfully ejected" them from their reservation (IND 1st, 1:147) were appointed as their very guardians by the General Assembly.[4]

Although reservation communities engaged in struggles to protect their lands did in some instances appear to have Anglo friends or sympathizers to whom they could look for assistance, legislators responding to Natives' petitions or committees appointed to look into complaints against encroachment often revealed themselves to be more concerned with protecting the interests of other colonial landholders or increasing their own holdings, rather than protecting Natives' land rights. Committees assigned to investigate encroachment on reservation lands were required to submit reports to the General Assembly, but they also made recommendations for the resolution of particular disputes, which legislators were likely to accept. Thus investigatory committees could have enormous influence on, if not wholly determine, the outcome of disputes over Natives' rights to reservation land. In effect, then, Native communities seeking to defend their reservation lands were subject to several tiers of colonial power: encroachers (among whom were land owners and proprietors in towns neighboring or encompassing reservation land), investigatory committees, and the General Assembly. Government-appointed Anglo overseers of reservation land, as well as missionaries, might also have an influential role in disputes over reservation land, and as in the case of Mashantucket Pequots' conflict with the town of Groton, overseers and missionaries sometimes sought to defend

Natives' land rights. Nonetheless, in the end it was generally the reports of government-appointed investigatory committees that held sway over the land rights of a reservation community besieged by encroachers.

Reservation communities did not necessarily succumb to the will of investigatory committees, however. In their petitions leaders of reservation communities sometimes contested committee reports and demonstrated a keen understanding of the forces that bore down upon their communities. An early-eighteenth-century petition from Eastern Pequot leader Mary Momoho informed the General Assembly of the threats posed to her community's reservation, established in Stonington in 1683, and took issue with the prediction of those Anglos who "tell us that when one or two more of us be dead the Lands will fall to them" (IND 1st, 1:73).[5] Mary Momoho responded: "we suppose that there will be some pleas made that wee are almost all dead & indeed so we be but yett wee have Thirty three men yet alive which belong to Momoho besides woemen & Children therefore we would begg the Honoured Courtt that they would take that prudent care of us as to Lett no Country Grants to be Laid upon our Lands" (1:73).[6]

The petition is signed "the sunk squaw which was the wife of Momoho and her men." In emphasizing the precise number of men in the reservation community – as well as her community's continuing connection to the former male sachem Momoho – Mary Momoho's petition suggests that she was aware of the fact that colonial officials would evaluate the reservation community's land rights according to the presence, or absence, of adult men among them. And indeed Native men in early-eighteenth-century southern New England were unlikely to exist in large numbers in reservation communities: the colonial wars of the seventeenth century and European diseases had taken a great toll on all Native populations in southern New England, and in the post–"Indian War" era Native men were compelled to seek out wage labor on colonial farms or in the whaling industry (see Brasser 1971:79–80; McBride 1990:107). Although recruited for military service in the imperial wars of the late seventeenth and early eighteenth centuries, Native men did not necessarily oblige colonial authorities willingly in these matters.[7] The account of a Captain Williams, who "command[ed] a company of Mohegan Indians" in Deerfield, Massachusetts, in 1724, indicates that the demands placed on Native men by colonial military service drew them away from matters important to the livelihood of their communities. Williams reported that

Mohegan men were "impatient to return and be at home, to gather their corn," and that they "will not be perswaded to stay there till the leaves fall from the trees" (CR 6:61).

The Eastern Pequot reservation community likely comprised more adult women than men at the time, but Mary Momoho's petition does not suggest that she had achieved her political authority within her own community by default. Nor is her petition entirely deferential to colonial authority; indeed, it opens with a reminder to the colonial government "of the former unity which was betwixt you and our Nation" during King Philip's War, when "Momoho was then the Pecot Saysjum and had sixty men under him and att all your expeditions of War was ready to serve you & doubtless was a guard to your nation" (IND 1st, 1:73).[8] Her petition's concluding line, which indicates that the male members of the Eastern Pequot reservation community are now "her men," is clearly an assertion of her political authority by her own community's standards, not those of colonial society. The General Assembly's response to the petition refers to her as "Momoho's Squaw" (1:74), rather than as a sachem or sunksquaw in her own right.

The General Assembly ordered that "some Suitable persons near the said Land" be charged with "inspect[ing] the state of this Affair" (IND 1st, 1:74). In 1723, however, Mary Momoho and eight other Eastern Pequot signatories submitted another petition to the General Assembly, indicating that what had been "inspected" was the reservation community, rather than the problem of illegal encroachment on the reservation land. The petition explains that the investigatory committee "sent by this Assembly last October . . . says, ye English Did Inform them [of] ye Number of ye Indians belonging to Mo-mo-hoe & his Company, that is now Extant or [descended] from them, And they Say, The English Inform'd them, that there was three men & four Squaws, & of Male Children twenty four, twenty of which are bound Servants to ye English" (IND 2nd, 2:22). Thus the committee had concluded that "a Small Quantity of Land would Suffice" for Mary Momoho's community and their "Posterity to plant upon" (2:22). Eastern Pequot petitioners challenged this report, asserting that "ye Descent of Mo-mo-hoe & his men, Male and Female which are now Surviving are above one hundred and thirty (as we shall set forth & demonstrate to this Assembly)" (2:22). The petition also emphasizes the importance of Eastern Pequot children to the life of the community, explaining that even those children who were then indentured servants in Anglo households would eventually attain their "freedom": "Though wee have bound out Some of our Children to ye English for Learning and Education; 'tis no other wise than ye English bind out their Children Each to other & c. Our Children are free at ye Same Age & time as ye English Children are, which are bound out" (2:22).

What is striking about this petition is that it makes what might appear to be two opposing arguments in defense of Eastern Pequots' rights to their reserved land. It indicates, first, that those rights reside in a distinct community, whose members "Male and Female" are bound by kinship to shared ancestors – "Mo-mo-hoe & his men." Moreover, the above comment regarding the Pequot children in servitude suggests that their spatial distance from the reservation and their immersion in colonial society has not severed their connection to the reservation community or obliterated their identity as Pequots. These Pequot children in servitude, whose lives are undoubtedly expected to benefit by exposure to English "Learning and Education," have remained "Our Children" to the petitioners. Yet there is also an appeal to the commonality of experience between Pequot and English children. And in that sense, the Eastern Pequot petitioners, who have been subjected to the colonial argument that theirs is a vanishing community whose land rights should be increasingly limited if not wholly denied, offer a cultural argument of their own, suggesting that in important matters of life – specifically, those concerning the education and future of one's children – their lives and those of "the English" are not so different, and that Eastern Pequots and their lands deserve comparable protection from the government.

That evocation of cultural similarity is bolstered by a more direct appeal to justice and legality. The petition indicates that the 1683 covenant with colonists, which had been intended to secure their rights to the reservation land, had not been forgotten: "This Court fixed ye [reservation] Land for our Fathers *(& as they have told us) wee & our Children for ever*" (IND 2nd, 2:22, emphasis added). What, after all, did the size of the reservation population have to do with the validity of that covenant? The colony's 1680 reservation law, which was to have preserved reservation lands in perpetuity, made no stipulation regarding the size of Native communities for which reservation lands were to be designated; nor, in fact, did it fix rights to reservation land solely in male members of Native communities. Nonetheless, Eastern Pequots appear to have been aware of the fact that the presence of adult men among them was being equated with their need for and rights to land, and thus the petition emphasizes the importance of male ancestors as the conveyors of that covenant.

If Eastern Pequots intended for the reservation land to be for "our Children for ever," the gritty details of reservation subsistence articulated in the 1723 petition make it apparent that their hopes for the future were not sustained by any romantic vision of a secure existence within the realm of reservation boundaries. Eastern Pequot petitioners argued that the General Assembly's investigatory committee had simply ignored the economic hardships endured by the reservation community, since their recommendation that "a Small Quantity of Land would Suffice for us" was made "not Considering what great Disadvantages wee are under for want of Dung! When wee have Wore out our Planting Land; Wee must always be breaking up new Land; So that a Small Quantity of Land will Starve us!" (IND 2nd, 2:22). Subsistence strategies were drastically limited by confinement to small parcels of land, but equally important here is the indication that Eastern Pequots were indeed attempting to make use of all the arable land within the reservation's boundaries. For New England's Native peoples, appropriate land use required that specific agricultural plots lie fallow periodically so that they could later be planted again (see Merchant 1989:76). However, colonial committees were likely to ignore local subsistence practices and to determine that land not being used or "improved" at the time of their inspection was abandoned land.

Investigatory committees' failure to acknowledge and address the specific economic conditions of reservation life may reflect their tendency to disregard the specificity of Natives' complaints against encroachers. In a petition of May 1737 Mohegans reported that the members of the committee appointed to investigate their complaints against encroachment "are so remote from us [that] it is difficult for them to obtaine true apprehensions of our affairs" (IND 1st, 1:158). Such "remoteness," however, was not necessarily a simple matter of geographic distance alone, but likely a matter of the particular agenda of the appointed committee members as well.

When Eastern Pequots petitioned yet again in May of 1749, the circumstances under which their community had been compelled to live had not improved. While this petition does not recount the actions of encroachers, stating only that Eastern Pequots have been "frequently in a great variety of Ways & Manners grievously Molested" (IND 1st, 2:40), the subsequent report of the investigatory committee gives greater detail. Ownership of the reservation land had been claimed by the two heirs of Stonington resident William Wheeler (son of Isaac Wheeler, see note 5), who had allowed Eastern Pequots only the "liberty to plant Indian Corn, & Denying them any Liberty to keep any Cattle, Sheep or hoggs" (2:41). The committee did not speculate as to who the actual owners of the reservation were, but instead wrote that they would "Refer to Your Honours [of the General Assembly] the Consideration In whom the Fee [i.e., colonial legal title] of said Land is, and whether any Thing is Needfull further to be Done by This Assembly" (2:41). While they concluded that the rights of Eastern Pequots had been violated, their report characterizes the reservation community in a way that would be unlikely to elicit government defense of Pequots' rights against the prominent Wheeler family. The committee concedes that Eastern Pequots "had Just Ground of Complaint, & that They have Just right to use & Improve so much as is Needful for Them," and offers this description of the reservation community: they "are in Number about thirty eight of old & young, & The Greatest part Females; Who are not disputed to be the proper Descendants of sd Momohor" (2:41).

The General Assembly was slow to respond, and in May of 1750 another petition from Mary Momoho, along with Samson Sokient and "all Indian Natives of ye Tribe of Momohor," reminded the General Assembly of their complaint in the previous year and of the prior committee's recommendation that William Williams and Nathan Crery, the sons-in-law of William Wheeler who claimed rights to the reservation, be billed for "the Costs and Charges of This Enquiry" (IND 1st, 2:41). Uncertain whether it was "Multiplicity & Urgency of other Business or Meer oversight or Inattention" that left the 1749 petition unattended by the assembly, the petitioners explained that the Eastern Pequot community "neither thro' Extreme Poverty can, nor (being ye Blameless Party) ought to be condemned in Cost which have Unavoidably been Occasioned in Said Enquiry" (2:42). The General Assembly once again put off the matter until their next session, in October, at which time William Williams and Nathan Crery were ordered "to Appear to Show reasons why the Costs mentioned in This Memorial Should not be Taxed against Them" (2:42). It was not until October of 1750 that yet another committee made its report on the 1749 complaint. In this instance Eastern Pequots had requested that the committee come to the reservation. The committee complied, and their report states that Williams and Crery had put a fence across the reservation

> at which the Indians were Disturbed and had thrown the sd Fence Down, we also found that there had been Considerable Timber Cutt on ye sd lands by sd Williams and Crery (as ye Indians Informed us) the said Williams and Crery being present asserted their Right to Cutt and Improve as they Please only allowing the Indians to Plant in Small Yards of Inclosures and to Secure their Corn by fencing within their Large Pasture which they (viz) the said Williams & Crery Challing [challenge] to be their own property in fee[.] they also dispute the bounds of ye Lands claimed by ye Indians – and Since we were at Stonington Several of ye Tribe in behalf of ye Rest, have been with us at Norwich and Complain and Say that said Williams and Justice Minor put their unruly horses Cattle and Sheep into the sd Large pasture and have Eat up & Destroyed good part of their Corn & beens. They assert also that ye Indians have attempted to fence in some of their land for pasture, but have been beaten off from it and their fence thrown down; and that sum of them Did Plant a field of about an acre with Corn & beens[,] which one Nathaniel Holaredge Chalinging the Improvement of By force of a lease from sd Williams did Weed and Hill [hull] ye Corn, and Now have Gathered and Carried away the same; all which Facts according to the best lite and knowledge that we can gain are true, the Indians are very Desirous that your Honours Would appo[i]nt an officer to Come and Run the Lines of their Lands and assertain their Bounds and also to make Some further acts by which they may be more Efectively Enabled to take the Profits of ye land for the Necessary Support of them selves and Familys. (2:44)

The committee's report bears citing at length since it offers a detailed picture of the everyday struggles of reservation communities at the time. Protecting reservation resources and agricultural plots from pillaging was clearly a central problem. Pequots, as well as Mohegans and Mashantucket Pequots, entreated the General Assembly to acknowledge and enforce reservation boundaries, but as in this case, the officials assigned to this task assessed reservation boundaries in collaboration with those who had been charged with encroachment. Eastern Pequots thus had little meaningful government protection to rely upon and surely appeared extremely vulnerable to those Anglos who sought to acquire their lands and who had dismissed them, in any case, as "almost all dead." In light of the above account, and considering that the Eastern Pequot community was at the time led by a woman, researchers today can only speculate about the degree of violence that colonial encroachers may have presumed they could inflict upon the reservation community with impunity: one wonders, for instance, upon how may occasions Eastern Pequots who were engaged in the task of building or repairing fences to protect their crops were "beaten off" by those who desired their lands. Indeed, since the General Assembly had been slow to act on the May 1749 petition, Williams and Crery may have assumed there was little government interest in protecting the land rights of a small Indian community, particularly if that community was perceived as doomed because of the absence of men and male leadership.

In response to the charges of violence made in the 1750 committee report, the General Assembly appointed yet another investigatory committee – John Bulkley of Colchester and Jonathan Trumbull of Lebanon – who were ordered to "make [an] Agreement & Settlement with sd Williams & Crary as they . . . Shall Think Just and Equitable" and were "Authorized and Impowered in ye Name of ye Governour & Company of This Colony to Take and Give Deeds of Release Grants or Privledges" as they saw fit (IND 1st, 2:45). The General Assembly did not order the committee members to consult with Eastern Pequots regarding the "agreement and settlement" that was to be made with Williams and Crery; they were directed simply to "repair to sd Stonington, To view ye Premises and Consider ye Circumstances of ye whole Case" (2:45).

The subsequent report by this committee, dated May 1751, indicates that their investigation entailed no consultation with Eastern Pequots; neither does their report acknowledge the prior complaints made by the reservation community. According to their own record of their investigation, the committee met only with Williams and Crery, at which time they "agreed" with Williams and Crery on what the bounds of the reservation were, without input from any members of the Eastern Pequot community. Williams and Crery, "& Their Heirs & Assigns," were granted "Thirty five Acres of Land at the Southerly End" of the reservation, as well as "Twenty Acres more laid off to them on the East Side" (IND 1st, 2:46). Finally, the committee determined that Williams and Crery should "pay the costs" of the 1749 committee and any costs incurred as a result of the inquiry. The General Assembly approved the report, ordering that Williams and Crery were to "release" their claim to the reservation to "ye Governour & Company and their Successors" (2:48). This action was apparently intended to resolve, or bury, the question of legal title to the reservation. Neither the General Assembly's decision nor the report of the investigatory committee acknowledged the original terms of the covenant that Eastern Pequots had invoked in 1723: namely, that the colonial government had "fixed ye Land" for "wee & our Children for ever" (IND 2nd, 2:22).

By May of 1751, after Eastern Pequots submitted four petitions attesting to a thirty-year struggle to protect their land rights, the initial reservation covenant had been written out of the colonial legal proceedings regarding the dispute over the reservation. A succession of committees and committee reports provided the appearance of legitimacy to the colonial government's handling of the dispute, yet the grievances of Eastern Pequot petitioners were finally ignored, as was the 1680 reservation law. This "committee game," as it might be termed, was thus a means of enabling, if not offering incentive to, encroachers.[9]

The undermining of Native rights to reservation land was propelled by more than colonial land hunger and the biases of particular colonial officials. Eighteenth-century Indian policy reflects the formation of a distinctly racialized social hierarchy (see Warner 1935:327–29). Historians have pointed out that Anglo-American hostility toward Native people in southern New England intensified in the aftermath of King Philip's War. Indians "were watched and hunted as thieves day and night," one historian contends (Crane 1904:223). "By 1680," Peter Lloyd argues, "feelings ran high against all Indians, Christian and Pagan alike" (Lloyd 1975:153). During the eighteenth century a system of "wholesale racial subordination and segregation" would become firmly entrenched in southern New England, structuring the lives of Native people "through the remainder of the colonial period and into the national era" (Salisbury 1985:457; see also Liggio 1976). Laws concerning treatment of slaves, which were "continually growing harsher" by the end of the seventeenth century (Steiner 1893:382), reflected the salient racial categories of the era as well as the degree to which racism infused official assessments of the rights of both Native American and African American people. In 1690, for example, Connecticut instituted a "black code," which stated that a " 'negro, mulatto, or Indian servant' found wandering out of the bounds of the town to which he belonged, without a ticket or pass from an Assistant, or Justice of the Peace, of his owner, shall be accounted a runaway and may be seized by any one finding him, brought before the next authority and returned to his master, who must pay the charges" (382–83).

When Connecticut prohibited the importation of enslaved Indians in 1715, "this measure was not prompted by affection for the slaves," Steiner argues, "but by fear of them" (1893:385).[10] This 1715 law depicts Indianness as an ever-present threat to colonial society: it would be "of pernicious consequence," the act states, to allow an "overgreat number" of Indian slaves into the colony, since "diverse conspiracies, outrages, barbarities, murders, burglaries, thefts, and other notorious crimes at sundry times and, especially of late, have been perpetrated by Indians and other slaves . . . [who are] of a malicious and vengeful spirit, rude and insolent in their behavior, and very ungovernable" (cited in Steiner 1893:385). The law thus fashions a colonial world infused with the imminent terror of "Indians and other slaves," whose inherent, immutable savagery cannot be made "governable" even by slavery – which, of course, classified Indians and Africans as chattel and not persons. Attesting to such dehumanization of Indian and African people in eighteenth-century New England, Chief Justice of Massachusetts Samuel Sewall noted in a diary entry of June 1716 that he had tried "to prevent Indians and Negros being Rated with Horses and Hogs; but could not prevail" (Sewall 1973:822).[11]

The construction and elaboration of racial categories in colonial laws suggested that indigenous peoples in southern New England, though militarily conquered, required vigilant surveillance. In early-eighteenth-century Connecticut, Native populations were subjected to stringent laws that were intended to confine them geographically and that cast those who transgressed designated boundaries as "enemies." Although the legacy of King Philip's War continued to fuel colonial ideas about imminent "Indian treachery" into the eighteenth century, the threat of both Indian and French conspiracy during the imperial border wars was the ostensible justification for the Connecticut government's establishment of laws restricting the movements of Native populations.[12] In 1723 Connecticut officials feared that "about three hundred French Indians were come over the lake towards Connecticut," and that "divers parties of those Indians [were] waiting to do mischief on the frontiers" of the colony. The General Assembly issued the following orders to be "sent to the sachems and several bodies of Indians in this Colony" as of August 1723:

> requiring them forthwith to call in all their Indians that are out a hunting in the woods, and that they do not presume to go out again into the woods to hunt, north of the road that goes from Farmingtown through Waterbury, and Woodbury, to New Milford, or north of the road from Hartford through Coventry and Ashford to New Roxbury [essentially the entire northern half of the colony], before the meeting of the General Court in October next, or without leave first had of the Governour and Council; and that they publish it to all Indians, that such as are found north of the said paths in the woods, after the 20th of this instant August, must expect to be treated by the scouts, and all others, as enemies. (CR 6:407–8)

In May of 1724, similar restrictions on Natives' movements were reiterated in "An Act for better Securing our Frontiers against the Skulking Parties of Indians," which indicated that colonists who were to kill any "Indian enemy" and "produce the scalp of such Indian enemy to the Governour and Council, or to the said Committee of War, shall immediately be paid out of the publick treasury the sum of fifty pounds" (CR 6:464). The act does not require that colonists who turned in scalps must prove by some means (witnesses, for example) that their victims had violated any law. Moreover, although colonists were likely to be made quickly aware of laws that entailed such handsome rewards for their services, it cannot be assumed that local Native communities were well informed of the potentially deadly implications of these laws. Even if they had been "published" to or distributed among Native communities, Native men engaged in a hunt, for example, surely could not be certain when they had entered officially forbidden territory at any given moment (e.g., "southward of the dividend line between [Connecticut] and the Province of Massachusetts, northward of the road that goes thro' the towns of Farmington, Waterbury, New Milford, Danbury, and Ridgefield" [464]). Indeed, such legislation made Indian men in pursuit of wild game particularly vulnerable to being classified and killed as "skulking Indians."

In May of 1725 the General Assembly renewed "the bounds stated for restraining the Indians" in the May 1724 law, with the added incentive, for colonists, of a significantly increased bounty on Indian scalps: "if any number of effectual men, or any particular person, will sufficiently prepare themselves at their own cost and charge [that is, acquire firearms at their own expense], upon the news of the approach of the Indian enemy within this government, will go forth after them, and do take and recover any scalps of the enemy Indians . . . they shall receive the sum of one hundred pounds out of the publick treasury of this Colony for each scalp so obtained" (CR 6:535).

Restrictions on Native hunting were specified by the Connecticut government again in July of 1724, reaffirming the fear that "enemy Indians were waiting for an opportunity to do mischief, not only in the frontier towns of New Milford, Litchfield and Symsbury, but also near the towns of Ridgefield, Danbury, (below Milford,) Woodbury and Newtown, where our friend Indians commonly hunt." In this case, however, the legislation indicates that Anglo residents of these towns are "put to great distress, not being able to discern the enemy by their tracks, or to distinguish between friend and enemy Indians when they meet them in the woods," and that "the firing at deer, or other wild creatures" has made "false alarms . . . of pernicious consequence" – which presumably refers to the killing of "friend Indians" (CR 6:479).

It was thus ordered that "all persons . . . English or Indians" were forbidden to hunt or discharge a weapon "in the western frontier . . . till further order." A final warning is directed solely at those Native people who would, for any reason, enter the "frontier" region of the colony:

> And whereas if any of our friend Indians should be found in the woods about those towns, (especially now, since all hunting is prohibited,) they may be taken for enemies and be in hazard of their lives: It is therefore ordered that notice hereof be immediately given to the Indians inhabiting on the west side of Connecticut River, by the chief military officer in the counties of Hartford, New Haven and Fairfield; and that they be warned not to venture from the usual places of their abode into the woods, unless in company with the English; to prevent false alarms, and to preserve them from the danger which, in so doing, they will be exposed. (6:480)

In October 1725 the General Assembly appeared to concede that restrictions on movement that had been imposed on "the Western Indians" of Connecticut threatened their survival.[13] Measures were proposed that were to allow Native men more freedom to hunt but required no less severe restrictions on the daily existence of Native communities:

> But now this Assembly considering the Narrowness of their bounds [imposed by the law of the previous year], . . . [and] also considering

> the Danger there is of Setting [the Indians] Entirely at Liberty Do therefore order . . . That all the Indians abovesd . . . are to [be] convened [at which time] each Tribe shall chuse a Head or Chief who Shall be accountable for his Subjects And farther that, the Several Tribes under their chiefs Shall be obliged to Answer their names once every Fortnight [to colonial officials] . . . And also that no Indian be allowed to come on any account without a Certificate within the Bounds of Lichfield (or any other Town that shall publickly manifest to any Authority that they are unwilling sd Indians come to their Town) And that none of said Indians for the future be painted And that they be notified that if they come within the Bounds of . . . any Prohibited Town they may expect to be treated as Enemies, And that if any farther Suspicion of them arise they must be Immediately all confined . . . perhaps forever. (IND 1st, 1:117)[14]

The regular inspection and "marking" of "friendly Indians" (in this case, via a "certificate" permitting entry into "Prohibited Towns")[15] had been ordered in October of the previous year as well, when the General Assembly lifted hunting restrictions on the east side of the Connecticut River for "Moheags, Pequots, and all Indians of this Colony," "provided they give a list of their names to the chief commission officers of the towns where they belong . . . and that the said Indians shall wear a white mark on their heads for to distinguish them to be friends, and that they do not go northward of the line leading from Enfield to Woodstock, and that once in ten days said Indians appear and answer to their names before one of the commission officers in Stafford" (CR 6:486). In May 1725 colonial officials tightened the law on Indian inspections, stating that "if the D.[eputy] Governour and Council shall think best to order any companies of Indians to appear once a day or once a week before any English person or persons as they shall appoint, and give account of their ramble and business, the Deputy Governour and Council are desired and directed to make such orders, and appoint such penalties to any Indian or Indians that shall not conform thereunto as they shall conclude upon and appoint" (6:551).

As reservation communities were under siege by encroachers in the early eighteenth century, so too were all Native populations within the colony under government surveillance. To violate such laws – to be thus regarded as an "enemy" or "skulking" Indian – was to risk one's life. Such regulations posed a direct threat to the male members of reservation communities whose subsistence hunting took them beyond reservation boundaries. Native hunters might also be penalized for failing to adhere to colonial regulations concerning hunting seasons. Fines could be devastating to members of already impoverished reservation communities, as indicated in this 1717 petition from Mohegan leader Ben Uncas I to the Connecticut General Assembly: "Your petitioner being Ignorant of the Law prohibiting the Killing of Deer in the winter Season, his Son A young Lad did the last Winter kill with his dog, a Number of Deer, Incouraged thereto by Examples of the English, about Hebron and Colchester and other places" (IND 1st, 1:85).[16] Ben Uncas I was ordered "to pay 56 [pounds] to the Complanents, which is very grevious to me and greatly impoverishing to my family" (1:85). Not only the killing of "enemy Indians," then, but also monitoring and reporting on the routine activities of Native men could be profitable colonial ventures in early-eighteenth-century Connecticut.

Laws intended to both tightly control and dispossess Native communities were also proposed under the banner of the "civilizing" mission. A crucial example is an October 1717 act of the Connecticut General Assembly, "Measures for Bringing the Indians in this colony to the knowledge of the Gospell" (IND 1st, 1:87). In addition to requiring that the "Authority of Each [Anglo] Town" should annually "convene the Indians inhabiting each Town, and acquaint them with the Laws of the Government for punishing Such Immoralities as They Shall be guilty of," the measures also entailed an imperative of geographic control and cultural surveillance that reflected colonial legislators' interest in rendering even the internal dynamics of family life in Native communities more accessible to colonial authority. To ensure that Native men and women be "brought off from [the] pagan manner of living," they were to be "encouraged to make Settlements in Convenient Places, in Villages after the English Manner" (1:87). The particular means by which Indians' "pagan manners" were to be stamped out point to what was to become an increasingly important strategy for controlling reservation populations and undermining their land rights: that is, the practice of scrutinizing and evaluating the cultural legitimacy of reservation populations, particularly those whose members had resisted colonial encroachment and questioned colonial authority. In the 1717 act, government assessment of Indian cultural illegitimacy was directly linked to an implied "absence" of privatized, male proprietorship of land, as the following directive makes clear: "It is hereby resolved that measures shall be Used, to form Villages of the Natives; wherein ye Severall Families of them should have *Suitable Portions of Land appropriated to them, so that ye sd Portions, should descend from ye Father to his Children*, the more to encourage them to apply themselves to Husbandry" (1:87, emphasis added). Hence collective landholding, women's political authority, and kin-based ties to land (through matrilineal inheritance) were clearly marked as deterrents not simply to Natives' "conversion," but to one of the most fundamental expressions of colonial "civilization" – that is, "husbandry," or the cultivation of the earth in accordance with colonizers' cultural standards.

Seventeenth-century colonial law in Connecticut had not made such a direct effort to impose gendered prescriptions regarding land rights on reservation communities.[17] This particular aspect of the 1717 measures suggests that nearly a century of colonial domination in southern New England had not eradicated Native women's role as the primary agriculturalists in their communities (see Cronon 1983:44–45; Merchant 1989; Jensen 1994). Given that dispossession, the undermining of indigenous subsistence economies, and service in the imperial border wars compelled many Native men to leave their communities in the eighteenth century, it is likely that women and matrilineal kin groups not only sustained community life but also controlled agricultural plots on reservation lands.[18] From the perspective of colonial legislators, then, curbing Native women's economic power and political influence – via the imposition of patrilineal inheritance and privatization of land – may have been deemed a viable means of dismantling those communities (or "detribalizing" them, as it would come to be phrased in the parlance of Euro-American Indian policy) and thus eradicating their *collective* claim to a land base.[19] Indeed, the proposed "Native villages" would not have the same legal standing as reservations defined by the 1680 law, which clearly indicated that reserved lands were *not* to be the property of individual (or solely male) Indians but rather of "parcells of Indians," whose "heirs" (no gendered distinction is made in the 1680 law) retained their rights to those lands "for ever" (CR 3:56–57). Conversely, without the presence of adult men and male authority, the properly "civilized" Indian villages prescribed by the 1717 measures could not exist; thus there would be no Native land rights that the government would be obliged to acknowledge and protect. In effect, the 1717 measures provided a means of legislating reservation communities, and their land rights, out of existence.

The measures were aimed primarily at Mohegans, whose resistance to dispossession had elicited the intervention of the English Crown. The colony had ignored the 1705 decision of an imperial commission that reviewed Mohegans' complaints and ruled against the colony (see chapter 4 for further discussion). But as Connecticut's Governor Gurdon Saltonstall reported to his General Assembly in 1713, the Crown had not lost interest in the matter of Native land rights after 1705, for word had been sent to Connecticut that the queen planned an inquiry into "the Affair of Indian Lands" in the colony (IND 1st, 1:79).

As the colony's handling of Native lands was subjected to scrutiny from without, so too was there internal debate about the nature of Native land rights. At the time the "civilizing measures" were enacted, Connecticut legislators faced legal dilemmas caused by colonists who had purchased land directly from Native leaders without the approval of the General Assembly and in violation of colonial laws that prohibited this particular practice, which was referred to as the "purchase of Native right" (CR 1:402, 4:397; see also Bushman 1967:84).[20] A 1717 law forbidding purchases of "native right or Indian title" details the problems this practice created for the Connecticut government:

> This Assembly, observing many difficulties and perplexities arising in this government by reason of many purchases of land made of Indian titles without the preceding allowance or subsequent approbation of this Assembly: which to remove:
>
> It is hereby enacted and declared by this Assembly and the authority thereof, That all lands in this government are holden of the King of Great Britain as the lord of the fee; and that no title to any lands in this Colony can accrue by any purchase made of Indians on pretence of their being native proprietors thereof, without the allowance or approbation of this Assembly. So it is hereby resolved, That no conveyance of native right or Indian title, without the allowance or approbation of this Assembly as aforesaid, shall be given in evidence of any man's title, or pleadable in any court. (CR 6:13)

The law required that a committee be formed to "inquire into and gain a true understanding of all the claims [made by purchasers of Native right]" and to make compensation to those individuals in cases it deemed appropriate "either within the bounds of any town with the consent of the proprietors or elsewhere within the ungranted lands of this Colony" (CR 6:13). The General Assembly's primary concern was not to protect Native land rights but to maintain its own authority over the "settling" of land within the colony (see Jennings 1975:130). As it was explained in the act itself, the law and the committee's task were to make it possible for the General Assembly to "proceed to the settlement of all the undisposed lands in this Colony in such manner as shall then be determined, that all future troubles about our settlements may be avoided" (CR 6:13–14).

Confronting debates within, as well as pressures from without, on the matter of Native land rights, Connecticut legislators could not afford to ignore the presence of reservation communities or the legal implications of their claims to ancestral lands. In fact, the intent and content of the 1717 act had been debated among government officials. An initial proposal for the "civilizing" measures, presented to the General Assembly by Governor Saltonstall, contained a recommendation pertaining to the *protection* of reservation lands, a recommendation that was not preserved by the General Assembly when the 1717 measures were finally enacted. According to the proposal made by Saltonstall:

> the Lands which in any sort are Reserved or which ought to be reserved for the Use of the Indians be by the direction and Order of the Government in the best and most Effectual manner Secured to that End. Which Wee Take to be of great Necessity to the proposed End [i.e., Indian "conversion"] . . . in 2 respects[:] 1 Because This will Effectually Remove from the Natives the fears and Jealousies of those wrongs which they frequently make Complaint And 'tis to be feared Oftentimes not without Just Reason – They that possessed Large Countries heretofore are now Reduced to Such a Small quantity that they have but Sufficient, if that, for Such a Subsistance as it is to be wished they might have – 2ly Bec[ause]: The Securing to them Certain Meet parcells of Land against the Intrussions of all persons – under pretence of Right, where the Indians may Live in Quiet and have their Tillage preserved from Trespasses is the Liklyest way to put them into Circumstances in which they may more Easily be prevaild with, as to the great design which is proposed of perswading them to receive the Gospell. (IND 1st, 1:88)

Saltonstall's remarkable proposal reiterated the provisions of the 1680 reservation law and indeed emphasized the necessity for vigilant governmental protection of Native land rights. Equally important, it acknowledged, at least to some extent, the validity of Natives' complaints against dispossession, conceding that the Native peoples in the colony's midst did indeed have inherent rights to land, having "*possessed Large Countries heretofore*" that "are now reduced" to such a "small quantity" that they are barely able to sustain their communities. This was indeed an indictment of colonial encroachment, perhaps condemning it more as an immoral than an illegal act. Nonetheless it placed the onus of guardianship on the Connecticut government and may have recalled a bit too closely the colony's guilt in the matter of Mohegan dispossession as determined by the 1705 commission. Not surprisingly, then, the final version of the 1717 act omitted an important directive to the colonial officials who were to be appointed to begin implementation of the measures: that is, the governor's proposal that these officials should investigate colonial claims that had been made on reservation land "in opposition to ye sd Indians" (IND 1st, 1:88). The enacted 1717 measures thus entirely silenced the quite pertinent issue of Natives' resistance to dispossession and the problem of illegal encroachment on reserved lands.

It should be noted, however, that Saltonstall's proposal does not deviate from the prevailing colonial notion, clearly articulated by missionary John Eliot in his 1643 *New England's First Fruits* (see chapter 2) and also encoded in the 1680 reservation law, that Indians, as they existed in communities or "parcels," must be "set apart"; and certainly what Saltonstall prescribes here might be read as a prescription for tranquilizing Native communities, securing the boundaries of reserved lands so that "the Indians may live in Quiet," undisturbed by colonists but also prevented from "disrupting" colonial society.

Although the 1717 act identified no specific Native community by name, the town of New London (which encompassed the Mohegan reservation) was specified as the place where "there are now living, the largest Number of Indians, [that] live together in any one Place."[21] Thus the act ordered that judges of the superior court "visit the Indians" living upon the "considerable tract of land in the township of New London" – the Mohegan reservation – and

> take account of the number of their families and persons; of the quan-

> tity and quality of said land, with other circumstances thereof, in respect of any claims made thereto or possessions held thereon, and lay a plan of the same before the General Court for their further direction, and that they may be the better enabled to proceed in forming a village of the said Indians there, and bringing them to such civil order, cohabitation and industry, as may facilitate the setting up of the gospel ministry among them; and that they view and make report of all the land formerly sequestered to said Indians [that is, Mohegans]. (CR 6:32–33)

The committee charged with "visiting the Indians" in New London reported that they had "view[ed] the state of the Indians living at Mohegan" and determined the "number of the said Indians to be upward of two hundred, and that the land is sufficient for their comfortable subsistence, and that the said Indians have complained to them of several claims and entries made upon the said land, and damage sustained by them in their fields, and prayed that they would recommend them to the care and protection of the said court" (CR 6:77–78).

The Mohegan community may have been deemed to be in dire need of "civilizing," if not simply "quieting," but as colonial officials had come to learn, Mohegans were not to be easily manipulated. The General Assembly appointed a committee to investigate their complaints and "to do and act therein for the removal of all forcible entries" on their reservation (CR 6:78). Mohegans' effort to set the 1717 committee to the task of investigating encroachment did not, however, serve to divert government attention from the intent of the 1717 act. By October of 1719 the General Assembly ordered the previously appointed committee to enforce the "civilizing" measures, since it "*might prove a great blessing both to the English and Indians*" in New London (6:148, emphasis added). That intended "blessing," evidently, was to bring an end to Mohegans' complaints and to secure colonial control over Mohegan reservation land. In addition to assigning the committee with the task of "the settling of a minister" among Mohegans – who was to be given five hundred acres of Mohegan reservation land for his own farm and parsonage (6:193–94) – the General Assembly also empowered the committee members to act as Mohegans' "guardians" and authorized them to lease parcels of the reservation land "in their own [that is, the guardians'] names" in order to cover the expenses of the "civilizing" effort. The final paragraph of the order makes it clear that such an arrangement would serve to legitimize the whittling away of Mohegans' reserved land, since it added that "the whole charge [of implementing the 1717 measures] be supported out of the profit of said lands" (6:149).

The 1717 act is perhaps the most important colonial legislation regarding Native land rights in early-eighteenth-century Connecticut. Apparent in the stark contrast between the initial proposal and the enacted "civilizing" measures is that colonial officials continued to debate the matter of Native land rights long after military conquest, and that reservation communities' resistance to dispossession was of no small concern to the Connecticut government. Significantly, the government officials' shifting positions on the question of Natives' rights to reservation land posed problems for Anlgos as well as reservation communities.[22] In 1760, proprietors of the town of Groton, who sought to appropriate Mashantucket reservation land, expressed their dissatisfaction with the General Assembly's inability to resolve the enduring dispute over Mashantucket Pequots' land rights. "There has been a long controversy," they complained to legislators, "subsisting between proprietors and the said Pequot Indians respecting the Improvement of said Mashentucket Lands," which the proprietors deemed to be part of the town's common lands and thus under their own control. They warned the assembly that the "controversy appears likely to continue and the matter somewhat doubtful, how far said Proprietors have a right in said lands or whether said Indians have any more than a right to the use and improvement of sd lands according to their ancient manners of improvement of lands and not the absolute fee thereof – and the courts have judged variously relating thereto" (IND 2nd, 2:109). The proprietors of Groton finally requested the appointment of a committee to "determine, settle and quiet said controversy by setting out a sufficient Part of said Lands for the Improvement of said Pequot Indians" (2:109). What was considered "sufficient" for a reservation community's use, as I have explained, was to be determined solely according to the colonial committee's assessment of the viability of that community's population and its cultural practices, or "ancient manners."

In May of 1761 this committee urged that unless the dispute over Mashantucket Pequots' land rights was finally resolved, "it ever will be a discouragement to Good Improvement and Husbandry" (IND 2nd, 2:118). Like the 1717 measures, this assessment of the land dispute posed reservation land and the Native communities that endeavored to live upon it as a *cultural* problem, and more pointedly as a hindrance and disruption to "civilization"; in so doing, colonial officials deflected attention from the illegality of encroachment on reservation land. As Connecticut governor Joseph Talcott argued in the midst of the Mohegan case, to restore colonially appropriated lands to Mohegans would be to disturb "the peace and quietness" of the "several flourishing Towns . . . upon [that] land" (TP 1:335). Indeed in early-eighteenth-century Connecticut "civilization" was a work in progress. As Massachusetts governor Jonathan Belcher remarked in 1729, in a statement of support to the Connecticut government as it contended with the ongoing dispute over Mohegans' land rights, the colony of Connecticut had not yet wholly conquered its "wilderness," for a "great part of the lands in this Colony are still unclear'd and but a small part of it to this day thoroughly subdued and the Inhabitants of this place have hardly any other way of supporting themselves but by tilling and subduing the Earth, and the whole strength of the people of this Colony is employ'd in clearing and tilling the wilds of this Colony" (1:188). Opposing the particular exigencies of colonial "civilization" – notably private property and absolute male authority over political and economic activities – reservation communities could be cast, quite conveniently, as an intolerable cultural presence. Equally important, in their refusal to acquiesce to colonial demands for the last bits of their reserved lands, Native resisters challenged the presumed historical destiny of their conquerors, whose attainment of civilization depended upon the relentless "subduing" of the landscape.

Connecticut's Indian policy, as it was expressed in legislative acts as well as the arguments of encroachers, investigatory committees, and reservation overseers, took a decidedly cultural turn in response to Native resistance to dispossession in the early eighteenth century. Although in some instances the illegal acts of encroachers were acknowledged by colonial officials, their lawlessness and disregard for Native land rights was not examined or monitored as a social problem or breach of "peace and quietness." Instead, at crucial junctures in disputes over rights to reservation land, colonial authorities proffered the notion that reservation communities were culturally illegitimate entities, and as such required surveillance and specific measures of containment and control. In 1721, when the General Assembly approved an investigatory committee's recommendation that the Mohegan reservation be reduced to one-fourth its original size, the idea of the inevitable "extinction" of the Mohegan reservation community was formally introduced into colonial legal discourse on Native land rights. As it was forged in the 1721 decision, Mohegan "extinction" was the condition that was to free the remaining fragment of their reservation for colonial appropriation. The unfolding of that legislated Indian destiny – the imminent "degeneration" that would culminate in the "disappearance" of reservation communities from the colonial landscape – was a process that required monitoring as well. But precisely how "extinction" was to be assessed or "recognized" was open to multiple colonial interpretations. Would it be the "absence" of individual (male) Mohegan bodies from the reservation land, or the erasure of the Mohegan body politic (that is, communal existence and collective land rights) that would be required to declare their extinction and thus abolish the remaining reservation with some show of legitimacy? Or would it be the disappearance of a Mohegan identity – as construed by and thus "recognizable" to Anglos – that would be the definitive sign of "extinction"? Well before 1721 Mohegans had been cast as "inconsiderable Indians," whose population size and ways of life did not merit a stable, protected land base; but the idea of ineluctable "Indian extinction" opened new possibilities for cultural manipulations and denials of Natives' land rights. The anticipation of "extinction" and official assessments of it would thus shape Euro-American Indian policy, yielding a diversionary discourse that worked to focus Euro-American attention on notions of Indian cultural (and, ultimately, "racial") "illegitimacy" while deflecting and burying questions concerning the illegitimacy of colonial justice and the illegality of dispossession.

Yet contests over Natives' rights to reservation land in eighteenth-century Connecticut also yielded narratives that countered such discourse. The claimed truths of eighteenth-century Indian policy in Connecticut were contested by Mohegans and Mashantucket Pequots, who articulated important critiques of colonial authority as they pressed for their collective rights to land and to a future. In specific moments and expressions of resistance, Mohegans and Mashantucket Pequots argued that their reservation land was not only essential to community survival but was also a reminder of unfinished histories of struggle.

# 4

# "Only an Indian's Story"

## *The Mohegan Land Struggle, 1704–1738*

Although the legal proceedings of *Mohegan Indians v. Connecticut* have received some attention by scholars (e.g., Beardsley 1882; Conroy 1994; F. Morgan 1904:275–89; Smith 1950:422–42; Walters 1995; DeForest 1852:303–46), the historical significance of Mohegans' resistance to dispossession in the eighteenth century has yet to be adequately analyzed.[1]

The legal case was initiated in 1704, when Mohegan sachem Owaneco, the son of Uncas, petitioned the English crown to assert Mohegans' rights to lands claimed by the Connecticut government. In response, Queen Anne established a commission that met in Stonington, Connecticut, in 1705 to review the matter and render a judgment. Mohegans' complaints against Connecticut were heard, and the commission determined that the colony had unjustly appropriated the lands in question and must restore them to the Mohegan people. The Connecticut government refused to comply with the decision, however, and the legal case continued for nearly seventy years. By 1773 a decision of the British Privy Council brought the case to an end in the colony's favor (see Walters 1995:826–27).

But the legal case, and certainly Mohegans' defiance of colonial authority, had proved troublesome for Connecticut officials. This was a land dispute, but as it pressed on, a struggle over more than land rights ensued. For one thing, Mohegans' complaints posed a public relations dilemma for the colony: external authorities – the Society for the Propagation of the Gospel in New England as well as the Crown – had taken a serious interest in the matter of Mohegans' land rights. And Mohegans, particularly because their previous sachem Uncas had offered support to colonial forces in their assault on the Pequot nation in 1637, had served an important historical role as "Indian ally" to the colony. Arguing against the injustices they had endured at the hands of the Connecticut government as well as colonial encroachers who ignored their land rights, Mohegans compelled colonial officials to justify acts of dispossession. But legislators and investigatory committees also sought to quell Mohegan dissent by simply denying Mohegans' land rights, employing legislative actions intended to both diminish their reserved land and tighten colonial control over the reservation community.

This struggle over land rights became a struggle over political authority between Mohegans and colonial officials, as well as among Mohegans themselves. It was also a struggle that evoked the past, entailing contending accounts of conquest and Mohegan history. It demonstrates the complexity of power relations that shaped and were shaped by reservation communities that struggled to defend their remaining lands. Despite the fact that Mohegans, like members of other reservation communities at the time, endured a harsh and even desperate existence, they confronted and questioned colonial authority: for over thirty years after the colony's rejection of the 1705 decision, Mohegans rebuffed colonial officials who sought, by various means, to undermine their land rights and impose constraints on their lives.

Yet, in less than two decades after the 1705 decision, Mohegans' "sequestration" – their reserved planting land that initially encompassed over 20,000 acres in New London – was in one legislative act reduced to less than 5,000 acres. And in that act, colonial officials declared that what remained would belong to Mohegans until their "extinction," at which time the land would then belong to the town of New London. Colonial power thus imposed its will definitively and harshly, but still the Mohegan reservation community did not disappear, or acquiesce. Just as colonial assessments of Mohegans' existence and of their land rights were crafted in response to Mohegan resistance, so too did government officials seek to redefine the nature of the colony's relationship with the Mohegan body politic. In asserting their rights to their reserved planting land, Mohegan leaders reminded the Connecticut government that the historical relationship between Mohegans and colonists had been one of alliance, since Mohegan men had indeed performed military service on behalf of the colony from the time of the Pequot massacre.[2] But Connecticut's arguments against the 1705 decision disparaged Mohegans' role as colonial military ally and described Mohegans as "inconsiderable Indians" who had barely enough men among them "to make a hunt."

During the Mohegan case, colonial legal rhetoric evoked military conquest and asserted the idea that "Indian savagery" had been irrevocably subdued in the seventeenth century. Yet, although Connecticut contested the 1705 decision by arguing that the 1637 "Pequot Conquest" had rendered Mohegans a fully conquered people as well, at other critical moments in the legal dispute Mohegans' resistance was depicted as a threat to colonial society. These shifting representations should not be viewed merely as a colonial reflex, but as an important governmental strategy of diversion and control. Mohegans proved difficult to "quiet," and their complaints brought imperial authority to bear on the colony; as the legality of Connecticut's handling of Native land rights was questioned, colonial officials sought to direct attention to the "illegitimacy" of Mohegan resisters.

Although two recent articles offer important analyses of the legal aspects of the Mohegan case (Conroy 1994 and Walters 1995), neither includes a discussion of Mohegans as relevant political actors or explains Mohegan resistance as a driving force of the legal dispute. This may attest to the power of the Connecticut government's own depiction of Mohegans throughout the course of this protracted legal dispute, since their arguments cast Mohegans as pawns of self-interested Anglos – primarily their "guardians," the Masons, who also had a claim to a portion of Mohegan lands.[3] In a response to Owaneco's 1704 petition to the Crown, Connecticut legislators contended that "som[e] perticuler Persons that were too familiar with them [Mohegans] for their owne Private Interrest have Endeavrd to move them to such things as have given a great deall of Trouble to this Government and if not Prevented will be their [Mohegans'] ruin" (IND 1st, 1:61j). Later, in 1735, when Connecticut governor Joseph Talcott learned that Captain John Mason and Mohegan leader Mahomet II planned to go to London to deliver a second complaint against the colony, Talcott sought the support of Massachusetts governor Belcher in the matter, telling him that Mason "is making a tool of one Mahomett . . . to serve his purpose" (TP 1:329). Captain Mason's "purpose," as Talcott saw it, was to protect his own interest in Mohegan lands (1:328; see also Talcott's letter of February 17, 1736, in TP 1:335–37), the claim to which he inherited from his grandfather, Maj. John Mason, leader of the 1637 Pequot massacre and longtime adviser to Mohegan sachem Uncas. It may well have been true that the Masons, who had close connections with Mohegan leaders since the time of the Pequot massacre, were interested in perpetuating the legal case to secure their own claims to Mohegan lands.[4] However, a careful analysis of Mohegan resistance during the course of this dispute indicates that their motivation for opposing dispossession and contesting colonial authority was rooted in the condition of life, and in the history, of the Mohegan reservation community itself.

Mohegans' efforts to assert their land rights throughout the course of *Mohegan Indians v. Connecticut* were not carried out solely through their petitioning of the colonial or imperial governments. The most dramatic act of resistance engaged in by Mohegans during this struggle took place in September 1736 on their reservation in New London, when they held a ceremony to name a Mohegan woman, Anne, as *sunksquaw* in defiance of the Connecticut government and its sachem of choice, Ben Uncas II, whose allegiance had been cultivated by the colonial government (IND 1st, 1:173).[5] This ceremony, referred to by Governor Talcott as an attempt to "Set up a Queen or Imposter" (1:173), was an important challenge to colonial efforts to undermine Mohegans' land rights and control Mohegans' internal political affairs. This chapter traces the history of Mohegans' land struggle as it leads to this act of protest, and examines the intertwining of colonial legal and cultural strategies of rule.

## History, "Savagery," and the Implications of Mohegan Dissent

Owaneco's 1704 complaint to the Crown argued that the colony of Connecticut had failed to honor its agreements with Mohegans, which had provided for the protection of Mohegans' reserved lands. Further, Owaneco's petition charged that the colonial government had unjustly granted Mohegan lands to several Connecticut towns (*Proc.* 1769:4; see also Smith 1950:424–25).[6] The imperial overview of the matter was summarized thus by the queen's council in 1704:

> In relation to the charter colony of Connecticut, a complaint having been made to us in behalf of the Mohegan Indians, that the governor and company of the said colony had unjustly taken from the said Indians a tract of land, of which they were legally possessed; and it having been represented to us that the said Indians had always lived in a friendly manner and entertained a good correspondence with the English in those parts, and that having often applied to the governor and company for relief without being able to obtain any redress, they would be tempted to withdraw their obedience from her Majesty and

> join with the eastern or French Indians, which would be of evil consequence to her Majesty's subjects in those parts. (Stock 1930[1704]:77)

The queen's commission was intended to resolve the matter so as to "effectually prevent the defection and revolt of these Indians to her Majesty's enemies of Canada" (Stock 1930[1704]:77). The nature of Mohegans' status as a political entity – either as an independent, sovereign people who were allies of the Crown and colony, or as wholly subjected to the political authority of the colony itself – became an issue of legal and cultural significance in the context of the dispute. Mohegans themselves repeatedly evoked the history of their alliance with the colony in their complaints to the colonial government regarding encroachment, and that alliance had been the basis for Connecticut's claim to much of the land in the colony. Not only had some Mohegan men aided colonists in their attack upon Pequots in 1637, but as claimed in the 1736 petition of Mahomet II, "Sachem Uncas Entred into a firm League of Alliance and Friendship with the English whom he & his Descend[ents] & his whole Tribe have ever Inviolably kept faith, constantly assisting them in their Wars against the French & Indians, with 150 fighting Men, & Sometimes a far Superior No:, doing them many Signal Services, & from time to time making them free Gifts & Grants for small Cons[ideration] of Sev[eral] Tracts of their Land by [which] the Gover[nment] of Connecticut now holds 21 of their Towns, being the greatest part of their Colony" (TP 1:369).

After the 1705 decision Connecticut officials denied that Mohegans had possessed any political and historical significance as allies to the colony and argued that Mohegans did not exist as a politically autonomous, or culturally viable, people. On one level such depictions of Mohegans were a part of the colony's efforts to keep the imperial government out of its affairs. The fact that the Crown considered the Mohegan land dispute to be within its own jurisdiction and treated it as a "Suit that was in effect like one between 2 colonies" (cited in Walters 1995:810) was indeed threatening to the internal authority of the colonial government. Connecticut's position was that the proceedings of the 1705 commission were contrary to the powers bestowed to the colony by virtue of its 1662 royal charter. As Walters explains, Connecticut's argument against the proceedings of the 1705 commission relied upon the fact that the charter had rendered Connecticut " 'a Body Politique & Corporate' with legislative, executive, and judicial powers," such that the "boundaries of Connecticut established by charter included the reserved, or trust, lands claimed by Mohegans. The colony therefore argued that, whatever doubt might have existed before the charter as to land titles, after the charter the reserved lands were 'vested in the Govr and Company in full and Absolute Property and Right in Law' " (804). In response to the 1705 decision the colony's attorneys wrote that if the queen's commission were to assume the power to "enquire and judicially determine concerning the matter in controversy . . . we must declare against and prohibit all such proceedings, as contrary to law and to the letters patent under the great seal of England granted to this her majesty's colony" (*Proc.* 1769:33).

But Connecticut's claim of jurisdictional rights over the matter based on the charter was not the only argument offered in the colony's defense. Of equal significance was the claim that the 1704 complaint lacked legitimacy because Owaneco was "no Sachem or Gov[ernor]" and thus did not have the authority to speak for Mohegan people (cited in Walters 1996:811). Colonial officials also argued that Uncas had been neither an important ally to the colony nor a legitimate sachem. This claim was expressed in the accounts of Pequot conquest that were reiterated by Connecticut representatives throughout the course of the legal case, and that were intended to nullify the very notion that Mohegans were a people in their own right who possessed a homeland. As one Connecticut legislator contended three decades earlier, in his objection to the establishment of Mohegans' sequestered lands in 1671, the lands Mohegans claimed as their own "are Conquest Lands and so belong to ye English and not to Uncas" (IND 1st, 1:25). Connecticut legislators offered a detailed version of this argument in a proposed initial statement against Owaneco's petition in 1704, claiming that at the time of "the English planting [of] sd Colony," Uncas had been "Subordinate to ye Grand Pequod Sachem [Sassacus]," and that Uncas's "disgust of the said Sachem" led him to "put himself with som that followed him in the service of ye English against the Pequods": "the Pequods and all theire Adherents and Subjects, whereof all the Moheags were a part, were Conquerred, many killed, most dispersed, part of those yt remained were put under ye Managemt of sd Uncas *who for his Assistance was Constituted and made a sort of Sachem*" (IND 1st, 1:61, emphasis added).

After being "advanced" by the English, as it was termed, Uncas "pretended to the Proprietary of a smale Territory Called Mohegin, which was under the [colonial] Government and was the residence of the Grand Pequot Sachem [Sassacus]" (IND 1st, 1:61). The Connecticut government's claim to absolute ownership of Mohegan lands via both the Pequot massacre and the 1662 charter, as well as its particular depiction of Mohegan-Pequot relations in the seventeenth century, obfuscated the history of colonial relations with Mohegan sachems, particularly with regard to the question of Mohegan land rights.[7] Colonists continued to "purchase Native right" (1:84) – that is, Mohegan land – from Uncas and Owaneco after the Pequot massacre and after the 1662 charter. The colonial government had approved such purchases and acknowledged the sachems' authority (e.g., 1:84). As historian Richard Bushman points out, after 1675 "almost the entire country east of the Connecticut River claimed by the Mohegan sachem Uncas came into the possession of a few colonial leaders who were in the confidence of the natives [i.e., Mohegan leaders]" (Bushman 1967:84).[8] Although the colonial government's policy had been to control the acquisition and distribution of land, Connecticut became "liberal in allowing individuals to use Indian lands purchased privately": in the case of the "grants" or "purchases" colonists obtained from Uncas after 1675, "the Assembly confirmed these huge tracts to the recipients and allowed them to dispose of the land as they wished" (84).[9] Despite its argument to the Crown in 1705, then, the Connecticut government had acknowledged Mohegan land rights by its approval of individual purchases of Native right from Mohegan sachems (see Conroy 1994:399–400).[10]

When the imperial commission sat to hear testimony on the dispute, Connecticut's representatives refused to cooperate. The commission's judgment begins with this description of the initiation of the proceedings, for which Owaneco and Connecticut representatives were present:

> The court being opened, and Oweneco, the complainant, being present and ready to make out his complaint against the government of the colony of Connecticut, and other particular persons, proclamation was made for the commissioners of the governor and company of the said colony of Connecticut to come into court, and make answer to the complaint of Oweneco, Sachem of the Moheagan Indians, [Connecticut representatives] at first appeared, but afterwards made default, refusing to make any answer; after which a particular list of several

> persons that were complained against by Oweneco, for intruding into his lands, and who were summoned by the officer, were also called to come into court, and make answer to the complaint of Oweneco, who also all made default. Whereupon, the court, at the desire of Oweneco, proceeded to enquire and examine his complaint; and [made its decision] upon enquiry and examination of the several allegations and proofs of the said Oweneco. (Proc. 1769:27)

As subsequent arguments of Connecticut's representatives make clear, the very notion that Owaneco should have the floor, so to speak, and be allowed to challenge the claims of the colonial government was a scenario that colonial officials would not tolerate. Nonetheless "an Indian's story" about the impact of land loss on Mohegans, including testimony regarding specific instances of dispossession, was heard by the commissioners. By August 24, 1705, they ruled in favor of Mohegans, stating first that "Oweneco is the true and undoubted Sachem of the Moheagan Indians, being so owned by all of his tribe that were present at the court . . . and also acknowledged and treated with as the Sachem of the said Moheagan Indians in several leagues and treaties between the said colony and Uncas" (Proc. 1769:27).

The decision of the commissioners thereupon confirmed the validity of Owaneco's initial complaint to the Crown, determining that the colony had unjustly "granted away" both Mohegans' planting grounds and a considerable portion of their hunting grounds (Proc. 1769:28). The planting grounds in question, known as the "sequestered lands," comprised a thirty-two-square-mile tract of land (20,480 acres) between New London and Norwich (Mohegan Federal Acknowledgement Petition, vol. 1, 1984:77; DeForest 1852:297).[11] By 1704 the sequestered lands were encompassed by the newly enlarged town of New London (Proc. 1769:27–28). Mohegans' hunting grounds, which included "a large tract of land between Norwich and Haddam, Lyme, Lebanon, and Metabesset," were granted by the colony to the town of Colchester in 1699 (28; for grants of Mohegan lands made by the Connecticut General Assembly between 1687 and 1704 see also Smith 1950:424). The 1705 commission also acknowledged that a smaller tract of Mohegan planting land, including approximately eighteen square miles on the northern boundary of the town of Lyme, had been appropriated by that town "under pretense of their grant of their township from the colony" (Proc. 1769:27–28).

The sequestered lands, also called the "lands at Mohegan" (IND 1st, 1:153) and the "Mohegan fields" (1:122), were known by Connecticut officials to be the place where the majority of Mohegan people "dwell and plant" (1:122; see also Mohegan Federal Acknowledgment Petition, vol. 1, 1984:76–78). The history of the sequestered lands began in 1640 when, in the wake of the Pequot massacre, Connecticut colonists sought to solidify their control of the Native lands and Native populations in eastern Connecticut (see Conroy 1994:399). Thus an "agreement," as Connecticut historian Forrest Morgan referred to it (1904:279), was made between Uncas and the Connecticut government in 1640 by which Uncas purportedly "granted" the majority of Mohegan lands to English colonists and reserved a small portion for the Mohegan people. Uncas was remunerated with "5 yards trucking cloth, with stockings and other things" (Proc. 1769:152, 158).[12] The expanse of Mohegan territory at the time included what was to become "the northern two-thirds of New London County, and the southern two-thirds of Windham and Tolland Counties," encompassing approximately eight hundred square miles (F. Morgan 1904:282; see also Bowen 1882:26).

In 1659 Uncas and his brother Wawequa granted to Maj. John Mason and "his heirs or assigns . . . all our lands that do belong unto our territories, possessed now by us, or that has belonged unto our predecessors" (Proc. 1769:46). By this agreement the Masons were allowed "the one half the profit and value of all such lands, woods, ponds, minerals, herbage, rents &c. That shall at any time arise and accrue upon the premises"; in addition Uncas and his sons Owaneco and Attawanhood (also known as Joshua) were not to "make sale, or any way dispose of the premises . . . without the consent and allowance" of the Masons (1769:46). In May of 1671 Mason deeded a portion of these lands back to Mohegans, purportedly intending to protect the lands from alienation by grant or sale, while also preserving for himself and his heirs "the one halfe ye Profitts and value of all such lands, woods, Ponds, minerall, Herbage, Rentts &c that shall at any time arise and accrue upon ye Premises" (IND 1st, 1:26). According to this document, Uncas and his sons Owaneco and Attawanhood promised as well that neither they nor any other Mohegans "shall at any time make sale, or any waye dispose of ye Premises or any Part of ye same, without ye consent and allowance of him ye said Major Mason, his heirs and successours" (1:26). This reserved land created by

Mason's 1671 deed, and situated between New London and Norwich, became known thereafter as the "sequestered lands."

In 1680, at a meeting of Pequot, Niantic, Paugussett, and Mohegan sachems with a General Assembly committee, Uncas requested that the "bounds of his Lands may be setled before he dyeth," particularly the "Moheagon Feilds" – that is, the sequestered land that was to have been protected by Mason's deed – so as to ensure "peac[e] twixt his children & people and the english" (IND 1st, 1:39). While Uncas's statements at the 1680 meeting are recorded by the committee as a request rather than a complaint about encroachment, it seems clear that Uncas feared that Mohegans' rights to their reserved land would not be secured for the future unless the colonial government surveyed and recorded its boundaries. It should be remembered that this was the meeting that resulted in the establishment of the 1680 reservation law, which specified that "what land is allotted or set apart for any parcells of Indians within the bownds of any plantation" was to "be recorded to them and the same shall remayn to them and their heirs for ever" (CR 3:56–57). The 1680 law also declared "any alienations" of those lands by Native people or purchases by colonists "voyd and null" (3:56–57).

In March of 1684, after Uncas's death, Owaneco deeded "to his peapol . . . all the Lands called the Sequestration"; this deed was acknowledged and recorded by the General Assembly (TP 1:348; *Proc.* 1769:217). Despite Uncas's 1680 request, however, and Owaneco's apparent attempt to protect the sequestered lands, in 1687 the Connecticut government began to grant parcels of Mohegans' reserved lands to Connecticut towns (Smith 1950:424; Walters 1995:804). In 1698 the General Assembly granted some of the sequestered lands to Governor Fitz-John Winthrop and to Gurdon Saltonstall (who later was governor between 1708 and 1725), as well as other colonists (Smith 1950:424). But Mohegan leaders, most notably Uncas and Owaneco, also granted or sold parcels of Mohegan reserved lands to colonists, among which were transactions later called into question during Mohegans' legal case against Connecticut.

Among the most significant of these questionable transactions is colonist Nathaniel Foot's June 1699 "purchase" of Mohegan hunting grounds from Owaneco, the very same tract that the General Assembly had granted to the town of Colchester in the previous month. During the proceedings of the 1705 commission, a witness to the event, John

Prents, testified that Owaneco had been plied with liquor: "Whereas Mr. Foot did some years since obtain a writing from Oweneco, Sachem of Moheagan, *for a tract of land called Colchester*; I being present did say to Mr. Foot, that Oweneco was *not capable to understand what he did*, by reason, as I judged, *he was in drink*; Mr. Foot answered me it would be as good as other Indian deeds" (*Proc.* 1769:51, emphasis in original).

The validity of this deed was challenged subsequently by Mohegan attorneys before the imperial commission of review in 1743. In this instance John Chandler, a colonist who had "been well acquainted with the tribe of the Moheagan Indians for the space of about fifty years, and well knew Oweneco the chief Sachem," testified that he "apprehended no other but that the said deed was a jest, and designed to be improved no otherwise than to shew what an Indian would do when gratified with a little liquor and a little money" (*Proc.* 1769:232). This "transaction" had taken place at the home of Chandler himself, at which were present at the time – in addition to Owaneco, Chandler, and Foot – a "gentleman of the law" and "several other persons" engaged in "some chearful talk" (232). In contrast with Prents's testimony, Chandler claimed that none present were intoxicated. Instead, he explained that he perceived the transaction to be "in jest" because "the consideration paid was so very inconsiderable [it "exceeded not the value of about five or six shillings"], and Mr. Foot having often, in the hearing of this deponent [Chandler], spoken so very diminutively of native rights, which he deemed so utterly to despise" (232). Given such testimony, it is possible that Foot had been employed to obtain a deed for Mohegans' hunting grounds from Owaneco for the purpose of securing the General Assembly's expropriation of that tract.

The question of the conditions under which deeds to Mohegan lands were obtained from Mohegan leaders is among the most important issues to be raised by the Mohegan case. Nineteenth-century historian John DeForest notes that Mohegan sachems "at times complained, that advantage was taken of them when they were intoxicated, to beguile them out of lands which they never intended to part with" (DeForest 1852:290; see also Smith 1950:424). Ben Uncas II petitioned the General Assembly in October 1733 to complain that "Our Good is greatly obstructed by Reason of Strong Liquors being brought in such great Quantities into our Town, (Cyder by the Barrel, and Rhum by the Gallon)": "English Men," he charged, "often bring great Quantities of Strong Liquor up the River to us, and whatsoever we have that they want they purchase with it" (TP 1:91–92). A great deal of Mohegan land was acquired by purchase from Mohegan sachems, particularly Owaneco. Whether or not Owaneco had been, as Chandler reported in the case of the "sale" to Foot, in "a mind to get a little liquor and a little money" (*Proc.* 1769:233), such transactions may have regularly taken place without the consent or consideration of the larger community of Mohegans, if not in contempt (on the part of purchasers) and disregard (on the part of Owaneco) for Mohegans' land rights.

Anthropologist Laurie Weinstein-Farson has determined that Owaneco "made no less than twenty-five deeds of sale to the colonists between 1659 and 1710" (Weinstein-Farson 1989:7). She notes that "few deeds indicate that the Mohegan received monetary remuneration; instead, the deeds contained conditions which forbid the Indians from 'molesting' the colonists (that is, they were forbidden from returning to use their former lands)" (7). DeForest characterizes Mohegan land transactions in the latter half of the seventeenth century thus:

> The Norwich and New London records abound with deeds, conveying tracts, of usually from one to five or six hundred acres, to various persons of those towns. Some are signed by Uncas, some by Oweneco, some by both these sachems, and others have in addition the mark of Joshua or Attawanhood. In these deeds the sachems alledge various reasons for parting with the land: sometimes it is "out of love and affection for the grantee;" sometimes "on account of many benefits and kindnesses heretofore received;" sometimes for "a valuable consideration" now paid, or perhaps only promised. These grants often covered each other, often contradicted each other, and were the source of innumerable quarrels and litigations between the English and the Indians, and between the English and each other. (DeForest 1852:290)

Owaneco's September 1704 petition to the General Assembly, intended to notify the government of his grant of two hundred acres of Mohegan land to colonists John Plumb and Jonathan Hill, relates a suspicious scenario, suggesting that colonists' "friendships" with Mohegan sachems came at a hard price for Mohegan people:

> To the honored General Assembly . . . the Last fall I was In Great danger of being drowned fal[l]ing out of a Conow in the night, and had it not bin for my Loveing frinds John plumb and Jonathan hill both of New London who wth hazard of their own Lives ventured and so

> was a means of Saveing my Life when I was so far gon that I was for a time senceless: for wch kindness and good Servis to me In that time of emenent danger I have given them the sd John Plumb and Jonathan Hill one hundred acres of land apeace to be Laid out to them In my lands not yet disposed of to the Inglish. (IND 1st, 1:53)

Owaneco requested that the General Assembly give "their Confirmation" of this grant so that the land in question "may be theirs [Plumb's and Hill's] and their heirs and assigns forever wthout being disturbed by any body Lawfully" (IND 1st, 1:53). The "lands not yet disposed of" that Oweneco refers to here were within the realm of Mohegans' reserved planting grounds between Norwich and New London; and the designated acreage was subsequently surveyed and acquired by Plumb and Hill with the General Assembly's consent (*Proc.* 1769:51–52).

The colonial records are for the most part silent regarding the processes of decision making and disputation in Native communities that may have preceded or followed sachems' "sales" or grants of land to colonists. Indeed it is unlikely that Native leaders in New England held authority, as granted by their own people, to permanently alienate ancestral lands (see Snyderman 1951; Starna 1989; J. Strong 1985). The 1705 decision acknowledged not only the questionable nature of some of these transactions but also the testimony regarding the impact of land loss on Mohegan people. This was something that the Connecticut government had failed to do, despite the fact that Mohegan leaders had made formal complaints to colonial officials prior to the 1705 decision.

Mohegans' October 1703 petition, for instance, explained that despite their "complaints from time to time" the colonial government had "granted to New London & Coulchester all the Rest of our Lands" and that "we have noe Land eithere to plant or hunt upon" (IND 1st, 1:52).[13] It was in this petition that Mohegan leaders also detailed the acts and threats of violence against Mohegans who had attempted to continue living upon lands claimed by Anglos, the most significant being that Mohegans had been "thretned by them of Colchester . . . to be killed" (1:52; see chapter 3). In addition Mohegan petitioners charged that the Connecticut governor himself, Fitz-John Winthrop, "did in a time of snow Last winter turne our women & children of[f] our planting field claiming it for his own" (1:52). Although this petition is not included among the evidence submitted during the proceedings of the 1705 commission, evidence regarding the appropriation of this particular planting field – drawn from testimony by an attorney for Mohegans, Nicholas Hallam, and from the record of a meeting between Mohegan leaders and Connecticut officials in September 1703 – was submitted to the 1705 commission (*Proc.* 1769:57–58). In fact, it was testimony about the removal of Mohegan families from this tract of land, called Massapeage, that provided the commissioners in 1705, as it does researchers today, with evidence that Mohegans' legal dispute with the colony was not the result of manipulations by their "guardians."

Massapeage, which means "great-water land" or "land on the great cove" in Mohegan-Pequot language (Trumbull 1881:24), refers to "a fine tract of land on the [Thames] river, within the bounds of Mohegan proper" (Caulkins 1895:122–23). Uncas granted rights to Massapeage to colonist Richard Haughton in 1658, and Haughton subsequently petitioned the colonial government for approval of the transaction (*Proc.* 1769:168). The General Assembly deemed that Haughton "may have liberty to agree with Uncas" for this "neck of land called Massapeage," but legislators limited Haughton's rights: "provided the said Houghton or his assigns never make any further or other use of it but only to plant or sow thereupon in the summer, and to keep cattle thereupon in the winter, and that no swine shall be kept upon the premises at any time, neither shall be any other ways improved to the trespass or prejudice of Uncas in any such kind or trouble of this commonwealth" (*Proc.* 1769:169).

The language of the order indicates that the Connecticut government did not acknowledge or intend the "agreement" between Uncas and Haughton to grant Haughton legal title to the land. Nor is it likely that Uncas meant the grant to entail the absolute alienation of the land from Mohegan people. Although the recorded deed, written in the colonial legal language typical of the period, states that it was a "gift" from Uncas to a "well-beloved friend" (*Proc.* 1769:169), it too includes a provision that suggests that Mohegans, by virtue of the friendship that purportedly existed between Haughton and Uncas, did retain rights to use the land. That is, it stated that nothing was to be "demanded or received of" Haughton for the land, "but only such commendable laws as are provided between the English and the Indians, and in many such like occasions, as namely to satisfy one another in a just and loving manner" (169). Testimony to the 1705 commission indicates that Mohegan families had continued to live upon this neck of land, perhaps with the consent of Haughton and his family. Nevertheless, after Haughton died in 1682, his heirs sold Massapeage to Fitz-John Winthrop (Caulkins 1895:299–300) in violation of the General Assembly order concerning the 1658 transaction between Uncas and Haughton.

Hallam's testimony and the October 1703 petition indicate that both the 1703 enlargement of the town of New London and the loss of land at Massapeage were viewed by Mohegans as a threat to their survival and as an indication that the government had disregarded their rights to their reserved planting lands. Indeed, the colony's May 1703 "Act for the enlargement of New-London township" described Mohegans' reserved lands in a sufficiently vague manner to provide considerable incentive for encroachment, for it stated that "whatsoever proprieties, whether of English or Indians, that are within the said tract of land so granted and added, shall be and are hereby reserved and saved, for the respective possession, use, and improvement of the several proprietors of the same" (*Proc.* 1769:177). Although this act, like the 1704 New London patent that followed it, describes the newly established boundaries of the town, neither record the definitive boundaries of Mohegans' planting lands (177–81). That the boundaries of the reservation were subsequently defined according to the desires of colonists who sought to acquire or control the distribution of Mohegan lands is suggested in Hallam's testimony. He explained that he had been hired by Captain Samuel Mason, then "patron and trustee of the Moheagan Indians," "to assist in running the line between New London north bounds and the Indians lands, called Moheagan lands, belonging to the Moheagan Indians" (55). To this end, Hallam accompanied

> some of the Moheagan Indians, down to the river called Norwich river [i.e., Thames River], where the said Indians showed this deponent a rock in the said river, saying that was their bounds between New London and them; and that when this deponent came to the said river, *it being a cold snowy day, he met with about thirty or forty Moheagan Indians, men, women, and children, in a very poor and naked condition, many of them crying lamentably*; whereupon this deponent asked said Indians the reason of their being in that condition, who told this deponent, *that the governor had been up with them that day, and had drove them from their planting land, which they had enjoyed ever since the English came into the*

*country, and that they were not willing to leave the English, unless they were forced to it.* (55, emphasis in original)

Hallam explained that although New London's surveyors and Mohegans "could not agree" on what the boundary between Mohegan reserved land and New London should be, "*these persons that were on the behalf of New London* . . . did dig up trenches, and heaved up heaps of stones, and marked trees; and when they came to Norwich river it [the surveyors' boundary marker] *fell better than a mile above the rock*, commonly reckoned to be the rocks which was the bounds between New London and the said Indians, *which said mile was into the Moheagan lands*" (*Proc.* 1769:55, emphasis in original). Hallam also testified that Mohegan leaders had complained about encroachment on their reserved lands directly to the General Assembly in Hartford prior to the establishment of the imperial commission, "notwithstanding which, the said general assembly enlarged New London bounds, and run the same to Norwich bounds, which takes in all the lands commonly called the Mohegan Fields" (55).

The other significant testimony regarding Mohegans' dispossession at Massapeage was drawn from the colony's record of a September 1703 meeting between the governor and council and six Mohegan leaders, among them Ben Uncas I and Mahomet I.[14] This account is important not only because it includes Mohegan leaders' own assessment of the impact of dispossession, but also because it reflects their own understanding of the alliance that had existed between Mohegans and the colony, which Mohegans believed the Connecticut government had betrayed. At the September 1703 meeting, Mohegans questioned the government's demand that their "names should be [e]nrolled" (*Proc.* 1769:58) – that is, that Mohegans should sign their names to the official record of the proceedings of the meeting. Papepainte, "one of the [Mohegan] council" who was present, stated that "formerly there was no such thing as taking an account of our names; it seems strange that such a thing should be desired now; we desire for to know the reason" (1769:58).[15]

Statements from other Mohegan leaders present at this meeting indicate that Mohegans viewed encroachment on their reserved lands as a disavowal of the history of Mohegans' alliance with the colony, and as a violation of the obligations that this alliance continued to entail. Asnehunt, a member of the Mohegan council, stated that "The English *had turned them out of their houses in the time of snow from Massapeage, which occasioned their women and children to cry*; yet they have now sent out scouts [as a part of Mohegans' military service for the colony], as they and the English have been friends and brethren, so they are our brethren still." When Asnehunt was asked "who turned them out, he said *the governor last spring*." Another member of the Mohegan council, Appagese, added that "from a boy their ground and he grew up together, and they have always been friends to the English, *and why our ground and we should be parted now, we know not* (*Proc.* 1769:58, emphasis in original).

Mahomet's complaint, the last to be included in this account of the September 1703 meeting, responds to an incident in which Mohegans were treated by colonists as "enemy Indians."[16] Mahomet "said that there was four of his men taken at Colchester the last winter, and carried to New London, and there threatened to be hanged, when they had done nothing worse than they went into a cellar and warmed themselves by the fire, which he said seemed strange to him, and he was ashamed" (*Proc.* 1769:58). Mahomet may have been "ashamed" that Mohegan leaders' alliance with the colony had resulted, for his people, in the unexpected consequence of their alienation – both socially and geographically.

The 1705 commission made note of the incident at Massapeage in their decision, stating that "the said Sachem [Owaneco] and Moheagan Indians have been very unjustly dispossessed and turned out of a tract of planting ground, called Massapeage, lying within the township of New-London" and that this land was to be "restored to" Mohegans, along with "all their planting ground, lying between New London and Norwich," as well as "another smaller tract upon the north bounds of Lyme" and the "larger tract of hunting land between the bounds of Norwich and Haddam [which had been granted by the General Assembly to Colchester]." Moreover, the commission's decision described Mohegans as a people with an inherent right to a land base: "the said Moheagan Indians are a *considerable* tribe or people, consisting of one hundred fighting men, *formerly a much greater number*, and cannot subsist without their lands, of which they have been deprived *and dispossessed as aforesaid*" (*Proc.* 1769:29, emphasis in original).[17]

Having depicted Mohegans as a distinct people who had "formerly" been a significant military force, the 1705 decision thus suggested that Mohegan history mattered in the context of their present struggle, and that it was, indeed, a basis for their rights to land. And, of course, the decision also acknowledged the legitimacy of the evidence that had come from Mohegan people themselves. What it asserted, then, was not only that Mohegans had a right to a livelihood upon their own lands because they constituted a "considerable tribe or people" vis-à-vis the colony. Implicit in its validation of what one of the colony's defenders, William Samuel Johnson, would refer to decades later as "only an Indian's story" (IND 1st, 2:277) was a potentially troublesome challenge to colonial authority: the notion that the Connecticut government was neither the sole arbiter of justice for local indigenous peoples or the preeminent "interpreter" of Indian voices and histories.

The colony offered its own historical evidence – a narration of Pequot conquest, fashioned as a simultaneous Mohegan conquest – as a legal grounding for its claim to Mohegan lands and its caustic dismissal of Mohegans' complaints. Attacking the legitimacy of the former Mohegan sachem Uncas, Connecticut's representative Sir Henry Ashurst contended that prior to 1637 Uncas had been "subdued and conquered" by Sassacus, and that Uncas so "joined himself" with English colonists "against the said Pequot Sachem, and served them in no greater station than a pilot to steer their vessels upon the waters in those parts" (*Proc.* 1769:153–54). The appeal further argues that Connecticut colonists

> by *such* conquest [of Pequots], became absolute owners of the lands and plantations of Connecticut: howbeit, the said Uncas Sachem, having so joined in the wars against the Pequot Sachem, *intreated* to be *permitted* to possess some part of the said conquered lands, under such terms as your petitioners [the Connecticut government] thought fit; and thereupon your *petitioners, to obviate all further pretences, took an instrument in writing, whereby said Uncas Sachem did freely give and grant to your petitioners and their successors all the lands that ever had belonged to him, by what name soever called, whether Mohegan, Massapeage, or otherwise, for ever; reserving only for his own use that ground which at that present time was planted and improved by him*; which your petitioners aver was at that time very inconsiderable, he having but very few men, and not enough to make a hunt. And moreover, the said word reservation ought not to be deemed a reserving of any right that he had, but the *permission* of your petitioners, the *conquerors*, to *suffer* him to possess the same. (154, emphasis in original)

Thus Mohegans, like their sachem Uncas, are depicted as lacking legitimacy altogether: they did not exist in the past as a viable people ("having but very few men") and had been allowed the use of only an "inconsiderable" tract of planting land to avoid any "further pretences" by Uncas. In essence, Mohegans were to be viewed as "inconsiderable Indians," as Ashurst subsequently refers to them (*Proc.* 1769:155), whose claim to a history of alliance with the colony was a sham.

But Mohegans' assertion of their land rights had not been viewed as "pretence" by the Crown. Indeed the imperial directive to the 1705 commission had explained that Uncas's alliance with colonists had "permitted them [colonists] peacably to plant and settle a great part of their lands, which they granted to them for an inconsiderable value, reserving only to themselves a small parcel of land to plant and hunt in" (*Proc.* 1769:24). The meaning and intent of Uncas's 1640 "agreement" was thus an important issue in the legal dispute during and after the 1705 decision.[18] The fact that this agreement had not been recorded by the colony until 1736 was no small matter in itself (Smith 1950:438; IND 1st, 1:173). In 1743 a copy of the purported deed was produced by Connecticut's representatives as evidence to an imperial commission of review (*Proc.* 1769:xiii, 99; see also Smith 1950:438 n. 133). The recorded deed was crucial to the colony's efforts to reverse the 1705 decision (see Morris 1974:72), since it was the recordation of deeds by the appropriate colonial officials that bestowed validity to a colonial claim of land ownership, regardless of whether there was a disparity in time between when the land transaction occurred and when it was actually logged in the record books. As one legal historian has explained, the "system for registering and recording titles to land" was "one of the first American [legal] innovations." "Recording acts, and the recording system," Friedman notes, "were invented in New England, in the early days of seventeenth-century settlement. . . . The essence of the system was that *the record itself guaranteed title to the land.* An unrecorded deed could not stand up against a recorded deed, even though the recorded deed was issued later than the unrecorded deed." Friedman points out that the recording system "made it easier to govern and control the settlements," and adds that New England colonists "felt the need for a way to prove title to land" (Friedman 1985:63, emphasis added).

During the proceedings of the 1743 commission, Connecticut representatives submitted as evidence what they claimed to be the recordation of the "original deed by said Uncas" from 1640, to which Mohegans' attorney objected (*Proc.* 1769:99).[19] The commissioners subsequently allowed the document to be "admitted as an exhibit in court, and to be read" (108). In their final determination on the matter, three of the five commissioners, supporting Connecticut's claim that the document was legitimate, argued that it had "all the marks of the antiquity it is supposed to be of": it had purportedly been written by Edward Hopkins, "governor" of the colonists who were occupying the area at the time, and "the marks of Uncas and Poxon, an Indian witness thereto, appear by the heavy bearing of the hand on the paper, and the irregularity and stiffness in the turnings, to be made by persons not accustomed to form regular shapes or figures, and are done in such manner as is not easy for any person to imitate." Hence they determined that the document was "the genuine act and deed of Uncas" (138). Another commissioner dissented in part, stating that "it was not the intention of the parties to that deed to pass the absolute property in the Moheagan lands from Uncas to the governor and magistrates, but only to vest them with the sole right to purchase these lands" (141). Yet another of the five commissioners disagreed entirely that the document had any validity, arguing that "the marks thereon put for Uncas and the Indian witness Poxon (or Foxon) were not the marks by them respectively made," and that "the writing was entirely a copy, wrote by one and the same hand, viz. Governor Hopkins" (141).

Despite the opposition of the latter two commissioners, the document submitted by the colony was accepted, and the commission's final judgment upheld the previous decision, in 1738, which had overturned the 1705 decision. As in the colony's argument against the 1705 decision, the proclaimed legitimacy of the 1640 deed rested upon tenuous cultural assessments. The commissioners who deemed the colony's document authentic, displaying "all the marks of antiquity," described it as having born the heavy, inimitable hand of presumed savages – "persons not accustomed to form regular shapes or figures." Such a colonial depiction of Mohegan "savagery" might be dismissed as incidental or inevitable at the given moment, but particular constructions of Mohegan "otherness" were all too important to colonial efforts to subdue Mohegan resisters. Mohegans were not to be acknowledged as having a culturally or politically legitimate existence as *a people*. Yet Mohegan savagery, as colonial officials proffered it, was a malleable thing: that is, it was posited as evidencing the effects of absolute conquest (Mohegans were "an inconsiderable people"); but Mohegan savagery was also posed as a potential threat to colonial settlement (so the 1640 "agreement" was made to "obviate all further pretenses" to land on the part of Uncas). Thus Connecticut representatives could make what would seem to be an absurd argument for the legitimacy of their claim to Mohegan lands: that the recordation of the 1640 "deed" represented a "legal" and fair purchase from sachem Uncas; and, at the same time, that Uncas had been neither a legitimate sachem nor a true proprietor of the lands in question (IND 1st, 1:61). The eighteenth-century colonial notion of Indian savagery – as simultaneously subdued and threatening – made such logic possible. And as Ashurst's appeal to the Crown maintained, it was the conquest of the savages that had established and legitimized "such terms by which your petitioners [the colony] thought fit" to control conquered lands: Mohegans in eighteenth-century Connecticut thus lived upon land to which they had no historical right, only the "permission" of "the conquerors." In colonial officials' enmeshed vision of legality and history, the Pequot massacre was day one, and Mohegan existence – their posited cultural inadequacy and "otherness" – was to be rooted in that moment of conquest.

If the arguments of the Connecticut government proved anything during the course of the Mohegan case, it was that both colonial notions of savagery and narrations of Pequot conquest could be effectively manipulated and woven into their legal arguments to quell Native resistance and deny history to reservation communities. Mohegans' struggle to preserve their land rights had also elicited unabashed contempt from colonial officials, exemplified in William Samuel Johnson's 1771 argument on Connecticut's behalf, which scoffs at Mohegans' complaints against the colony and mocks the conditions of life that colonial expropriation of their lands had wrought. Referring to testimony that had been given to the 1705 commission on behalf of Mohegans, Johnson wrote "It is most of it h[e]arsay, only an Indian's story, the Indians said *the Gov[ernor] had turned them off [at Massapeage]* &c. What Act was done by him? None is mentioned – *The Indians were in a poor & naked Condition* – They were never otherwise. It is calculated to excite Compassion, but proves nothing" (IND 1st, 2:277, emphasis in original). It was thus the inherent condition of savagery that was to have denied Mohegans a history, making theirs a wretched life that was "never otherwise."

In 1713 Governor Saltonstall informed the Connecticut General Assembly that "there will be speedily made, by her Maj[esty's] Command, an Enquiry into 2 things Particularly. 1. The State of our Ports and Trade 2. The Affair of the Indian Lands" (IND 1st, 1:79). "As for the Indian Affair," Saltonstall wrote, "this Complaint was of being wrong'd of the Land they had reserved to themselves in new London & Colchester" (1:79). He added that he was uncertain as to the current status of the legal dispute over Mohegan lands: "as for what they claimd in Colchester, I know not what has been done since the Court for Indian Complaints at Stonington [i.e., the 1705 commission]; possibly the Representatives of that Town may readily inform You, so [that] by turning to the Records, You may presently See the present State of the Affair, and be enabled to give Direction thereon, and If need be make some further Regulation" (1:79).

If government officials were to claim ignorance concerning the "State of the Affair" in 1713, several years after Saltonstall's warning, Connecticut legislators' "further Regulation" was manifested in the 1717 act ordering that Mohegans were to be Christianized and confined to "settlements in convenient places, in villages after the English manner" (CR 6:31–32; see chapter 3). The 1717 "civilizing" measures were intended to divide Mohegans' reserved land into "suitable portions" for individual families, requiring that "the said portions should descend from the father to his children" (6:32). In order to impose this system of allotment, the General Assembly ordered that several judges of the superior court of New London were to

> make a view of the said tract of land [in New London], visit the Indians living on it, take account of the number of their families and persons, of the quantity and quality of said land, with other circumstances thereof, in respect of any claims made thereto or possessions held thereon, and lay a plan of the same before the General Court for their further direction, and that they may be the better enabled to proceed in forming a village of the said Indians there, and bringing them to such civil order, cohabitation and industry, as may facilitate the setting up of the gospel ministry among them; and that they view and make report of all the land formerly sequestered to said Indians. (6:32–33)

That legislators sought to subsume the legal issue of Mohegans' land rights into the project of saving Mohegan souls is not so thinly veiled here; nor is the suggestion that a more direct effort to "civilize" Mohegans – that is, to more carefully control and confine Mohegans' activities – would stifle their opposition to dispossession. But the officials charged with implementing the measures reported in 1718 that Mohegans "have complained to them of several claims and entries made upon their fields, and damage sustained them in their fields, and prayed that they would recommend them to the care and protection" of the colonial government (CR 6:77).

In October 1718 the General Assembly appointed James Wadsworth, John Hooker, and John Hall to investigate this complaint against encroachment and subsequently named them as Mohegans' "guardians": with that they were bestowed with the power to lease out Mohegan lands, in their own names, to cover the costs of the Christianization effort as well as the fee for their own services (CR 6:148–49, 256). As it was phrased in the General Assembly's order, the committee members were to ensure that "nothing shall be done that may bring any charge upon the government, but that the whole charge be supported out of the profit of said lands" (6:149). Moreover, the committee members were given the authority to make the final "conclusions and determinations and orders" regarding "the quieting and better settling" of the lands in question (6:256). As a consequence of this committee's reports, between 1718 and 1719 the General Assembly ordered that five hundred acres of the sequestered lands be appropriated for the purposes of implementing the 1717 measures: two hundred and fifty acres "for a farm, to be the ministers who shall first be ordained their; and also two hundred and fifty more for a parsonage" (6:193–94, 256).

In 1720 Wadsworth, Hooker, and Hall were reappointed and again charged with task of fulfilling the 1717 measures, as well as ensuring "the quiet settlement" of the "north parish in New London," which encompassed Mohegans' reserved planting lands (*Proc.* 1769:188).[20] The committee was thus directed

> to endeavour a final settlement of the controversy respecting the land in said parish; and, if the said commissioners, upon hearing the pleas and arguments of the parties, shall be able to settle the whole matter by a composition, then such agreement shall be brought to this assembly . . . for their confirmation. . . . But if, upon the endeavours of the committee, no agreement can be gained from the parties, then the

> committee are to make a settlement of that whole affair, and lay the same before this assembly as soon as may be, for their confirmation; and also, that no charge arise to the colony by this act. (188)

The committee game, as I have termed it, may have left an official paper trail to provide evidence of government attention to Natives' protests against encroachment, but it did not necessarily convince indigenous communities themselves that the appointed officials had adequately and fairly investigated their complaints. Mohegans did not rely on the "guardianship" of Wadsworth, Hooker, and Hall. In October 1720 Mohegan leaders met with Governor Saltonstall to make a formal complaint against individual colonists who had encroached upon their reserved land. This was an important moment in the history of Mohegans' dispute with the colony since, once again, Mohegans' own views regarding their land rights, as well as their specific charges against colonial encroachers, were presented and put on the record in the presence of government officials.

Saltonstall arranged for the meeting to be held "at the publick Home [i.e., tavern] kept by ye Widow Prentts in New London" (IND 1st, 1:90). The governor's chosen location was clearly not a "neutral" meeting ground, but Mohegan leaders appeared there to make their argument nonetheless. Cesar Uncas, grandson of Uncas, was then sachem, having replaced Owaneco after his death in 1715 (1:90; Fawcett 1995:40). According to Saltonstall's report, Cesar, along with Ben Uncas I and other Mohegan leaders who were present, had "complaind to me in Council, that They are disturbed in the Enjoyment of their Lands in Moheagan, lying within the Bounds of the Town of New London, by Several Persons, who had intruded upon the Land there, which was reserved for their Use; and particularly against Stephen Maples, Jonathan Hill, Ralph Firgoe, Joshua Baker, Alexander Baker, & John Nobles, all of New London, for so doing" (IND 1st, 1:90). Ben Uncas charged that Jonathan Hill, who was present at the meeting, had offered him and Cesar "four pound a piece to be quiet & not complain against him. Which Jonathan Hill being present Said he had offered it only for peace Sake. *Upon which the Indians declared, that the Land was not theirs to dispose of, but it was to descend to their Children*" (1:91, emphasis added).

Saltonstall's report does not indicate what discussion might have followed Mohegan leaders' assertion about the inalienability of the sequestered lands, but this declaration suggests that Cesar and Ben Uncas I sought the government's formal acknowledgment of Mohegans' *collective* rights to their existing land base. Their statement was a claim about Mohegans' existence as a people whose children were to inherit the Mohegan homeland. Eastern Pequot leader Mary Momoho also made this assertion with regard to the land rights of future generations of Eastern Pequots (see chapter 3).

Following Mohegans' pronouncement that they would agree to no further "disposal" of their reservation land, Hill "declined to give any [account] of ye Right he had to the Land the Indians complained against him for intruding on" because "he had formerly given it" to the General Assembly (IND 1st, 1:91). The other alleged encroachers at the meeting also claimed to have previously "shown their titles" to the General Assembly (1:91). The governor and council, unprepared to resolve the matter on the spot, ordered that those whose claims to Mohegan land were in dispute "should be required to give the next Generall Assembly, an Account of their title to the land" and that "if it appear to the sd Assembly they have a Just Right there, the Indians may be made Sensible of it, and they [the colonists] may be quieted in their Possessions there" (1:91).

What appears to have been an effort on the part of Mohegans to bypass their "guardians" was unsuccessful, for the matter was ultimately handed over to Wadsworth and Hall, who swiftly made Mohegans "sensible of" the demands of encroachers. In February 1721 Wadsworth and Hall arranged a meeting at which, pursuant to the General Assembly's order of 1720, they were to have "endeavoured an agreement among the claimers" of Mohegans' sequestered lands. "Caesar, Ben Uncas, and the rest of the Indians present," were assisted by interpreters Captain Robert Denison and Thomas Stanton (*Proc.* 1769:189). The report by Wadsworth and Hall explains that they

> acquainted the Indians . . . that that [eastern] part of the Moheagan lands . . . shall be for ever settled to the Indians and to their benefit, to be under the regulations of a committee so long as there shall be any of the Moheagan Indians found, or known of alive in the world, only some little parcels thereof, viz. Mr. Hill's, and some other little pieces, upon consideration, shall be settled in their [Hill's and other

> colonists referenced] possession. And the Indians earnestly desire, that they may be restrained from parting, or any way selling the land, that shall now be settled upon them. (189)

Hill agreed to pay Cesar and Ben Uncas I twelve pounds, "provided that may be an end of the whole controversy, and that he may be quieted in his land" (Proc. 1769:189). The report also asserts that Cesar and Ben Uncas stated "that they are greatly desirous of a final settlement of the controversy about their lands, and that they are free to part with some little pieces, upon consideration, because they think it may be for the peace; and that they don't want the land, and thereupon desire the committee [i.e., Wadsworth and Hall] to view those lands, that they may be described in the settlement to be made" (189).

The claim that Cesar and Ben Uncas "didn't want the land" stands in stark contrast to their statement to Saltonstall in October 1720. There can be several possible interpretations, not the least among which may be that Wadsworth and Hall, along with the interpreters, ensured that the official report protected the interests of the Connecticut government rather than Mohegan land rights. The committee, in fact, awarded Robert Denison, one of the interpreters, a parcel of land in the western section of Mohegans' sequestration (Proc. 1769:191). It was surely apparent to Cesar and Ben Uncas that their supposed guardians – bestowed with full power to determine the extent, or nullification, of their land rights – intended to put an end to the land dispute once and for all. If it is true that these Mohegan leaders told the committee "that they don't want the land" that had been encroached upon, it may have reflected their exasperation, as well as their hope that their acquiescence to the committee's demands might finally ensure peace for Mohegan people in the future.

The remainder of the report details the distribution of various "pieces" of Mohegans' planting lands. Upholding the claims of Hill and five others named as encroachers by Mohegan leaders in October 1720, Wadsworth and Hall also approved claims or "country grants" made on the reserved land by government officials, including Governor Saltonstall (Proc. 1769:189–91; see also DeForest 1852:315). Their report recommended that the General Assembly "ratify and confirm, all the sales of lands made by Uncas or Oweneco" before May 1710 (Proc. 1769:191).

Only the "eastern part of the Moheagan lands," which had not been "already disposed of by the committee" was to remain in the possession of Mohegans (approximately one-fourth of the original sequestration, or four to five thousand acres; see Mohegan Federal Acknowledgment Petition, vol. 1, 1984:79; DeForest 1852:351). Finally, Wadsworth and Hall declared that this fragment of the Mohegan sequestration

> *Shall for ever* belong to the Moheagan Indians, from time to time, and from generation to generation for ever, so long as there shall be any of the Moheagan Indians found, or known of alive: and when the whole nation, or stock of said Indians are extinct, and none of them to be found, *and never before*, the said eastern part, which is now settled upon the Indians, shall *for ever belong to the town of New London* . . . And it is further provided, that if it shall so happen at any time that the said Indians and all of them be gone, and not known of, supposed to be extinct, then the said town may enter upon said land, and improve the same. (*Proc.* 1769:194, emphasis in original)

Approved by the General Assembly, Wadsworth and Hall's proposed final solution to the dispute over Mohegan lands encoded the anticipated "extinction" of the reservation community in colonial law, lending it a façade of validity. Thus the notion of impending Mohegan extinction here makes a new and incisive official determination regarding Mohegans' historical possibilities. The 1717 "civilizing" measures were aimed at abolishing Mohegans' collective land rights and dismantling the reservation community, but in 1720 the complaint of Cesar and Ben Uncas I made it clear that the 1717 measures were not to be quickly realized. The 1721 action dismissed the plan to "civilize" Mohegans altogether (since such a plan anticipates, of course, not simply that those who are to be "civilized" will be around for some time but indeed that their future will be made more secure by the very condition of "civilization"). In that sense, then, the 1721 act was as much a caustic retort to the 1717 measures as it was to the 1720 complaint of Cesar and Ben Uncas I, effecting the immediate expropriation of most of Mohegans' sequestered lands while simultaneously "legalizing" a grim historical destiny for the reservation community. Mohegans seeking to secure a life for themselves and their children on their reservation were not just to be a conquered people whose lives and lands were under the thumb of colonial government and subjected to the exigencies of colonial land hunger: it was now a governmental decree that Mohegans were a doomed people. Conversely, the 1721 action proclaimed implicitly that the townspeople of New London were destined to flourish and expand onto Mohegans' remaining lands.

It is no small point, however, that Mohegans had not articulated such a vision for themselves or their descendents. Nor had their protests against encroachment, as the 1705 commission learned, indicated that they viewed their relationship between themselves and colonists as one between conquered and conquerors. Mohegan leaders in 1703 asserted alliance and friendship as the nature of their relationship with "the English": as Appagese had phrased it, he had grown up with his land *as well as* the English, "*and why our ground and we should be parted now, we know not*" (*Proc.* 1769:58). This was an argument that claimed a similarity and even overlap in the ways of life and the histories of Mohegans and colonists, not unlike the argument made by Mary Momoho when she exhorted those who suggested her reservation community was dying out, maintaining that while some Eastern Pequot children were "bound out" to English households "for Learning and Education, 'tis no other wise than ye English bind out their Children Each to other. . . . Our Children are free at ye Same Age & time as ye English Children are" (IND 2nd, 2:22). Mohegans, like Mashantucket and Eastern Pequots, insisted that their reservation land was essential to the survival of their communities; but their protests against dispossession did not necessarily suggest that they viewed reservation boundaries as rigid cultural demarcations. That is, their protests suggest that the defense of reservation land did not emerge from Natives' assessment of themselves, or colonists, as inherently and irrevocably "other." And having lived – as their petitions declared – not in isolation from the colonial world but fully immersed in it and subjected to the particular problems of co-existence with colonists, reservation communities and their lands were thus entitled to government protection.

This was a powerful argument, and making such arguments to colonial authorities was all that reservation communities could hope to do to defend their land rights. Mohegans' protests *had* had an impact on the course of events in the early eighteenth century – as the 1705 decision made plain – and again in 1718 when they responded to the committee deployed to implement the "civilizing" measures by directing their attention, at least momentarily, to the problem of illegal encroachment.

Moreover, in 1720 Mohegan leaders had conveyed to the Connecticut governor that they did indeed intend to provide for the future of their children. Whether Owaneco's many "sales" or "grants" of Mohegan land had been frivolous coerced, Cesar and Ben Uncas I indicated that they meant to call a halt to such land transactions for the sake of their descendants.

In the aftermath of the 1705 decision, then, colonial officials learned that dispossession, impoverishment, and various strategies for "quieting" Mohegans had neither effectively silenced them nor ended the potential legal problems of the land dispute. If Mohegan leaders had argued that their lives were not detached from colonial society, and if their accounts of the past insisted that conquest had marked the beginning of alliance and initiated an overlapping of their history with that of colonists, then certainly their rights to land deserved legal justice comparable to that of their colonial neighbors. The 1721 action, however, was a wholesale erasure of Mohegans' defense of their land rights and of their pleas for just treatment. But legitimizing the erasure of *Mohegan people* required more than the pretense of legal documentation, for instance, or the protocol of government officiating over the "release" of Mohegan reserved lands to their Anglo neighbors. Indeed it would require an idea of broad cultural and political significance for colonial society, one that would enhance colonial demands for unimpeded access to indigenous lands and, concomitantly, amplify the colonial claim to an unimpeachable historical destiny. The rhetoric of the 1721 act did that and more: it intertwined "scientific" detachment and cultural distancing, describing Mohegans as "the stock of sd Indians" and thus insisting upon the rigidity and obviousness of their otherness as well as their ready access to colonial surveillance. What could more fully demarcate Mohegans from their presumed conquerors, and irrevocably oppose their historical destinies, than the notion of ineluctable Indian "extinction"? The very terms "stock" and "extinction," when applied to human communities as opposed to plants or animals, point to the emergence of a distinctly racialized discourse on Indianness; and here the shrunken reservation was to be the colonial petri dish within which the externally defined Mohegan "stock" was destined to languish, degenerate, and die – under the supervision of the colonial government. Yet, as I have argued, Mohegans had an alternative vision of their future.

## When "the People Were All Together"

It is difficult to imagine that the events of 1721 could have been anything other than immensely disheartening and destructive to Mohegan people. But Mohegans had to continue to conduct their lives nonetheless, to raise their children, to plant and attempt to harvest their fields, and to deal with the intensifying threats to their land and livelihood.

Mohegan leaders had face-to-face encounters with colonial authorities, and the colonial records that recount those meetings, along with their petitions, provide insight into the strategies that these leaders employed and the knowledge and experiences they drew upon in their responses to and critiques of colonial power. Their authority was rooted in their own community, but leadership among Mohegans was monitored and disrupted by colonial officials in the eighteenth century, and particularly so in the case of the Connecticut government's co-opting of Ben Uncas II in the 1730s.[21] Yet Mohegans did not relinquish control over this aspect of their lives as the land dispute with the colony wore on. Many opposed Ben Uncas II, in defiance of the Connecticut government; and despite government efforts to intrude into and manipulate their lives after 1705, Mohegans continued to hold ceremonies during which leaders were named and celebrated and in which members of neighboring Native communities participated.[22]

Colonial observers were present at these celebrations, and some of those who had witnessed these events described them in 1738, during testimony to the second imperial commission appointed to review the Mohegan land case. Jonathan Wickwere of Norwich, for instance, told the commission that "he was there present at the Time when [Cesar, Owaneco's son] was invested with the Sachemship [in 1715] with much Pomp Expressions of Joy & by universal Consent of all the Moheegan Indians & other of ye Neighboring Indians to the Number as near as I Can guess of five Hundred or thereabouts" (IND 1st, 1:173).[23] Likewise, Thomas Rose testified that he had gone "too or three Times amongst them" when "Mohegans, Pequotts & Nihantick Indians gathered themselves together at Moheegan to make a Sachem" (1:173). Colonial officials were also dispatched to these ceremonies "to keep order among the Indians," as was the case in 1723, when the General Assembly granted Mohegans permission "to meet in a convention of Indians from divers parts of this Colony, at Mohegan, to install as their sachem Major Benn

Uncas [Ben Uncas I]" (CR 6:408–9).[24] According to the government's report, the ceremony lasted seven days and was attended by approximately "four hundred men and women," among them "Moheags, Pequots, Nianticks, Shoutucketts, and Hartford Indians" (Proc. 1769:202).[25]

By 1738, when a second imperial commission convened to respond to the 1736 complaint Mahomet II delivered to the Crown, Connecticut officials had attempted to take full control over Mohegan leadership, casting Mahomet II as an "impostor" and denying Mohegans' right to name their own sachem, Anne, in Mahomet's absence. Colonists gave testimony to the commission on the issue of Mohegan leadership: Mohegan complainants, on the other hand, were not allowed to make their own argument before the commissioners (see the next section).

The relationship of Ben Uncas II, Mahomet II, and Anne to prior Mohegan sachems bears a brief recounting. According to Mohegan Tribal Historian Melissa Fawcett, sachem Uncas held authority from 1635 to 1683, followed by his son Owaneco, who was sachem from 1683 to 1715 (Fawcett 1995:40). Owaneco was the father of both Cesar (who was sachem from 1715 to 1723 [40]) and Mahomet I, whose death preceded that of Owaneco (IND 1st, 1:173). Ben Uncas I, also a son to Uncas and known by colonists as "Major Ben Uncas" (see "Uncas Genealogy," unnumbered figure at the opening of vol. 2 of TP; see also Fawcett 1995:40), had been named as sachem by Mohegans in 1723. But several colonists testifying before the 1738 commission claimed that Maj. Ben Uncas, father of Ben Uncas II, had been looked upon unfavorably by Owaneco. Thomas Rose told the commission that Ben Uncas I "was born of an inferior Squa," and that when "sd Ben grew up he took Asnehunts Daughter to be his Squa and Owaneco us'd to Speak very diminutively of the Sd Ben Uncas [I] & his Squa" (IND 1st, 1:173). Rose's testimony thus suggests that Owaneco, Uncas's eldest from his marriage to former Pequot sachem Sassacus's daughter ("Uncas Genealogy," TP, vol. 2) and Ben Uncas I were not simply rivals, but that Ben Uncas I was disdained by Owaneco because of the supposed "inferiority" of his mother. This may have been a distorted colonial assessment of the relationship between Owaneco and Ben Uncas I, and the derogatory term "inferior Squa" is undoubtedly Rose's own. Ideas about gender had been infused into the struggle over Mohegan land rights when colonial legislators enacted the 1717 "civilizing" measures and, in an overtly defiant gesture from Mohegans, the gendering of political authority was again emphasized when "a very great number of Moheagan Indians" denounced Ben Uncas II and proclaimed Anne, daughter of Cesar, as their *sunksquaw* in September 1736 (*Proc.* 1769:235–36; IND 1st, 1:173q). Thus Rose's account may reflect something of the way kin ties and notions of gender were asserted and contested by Mohegans as they struggled to defend their land rights and ensure a future for their community within the strictures of a patriarchal and increasingly hostile colonial society.[26]

Ben Uncas II had been officially recognized as sachem by the General Assembly in October 1726 (IND 1st, 1:129), but according to the accounts of several colonists, he had not been readily accepted by all Mohegans even then. Jonathan Barber, missionary to Mohegans and "resident in Moheegan" during the period of the dispute over the leadership of Ben Uncas II, claimed that after the death of Ben Uncas I, "there was a time appointed by the Indians & many of them Gathered at that Time in Order to Crown this Ben Uncas [II], but . . . he behav'd Himself after such a Manner [that] some if not many of The Indians present refus'd actually to Crown him" (1:173).[27] Barber added that from that time on Ben Uncas II had nonetheless "been Call'd Sachem by most of The People in this [Connecticut] Government that he had been acquainted with, & [that] the Taxes of the Moheegan Lands which the Government have Leased out, have been paid to Him, & [that] Some of the Indians have own'd Him to be Sachem & Some denied him as Such" (1:173). Thomas Rose's testimony held that Mohegans intended to name Mahomet II as their sachem rather than Ben Uncas II, "but the Indians sd Old Ben (the Father of the present Ben) would kill Young Mahomet if he should be made Sachem, & therefore Young Mahomet would not accept the Sachomship, & Capt. [John] Mason Understanding the Difficulty amonst the Indians & to prevent Murder Amongst them persuaded the Indians to make Ben their Sachem" (1:173; see also the testimony of Thomas Waterman, 1:173). The testimony of John Richards, however, differed from these accounts, asserting that Ben Uncas II was "universally received" as a sachem among Mohegans (1:173).

Regardless of the extent of internal debate over the leadership of Ben Uncas II in 1726, he was subsequently publicly repudiated by Mohegans and by their Pequot and Niantic supporters. In the early period of his leadership, however, it appears that he had not been compliant with the Connecticut government, and that he intended to both assert control over Mohegan lands and assign *Mohegans* as reservation guardians. In a 1726 petition to the General Assembly, Ben Uncas II named four Mohegans as "Trustees or over seers for the Moheag Indians" (IND 1st, 1:128). He also appointed Jo Weebucks, "son of Peter Weebucks of sd Mohegen," to "be our True and Lawfull Attorny for us and on our own behalfes, as well also as for all the mohegen Indians in sd new London and in our Names to Ask demand Sue for Recover and Require of Any person or persons whomsoever Any Land Rents or herbage that are witholden from us" (1:128). This would appear to be a response to the 1721 action and the government's disregard for Mohegans' complaints against encroachment. The petition suggests that Ben Uncas II and the newly established *Mohegan* "trustees or overseers" were determined not to allow colonially appointed "guardians" or committees to make determinations, as Wadsworth and Hall had done, that would further undermine Mohegans' land rights.

But the General Assembly's response to the 1726 petition ignored Ben Uncas's assertion of political authority over Mohegan affairs. Instead, Wadsworth and Hall were again granted "full power . . . to take upon them the Guardianship of the sd Mohegan Indians" and were instructed to fulfill the assembly's act of October 1719, which ordered "the conversion of the Indians to the faith of Christ" and "the civilizing of them" (CR 6:148–49). Moreover, Wadsworth and Hall were "directed and impowered to raise a School house . . . in the Most convenient place in the sd Mohegan lands [and] the cost of sd School house shall be paid out of ye publick Treasury of this Colony Unless the sd Committee shall find [that] Some part of the Rents of ye sd Indian Land May be Appropriated to ye Service" (IND 1st, 1:129).

Thus the General Assembly moved to further tighten its control over the reservation community and its land. The fervor to "civilize" Mohegans was emphasized again in a 1730 order to their guardians, who then included Samuel Lynde and Stephen Whittlesey as well as James Wadsworth: the "Gardians of sd [Mohegan] Indians . . . are hereby directed & fully Impowered to Inspect the carryage & maners of sd Indians, and use theire Indevours that the sd Indians be christianised if possible, and also Incorage Industry amongst them, and the sd Gardians Shall & they are hearby Impowered to lease out, for a term of yeares, Such percells of the Mohegan Lands as they Shall thinke proper, provided there be not any charge brought on this Colony by the doings of sd Gardians" (IND 1st, 1:154).

The fact that the General Assembly continued to grant colonial guardians such power over the Mohegan reservation community, demanding that they "inspect" Mohegans' behavior, suggests that legislators were wary of the possibility that Ben Uncas II and other Mohegans might be planning to re-ignite their legal case against the colony. In fact, the Connecticut government had been reminded of the 1705 decision by Captain John Mason not long after the 1721 reduction of Mohegans' sequestration in 1721. Mason, whose role as guardian and adviser to Mohegans had been acknowledged by the General Assembly in 1723 at the request of Ben Uncas I (TP 1:9), petitioned in 1723 and 1725, presenting the assembly with "copies of the proceedings and Judgment" of the 1705 commission (IND 1st, 1:126) and declaring that he had "patiently waited these 17 or 18 years" for the colony to respond to the commission's decision (1:123).

The 1721 decision had not closed the Mohegans' legal case against the colony, then, and Ben Uncas II had shown himself to be potentially disruptive to the General Assembly's plan to finally quiet and "civilize" Mohegans. The missionary endeavor had begun to gain momentum in southern New England in this period, however, and it generated public interest in the cause of Indian conversion (Love 1899:189). Experience Mayhew's "visitations" to the Native peoples of southern New England in 1713–14 lent incentive to this mission, though he had been for the most part rebuffed by Mohegans and Pequots (25–26; see also chapter 2 here). The famous Mohegan preacher Samson Occum was born in 1723, when, as Love phrased it, Mohegans were still "heathen" (Love 1899:24). Captain John Mason, encouraged by the Connecticut government, established a school at Mohegan in 1727 at which he remained as schoolmaster into the early 1730s (27–28).

A letter from Mason to Governor Talcott in October 1733 attests that the endeavor to "civilize" Mohegans had begun to have an impact on Ben Uncas II, whom he describes as "of late greatly Reformed," along with "some of his People": "He has himself and his Wife, of late began to learn to Read, and they give their Minds to learning, and have for the time they have been learning made great progress. Some other Elderly Persons have begun to learn to Read, and many Youngerly Persons can Read in their Bibles. Since they had a Minister (which is About Seven Weeks) they have attended Publick Worship the greater part of them, and they give Good Attention to what is said unto them, & some have learned to be Effected" (TP 1:290).[28]

Along with his letter to Talcott, Mason included a petition from Ben Uncas II that sought the General Assembly's protection from "English Men [who] often bring great Quantitites of Strong Liquor up the River to us" (TP 1:291–92). "Whatsoever we have that they want they purchase with it," lamented Ben Uncas II (1:292). In a subsequent "Act for the More Effectuall preventing the Selling Strong Drinke to the Moheagin Indians," the General Assembly acknowledged that "there is Continually Much Strong Drink Sold to the Mohegin Indians," and claimed that the peddlers of liquor had "Impoverished" Mohegans' "estates" and "debauched their Manners" such that Mohegans were "rendered More intractable to receive the Christian Faith" (IND 1st, 1:164).

If Ben Uncas II had become a "most prominent friend of the Christian religion" (Love 1899:30) after he was named as sachem, he had not necessarily lost interest in Mohegans' land rights. And although the reservation community and its lands were preyed upon by peddlers of liquor, their opposition to dispossession continued. Love, in fact, remarked that Mohegans' land dispute with the colony "had been bred in the bone of the Indians of [Samson] Occom's generation" (119). The refurbished Christianizing mission in the early eighteenth century had not deadened Mohegans' connection to their land or to their history of struggle.

In November of 1734 a complaint from Mohegans was presented at a meeting of the commissioners of the Society for the Propagation of the Gospel in New England, explaining "that great part of their land had already been taken away from them, and that they are still in danger of further encroachments." According to the minutes of the meeting, the complaint was "presented from Uncas, Sachem of the Mohegans, and Capt John Mason, in behalf of said Indians" (TP 1:310n). Presumably, it was Ben Uncas II to whom the report referred. Captain Mason and Reverend Barber also brought a complaint to the Society on Mohegans' behalf in 1735 (1:327). The urgency of the matter had been brought to the attention of Revered Eliphalet Adams of New London, the society's "agent with the Indians in the eastern part of Connecticut" (1:107n), by Benjamin Colman of Boston, a commissioner for the society:

> The Complaint I fear will fall heavy at Last upon your colony, for the Injury done the Indians in their Laws. I have as high a Resentment

> of such Injustice as any one, and Againe am as loath to apply home [to England] in any complaint for a Relief to the poor Natives, always friendly and faithfull to us, never to be Enough Acknowledged by us. We have complained to Your Gov[ernment] in Vaine. I know nothing more threatening to your charter than a wrong of this Nature, well proved, but what heart or hand can I willingly have in a piece of Justice which may bring on you so heavy a Revenge. What would it be for Your Province to do the Indians Right, and bear the loss among them. I beseech you beg Your Rulers to Consider on it, and that timely (1:327–28)

Thus did Colman raise the question that had been addressed by the 1705 commission, and that had been perceived as such a threat by Connecticut officials: that is, the question of what it would mean for the colony "to do the Indians Right." By January 1736, colonial officials knew that this question was to be put to the Crown once again, for as Governor Talcott reported, Mahomet II and Captain Mason were journeying "for Great Britain, to enter a Complaint in the name of the Indians against this Colony, that they have wronged the Indians in their lands" (TP 1:328–29). In several letters he sent to solicit support for the colony from officials in Boston and London, Talcott claimed that Ben Uncas told him "Capt Mason was now conspiring with one Mahomet, to set him up for the Sachem of the Moheagues, and so by that means to revive the old controversy" (1:336; see also 1:338–44).[29] Talcott's letter to Massachusetts governor Jonathan Belcher hinted at the manipulations of Mohegan leadership that were underway. Diverting Belcher from the question of whether or not injustice had been done to Mohegans, Talcott instead offered a defense of what he suggested were Mohegans' political traditions, now threatened by the purported "mischief" and deceit of Mahomet II and Mason:

> Capt Mason is making a tool of one Mahomett, that is of the family of Owanaco, to serve his purpose [namely, Mason's own claims to Mohegan lands], and designs to carry Mahomett with him to Great Britain, as the Sachem of said Indians. This, if not prevented, may prove of mischievous consequence, for there have been three succeeding Sachems of the Moheags solemnly installed by the Indians, and approved of by our Assembly, contrary to the pretensions of Capt Mason about this Mahomett, and Ben Uncass the present Sachem is now in the full

> possession of the Government, and has the hearts of his people. If Capt Mason should any ways prevail to make any alterations [in] their Government, it would undoubtedly produce much hatred and many murthers amongst them and hinder and divert them in their present inclinations to receive the truth as it is in Jesus. (TP 1:329)

Talcott thus implied that it was not Mohegans' land rights that were at issue, but the internal violence supposedly ready to erupt among them should there be any disruption of the status quo at Mohegan. And if Mohegans were such a volatile people – prone to "much hatred and many murthers" and hence to *self*-destruction – what they needed was Christianization rather than further involvement in a land dispute.

Discrediting Mahomet II appears to have been essential to Talcott's effort to elide the legal problems posed by Mohegan resisters and to prevent an investigation by another imperial commission. But Mahomet was to be depicted as a presence more troubling than simply the "tool" of an outside agitator. The story Talcott conveyed regarding Mahomet's illegitimacy as a sachem concerned his purportedly dubious parentage. Mahomet's father, Mahomet I, allegedly committed a murder and was, according to Talcott, subsequently killed in revenge (TP 1:340). Mahomet I was thus depicted as an outcast, his "intolerable pride and cruelty" earning him "the general indignation" of Mohegan people. Likewise, Talcott claimed, Mahomet II "has been utterly rejected by them" (1:340).

Talcott's own investigation into the matter of Mohegans' "rejection" of Mahomet II did not bear out these contentions, however. He employed Captain Benajah Bushnell of Norwich to go to the Mohegan reservation to obtain evidence from Mohegans regarding "Mahimit's Turblent Carriges and Insultings among his people" and to prove that Ben Uncas II was the rightful sachem. In February 1736 Bushnell reported that "the Indians are very Loth to Give any Evidence" against Mahomet II, and that "I cant git one to speake in that Case" (TP 1:350). In attempting to provide evidence supporting the sachemship of Ben Uncas II, Bushnell explained that "Ben the 2 saith that he hath Raigned about 10 years. I Cant git no Evidences of there Discarding of Mahamit the 2" (1:350). The rest of Bushnell's report to Talcott bears citing in further detail, since it reveals the way in which notions of gender and cultural illegitimacy shaped colonial assessments of the Mohegan "stock" as the legal case was revived:

> On Wednesday I met Mr. [John] Richards [town clerk of New London] att Mohegen, and went to Ben's wigwam, and asked him Several Questions, which he Answered. All which Mr. Richards will give your Honer an accompt of att Large. We found but 7 ffamilies att Mohegen, and but 6 men, (beside Ben), 2 of them Declared themselves well satisfyed in the present Raigne under Ben, & said they thought yt the people were all well satisfyed. The others said that they did not care to Declare or say anything about it, without the People were all together. Since that I have Examined Ned & Jo: Webux, who say they are very easy in the present Sachem, & think it not worth a while to Change. . . . I have Examined Several of the Indians, Concerning the number of all the ffamelies that belong to the whole Tribe of them, and they have Reckoned them up, and Cant make more than 28 of them, & Several of them are non Residents, and seldom Live there. And there are several Widdows that keepe house, which they Reckoned as ffamilies. And they are not only a few but miserable pore, that I think if our Soveraign Lord the King knew their Circomstances well he would hardly put himself much out of his waie to obtain an alliance with them. (1:350–51)

Bushnell's report offered Talcott nothing in the way of hard evidence to undermine Mahomet II, but it did represent the reservation community – because of its poverty, its small population, and the purportedly insufficient presence of adult men – as degenerating and unworthy of imperial concern. Here was a response to Mohegans' complaints against dispossession that picked up the theme of the colony's prior argument against the 1705 decision, and that also indicated that the prophecy of the 1721 action was being fulfilled. Mohegans are depicted as "inconsiderable Indians" here, but in Bushnell's obvious disdain for Mohegan people there is something more insidious yet: the suggestion that Mohegans' own "reckoning" of family requires monitoring and adjustment. Counting Mohegans is clearly deemed essential to evaluating the viability (according to colonial cultural standards) of the reservation community and thus their entitlement to land and government protection; but *how* to count them is a problem for colonial assessors, and the "several Widdows that keepe house, which [Mohegans] Reckoned as families," are representative of that problem. Indeed how were *Mohegan women* – who presumably were present on the reservation in greater numbers than men at the time of Bushnell's investigation – to be "reckoned" by colonial authorities at this juncture in the legal dispute?[30]

What Bushnell's account distorts and silences is as significant as what it seeks to convey. For one thing, since he reports that Mohegans had not readily yielded to his interrogation, and that he was unable to acquire evidence against Mahomet, it is apparent that Mohegan women were among those who had not "discarded" Mahomet II and who had refused to respond to Bushnell's questions. More importantly, it is clear that among Mohegans themselves the presence of women on reservation land was indeed important, and despite the pressures of Christianization and the colony's attempt to reorganize the reservation community into patrilineal households via the 1717 "civilizing" measures, Mohegan women were not required to have husbands to be "reckoned as family" and thus to have rights to the reservation land. Women as well as men constituted the Mohegan body politic – "the People" who, when together, would decide the matter of their own leadership. So while Bushnell had disparaged the Mohegan reservation community, his report nonetheless reveals something subversive – a thwarting of colonial intrusions and an implicit challenge to the claim of "extinction" – emanating from the internal workings of kinship, gender, and community at Mohegan.

Although Talcott had not gained the evidence he sought from Bushnell's investigation, by April of 1736 he had in hand two documents, both written in the colonial legal parlance of the time, that were to be submitted to the Crown as evidence discrediting Mahomet's petition. The first, entitled "Declaration of Ben Uncas, Sachem of Mohegan, 10th April, 1736," offered the colony's argument against the 1705 decision and depicted Captain John Mason as a self-serving instigator of Mohegans' complaints against Connecticut (TP 1:361–63). The second, entitled "Declaration of 9 of the Prime Mohegan Indians, dated 17th April, 1736," focused on the issue of Mohegan leadership and detailed the supposed illegitimacy of Mahomet II. This declaration attests that Ben Uncas II was Mohegans' "Rightfull Sachem . . . Elected into that Office According to the Antient Custom," which was described as follows: "altho' their Predecessors had had regard in the choice of their Sachems to the family of their late Sachems, Yett their Predecessors never Supposed themselves obliged to Elect the next Heir Male of the sd Sachem, but to choose the most worthy and promising Branch of the ffamily, and that the Gov[ernment] of sd Colony had never molested or hindered them in this their Antient Custom & Usage" (1:364).

However, as the General Assembly made clear to Mohegans at their 1723 ceremony appointing Ben Uncas I as sachem, the colonial government would allow Mohegans to name their own leaders provided they understood that "the government would justly expect from them that their love and friendship to the English should hereafter be manifested on all occasions" (*Proc.* 1769:201). The Connecticut government's recognition and approval of Mohegan leaders, then, was contingent upon their deference to colonial authority. Mahomet II had, of course, defied this colonial expectation by submitting a complaint to the Crown. Ben Uncas II, on the other hand, ultimately complied with colonial authority, perhaps having been drawn in that direction by the Christianizing mission or, equally likely, by the General Assembly's utter disregard for his initial petition to them in which he asserted Mohegans' political autonomy.

If Mahomet's petition to the Crown was to draw imperial attention once again to the illegality of colonial appropriation of Mohegan lands, Governor Talcott produced documents intended to draw attention to the purported illegitimacy of Mahomet II, for if Mahomet II was an "impostor" (TP 1:337) who did not represent Mohegan people, his complaint could have no validity. Talcott's "Declaration of 9 of the Prime Mohegan Indians" claimed that Mahomet II had no right to the sachemship not only because his father had supposedly been "banished" by Owaneco for his "Cruelty & barbarity," but *also* because of his parentage on his mother's side:

> Mahomet [I] took to Wife a Woman of the Royall Blood, according to the Custom & practise of that Nation & dwelt w[ith] her Some Years, during w[hich] time he took *a Concubine of a Mean Extract*, by whom he had Issue Yeomanum [alias] Mahomet [II] & Some Short time after the birth of sd Yeomanum the sd Mahomet discarded the sd Concubine Woman & her Issue, & banished them from him, & they dwelt in Exile from him to the day of his death, & never to that day returnd into the Dominion of the Mohegans, but had been always looked upon as a *Stranger & an Alien*. (1:365, emphasis added)

This genealogical assessment of Mahomet's political "illegitimacy" brings into relief a crucial aspect of the leadership ceremony that took place several months later at Mohegan, during which Cesar's daughter Anne was appointed as a new leader. The naming of Anne not only challenged the authority of Ben Uncas II as well as that of the Connecticut government, but it also defied colonial derogations of Mohegan women, asserting their importance to the preservation of Mohegans' land rights and community life. Colonial notions of gender hierarchy and the government's disregard for the political and social relevance of Mohegan women had been made explicit in the 1717 "civilizing" measures, as well as Bushnell's report on the reservation community submitted to Talcott earlier in 1736. The April 1736 "Declaration," presented as an evaluation of Mahomet II by supposed Mohegan *elites* (the unnamed "9 Prime"), reflected the colonial government's gendered and now distinctly class-based prescriptions regarding political leadership within the Mohegan reservation community, notions neatly embodied in the juxtaposition between "*Woman of the Royal Blood*" and "*Concubine of a Mean Extract.*" This colonial construction of the standards of Mohegan cultural and "biological" legitimacy was to render Mahomet II a false sachem, as well as an ersatz Mohegan – a "*stranger*" and "*alien*" to Mohegans themselves. And, of course, this construction relied ultimately on a derogatory representation of Native women who lived an impoverished or "mean" existence.[31] Since, according to Bushnell's characterization, *all* Mohegans were "miserable pore," this was a characterization that colonial officials might readily apply to all Mohegan women. Hence this effort to root legitimate Mohegan identity and political authority – and thus Mohegan land rights – in the wombs of women of colonially concocted Mohegan "Royal Blood" hinted at the possibility that far more Mohegans could be disqualified, or "unrecognized," via the government's own calculations of the absence of such "blood" in the reservation community. With Mahomet II gone to England, and the colonial campaign to discredit him underway, what was to be done by Mohegans at home? The prior three decades had shown the reservation community that the Connecticut government was no protector of their land rights, nor had colonially appointed guardians of the likes of Wadsworth and Hall proved to be friends. While Mohegans' protests against dispossession had evoked a history of alliance and beseeched the colonial government to acknowledge Mohegan land rights as it would those of their colonial neighbors, the 1736 ceremony suggested that Mohegan people sought now to convey a different message to colonial authority, one that rejected this alliance, and the notion that it linked the lives of Mohegans and Anglos.

Mohegans' naming of a woman as their leader, at this particular moment, was a most blatant gesture of defiance to colonial authority, but Anne, it must be remembered, was the daughter of Cesar, a leader whose legitimacy the Connecticut government had never disputed, and who was depicted in the April 1736 "Declaration" as a sachem whose position of authority had been rightfully inherited from his father, Owaneco. That document also noted that Cesar had died "without Issue Male" (TP 1:366), but that did not mean that his daughter was never to be made a leader by her own community. Colonial officials in Connecticut knew that Native women could and did become sachems or *sunksquaws* of reservation communities, and indeed Mary Momoho, leader among Eastern Pequots at Stonington, had made her presence known to the General Assembly in the early eighteenth century.

There is no record of Mohegans' requesting government permission to hold the September 1736 ceremony, but there were two colonists present who later reported on the event, Jabez Crocker and Joseph Tracy Jr. of Norwich. Their account was submitted as testimony to the 1738 commission:

> on the 10th day of September, A.D. 1736, they were on the Indian land at Moheagan present with a very great number of Moheagan Indians, as we supposed universally met at a meeting which they call a black dance: and whereas they were then informed that endeavours were made by some English persons to prove that Ben Uncas was their rightful Sachem, and being importuned by the said Indians in general, but especially by some of the chief of the said Indians, which were said to be Moheags, to take notice of their minds in that affair; and accordingly the matter was put to vote among said Indians by said Indians, and the vote was universal in the favour of Mahomet, grandson of Oweneco, late Sachem of Moheagan, to be their Sachem, whom the deponents understand to be the same Mahomet which was then in England, and there died; which Mahomet they understand to be the great grandson of Uncas, the former Grand Sachem of Moheagan, and that the said meeting was in Moheagan, the general seat and rendezvous of the said Indians, and that the deponents then inquired of the said Indians, whether they desired that Mahomet should take the measures that he then did? they answered, they approved of Ma-

> homet's proceedings in his memorial in their behalf in England; and farther signified the one principal cause of their meeting or dance was to establish Anne the daughter of Caesar, which Caesar was younger brother to Mahomet, father of the aforementioned Mahomet, to be their ruler until Mahomet returned, and for him to be chief when he returned; for they entirely denied Ben Uncas to be their Sachem. (*Proc.* 1769:235–36; see also IND 1st, 1:173)

Governor Talcott's response was to name this act an attempt by Mohegans to "*set up a queen or impostor*," as missionary Jonathan Barber later testified (*Proc.* 1769:237). Barber also explained that, not long after the ceremony, a rumor had circulated that "Eastward Indians" were planning to attack Mohegans, "which caused the Indians a very great fear, even so great that they did many of them begin a fort for their defence" (*Proc.* 1769:237; see also IND 1st, 1:173).[32] Since Mohegan men had served as military allies to colonists in all the major colonial wars, Mohegans "sent [a message] to his honour our governor [Talcott], desiring that they might have provision from the English or government if their enemies should assault them. Upon which his honour sent this letter," which Barber summarizes:

> He first reminds them of former leagues or agreements that they had entered into with the government of Connecticut, and that the government had always treated with them in and by their Sachems. Further he informs them, that he had heard that many of them had been active in setting up a queen among them, and had forsaken Ben Uncas their Sachem. His honour manifested a displeasure at their proceeding, and did exhort them to peace and unity . . . and his honour told them in the letter, that if they would set up a queen or impostor, and not own Ben Uncas for their Sachem or king, that they would protect only Ben and his family, with those that adhered to him. And further he said, that if they would return to Ben, and own him for their Sachem, that he did not know but that he or the government might protect them. (*Proc.* 1769:237)

Talcott's warning does not acknowledge Anne by name, as if to signal an absolute erasure of her existence.[33] But there is evidence that Mohegans' naming of Anne had been discussed by colonists: Samuel Leffingwell of Norwich told the imperial commission that he "heard, when

Mahomet was in England, that some of the Indians were about to set up Anne, the daughter of Caesar, to be Sunkee Squaw" (*Proc.* 1769:204).

Ultimately Connecticut officials sought a more direct, and surely more conventional, means of silencing Anne: an arranged marriage. As colonist Samuel Avery later explained, "some time in the Year 1737 it was Proposed and Thought Convenient that Ben Uncas, Junr. [son of Ben Uncas II], who was then an Indented Apprentice . . . in the Province of Massachusetts, should be Sent for . . . And Marryed unto Sachem Cesar['s] daughter" (IND 1st, 1:236). In his petition to the Connecticut General Assembly requesting reimbursement for his services, Avery stated that he had performed "Said Service in obedience" and brought the son of Ben Uncas II home, though he complained that he "bore All the Charges and have Never Rec[eived] any Satisfaction . . . but alwaies Expected that I should" (1:236). According to colonial accounts, the marriage did take place (1:236, 173; TP 2:198).[34]

Anne was to be silenced, then, and her political influence usurped, through a colonially imposed leadership marriage. But colonial officials could not hide the fact that the ceremony had indeed taken place, without the consent of the Connecticut government. And Talcott's threat to Mohegans suggests that their act of rebellion was viewed as intolerable. There are a number of things that the September 1736 protest implied about how Mohegan people understood the history of their land struggle and their possibilities for a future. In one sense, the event may have been a means of commemorating the previous three decades of Mohegans' resistance to dispossession, for indeed Anne's name recalls that of the English queen who had established the first commission to hear Mohegans' complaints against the colony in 1705. Thus Anne's leadership may suggest a compelling irony – invoking imperial authority in order to remind the Connecticut government of the 1705 decision. In fact, Talcott claimed in 1736 that although he knew that the queen's commission had "determined that sundry lands should be restored to Oweneco," he "never saw" the colony's record of the 1705 commission, "nor can I tell anywhere to find it" (TP 1:335).

It is also important to note the significance of the season during which this event took place: late summer was the time of green corn harvesting, and hence the establishment of Anne's leadership may have coincided with the Green Corn Ceremony, a celebration that highlighted Native women's role as agriculturalists (see chapter 1). Thus Anne's ceremony may have been a means of confirming the importance of women not only as cultivators of corn and reproducers of community life, but as purveyors of Mohegans' historical ties to their reserved planting land, the land that remained "the general seat and rendezvous" of Mohegan people (*Proc.* 1769:236).

The 1736 ceremony also demonstrated that Mohegan resisters were as focused on the present, and the future, as they were mindful of the events of the past. The ceremony conveyed Mohegans' intent to perpetuate their own "Antient Customs" regarding leadership – without, and against, colonial supervision. In effect, the naming of Anne as sunksquaw denied the Connecticut government the right to define Mohegans' political traditions: it asserted that Mohegan leadership was a local matter, its legitimacy rooted in the reservation community – and in Mohegan land – rather than in the halls of the Connecticut General Assembly. And if Mohegans at the ceremony did, in fact, refer to the event as a "black dance," that name too may have had a timely political and cultural significance. Evoking as it does the colonial notion of Indian "savagery" as a diabolic, anti-Christian force, such a designation suggests that the ceremony expressed Mohegans' rejection of the multiple trappings of colonial "civilization." Given Governor Talcott's attempt to control Mohegan leadership and deny Mahomet's Mohegan identity, Mohegan resisters may have intended for the "black dance" to proclaim their *otherness* – to articulate Mohegan identity as existing in opposition to colonial society and in defiance of governmental control.

## The Unspeakable

According to Crocker and Tracy's account of the September 1736 ceremony, the Mohegan participants were not aware at the time that Mahomet II had died of small pox in England in the previous month (TP 1:374). Had he returned, the events that followed, and the proceedings of the 1738 commission, may have gone differently. As one historian remarked, Mahomet's "decease rendered unnecessary a vigorous defense by the colony" before the 1738 commission (Smith 1950:430). Though Mahomet was not to have an opportunity to challenge the leadership of Ben Uncas II before the commission, and the sachemship of Anne was quashed by Governor Talcott, opposition to Ben Uncas II continued. By

May of 1737, Mohegans petitioned the General Assembly to complain against Ben Uncas II for assisting encroachers whose livestock had damaged Mohegan crops. The petition was signed by Wemus Chum, Sam Uncas, John Comoush, and John Uncas Jr., who was the next Mohegan leader to challenge the position of Ben Uncas II (IND 1st, 1:173). The petitioners stated that Ben Uncas II "utterly Denies to ask us any Councill in any of ye affairs but Does as he is Directed by them whome we think to be our Trespassers" (1:158). "Since Capt. Mason hath been gone [to England]," the petitioners explained, and the reservation's "Care [has] Come into the Hands of others"

> we have sufforrd great Damage, for our Hogs are not allow'd to [go] in the pasture and when any Hoges get into our fields and wee putt them into the pound Ben will turn them out and Deliver them to their owners without [them] paying any Damage. . . . And Ben we are Informed sais he Cares Not for us but is about to Lett out all our Lands from us and receive the proffits to his own use, which . . . we Can by No Means allow of for we rec[k]on We have Each of us an Equal Intrest With him. We Subscribe in ye Behalf of all the Moheag Indians Except Ben and Some few yt are in ye Woods Hunting: And what we have written is the Desire of twenty four of us. (1:158)

Over thirty years after the 1705 decision, this petition attests that the lives of Mohegan people who sought to live and plant on the sequestered lands still entailed a continual struggle against encroachment and the threats it posed to their livelihood. Nonetheless, as the 1736 ceremony made clear, many Mohegans were resolved not to surrender their remaining lands, or their lives, to the control of colonial authorities. Thus the petitioners did not ask for a "guardian" to be appointed to replace Mason, nor did they seek the colony's approval of the leadership role they had taken.

The Connecticut government continued to uphold Ben Uncas II, however; by June of 1738, when the next imperial commission sat in Norwich to review Mohegans' legal case against the colony, among the evidence offered in defense of the colony was a document, signed by Ben Uncas II along with seventeen other men, which declared that Mohegans quitclaimed their rights to all but their remaining reserved lands (those lands that were left after the 1721 action) and "released" the colony from the 1705 judgment; in addition, the document referred to Mahomet II as having been "of Niantick" and thus not a Mohegan (*Proc.* 1769:197; see also IND 1st, 1:173). By this allegation, the colony sought once again to discredit the 1736 complaint to the Crown by depicting Mahomet as an "alien" among Mohegans, having no authority to speak for them. As it turned out, however, Mahomet's death had not left Mohegan resisters entirely on their own, for they had gained the support of members of neighboring reservation communities – Pequots and Niantics – who joined Mohegans in September 1736 "at a general meeting" at which "the whole body of them did renounce Ben Uncas [II] as Sachem" (*Proc.* 1769:218). This act of cooperative resistance suggests that the reservation communities of New London County acknowledged their common struggle against dispossession and perhaps recognized that Mahomet's complaint to the Crown had created an opportunity for all of them to be heard and thus to change the circumstances of their lives. As Talcott would have it, however, Mohegans' Pequot and Niantic supporters (some of whom attended the proceedings of the 1738 commission) were also *impostors*. He argued not only that the Mason family had been "feeding [Mohegans] with hopes to Gain the whole Country to themselves" (TP 2:60) but also that the Masons had "set up the Indians he could prevail upon" and induced "many of the Pequods, Nayantiks and Other Indians" to pose as Mohegans and thus make their "party appear Great" (2:55, 54; see also 2:108–9). Just as Mohegans' resistance was characterized as a mere pretense, concocted by the Masons, so too was the alliance between Mohegans, Niantics, and Pequots labeled a sham. Indian "impostors" thus abounded in Connecticut by 1736. And for Talcott, any Mohegans who had opposed both Ben Uncas II and the Connecticut government were not to be recognized as Mohegans: as he assured Francis Wilks, the colony's agent in London, in a July 1738 letter, the "proper Moheags" were those who supported "their King," Ben Uncas II, and who were thereby allied with the colony (TP 2:63).

Not surprisingly, the 1738 commission took upon itself the task of deciding who Mohegans' rightful sachem was before Mahomet's complaint might be considered. In making that determination, a majority of the commissioners, who supported the colony (Smith 1950:431), denied motions made by Mohegans' attorneys that "the Mohegin Tribe," or at least those Mohegans present in the courtroom, be allowed to testify on the matter of Mohegan leadership (TP 2:55–59). Talcott feared that if the Mohegan "Nation as a Nation might Now Come in and . . . renounce their Sachem" (Ben Uncas II), such testimony might "set up the tribe as owners of the Country": "if by their Declaration they can bring the Court to Determine Ben is no Sachem, they may by the same Means obtain the Like Judgment of the Court that nither Uncass nor Owanaco were Sachems, for they have nither of them more to show for their title than Ben hath. This would be to Defeat all our Deeds & Releases from the former Sachems, and lay us Lyable to be turned out of the Countrey by the Tribe, who never pretended to a Title till now" (2:58–59).

Thus Talcott surmised that if Mohegans were to have the floor, they might use the colony's own prior argument about Uncas "illegitimacy" to their advantage. Talcott had nothing – other than the "Deeds & Releases" the colony produced as evidence before the commission – upon which to base his assertion that the Mohegan people had "never pretended title" to their ancestral homeland or that they had renounced their collective right to the sequestered lands. Talcott did have grounds, however, to suspect that if a majority of Mohegans were to testify, a good number of them might contest the validity of some of those "Deeds & Releases" *as well as* the right of previous sachems to sell or grant Mohegan lands to colonists.

Having silenced Mohegans, the commission declared Ben Uncas II "to be the chief Sachem of the said Indians" and accepted the document produced by the colony that absolved it of any wrongdoing in appropriating Mohegan lands. Hence the 1705 judgment was overturned (*Proc.* 1769:7). But this action was appealed by John and Samuel Mason, sons of Captain John Mason, who petitioned the Crown "as the Trustees and Guardians" of Mohegans (TP 2:139). The Masons pointed out that when the commission of review met in 1738, Connecticut representatives objected to the 1705 decision being read, and hence the 1705 judgment was neither acknowledged nor addressed by the commissioners (*Proc.* 1769:6). Yet another commission of review was appointed in 1742, the Crown having determined that the proceedings of the 1738 commission were "very irregular" (1769:7). The orders to this commission stated that the previous commissioners had erred in refusing to examine the 1705 judgment and in "refus[ing] to hear the Indians in their own behalf, whom they had summoned, and who were present in court and desired to be heard" (7). This commission upheld the 1738 judgment nonetheless, and despite another appeal against that ruling, the legal case was brought to a close in 1772 when the British Privy Council found in favor of the colony (see Walters 1995:826). Samson Occom, who in 1764 returned to the reservation from his missionary travels, was much disheartened by the outcome of the dispute. According to Love, it "led Occom to see and to assert, as he did many times, that his people would never accept the Christian religion until they were treated with more justice by their neighbors." Love recounts that "it was said that a desire to conciliate the Colony in a distracted time had much to do with this result" (Love 1899:122). As Occom himself wrote, the final judgment from London was "a pure favour" to the colony (cited in Love 1899:122).

Talcott remained apprehensive about the potential legal implications of Mohegans' complaints. Indeed, he learned that not long after the 1738 commission rendered its decision, "about 40 or 50 Moheegs" had signed a petition to protest the "unjust proceedings of the commissioners" and the "management of the affaire between the Colony of Connecticut and the Moheegs" (TP 2:104). Consequently Talcott sought the advice of London attorney John Sharpe, to whom he sent the colony's record of the commission's proceedings. As Sharpe interpreted it, the attending commissioners denied "very rightly" the request by Mohegans' attorneys that those Mohegans present in the court be allowed to speak and identify their rightful sachem. "Was ever such a thing heard of before," Sharpe wrote, "as for a whole Tribe, or Nation, to come into a Court, & to insist to be heard by themselves[?]" (2:111). Allowing the Mohegan complainants to speak for themselves would be "against all Rules of Proceeding"; more dangerous, Sharpe suggested, was the fact that the *identity* of these Mohegans, as with "other Indians," was suspect: "What assurance cou'd there be that these Indians were really of the Mohegan Tribe, & that they were not pequat, Nihantick, or Narrogansett, or other Indians, brought there to answer this Particular Purpose? . . . Suppose some of the Indians had declared for Ben & some for John Uncas, What must have been the Consequence? Were they to have fought for the Mastership? Who cou'd have answered [what] might have ensued, or [what] danger might have been hereby br[ought] to the Court itself?" (2:108–9).

Sharpe argued the same point to Talcott that Talcott sought to convey to Massachusetts governor Belcher in 1736: Mohegans and "other Indians" were ever poised to erupt in violence, to degenerate into a chaotic throng. It was Indians who required monitoring, not the colony's handling of their land rights. Sharpe's response thus affirmed Talcott's de facto policy of sabotage that had been directed at Mohegans' expressions of political autonomy. If Talcott had feared that Mohegans' legal case against the colony might discredit colonial authority and its claims to the Indian territories in its midst, then Sharpe's forceful defense of the commission's actions in 1738 assured him that the muzzling of Mohegans was an absolute necessity precisely because the collective testimony of Mohegan plaintiffs – and the implicit recognition that they possessed a voice as "a whole Tribe, or Nation" – would serve to "put the Indians in the Place of the Comm[ission]" (TP 2:110). As Sharpe saw it, this could have disastrous consequences: "And [if] the Comm[issioners] were to have Governed themselves not by the Proofs & Evidences in the Cause, but by the Voice of the Indians, the Commission, And all the Powers thereby given to the Court, would at once have been undermined. . . . And could this be done with any other View than to brow beat, insult & menace the Court, and to overawe and terrifye 'em into a Complyance with their unreasonable Demands" (TP 2:110).

There is a rather telling irony here that should not go unmentioned. In juxtaposing the established order of English judicial proceedings with the threat of violent rebellion presumed to be simmering in the Indian body politic – the collective voice of which might alone serve to "overawe and terrifye" the court and thus obstruct the conventions of colonial authority – Sharpe's rhetoric points to the political malleability of this colonial construction of "Indian savagery," and its historical relevance as a signifier of Euro-American identity. For certainly it was readily appropriated later in the century by colonial radicals who sought to establish a "recognizable" face for their own rebellious actions and claim to political autonomy vis-à-vis imperial authority: it was the "savage" costume that offered a culturally embedded display of "legitimacy" for the Indian impostors who perpetrated the 1773 "Boston Tea Party," which served up its own message of "insult and menace" to the English Crown.

In his evaluation of the actions of the 1738 imperial commission, Sharpe played the wild card of "Indian savagery" to discredit Mohegans' complaints and to cast them as "illegitimate" Indians. Though he mocked it, however, Sharpe seemed also to fear that "the Voice of the Indians" did indeed have an argument to make, one that might have been "introductive of the most dangerous consequences" in that it could "render all [colonial] property precarious" (TP 2:110). As Mohegans' legal struggle against the colony garnered the support of Pequots and Niantics, Talcott was confronted with converging voices of Indian resistance, embodying multiple challenges to the legitimacy of colonial justice. The following chapter focuses on the discourse and confrontations that shaped the concurrent dispute over Mashantucket Pequots' reservation lands, examining Mashantuckets' opposition to dispossession and the interwoven contests over land rights, cultural legitimacy, and colonial justice it incited.

# 5

# "Now They Make Us as Goats"

## *The Mashantucket Pequot Land Struggle, 1709–1804*

In the context of the Mohegan land dispute, the identity of Mohegans who dared defy colonial rule was to become the subject of governmental scrutiny and manipulation. Mahomet II was depicted not simply as an illegitimate leader, but as an *illegitimate Mohegan*: an "impostor" in the fullest sense, whose genealogy was to be as scandalous as his act of political rebellion. Colonial arguments and legislative actions meant to silence Mohegans and bring an end to the legal case deployed particular notions of cultural and political illegitimacy that posed Mohegans, and not the violation of their land rights, as the problem that required monitoring. The colony's "official" or "legal" discourse on Mohegan land rights was thus a discourse of diversion and denial, telling a story about Mohegans that constructed and extolled the rights of their presumed conquerors. From the very inception of their legal dispute with the colony, however, Mohegans had interjected a counternarrative, one that not only contested the right of the Connecticut government to control the Mohegan reservation community and its lands but that also reflected Mohegans' own understanding of the past. Reminding colonial officials of the role of Mohegan ancestors as colonial *allies*, Mohegans argued that their history remained important, and that the colony had betrayed the alliance long ago forged between Mohegans and colonists. This had been a powerful argument, particularly as it was given voice in the decision of the 1705 commission. Mohegans' challenge to colonial authority was to be further complicated by Mashantucket Pequots' opposition to dispossession during the eighteenth century.

In a letter to Colonel Adam Winthrop of Boston, a commissioner of the Society for the Propagation of the Gospel in New England, dated February 17, 1736, Governor Talcott wrote:

> The Pequots were a nation conquered [in] 1637, and thereupon had no pretence to lands. Yet you will see what care the Government has

> taken to secure Mashantuxet to them, which being in quantity more than they could improve, and some of it so stony that it was not fit for their service, the English are allowed to improve some of it, for which they are to keep the Indians field sufficiently fenced, free from cost, which was judged to be the best use those lands could be put to for the Indians, they being a slack people in fencing, used to receive much damage, make many complaints. (TP 1:338)

Talcott's comments were a response to an inquiry initiated by the Mohegans' 1734 complaint to the Society concerning the colony's appropriation of their reserved lands (TP 1:310n). His letter opens with several paragraphs expounding on the delicate balance between Winthrop's supposed "friendship to this Colony, and faithfulness to the Indians." Talcott professes his certainty that Winthrop has made this inquiry to serve both these interests, rather than to "make me an instrument to provide you with materials to oppose this Colony":

> the thing that you choose, hope for, and should rather rejoice in, is that by me you may be informed that this Colony hath been a candid protector of the Indians, and hath secured for them lands sufficient for their husbandry, &c. And this is equally an agreeable task for me to perform. We both serve one Great Master here on earth, and a Greater still in heaven. Our interest is the same, and we are assured our labour of love shall not be in vain. I have therefore herewith sent you the enclosed copies, containing the evidence of these matters, as far as I can at present come at them. Doubtless more might be found with respect to their lesser tribes, but having no complaint about them, I have concerned myself principally about the Moheags and Pequots. (TP 1:338)

The themes evoked in Talcott's description of the Connecticut government's relations with Mashantucket Pequots are similar to those that were expressed in the colony's arguments during the Mohegan case: namely, that the history of the colony's treatment of the indigenous people of the region was one marked by acts of kindness; that indeed the colonial government had not denied land rights to Native people but rather had bestowed them. Equally important, just as Mohegans were cast as "inconsiderable Indians," so too were Pequots disparaged and the validity of their resistance to dispossession denied.

Talcott's depiction of Mashantuckets as "a slack people in fencing," who thus require, if not invite, the colonial government's supervision, is not simply a reflection of prevailing colonial attitudes toward Indianness, but an obfuscation of the history of struggle against encroachment that Mashantuckets had articulated in their petitions to the Connecticut government. Indeed, as Mashantucket Pequot sachem Robin Cassacinamon's 1721 petition to the General Assembly indicated, Mashantuckets had not found a "guardian" in the Connecticut government, as Talcott's letter to Winthrop would have it, nor an accurate acknowledgment of history. Instead, Cassacinamon argues that colonial land hunger had had dehumanizing consequences for Mashantucket people, who, like Mohegans, had served the colony as military allies[1]: "The English in ye time of ye war Called us brethren: & Esteemed us to be Rational Creatures: but behold now they make us as Goats by moving us from place to place, to Clear rough land: & make it profitable for 'em" (IND 1st, 1:95).

The counternarratives articulated in such petitions, and in other acts of resistance – such as the 1736 leadership ceremony at Mohegan – hit at the core of colonial authority in early-eighteenth-century Connecticut. If Cassacinamon's petition conveyed a scathing critique of colonial justice, Talcott's letter stands as a classic example of the colonial rhetoric of justice. As Talcott would have it, the Connecticut government's "labour of love" with respect to Native land rights is most evident in its treatment of Mohegans and Mashantuckets – the only two Native populations in the colony that Talcott acknowledges in the letter. Mohegans and Mashantuckets may well have been the most "visible" reservation communities to colonial officials at the time: their reservation lands were by far the largest in the colony, and their location – in New London County, a main hub of eighteenth-century colonial society – perhaps made those reservation lands the most coveted by Anglos. According to Talcott's 1725 population figures, the Mohegan and Mashantucket Pequot reservation communities were the largest in the colony as well (see TP 2:397–402; chap1n1; chap5n7). Mohegans and Mashantuckets were thus placed at the top of Talcott's hierarchy of Connecticut tribes, while the "lesser tribes" are by that very phrase rendered irrelevant. In omitting the other reservation communities whose lands were threatened by colonial encroachment – including Eastern Pequots in Stonington (see chapter 3), for instance, and Niantics in the town of Lyme (see IND 1st, 1:168, 132)[2] – Talcott's letter obscures the multiple, intertwined struggles against dispossession that were being waged by reservation communities in Connecticut at the time.

Mashantucket Pequot expressions of resistance during the early eighteenth century raise important questions about the possibilities for defying the varied silencing maneuvers of the Connecticut government and for subverting colonial claims to benign authority over Native peoples and their lands. Because of the ongoing Mohegan case and the unprecedented decision of 1705, Mashantuckets' opposition to dispossession – articulated in their petitions of 1713, 1721, and 1735 (all prior to Talcott's letter to Winthrop) – must be viewed as a part of a broader struggle over Native land rights in the eighteenth century. Indeed, efforts at resistance to dispossession by any other reservation communities in eighteenth-century Connecticut must be understood in terms of the impact that the Mohegan case had on the colonial government and its Indian policy. Nevertheless, *as Pequots*, Mashantucket resisters also confronted the colony with a singular cultural and political dilemma, an unforeseen challenge to the colonially lauded meaning of conquest: the supreme Indian nemesis of the seventeenth century had endured and had a substantial population (compared with other contemporaneous Native communities). By the early eighteenth century, Pequots had not only questioned colonial tactics of dispossession but challenged colonial accounts of Pequot history.

Mashantucket Pequots' struggle against encroachment on their reserved lands contested the colonial construction of Pequot conquest as the definitive act of Indian "pacification" and the crucible of colonial legitimacy. Like Mohegans, Mashantucket Pequots argued that the past mattered. They had survived military conquest, and in their planting fields as well as the very persistence of community life, Pequots continued to inscribe their presence, and their history, on the landscape. What, then, could their existence mean for colonial history and for an eighteenth-century colonial world from which the "head kingdom" (Hoadly 1932:66) of the Indians – that is, the Pequot nation – had not been finally and irrevocably eradicated? If the 1637 "vanquishing" of the Pequots could be claimed by seventeenth-century Connecticut officials to have stood for "the subdueing of the whole" of the indigenous population within the colony (66), could not Pequots' refusal to disappear and the audacity of their ongoing resistance be construed as evidence of a more widespread Indian insurgence?

Hence the irony in the publication early in 1736 of Maj. John Mason's *Brief History of the Pequot War*, described to Talcott as a "new book" (Bushnell to Talcott, February 29, 1736, TP 1:350). As Connecticut's argument against the 1705 decision in the Mohegan case demonstrates, Pequot conquest was invoked and manipulated in an effort to quell the increasingly troublesome matter of Mohegan land rights in the post–Indian War era. In fact, Mason's account of the massacre was put on the legal record in the Mohegan case when it was formally submitted as evidence by the colony to the imperial commission of 1743 (*Proc.* 1769:xiii, 253–77). In the first half of the eighteenth-century, then, the re-authorizing of Pequot conquest had become an urgent matter to Connecticut officials contending with Mohegan resistance to dispossession. Yet while the colony was proffering Pequot conquest as crucial evidence in its legal dispute with Mohegans, Mashantucket Pequots' defense of their land rights questioned the most basic assumption of the colony's master narrative: that is, that colonial supremacy and colonial justice had been established via the extinguishment of both the Pequot presence and the Pequot homeland. Evoking Pequot ancestors and emphasizing the importance of the history, and the labor, of a Pequot community that had never relinquished their homeland, Mashantucket resisters defied the colonial construction of Pequot identity as solely a referent of colonial supremacy. Talcott's February 1736 letter to Winthrop suggests that, at that moment, as Mahomet II delivered Mohegans' second complaint to the Crown, the dissenting voices of Mashantucket Pequots had likewise chafed at the claims of colonial authority and called for a retort.

As evidenced in the Mohegan case, Native-Anglo land disputes in eighteenth-century Connecticut embodied debates about the meaning of conquest, as well as the historical possibilities of reservation communities. In the dispute over Mashantucket Pequot reservation land, the idea of Pequot conquest shaped the way in which encroachers as well as government officials assessed the reservation community's land rights and its cultural legitimacy. As Groton's town proprietors had argued in October 1731, Pequots "were originally Captives in and Surrenderers upon ye Close of ye Pequod War," and as such they were merely "allowed and tollerated [in] ye improvement of Certain tracts of land in sd town" (IND 1st, 1:139). This depiction of Pequots as "*captives*" and "*surrenderers*" was precisely the representation employed by the General Assembly in 1714 when Mashantuckets' rights to their reservation at Noank were denied (1:83). Weighing upon Mashantucket resisters, then, were not simply the material effects of dispossession, but a colonial version of history that demanded their perpetual "captivity."

In recounting their own history of struggle, Mashantuckets critiqued the discourse of conquest, and their early eighteenth-century petitions offer insight into how they understood their relationship to their homeland and envisioned their future in the postconquest colonial world. They suggest, as well, that the political consciousness of Mashantucket resisters was informed by relationships over which the colonial government did not have complete control, and by historical events imbued with meanings that emerged out of the context of daily life in the reservation community. Focusing on their petitions to the Connecticut government between 1713 and 1735, this chapter explores the local knowledge and historical experiences that fueled Mashantuckets' struggle against dispossession and sustained Pequot identity.

## *Dilemmas of Resistance*

*Psal. XIV:1–3. We have heard with our Ears, O God, our Fathers have told us, what Work Thou didst in their Days, in the times of old: How thou didst drive out the Heathen with thy Hand, and plantedst Them: How Thou didst afflict the People and cast them out.* — Maj. John Mason, *Brief History of the Pequot War* (in *Proc.* 1769:253)

On May 14, 1713, the Mashantuckets submitted a petition that was "The humble Representation and Complaint of Scaudaupe, Robin Cassacinament [II], Negnanute, Waubeau, Oquacuim, & others in behalfe of themselves and the Rest of the Pequott Indians under their care and inspection." The petition stated:

> Whereas our Predecessors & Fathers for the better Accomodation of ye New Settlement of the English *at Pequott (now New London)* were willing to leave their planting Ground [at Nameag] to them, and remove to the East Side of *ye Pequott River* [later named Thames River by colonists] . . . [they] were about that time accordingly, by the Honourble John Winthrop Esq, yer first Govr who began the *plantation at pequott (and afterwards named it New London)*[3] Settled on a place called Newayonk being convenient for fishing and fowleing (as well as plant-

> ing) wch is a great part of o[u]r Subsistence and wch We know not how to live without there being no place where we can come to the Sound, or Salt Water to Fish & Fowle wth out Trespassing on the Rights & propetyes of the English. Besides this: wch was one great Reason as we have understood alwayes from ye English, as well as from o[u]r Predecessors, why Govr Winthrop placed them there, *that they might Never be hindered from fishing or Fowling, as well as planting, it being all Rocky Land not fitt to plow, but only for the Hoe.* It is true we had a father Accomodation apointed for us at Mashantuxet [in 1666], when the Wood failed at Newayonck and the Land was worne, but we never deserted it, but some of us have had aboad there allways, And we all depended on that place for o[u]r Fishing &c and what we did not plant, our Neighbors ye English have had the use of as a common for their creatures to feed on, And we are still willing that such part as we Shall not inclose for our owne conveniance may always lye common for them. (IND 1st, 1:75, emphasis added)

Most immediately striking in Mashantuckets' 1713 petition are the repeated references to a distinctly Pequot landscape. Acknowledging that specific geographical areas have been renamed by colonists, the petition nonetheless emphasizes Pequots' enduring historical connection to the land, a connection manifested in the subsistence practices upon which community life depended. Military conquest is not denied by the petition: in fact, the opening statement of the petition concedes that "our Predecessors . . . after the Pequot Warr had surrendered themselves to the English" (IND 1st, 1:75). But the petition does not suggest that Pequots viewed themselves as colonial "captives." Instead, the petitioners contend that the "Pequot Warr" marked the beginning of an alliance between Pequots and the colonial government.

Although the petition states that Mashantucket ancestors had been "permitted" to live at Nameag and were "protected" there,[4] this acknowledgment of colonial authority is immediately followed by a reminder to the Connecticut government of Pequot service on its behalf during colonial wars: that is, the petitioners note that "we shall always bear a Gratefull Remembrance and Acknowledgment [of the English] which we and our fathers have also shown by our ready and cherfull Obedience to the comands of this Govermt whenever they have had Occasion to order us out Against the comon enemy" (IND 1st, 1:75). Thus, it was argued that alliance, rather than conquest, defined the historical relationship between the Connecticut government and Mashantuckets.

In recounting Pequot postwar history, the petition emphasizes the significance of the Noank reservation to Pequot survival.[5] Noank, a peninsula on the west side of the mouth of Mystic River in the town of Groton, lies within the realm of Pequot ancestral land (see McBride 1996:86).[6] When the five-hundred-acre Noank reservation was established in 1651, the Mashantucket population may have included three to five hundred people.[7] Not long after its creation, the reservation was besieged by encroachers. Colonist John Packer, for example, "fixed his habitation, about the year 1655, in close proximity to the Pequot Indians, who had congregated at Naiwayonk," then within the bounds of the town of New London (Caulkins 1895:324). By 1665, at a New London town meeting, Packer requested that two representatives from New London might intercede "in the contest between him and the Indians at Naiwayunke and to compound with them in the best way they can with land to the satisfaction of the Indians and Goodman Packer" (minutes of town meeting cited in Caulkins 1895:138). Caulkins points out that Packer's son, James, "inherited from his father a controversy respecting the extent of his lands at Nawayonk, which commenced with the Indians before their removal" (325).

Pequots at Noank had a more well-known foe as well: namely, Maj. John Mason, who had led the 1637 attack on the Pequots' fort in Mystic. The town of New London granted Mason an island in Mystic Bay and "one hundred acres of land on the adjoining main-land" in November 1651, "as a bounty out of the conquered territory."[8] The town also included a "gratuity" to Mason, consisting of an additional hundred acres, and at a later date "they extended his boundary still further to the eastward." Caulkins states that Mason "was at the time intent on obtaining the removal of the clan of Indians that had settled under the rule of Cassasinamon [I]" at Noank, "opposite [Mason's] Island."[9] Hence in 1651 Mason, along with other New London residents, drafted a proposal to be presented to the town which declared that Mason and the other townsmen "have special use for the land and the Indians must be removed" (Caulkins 1895:78–79). Caulkins notes that it is uncertain whether the proposition was actually put before the town at the time; and indeed it was not until the early eighteenth century that the General Assembly decided to abolish the Noank reservation. Nonetheless, the "agreement" that was made in November 1651 between the town and the reservation community predicted that life at Noank was to entail a continual struggle: for it stated that "what damage shall come to any of their [Pequots'] Corne by any English Cattle or hoggs they shall bear the damage of it themselves, and shall make good any hurt that shall be done to any English Cattle or hoggs by themselves or any other Indians that shall live amongst them" (IND 1st, 1:2).

As Mashantuckets pointed out in their 1713 petition, Noank's rocky land had presented problems for cultivation, and by 1658 Mashantucket Pequot sachem Robin Cassacinamon I pressed the colonial government for additional planting land (McBride 1996:86; 1990:105–6). According to archaeologist Kevin McBride, by 1666, when the reservation known as Mashantucket was established, a substantial portion of the Mashantucket Pequot population had already moved to this area (approximately ten kilometers north of Noank, along the Mystic River), where they had planted corn and orchards since 1658 (McBride 1996:79; 1990:106). Those Mashantuckets who moved northward from Noank were no doubt urged by the threat of continual encroachment and the destruction wrought by colonists' livestock. But the 1713 petition attests that there was a resident community that remained at Noank long after the Mashantucket reservation was established.[10] Cassacinamon I lived at Noank until his death in 1692, having preferred, along with the other Mashantuckets who remained there into the eighteenth century, to be at the coast and "nearer to their fishing places" (Wheeler 1887:19).[11]

The description of Mashantucket life at Noank in the 1713 petition suggests that they had long accommodated colonial use of the reservation, since the petitioners explain that "what [Noank land] we did not plant, our Neighbors ye English have had the use of as a common for their creatures to feed on, And we are still willing that such part as we Shall not inclose for our owne conveniance may always lye common for them" (IND 1st, 1:75). Thus Mashantuckets expressed their willingness to use the reservation land cooperatively, in contrast with the exclusionary "Rights & propetyes of the English," which Pequots dare not violate (1:75). Although they were required to "bear the damage" done to their crops by their Anglo neighbors' roaming livestock, the petition indicates that Mashantuckets did not consider their accommodation of such intrusions as a concession of their land rights.

The 1713 petition attests that it was both the continuity of community life and the routines of subsistence activities that the Noank reservation had helped to sustain. The importance of access to the coast for harvesting "Fish & Fowle" is emphasized and was perhaps meant to remind Groton townspeople that Mashantuckets "never deserted" this land that "we all depended on . . . for o[u]r Fishing &c" (IND 1st, 1:75). And since the land at Noank is "not fitt to plow, but only for the Hoe" (1:75), the petitioners suggest that it is, in fact, Pequots who are able to make the most productive use of the land agriculturally.[12]

In effect, then, the petition argues that Mashantuckets' right to Noank is grounded in the economic needs that the land serves and Mashantuckets' productive use of its resources; but it also implies that Pequots acknowledged that their own history overlapped with that of colonists, and that a Pequot-colonial alliance was necessary for their own survival. Indeed, the petitioners suggest that, given their history, the colonial government is obliged to protect Pequot land rights, as it had in 1709 when the governor and council affirmed that Noank had been "antiently set out and appointed to" Mashantuckets and ordered encroachers to "remove themselves" (CR 15:566). The final passage of the 1713 petition thus calls upon legislators to adhere to that obligation and defend Noank against those Groton residents who have paid no heed to the 1709 order:

> Now may it please this Honrble Court our Complaint is this, that at a Towne Meeting as it is called in Groton [on] May ye 22nd Some of the inhabitants have taken Upon them to Voat away this our land at Newayonk to all their Inhabitants an Equall Share: as may appear by the record of Groton, And many, or most of said Shares are bought up by Nehemiah Smith, and his Son and Edward Yeoman and some others we understand, who are going forthwith to fence and build on it; which has been possessed and improved by us and our predecessors more then Sixty years [with] ye consent of the Authority, and the Towne of New London, And their voat seems to allow us our right as formerly, yet how shall we, that are poor Indians make use of it as formerly when these Men have fenced and built on it, and outed us of it, w[hi]ch clause in the voat was contrived to put a sham on us, and our Rights. (IND 1st, 1:75)

Pitting the lawlessness of encroachers against "poor Indians," the petition effectively turns the rhetoric of Pequot conquest on its head, suggesting that if Pequots are a conquered people, and as such rendered powerless, then it is their rights, rather than the desires of land-hungry Anglos, that require the devoted attention and protection of the colonial government. This was a retort to Pequot conquest that did not deny the power of the conquerors but rather requested a demonstration of their claimed benevolence, which the concluding plea of the petition clearly articulates:

> We humbly pray therefore that this Honrble Court would put a Stopp to the unjust proceedings of those people of Groton, and make voide all their Towne Voats wch so Unjustly invade ye Rights Wee have so long possessed and Enjoyed; We look on this Honorble Court to be our Patrons Who will still protect us in our just Rights we being poor helpless Indians and not able to help our Selves against such Designing Men, who w[i]th cunning contrivances are o[u]ting us of our just Rights, and think our poverty and ignorance, will not lett us defend our Selves at the Common Law. We understand that the Neighboring Govermt of the Massachusetts takes the immediate care of their Indian Natives when their Generall property is invaded without putting them to the charge and trouble of the Law; wch it is impossible for us to understand, or enter into the Law. And we understand has been the Ancient Custom of this Govermt also with Respect to us, wch [we] hope will still be continued; which will farther Engage us to doe what we are able for yor service at all times. (IND 1st, 1:75)

It seems clear that Mashantucket petitioners sought to convey a broader set of problems before the Connecticut government than solely that of encroachment on the Noank land. Legislators are asked not only to reflect on Pequot history and the history of the Connecticut government's own policy regarding Native land rights, but also to consider the fact that Indians themselves were pondering the meaning of colonial justice and taking into account the way it had been administered elsewhere. In addition, Mashantucket petitioners may have intended to remind colonial officials that external authorities had of late shown concern about the matter of Native land rights in Connecticut. It is likely that Pequots were aware of Mohegan's 1704 complaint to the Crown, and there is evidence that they sought to use that knowledge as leverage with the Connecticut government. In April 1741, in fact, when Mashantuckets petitioned the General Assembly to protest the vandalizing of their reservation's timber and corn fields by Groton residents, they alluded to Mohegans' legal case against the colony, stating that they "hope[d] for relief" from the government "sence we have not like our Neighbors given your Honours vast trouble by repeated applications on 'tother side [of] ye water" (IND 1st, 1:231).

It was not only the Mohegan land dispute that had caught the attention of authorities external to the colony. Connecticut officials learned that Mashantuckets did indeed have support from outside the colony. In a letter of May 1714 the Reverend Samuel Sewall of Boston informed the Connecticut General Assembly that he knew "the Indians have been molested in their Improvement on Newayonk," and that "I earnestly desire you will do all you can to vindicate them, whereinsoever they are injured. And I hope that tho the Natives are at present so thin/d, as to become like two or three Berries in the top of the uppermost bough; yet God will hasten the Time of their Reformation and Increase: and therefore with this Prospect the Honble General Court will preserve for them Entire all that is already assigned to them; and make further Additions as the matter may require" (IND 1st, 1:80). Sewall's reference to the Mashantucket Pequot population as "so thin/d," however, may have served the intentions of legislators who ultimately denied their rights to Noank in 1714, determining that their inland reservation, at Mashantucket, was "sufficient" for their use (1:83).

Mashantuckets were not isolated in their struggle to protect their reservation, and colonial accounts of Pequots' presence at Mohegan leadership ceremonies (see chapter 4) indicate that members of neighboring reservation communities did indeed collaborate in ceremonial activities that evoked the enduring political significance of kin ties and shared historical experiences. The account of missionary Experience Mayhew, who met with members of reservation communities in southeastern Connecticut in 1713 and 1714, reveals that kinship continued to bind Pequots, Mohegans, and Niantics in the eighteenth century. Mayhew had obtained the services of a Pequot man, Joseph, who was to act as an interpreter for him, and with whom he "discoursed largely . . . concerning the state of the Indians thereabouts" (Mayhew 1896:112–13). Mayhew was "exceedingly pleased" with Joseph not only because he "knew him to be a person of good parts, and of very good quality among the Indians," but also because "he stood related in one way or other to every company of them": "for I was enformed that he was a Pequot by blood, and a Sachim's son; and that the Nahanticks, a considerable

Company of Indians in the Town of Lime had chosen him to be their Sachim, and had a great love for him; Also that Coesar ye young Sachim of the Moheges had marryed his Daughter, and would probably be much Influenced by him" (102–3).

Mayhew explains subsequently that Joseph was the son of Cattapassett, who had been a sachem among Pequots at the Stonington reservation in the late seventeenth century (see CR 4:86). It was through Joseph that Mayhew learned of the Mashantucket Pequot dispute with the town of Groton. Having sent Joseph in October 1714 to entreat Mashantucket sachems Scattup and Robin Cassacinamon II to "give [Mayhew] a meeting," Mayhew learned from Joseph that Mashantuckets were "so out of frame with the trouble they had lately met with, and were still under" that they refused to meet with Mayhew (Mayhew 1896:113). Indeed, Joseph had related to Mayhew some of the recent details of the Mashantucket struggle to protect their Noank reservation. He explained that Mashantuckets had "pulled up and removed some ffence that the English had made there, were sued for it, & damages and charges recovered of them to the value of seaven or eight pounds; that for this, execution had been lately brought upon the Estate of the two Sachims, and that one of the Sachims [Scattup] being something of a Dealer in Smithery had by the officers, his Anvill and some other of his tools taken from him &c" (114). It is possible that Cassacinamon and Scattup may have hoped to turn the tables on Mayhew, perhaps enlisting Joseph to make use of his connection to Mayhew to seek support for Mashantucket rights to the Noank reservation. Perhaps Joseph had this mission in mind when he conveyed these details of the Mashantucket dilemma to Mayhew, though Mayhew acknowledged only that what Joseph related was "a very unhappie obstruction in my way" (114).

It is clear from Mayhew's account that intermarriage among Pequots, Mohegans, and Niantics was a conduit for information as well as an incentive for intercommunity political cooperation. Thus Mayhew comments that Joseph, as a father-in-law to Cesar, would probably have "much influence" on the Mohegan sachem. The shared struggle to protect reserved lands may have highlighted the importance of kinship and its attendant obligations among members of reservation communities. And as the 1713 Mashantucket petition suggests, the routine activities of community life, as well as an awareness of the immediate relevance of their own history, imbued reservation land with meaning.

Responding to the 1713 Mashantucket complaint, the General Assembly appointed a committee to "survey the land which the said Pequot Indians do now live upon and improve" and to "report to the Assembly . . . both the quantity and quality of the said parcels, with the number of the said Indians" (IND 1st, 1:71). The assembly's subsequent decision regarding the Noank reservation, issued in May 1714, does not state what the committee may have reported with regard to the numbers of Mashantuckets living at Noank or their use of the land there; nor does the ruling refer specifically to any aspect of the argument Pequot petitioners made for their rights to Noank in 1713. Identifying Pequots as "captives" and "surrenderers," the ruling held that "the said Indians have a very sufficient quantity of lands at the said Mashantucksett for their subsistence and livelihood" (1:83). The decision also stated that Mashantucket Pequots were to be "allowed for their conveniency of clamming, fishing or fowling, to come to the sea or salt water upon Nawayunk neck" (1:83); but as Mashantuckets had argued, without the colonial government's vigilant protection of their rights, such "agreements" with the town of Groton were tenuous at best.

By May of 1721 Mashantucket Pequot sachem Robin Cassacinamon II[13] petitioned the General Assembly to protest encroachment by Groton residents on what was now their sole reservation, known as Mashantucket:

> The memorial of Robin Cassinnamint Sachim of the Pequot Indians Living at Mashuntuxitt (in Groton) in behalf of myself & my People, humbly Sheweth to your Honours
>
> 1st. In ye first place being mov'd off from our right at Nawwayunk, & where wee & our Fathers Liv'd & improv'd Many Years (& thought it was our own & had a good right to ye same) Nevertheless ye Town of Groaton took it from us & Lotted it out which was greatly to our dissatisfaction, as your Honrs may Remember, by our Complaint to this Assembly
>
> 2dly. In ye Second place (upon our Complaint to this Assembly) your Honrs took Care for us, & ordered some Gentmen to Lay out Mashuntuxit where our Predicessors anciently dwelt, And Improved, by Planting both Corn & orchards: & our orchards are of great worth & value to us by reason our Grandfathers & fathers Planted them & the Apples are a great relief to us.

> 3ly. ye sd Gentlement measured ye Land to us at Mashuntuxit, which was greatly to our satisfaction.[14]
>
> 4ly. Groaton Gentmen Especially old Justice Smith which we much depended upon told us yt they would never move us from ye aforesd Mashuntuxit, nor lott it out as they had Nawayonk.[15]
>
> 5ly. ye Town of Groaton has been & lotted out ye best of our lands, at the aforesd Mashuntuxit, including our Orchards by fencing in of our sd Lands (& Building likewise) which is to Our great wrong and Dissatisfaction.
>
> 6ly. the English in ye time of ye war Called us brethren: & Esteemed us to be Rational Creatures: but behold now they make us as Goats by moving us from place to place, to Clear rough land: & make it profitable for 'em. (IND 1st, 1:95)

The Mashantucket reservation, situated within the "common" or "undivided" lands of Groton, comprised 2,000 acres at the time of Cassacinamon's petition (see 1714 survey, IND 1st, 1:105).[16] The committee appointed to investigate Cassacinamon's complaint reported in October 1721 that 500 acres of the 2,000-acre reservation, including part of Mashantuckets' orchards, had been claimed "some years ago [by] Mr. Winthrop of [New] London upon pretence of an ancient grant to his predesessor" (1:96).[17] The committee was told by Groton's representatives that this "alarmed the Indians, and thereupon they [Mashantuckets] desired the Inhabitants of Groton to take sd land & defend it against sd Winthrop, whereupon the Inhabitants of sd Town, made an exchange of land with the Indians and run the line at a place pitched upon by the Indians, and in consideration for the lands taken of from Mashentuxett, the Indians were allowed 600 acres at Wallnut tree Hill" (1:96). Groton officials also claimed that "the Indians had no Right to any lands in their town before," thus indicating that they acknowledged neither the order that established the reservation in the seventeenth century nor the assembly's 1714 confirmation of the reservation and its boundaries (1:83). Through the recent "exchange of land," the committee was told, Groton had given Mashantuckets "a legal right by deeds" to a reduced reservation (1:96). The committee reported that the Mashantucket reservation had "contained 2000 acres, and now by the late agreement there is but one 1000 left for the Indians, and but 600 acres in the leiue [of the 1,000 acres that were 'exchanged' "], only the Indians had sum libertie to Improve theire orchards (which were parted of by the sd new line)" (1:96).

In the "exchange," then, Groton officials required Mashantuckets to relinquish to the town 1,000 acres of the 2,000 contained within the bounds of the 1714 survey, for which Mashantuckets were then "allowed" the Walnut Hill parcel, while retaining the remaining 1,000 acres of the reservation.[18] Part of the land Mashantuckets "exchanged" with Groton included a section of Mashantucket orchards, "which were parted by the s[ai]d new line" drawn by the town through the existing reservation (IND 1st, 1:96). According to the above mentioned "deed," executed by the town of Groton in 1720, Mashantuckets were to retain their rights to this reservation "untill the Indians would sell the [land], or they were dead" (1:96). Like Mohegans, Mashantuckets were deemed ripe for disappearance from the reservation land; and like the legislative act that approved Wadsworth and Hall's 1721 reduction of the Mohegan reservation, Groton's 1720 deed to Mashantuckets ensured that their remaining reservation could eventually be expropriated by the town via "legal" means, or simply an official verification of the "death" of the reservation community.

Unstated in the report of the 1721 committee is the fact that the transaction took place shortly after the town of Groton voted, in 1719, to divide their common lands for distribution to Groton residents, "reserving to the Indians lands at Masshantuxett, to live on, plant, and get firewood" (CR 7:411). Consequently a committee appointed by the town obtained a quitclaim to part of the original Mashantucket reservation, which was signed by some, but not all, Mashantuckets (IND 1st, 1:100; see also CR 7:411). The "deed" then given to Mashantuckets in return included a total of 1,737 acres, "which is very rocky and hilly, and considerable part of it fit for pasturing only" (CR 7:411). The reservation land Groton had appropriated and "lotted out" included Mashantuckets' planting land – which Cassacinamon described as the "best of our lands" – at least part of which had been cleared already by Mashantuckets, thus making it more desirable to the encroachers (IND 1st, 1:95).

The committee that had been chosen by the town to execute the division of what the town deemed its common lands included Nehemiah Smith Jr., whom Cassacinamon describes as one of the "Groaton Gentmen [who] told us [that] they would never move us from . . . Mashuntuxit, nor lott it out as they had Nawayunk" (IND 1st, 1:108; 1:95). Lots on the Mashantucket land were assigned to twenty-eight Groton residents; in addition, Smith had three lots laid out to himself (1:107–8). Mashantuckets' overseer Captain James Avery later reported to the General Assembly that he searched "into the Records of sd Grotton" and found that "the number of acres in each lot is not mentioned in ye Record but it is well known that the lotes one with another containe twenty acres each" (1:109).

Not only did the town's actions violate the 1680 reservation law (CR 3:56–57),[19] but the signatures on the 1720 quitclaim may have been acquired by nefarious means. This too was reported by James Avery, who explained in a petition of May 1722 that Mashantuckets had complained repeatedly to him about encroachment on the reservation, and that "some of the people of said Groton have seemingly stopt the mouths of some of the said Pequet Indians by such means as they have seen cause to use and brought them to sign something, but some of them say to me [that] they did not know to what" (IND 1st, 1:101). Presumably, Avery refers here to the quitclaim. Moreover, he reported to the General Assembly that these recent events had "made a great division amongst the said Indians that they are become as it were two parties"; some Mashantuckets were so "much disturbed . . . that they should be forc'd from off the land which they and their Predecessors have so long a time possess'd that they have been some times apt to say it would be better for them to march off from out of the hearing of those things" (1:101).

The internal dispute among Mashantuckets, incited by Groton's intrusion onto the reservation land and manipulation of Mashantucket land rights, is evidenced in the fact that Scattup, who had been a signatory of the 1713 petition, did not sign the 1721 petition along with Cassacinamon. Indeed, Scattup and several other Mashantuckets submitted a brief petition to the General Assembly in May of 1722 to counter Cassacinamon's 1721 complaint, alleging that James Avery had "stirred up" Cassacinamon and had "incurriged him to make compla[i]nt to your Honours Contrary to ye minds of the Rest of ye Pequots." Scattup thus requested that the General Assembly "put in some other man" to replace Captain Avery (IND 1st, 1:104).

Here, as in the Mohegan case, a dissenting Native leader – Cassacinamon – is alleged to have been instigated by an outsider, the non-Indian reservation overseer. Scattup may have believed this to be true, or he himself may have been encouraged by town officials to make the charge in order to silence Cassacinamon. But it is certain that government officials had already attempted to dismiss Mashantucket complaints as a pretense. Governor Saltonstall told Experience Mayhew in 1713 that Mashantucket complaints about encroachment on the Noank reservation had been incited by "certain English men, [who] had too much countenanced and encouraged them in their discontent" (Mayhew 1896:117). If it is true that Scattup and his followers were "more prepared to accommodate Euro-American desires" than was Cassacinamon (McBride 1993:68), that may have been due to the fact that Scattup had so keenly felt the sting of the colonial government's reprisal to actions Mashantuckets took against encroachers at Noank. For as Experience Mayhew reported in his journal, when Mashantuckets had "pulled up and removed some ffence that the English had made there [at Noank]," they were "sued for it"; the suit was then exacted "upon the Estate of the two Sachims," and Scattup, "being something of a Dealer in Smithery had by the officers, his Anvill and some other of his tools taken from him &c" (Mayhew 1896:114). Perhaps Scattup opposed Cassacinamon's petition and acquiesced to the town's demands in an effort to ensure a more peaceful life for his community, or a less troublesome one for himself. It is also quite possible that Scattup believed, or was told, that he would be rewarded for his compliance. This appears to have been the case with Ben Uncas II, who, as the colony's Mohegan sachem of choice, received the payments from those colonists who "leased" Mohegan planting lands; and in 1737, after the death of Mahomet II, members of the Mohegan reservation community complained to the General Assembly about Ben Uncas's lack of concern for the well-being of the reservation community, charging that "he Cares Not for us but is about to Lett out all our Lands from us and receive the profits to his own use" (IND 1st, 1:158). Obeying or colluding with the town of Groton may have seemed far more beneficial to Scattup than joining with Cassacinamon to oppose encroachment on the Mashantucket reservation – a battle they were likely to lose.

A subsequent committee report indicates that Scattup and other Mashantuckets, perhaps his followers, had signed the 1720 quitclaim of 1,000 acres of Mashantucket land and agreed to the "exchange" for the "sixteen or seventeen Hundred acres secured to them by Groton" (IND 1st, 1:100). Cassacinamon had not signed this document. The committee members, Richard Bushnell and Joseph Backus, met with Scattup and "several Elderly men with him" in April 1722 to investigate Cassacinamon's 1721 complaint. Cassacinamon "was not there, [nor] like to come, for he was in ye woods lame with ye Gout" (1:100). Bushnell and Backus reported that they read to Scattup and his men, and the one representative who had come from Cassacinamon's camp, "all ye papers" regarding the 1720 exchange, and "made them to understand it" (1:100). Scattup, they claimed, "said he liked all that was done very well," while Cassacinamon's representative said "he knew little about it" (1:100).

If Scattup and his supporters had come to accept the loss of reservation land as unavoidable, the blatant theme of betrayal in the 1721 petition attests that the 1720 quitclaim had both fractured the reservation community and intensified opposition to dispossession among those Mashantuckets who continued to resent the Connecticut government's expropriation of the Noank reservation in 1714. In fact, McBride contends that some Mashantuckets continued to live on the Noank land after 1714.[20] Opening with the reminder that Mashantuckets had objected to the abolishment of the Noank reservation, and stating that they had considered it a violation of their rights, the 1721 petition identifies Noank as an important site of Pequot resistance. It should be remembered that the Noank reservation was the location at which Pequots, Mohegans, Narragansetts, and Eastern Niantics had come together in 1669, when they were suspected of "plotting to kill all the English" (IND 1st, 1:17; see chapter 1 in this book). The General Assembly's denial of Mashantuckets' rights to the Noank reservation in 1714 may have incited tensions among Mashantuckets, who were compelled to contend with intensifying restrictions on their subsistence activities and the imminent threat of prosecution for "trespassing" on land they believed to be their own.

Although the 1720 quitclaim and the 1721 petition reflect the intensity of the internal dispute among Mashantuckets, the 1721 petition nonetheless makes the point that bonds of kinship, as well as a history of struggle, bound Mashantuckets to their reserved lands. Just as Noank's value lay in its history as a place "where wee & our Fathers Liv'd & improv'd Many Years," so too are the planting fields of the Mashantucket reservation imbued with history, representing not only the labor of the living community but that of the ancestors as well.

Cassacinamon's articulation of the reservation community's relationship to its homeland and its ancestors also suggests that he may have sought to appeal to the patriarchal sensibilities of colonial authority, since it is Pequots' connection to land as sustained by the agricultural labor of *fathers and grandfathers* that is stressed in the 1721 petition, while the agricultural role of women, particularly with regard to the cultivation of the staple crop, corn, is unmentioned. Apples, a colonially introduced crop, had become a significant source of food for Mashantuckets by the mid-seventeenth century (McBride 1990:109), and it is likely that the labor of women as well as men would have been required to tend and harvest the orchards.[21] Nevertheless, Cassacinamon's emphasis on agriculture as practiced by men obscures the historical importance of women's role as cultivators and as ancestral links to their homeland.[22] This may indicate that Cassacinamon was aware of the General Assembly's 1717 "civilizing" measures, which were intended to impose a privatized system of land tenure on reservation communities whereby the "portions should descend from ye Father to his Children, the more to encourage [the Indians] to apply themselves to Husbandry" (IND 1st, 1:87; see chapter 3). If there were more women than men living on the Mashantucket reservation at the time (see McBride 1990:107), Cassacinamon, like his contemporary Mary Momoho, may have understood that colonists had begun to assess Native rights to reservation land in terms of the "absence" of men in reservation communities. In emphasizing male prominence in what colonists termed "husbandry," Cassacinamon may have hoped to secure government protection for the reservation land at Mashantucket.

Cassacinamon, Eastern Pequot sunksquaw Mary Momoho, and Mohegan sachem Cesar likely knew that they and their communities were engaged in a common struggle to defend reservation land and ensure a future for their descendants, and colonial officials could not have missed the fact that the leaders of these neighboring reservation communities had charged their Anglo neighbors with lawlessness and had made a common appeal to the General Assembly to demonstrate justice. In petitioning for the government's protection and redress against encroachers, these Native leaders pursued a colonially sanctioned means of resisting dispossession, and legislators were thus compelled to take a position on the nature of Native rights to reservation land. Between 1705 and 1721, the government's responses did not bode well for either Mashantucket Pequots or Mohegans. But Cassacinamon's 1721 complaint – which coincided with the General Assembly's approval of the drastic reduction of the Mohegan sequestration in May of 1721 – interjected a timely critique of colonial justice and Connecticut's Indian policy, one that could be applied to what befell Mohegans at the hands of the General Assembly and their "guardians," Wadsworth and Hall.

In contrast with the 1713 petition, which stressed Mashantucket interest in maintaining alliance with colonists, the prevailing theme of Cassacinamon's 1721 petition is colonial betrayal of that alliance. But as the sixth point of the petition makes clear, the betrayal attested to here goes beyond the problem of colonial encroachment on Mashantucket reserved land. Cassacinamon charges that Pequots' systematic dispossession had culminated in the dehumanizing practice by which Mashantuckets were exploited as livestock by their colonial "brethren," who had used Mashantuckets as they would goats, to "clear rough land" and "make it profitable" for themselves. Colonists in Connecticut did indeed "let goats go at large to subdue rough land and bring in pasture" (Bushman 1967:34). Cassacinamon and other Native leaders no doubt recognized that this practice aided encroachers who may have relied upon their livestock's destruction of Natives' crops as a means of "clearing" Native communities from desired lands. [23] Cassacinamon's petition thus constituted a bold and astute challenge to colonial legislators and indicated that he, and surely other Mashantuckets, had come to have a keen understanding of the relationship between colonial land hunger and colonial Indian policy.

The conclusion of Cassacinamon's 1721 petition evokes the precise language of the 1680 law and its stipulation that individual colonists' purchases of reservation land "shall be voyd and null" (CR 3:56–57): "I in behalf of my self & People do humbly Pray this Honble Assembly that your Honrs would be pleas'd to do us Justice by nulling & making void what Groaton Gentmen have done in lotting out, & fencing [our land] as aforesd & [that] your Honrs would be pleased to Confirm, & Give us in our Ancient possessions, at Mashantuxit" (IND 1st, 1:95). Cassacinamon thus proclaims that this is not simply a matter of the government's obligation to protect "poor Indians," as the 1713 petition suggested: the reserved lands at Mashantucket are Pequot lands – "our Ancient possessions" – held collectively by the Mashantucket Pequot people. And indeed legislators had pledged to protect that land in 1714, when the Noank reservation was abolished, promising Pequots that "should [they] be at any time molested and disturbed in their planting or improvement on the said Masshantucksett Lands upon their application made to this Court

[they] shall be heard and relieved by this Court" (1:83). The 1721 petition argues, then, that Mashantuckets have both law and history on their side.

The General Assembly appointed a committee to investigate the 1721 complaint, and the committee's report of October 1721 indicates that in the 1720 deed "given to the Indians" by the town of Groton,

> there is no mention made of any Grantees by name but only the pequot Indians. And there se[e]meth to be the nessesary words wanting in the Instrument [i.e., the deed] to pass the fee and there is libertie reserved for the grantors [Groton] to see sd land, that which lyeth comon at any time, and after harvest that which is fenced may also be fed [used for grazing] and there is also an incumbrance of highways upon the sd Walnut tree Hill [the six-hundred-acre parcel Mashantuckets received in the "exchange"]. And upon the whole we feare if the Indians be not cared for and protected by this assembly, they will be wronged. (IND 1st, 1:96)

The committee suggests that Groton's failure to list "any Grantees by name" renders the deed legally inadequate as a means of transferring the title of the lands in question to Pequots. And if the town officials who executed the deed intended for the land to belong to the town eventually, either through "sales" or Pequot deaths, naming "the Pequot Indians" as the grantees kept their title sufficiently vague to facilitate the town's appropriation of the remaining reservation land.

By May 1723 the General Assembly ruled on Cassacinamon's petition, acknowledging that in 1714 the government had "promised to relieve [Mashantuckets] when wrong'd" (IND 1st, 1:110). Overseer James Avery was then ordered to "prosecute" those who had by any "pretence whatsover enter[ed] upon the sd land" (1:110). In April 1725 a survey of the 1,737 acres that had been deeded to Mashantuckets by the town of Groton in 1720 was done by John Plumbe, who claimed to have been "assisted" in this endeavor by "the Sachem ScoteTanbe [Scattup]" (1:136).[24] Plumbe's report is not signed by any Mashantuckets but asserts that the survey of the 1,737 acres "was made to the good Satisfaction of the pequett Indians" (1:136). By May of 1725 Scattup, along with sixty other Mashantuckets, petitioned the General Assembly to request that "the seventeen hundred accers of Land well secured to us by Groton . . . be Recorded in the Colony Records for our Security & our Children after us"

(1:116). For good reason, Scattup may have had little faith in the General Assembly's promise to protect the Mashantucket reservation and so appears to have cast his lot with the town of Groton.

By 1727 Mashantuckets' overseer brought another complaint to the General Assembly, arguing "that [Mashantuckets] were wronged by the English Incroaching on there lands" (IND 1st, 1:134, 135). The committee appointed to investigate the complaint assessed the bounds of the reservation according to Plumbe's 1725 survey, rather than the General Assembly's 1714 survey, and reported in October 1728 that they "found no Considerable Incroachmt made upon [Mashantucket land] except on the So[u]thSide thereof [where there was] about Thirty nine Acres of Land Laid within their [Mashantuckets'] Bounds" (1:135). But as the Mashantucket petition of October 1731 attests, the problem of encroachment only worsened (1:138). Now Groton proprietors petitioned the General Assembly seeking government sanction for their use of Mashantucket land that they claimed via the 1720 deed. Describing Mashantuckets as "captives" and "surrenderers" whose presence the town had merely "allowed and tolerated," the proprietors requested that the Assembly "allow us to sell & buy rights in sd Land to Divide & fence the same to have ye summer feed or herbage and ye winter feed after indian Harvest and to Cut timber thereon or get Stones only for fencing ye Same. Saving to sd indians Nevertheless free Liberty to fence what they please for planting & c" (1:139). In response, the General Assembly dismissed the 1731 Mashantucket petition, and by 1732, following the recommendation of an investigatory committee that failed to acknowledge Mashantuckets' repeated protests against encroachment, the General Assembly determined that "one half of said lands [the 1,737 acres] is fully sufficient for the Indians to dwell on and cut firewood" (CR 7:412). It was thus ordered that half of Mashantuckets' remaining reservation land was to be

> laid out in fifty acre lots . . . and the English allowed to fence the same, so as to secure themselves and the corn of the Indians growing on such lots, and their apple trees, and . . . the proprietors were [to be] allowed to clear said lots, only allowing ten acres in every fifty acre lot . . . [to remain] forest for firewood for the Indians, and the Indians allowed to plant in one or more of said lots as it may be needful for them, and be also allowed to remove their planting to other lots once

> in three years if they desire it, and the other half of the lands remain unsurveyed and unfenced as it doth now, for the Indians to live on, plant, and get firewood, [which] would very well accommodate the Indians, and be a greater benefit to the proprietors. (7:412)

Mashantuckets knew well this decision was a threat to their community's survival. Their next petition, dated September 1735, is addressed solely to Governor Talcott. It includes neither an account of Mashantucket history nor any reference to government promises in the past. Instead, the petition focuses on the tenuous circumstances of the present and the varied and immediate threats that the reservation community confronted:

> some People that make Possessions of our Land . . . destroy So much of our timber for fenceing and for oather uesses that wee shan[t] in a Little time have a nofe for firwood, and Espechely for fensing for we find it is in vane to Plant within thare encklosers for wee planted th[ere] Last Spring, and our Corn was Destroyed by the English Cretors and by fensing in of our Land thay take away in a Great mesure the Priviled [privilege] of our orcherds for that Let their o[own] Swine go in and eat up our appoles and bed Down and if our Swine accedenttoly geot in they Commit them to the Pound [and] wee Cold not subsist without ceoping some Cretors wee shold be glad if wee Cold have more of the Produse of the Land to keep oather Creters . . .
>
> In as m[u]ch as wee Sea Plainly that thare Chefest Desir is to Deprive us of the Privelidg of our Land and drive us off to our utter ruin It maks us Conserned for our Children what will be Com of them for thay are about having the gospell Preched to them, and are Learning to read and all our young men And woman that are Cappell of Lerning of it and thare is Some of our young men wold be Glad to bild housen upon it [the reservation] and Live as the English do Cold they have a Sufficiancy of the Produse of the Land. (IND 1st, 1:227)

The petition is signed by thirty-one Mashantucket men, none of whom are distinctly identified as sachems.[25] Mashantuckets had by this point lost the support and assistance of their former overseer Captain James Avery, who died in 1731 (DeForest 1852:428).[26] The appeal to Christianity in this petition and the assertion of Mashantuckets' willingness to "Live as the English do" perhaps suggests the desperateness of the reservation community to secure the protection of the General Assembly. As the petitioners explained, when Mashantuckets had asked encroachers to "Ceep out thier Creters," they "thretten us if wee don't hold our tongs to beat our Brains out," and told Mashantuckets "that wee shant Plant thare anoather year" (IND 1st, 1:227). Likewise, Eastern Pequot leader Mary Momoho had informed the General Assembly in an earlier petition that Stonington residents confronted her community with the same bleak promise, "tell[ing] us that when one or two more of us be dead the Lands will fall to them" (1:73).

Like Mashantuckets, the three other reservation communities in New London county – Mohegan, Niantic, and Eastern Pequot – had brought complaints to colonial authorities that attested to the particularly dire conditions of life for reservation communities at the time and to the intent of encroachers to "drive us off to our utter ruin," as Mashantuckets expressed it 1735 (IND 1st, 1:227). The ruination wrought by encroachment was not confined solely to theft and destruction of reservation communities' resources and threats to their safety. Indian labor was under assault by encroachers, whose actions indicate that they sought not simply to degrade the material existence of reservation communities but to extinguish their will to continue living on reservation land. According to Native accounts, encroachers employed the tactic of destroying maturing or matured crops, thus ensuring that reservation communities would witness the destruction of the fruits of their labor, from which they were not to benefit. As Niantics explained in a May 1728 petition, they had long acquiesced to the demand of the proprietors of the town of Lyme that the town's residents "shall have the herbage" of Niantic agricultural fields for grazing livestock after harvest, but

> Instead of the sd English there haveing the herbage of sd Land after the Cropps is taken off Severall of them have from Time to Time for the Space of Twenty Years last past, when the Indian Corn beans &c. Was Come up . . . Turned in there Cows horses Swine Sheep &c. And have wholly destroyed the sd Indians Crops So that Your poor distresed Memorialists have not for the Space of Tenn Years had one Crop of Corn and are now Even Discouraged from planting Any more Since their Labour hath proved lost, for this Seven Years So that we have had no Ripe Corn. (1:132)

The 1735 Mashantucket petition points out that encroachers did not always rely on livestock to accomplish this end, since "some people cut our Stoaks [cornstalks] som time when the Corn is in the milk [and] wee Shold be Glad if thare Cold be a Stop Put to it the Stoake being our own Labbour wee Shold be Glad to have them for our own use" (IND 1st, 1:227). In an April 1741 petition Mashantuckets complained once again that Groton proprietors had not only "destroyed almost all ye timber" on the reservation, which the General Assembly had ordered to be reserved for Mashantucket use (see 1732 decision, CR 7:412), but that "they have also sometimes cut [our] stalks . . . before ye corn was hard by which ye corn was almost spoiled" (IND 1st, 1:231b).

The emphasis in these petitions on the agricultural labor expended by reservation communities – but lost to the strategic pillaging of encroachers – countered colonial notions about the failure of reservation communities to "improve" their own lands. But these petitions also attest to the fact that such practices of encroachment had taken an enormous toll on reservation communities, worsening their impoverishment and undermining their hopes for a viable future for their descendants.

As obliging as the appeal to Christianity and "English ways" seems in the 1735 petition, Mashantucket Pequots, like Mohegans and Eastern Pequots, continued to assert their collective rights to their reservation land. They did not request that their lands be divided into privately held plots for individual families within the reservation community, which would have signaled acquiescence to one of the supreme demands of colonial "civilization" – that is, the commodification of land as private property. Native petitions reveal that community life, identity, and collective rights to reserved lands were intertwined. This was quite simply expressed in the 1741 Mashantucket petition, which closed with the request from "Your Honours Pet[i]tioners" that "they may be restored to the injoyment of there land [so that] they may be Able to live near together" (IND 1st, 1:231). And as some petitions indicate, it was the lives of children in reservation communities, and the threat dispossession posed to their futures, that had been the most compelling impetus for Native resistance. "Consern for our Children" and "what will be com of them," as Mashantuckets explained in their 1735 petition (1:227), was on their minds as they sought the government's protection of reservation land (see also Eastern Pequots' 1723 petition [IND 2nd, 2:22] and Niantics' May 1743 petition [IND 1st, 1:251]).

Like Mohegans, Mashantuckets argued that their reservation land was essential to the perpetuation of community life. Mohegans had expressed this most dramatically at the September 1736 leadership ceremony, and Mashantucket petitions made the point that the routine activities of life as lived on reservation land – the maintenance of the orchards at Mashantucket, for instance – and the knowledge those experiences embodied and produced, served to bond people to each other and to a history that had been hard fought but was yet undecided.

## Pequot Conquest Born Again, 1761

Mashantucket Pequot resistance to dispossession challenged the claims of Pequot conquest. They had continued to live upon land that they described as their "ancient possessions," and in their pleas for justice they recounted a post-1637 history in which they had been both military allies and impoverished, dependent subjects of the Connecticut government. Their reservation land was the locus of community life as well as a site of struggle from which Pequot history was evoked, interpreted, and indeed *produced*. That was a crucial point conveyed by Mashantucket petitions: Pequots *had* had a history since 1637, and their protests against encroachment indicated that they understood its significance to their ongoing dilemma of defending a Pequot homeland encompassed by a colonial society that had denied their rights to such a place. Pequots confronted that reality as they endured the pillaging and threats of encroachers. But if Mashantucket petitions had acknowledged that the reservation community depended upon and, in fact, expected the protection of the colonial government to which it was subjected, they did not suggest that military conquest had doomed Pequots or rendered them a people devoid of inherent rights. Colonial narrations of Pequot conquest insisted that conquest was a discrete historical moment in which English colonists had established their right to control indigenous peoples and appropriate their lands (see chapter 1). Equally important, in the context of struggles over Native rights to reservation land, Pequot conquest had been evoked to affirm the inevitability of the *conquerors'* history – a history that demanded the abrupt end and continual silencing of indigenous histories. The protests of Mashantucket Pequots revealed an alternative history, one in which conquest was not merely a military act finalized in a distant past, but an ongoing contest over land rights and the meaning of justice, and thus it was a contest that implied historical uncertainties.

While Groton proprietors and colonial legislators obscured the problem of illegal encroachment in their depiction of Pequots as "captives" and "surrenderers," Mashantuckets reminded colonial officials that they had been victims of colonial lawlessness, but *also* that they had attempted to accommodate and coexist with the very colonial neighbors who denied their land rights and threatened the future of their reservation community. Mashantuckets had not just called into question the idea of an absolute conquest that was to have established an irrevocable historical trajectory for the conquerors while necessitating the inevitable "disappearance" of the conquered; they had called attention to the implications of that idea of conquest in the present, as it structured and devastated the lives of Pequot people living upon increasingly constricted reservation land.

Mashantuckets grappled with the living reality of conquest, and their assertion of their land rights suggested that this reality had shaped a historical consciousness that did not assume or insist upon the separateness of Pequot existence, but rather one that perceived Pequot history as enmeshed in the colonial world, just as their vastly diminished homeland had been enveloped by colonial society. Pequots had surely opposed encroachment on their reserved lands, but their petitions, which had emphasized the importance and persistence of Pequot labor upon the land, also revealed that they had lived with and accommodated conquest. Would the colonial government then defend their right to exist and likewise defend the reservation land upon which that existence depended?

The General Assembly's 1732 ruling may have been intended to finally resolve the dispute over Mashantucket Pequot reservation land and to bring an end to Mashantuckets' "many complaints," as Governor Talcott wrote in his February 1736 letter to Colonel Winthrop of Boston, but Mashantuckets' 1735 complaint offered a jarring contrast to Talcott's claim that the Connecticut government had been "a candid protector of the Indians, and hath secured for them lands sufficient for their husbandry" (TP 1:338). Mashantuckets went on to remind the General Assembly that it did not adequately monitor the officials it appointed as "guardians" of reservation land. In May 1741 Mashantucket Pequots charged that their current overseer and his relatives "are interested in our lands" (IND 1st, 1:234). In May of the following year Mashantucket petitioners complained that although the government had "appoint[ed] men to take care of us & our lands from time to time . . . those men your

Honours employed last year tho honest men yet they live a great way from us & know very little of our affairs & upon [that] account are not likely to be so beneficial to us" (1:239). Petitioning in 1750, Mashantucket Joseph Wyoke explained that the committee appointed to investigate his community's 1747 complaint against encroachers failed to do so, "so [that] ye sd enquiry has never been made nor any method taken to redress ye Grievances of ye Memorialists" (April and May 1747 [1:231, 234] and May 1750 [IND 1st, 2:51]).

Neither did the town of Groton resolve to acquire what remained of Mashantucket reservation land by gradual encroachment. In 1760 Groton proprietors petitioned the General Assembly to complain that the "controversy [over the Mashantucket reservation] appears likely to continue and the matter somewhat doubtful, how far said Proprietors have a right in said lands [as per the 1732 order; CR 7:411–12] or whether said Indians have any more than a right to the use and improvement of sd lands according to their ancient manners of improvement of lands and not the absolute fee thereof – and the courts have judged variously relating thereto" (IND 1st, 2nd, 2:109). Thus the town sought a final legal decision from the General Assembly that would clearly define, or nullify, Mashantucket land rights.

The question of who held the "absolute fee," or legal title, to the remaining reservation land at Mashantucket was no small matter. If, as the 1680 law held, reservation land was to be acknowledged as the *collective* property of a Native community "*and their heirs for ever*" (CR 3:56–57), then Groton proprietors would be left to contend with what had become an increasingly troublesome legal problem of trespass on reservation land – troublesome, of course, solely because Mashantuckets had continued to resist. It had been, after all, forty years since the penning of the 1720 "deed," which had anticipated that Mashantuckets would retain their reservation land only "untill [they] would sell" or "they were dead" (IND 1st, 1:96). Though Mashantucket "extinction" had been predicted in 1720 by Groton proprietors, as it had been for Mohegans in 1721, it had not been borne out.

In response to Groton's 1760 petition, the General Assembly appointed an investigatory committee that was ordered to "repair to sd Groton to view and enquire into the Circumstances of the Said Mashuntuxit Lands and *to examine and consider all former Acts of this Assembly respecting the Said Lands and the Claims and Improvements of the sd Memorialists* [*Groton propri-*

*etors] and of the said Indians* . . . and all other Matters relative to the Right or Improvement of said Lands as referred to in said Memorial [from Groton proprietors] (IND 2nd, 2:25, emphasis added). The committee arranged for an inquiry to be held at a public inn, "the House of Mr. Nathan Beans Innholder" (2:118), at which the committee purportedly heard the arguments of the proprietors of the town of Groton and their attorney, and "some of the [Mashantucket] Chiefs assisted by Matthew Griswold Esq[uire] and Capt Thomas Seymore as their Counsell" (1:118). The committee reported on the meeting as if it were a trial, over which they presided as judges; but, of course, they were not a court of law, and Nathan Beans's tavern was certainly not a neutral setting for Mashantucket Pequots' presentation of their complaints. Yet, as in the case of the Wadsworth and Hall "investigation" that yielded the 1721 reduction of the Mohegan reservation, this committee was endowed with the power to decide the fate of Mashantucket land rights.

In 1761 the committee issued a report on the dispute over Mashantucket Pequot reservation land that offered as "Exhibit No. 1" the "Articles of Agreement" of 1638 (i.e., the Treaty of Hartford). The report explained that the 1638 "agreement" held that "the Pequots were to be Distributed between the Narrhagansets and Mohegins and No longer to Retain their name nor Dwele in their Country" (IND 1st, 2:118). While the Treaty of Hartford had no technical legal relevance to the General Assembly's 1732 ruling that reduced the Mashantucket reservation – the validity and implications of which were the actual legal issues at hand in 1760 – the immense political significance of the evocation of Pequot conquest at this historical moment is obvious enough: it provided a justification for the expropriation of Pequot reservation lands, implying the a priori disqualification of any arguments Mashantuckets had made in defense of their land rights. And just as the 1680 reservation law was ignored by Connecticut representatives in the Mohegan case, so too did the 1761 committee report fail to acknowledge the existence of that law.

The 1761 report also obfuscated the recorded legal history of Mashantucket reservation land, suggesting that certain key documents were missing or simply did not exist. For instance, the report stated that the committee did "not find any Return [i.e., report]" that verified the establishment of the Mashantucket reservation and the surveys of its boundaries according to previous orders of the General Assembly (IND 1st, 2:118), including the 1714 survey that indicated that the reservation at that time constituted 2,000 acres (2:118). In fact, the 1761 report makes no reference to the reservation's acreage as it had been affirmed by legislators in 1714, nor to the fact that the General Assembly had promised at that time to preserve the 2,000-acre reservation for Mashantuckets in perpetuity. Instead, the report contends that Groton's 1720 deed to Mashantuckets for half of their 2,000-acre reservation "is the only Establishment we can find for the Indians under an English Title & Covers the Land called Masshantuxet Land Estimated in sd Deed at 1000 acres and is Exclusive of ye 600 acres at Walnut Hill" (i.e., the west side of the reservation, which was to have been secured to Mashantuckets as a part of the 1720 "exchange of land") (2:118). Cassacinamon's 1721 petition, which protested the 1720 transaction, is not mentioned in the 1761 report; nor is the fact that the validity of the 1720 "quitclaim" was disputed by Mashantuckets' overseer James Avery.

The "absence," or silencing, of particular legal records had its strategic significance in the Mohegan case as well. As noted in chapter 4, Governor Talcott claimed in a February 1736 letter – written as Mahomet II carried Mohegans' second petition to London – that he had never seen the 1705 decision of the imperial commission, "nor can I tell anywhere to find it" (TP 1:335). When the next imperial commission sat to review the Mohegan case in 1738, the majority of the commissioners refused to allow the 1705 decision to be read or entered into the proceedings (*Proc.* 1769:6). Two of the commissioners, however, "protested against these proceedings, and then withdrew," but the 1705 decision was reversed nonetheless (5–7).

For Mashantuckets, the strategic omissions of the 1761 committee report produced a similar outcome. Accepting the committee's conclusion that the enduring dispute over Mashantucket lands had been "a discouragement to Good Improvement [and] Husbandry," the General Assembly agreed with the recommendation that Mashantuckets should "hold the Land Yet Undivided [the remaining "Nine hundred Eighty nine Acres and 68 rods" of the reservation] free from all Incumbrances" (IND 1st, 2:118, 2:123). By May of 1762, Mashantucket leader Joseph Wyoke petitioned to contest the 1761 committee report, arguing that the "sd committee have not considerd nor determined nor found any facts from which any conclusion with certainty can arise that the English Proprietors [of Groton] had an Equitable Right in the [reservation] Lands proposed to be confirmd to them" (12:119). Moreover, the petition explained that Mashantucket complaints had been excluded from the committee's account of "the controversy that have happend there between the English and Indians about sd Lands" (2:119).

Joseph Wyoke's complaint went unheeded, and in 1766 the Reverend Jacob Johnson of Groton, who preached on the reservation at the time, reported to the General Assembly on "the miserable & suffering condition of the Indians in the town of Groton" (IND 1st, 2:238, 237). Yet another committee was appointed to "enquire into the condition and circumstances of sd Indians and their lands, and what is necessary to be done for their relief," and to ensure that measures were taken to "Civilise instruct and Christianize them" (2:237). Like the 1717 measures directed at Mohegans, this order to "civilize" and "Christianize" the embattled Mashantucket community diverted the question of illegal trespass upon the reservation land.

This committee's subsequent report on the condition of the Mashantucket community claimed that it included approximately one hundred people, "the greater part of them under sixteen years of age," many of them "po[o]r & needy [and] sundry of them Widows who Lost their Husbands in the late Warr" (IND 1st, 2:238). This is no doubt a reference to the "French and Indian War," during which Pequot men from the Mashantucket and Stonington reservations were recruited for service. According to Wheeler, "so many of them were killed in battle and died of disease, that the women and children at home were well nigh reduced to starvation" (Wheeler 1887:20). The General Assembly allotted the committee the sum of 20 pounds to aid the Mashantucket community, which "provided them some quantity of cloathing [to be] distributed among the poorest Children as also some School books." The report added that Mashantuckets "will stand in need of some further help from some quarters to enable [them] to attend the School through the winter," and that the Reverend Johnson should also be paid more for his services, "considering his attention to them in sickness & attending [their] funerals" (IND 1st, 2:238).

Still Mashantuckets persisted in their complaints against encroachment. In May 1773 Daniel Quocheats petitioned the Connecticut government to explain that the survey that was to have secured the 989 acres of the remaining reservation "has ever since the sd act of [the] assembly [in 1761], been in the hands of the proprietors [of Groton], who conceal & secreet the same, & the boundaries of the sd 989 acres and

68 rods of land has never been assertained, & the English Proprietors are frequently encroaching on [our] lands." Quocheats thus requested a "judicious indifferent person or a committee" to establish the boundaries of the reservation as ordered in 1761 for Mashantuckets' "sole use and improvement" (IND 1st, 2:243). When the committee reported on its investigation in October 1774, they acknowledged that "no monuments were erected and established" according to the 1761 order, and that "many incroachments have been made" on the remaining reservation land (2:246). Moreover, the committee explained that they had been unable to establish the bounds of the reservation because the survey "is either lost or secreted by some persons" (2:246). By 1785, Mashantucket petitioners again informed the General Assembly that the bounds of the reservation as ordered by the 1761 decision had not yet been established, and that "the said tribe are interrupted in their possessions & c by the People round about destroying their timber and c[row]ding in upon their lands" (2:249).

Though, finally, the survey for the 989 acres was done in response to the 1785 Mashantucket petition (IND 1st, 2:248), the General Assembly determined that Mashantuckets would have to pay for the survey, and hence in their petition of May 1793 Mashantucket leaders explained that "the Various Difficulties & hindrances" entailed in making the survey and exacerbated by "the Opposition of the Adjoining proprietors [of Groton]" resulted in a cost of "about 30 or 35 pounds [that] your Memorialists are wholly unable to make pay." Mashantuckets were compelled then to request the General Assembly's permission to sell "25 or 30 acres" of their remaining reservation land to cover the expenses of the survey (IND 2nd, 2:26). But the survey did not deter encroachers, and in May of 1800 Mashantucket overseers reported that "the proprietors [of Groton] have been in Possession and Improvement of about 70 or 80 Acres of the Indian Land [as defined by the 1761 order] for 39 years without paying anything therefor" (2:30). The overseers' report makes it clear that by the end of the eighteenth century, poverty and illness had devastated the reservation population, which was now also beleaguered by debts incurred to cover the cost of medical treatment (2:30, 32). The General Assembly subsequently ordered Groton proprietors to pay "the sums due the Indians" for the lands they had appropriated in violation of the 1761 order (2:30).

In May 1804 Mashantuckets' overseer Isaac Avery informed the General Assembly that "all Disputes with the Town and Indians are now Happily Terminated": Mashantucket medical expenses, Avery wrote, had been covered by the money Groton proprietors had been compelled to pay according to the General Assembly's order of May 1800. In addition, Avery explained that now Mashantuckets' "Dead are Decently buried out of the av[a]ils [i.e., sales] of their Lands." Thus did Groton proprietors – who continued, even then, to graze their livestock on the shrunken reservation land (IND 2nd, 2:32) – ultimately reap the anticipated benefits from Mashantucket deaths.[27]

## *New Directions for the Discourse of Denial*

Isaac Avery's 1804 summation of the dispute over Mashantucket reserved land is shocking not only in its obfuscation of the circumstances that had produced the devastating conditions of life then faced by the reservation community, but also in its total erasure of Mashantuckets' history of resistance to dispossession. Indeed, Avery's report seems to bear out the eighteenth-century colonial exigency of Indian "extinction," indicating that it was Mashantucket deaths and the much diminished population of the abjectly impoverished reservation community that had, at last, rendered the land dispute "happily terminated." But the documents that recount the history of Natives' struggles to preserve their reservation lands also reveal the role of government officials in creating and perpetuating this illusion of the inevitable (and blameless) "disappearance" of reservations and reservation communities.

As evidenced in Talcott's 1730 report on the "numbers" and "inclination" of the Native peoples in Connecticut, as well as in his 1736 letter to Adam Winthrop, during the early eighteenth century Connecticut's Indian policy moved toward rendering all Native populations "inconsiderable Indians," who were – from the perspective of Talcott's 1730 response to the imperial inquiry – both culturally degenerate and "docile": "The number of Indians amongst us are about 1600, of both sexes and all ages. They are inclined to hunting, idleness and excessive drinking. Some of their youth are now in a school at Mohegan, set up and maintained by the English for that purpose, and they give good evidence of their docibility" (CR 7:580–84). Like Groton proprietors' and colonial legislators' eighteenth-century evocations of Pequot conquest, such statements were intended to deny not only the legal validity of Native resistance to dispossession but their enduring histories as well.

"Docile" and imminently "extinct" may have been what Talcott's numbers were meant to convey about Native communities in 1730, but the conspicuous silences in his accounting of the colony's Native populations – the mentioning *only* of Mohegans here – makes it plain that there was a great deal that the colonial practice of counting Indians was meant to conceal. In the context of both Mashantucket and Mohegan struggles against dispossession, counting Indians and the introduction of Indian "extinction" as a "legal" matter to be assessed by colonial officials were crucial to a colonial discourse on Indianness that worked to legitimize and sustain processes of conquest in the eighteenth century. But the surveillance and control of reservation populations was problematic, for members of reservation communities sometimes defied colonial intrusions into their lives and refused to submit to colonial interrogations, as Mohegans had in 1736 when Governor Talcott dispatched an operative to Mohegan in hopes of obtaining evidence to use against Mahomet II. Reservations had become sites of resistance for specific Native communities and were also the locus of intercommunity relations, of overlapping histories and converging struggles. Thus they were problematic as cultural and political territories, defying colonially imposed boundaries that were intended to define, divide, and control indigenous communities and identities.

A 1731 report of a committee hired by Groton proprietors to investigate the reservation population at Mashantucket in order "to come to a true understanding of the Exact number of the Pequit Indians in Groton viz of all the males of sixteen years old and upward" reveals that relationships between reservation communities challenged the rigid and distinctly gendered calculus of the reservation "head count." Two Groton residents who claimed to have "knowledge of all the Said Indians dwelling in mashuntuckit by name" were appointed to attend to this task and made their report based on "the Information of severall of the most knowing of the Indians as well as of the English." The investigators asserted that "the number of the male Indians from Sixteen years old or upward liveing at Mashuntickit *whether Pequits Moheags or Narrowgansets or Compounded of them* to be twenty-two and we find not more and the number of those liveing among the English down by the Sea Side or in other parts of the Town by information as aforesd we we found to be nineteen and find noe more who worke wth the English & are Supported by these means; and we find that there is about ten or twelve boyes undr the age of Sixteen (IND 1st, 1:151, emphasis added). The women who constituted the Mashantucket reservation community are predictably obscured in this account, just as the political and cultural importance of women in the Mohegan reservation community was denied in Bushnell's 1736 report to Governor Talcott. Nonetheless, the certainty of counting Indians, as a tactic that expressed the "containment" of reservation populations as well as their accessibility and obeisance to colonial authority, is here countered by the presumed indeterminacy of the cultural identity of the reservation community.[28] The reported presence of Mohegans and Narragansetts on the Mashantucket reservation confirmed that reservation boundaries, as colonially imposed cultural parameters, were indeed permeable. This posed problems for colonial control and categorization of reservation communities: the committee may have intended to demonstrate that the apparently small number of men in the Mashantucket reservation community evidenced Mashantuckets' imminent disappearance, but the "compounding" between Pequots, Mohegans, and Narragansetts *on Mashantucket land* suggests not only that members of neighboring reservation communities were likely to share resources, including agricultural labor, but also that kin ties expanded access and, potentially, rights to reservation land for a larger Native population than that which was to have been confined to a single reservation.

Experience Mayhew's report on his 1713–14 visits to Connecticut attests that members of neighboring reservation communities continued to intermarry despite colonially imposed reservation boundaries, and that they remained involved in each other's political affairs. This was also demonstrated in accounts of Mohegan leadership ceremonies in the early eighteenth century. In a more overtly politicized expression of intercommunity collaboration, Mohegans, Pequots, and Niantics came together "at a general meeting" in September 1736, a crucial moment in the Mohegan case, at which "the whole body of them did renounce Ben Uncas [II] as Sachem" (*Proc.* 1769:218). Governor Talcott denied that there was any real alliance between Mohegans, Pequots, and Niantics in this case, claiming instead that this act was merely part of a scheme concocted by Captain John Mason, Mohegans' long-time friend and adviser. "Pequots, Nayantiks and Other Indians," Talcott declared, "have Nothing at all in the [Mohegan] Controversy" (TP 2:54). Later, in 1740, after Samuel Mason (brother of Captain John Mason) went to England to protest the 1738 decision of the imperial commission (2:104), Talcott continued to press this point, asserting that the Mason family had convinced Mohegans as well as Pequots and Niantics "that the Sachem [Ben Uncas II] gave up their Cause, the Country was theirs, and they might have it, if they would renounce their Sachem and Stand by ye Masons" (2:206).

There may well have been a good many Mohegans, Pequots, and Niantics who, by 1736, believed – with no need of encouragement from the Masons – that those who collaborated with encroachers "gave up their Cause," that much of the lands claimed by colonists were their own, and that renouncing Ben Uncas II might provide them with an opportunity to make their own case for their land rights. A century after Pequot conquest, the Mohegan-Pequot-Niantic alliance that Talcott denounced was surely an unanticipated and outrageous challenge to colonial authority. It may not have seemed so to Pequots at Mashantucket, however, who had long defended their reservation land because it was essential to the survival of their community and who had expressed through their petitions an understanding of the historical significance of reservation land, arguing that the land and the labor Pequots invested in it linked them to their ancestors and sustained Pequot identity.

Yet reservation land was not merely an economic resource and a reminder of the past: it was also to be preserved for future generations, who would be connected to their history and their community through the reservation land as well. In their efforts to preserve their land rights, then, Pequots had articulated a notion of historical continuity that did not deny the harsh realities of life for Pequots in the colonial world; nor did their descriptions of the rigors and disappointments of reservation life suggest that they had become mere "captives" and "surrenderers." Like Eastern Pequot leader Mary Momoho, Mashantuckets in 1735 indicated that they were defending the rights of "our children" – that is, the children of the reservation community, whom they envisioned as retaining their collective rights to land and livelihood. In their protests against encroachment, Pequots as well as Mohegans conveyed a sense of identity that was rooted in a conscious understanding of history as well as in their perpetually threatened reservation land. But reservation communities' shared struggle against dispossession also linked communities and identities across reservation boundaries, and thus, as the 1731 report of the Groton committee indicated, reservations were also shared homelands for neighboring Native communities. This would serve very practical purposes, such as the need for impoverished reservation populations to share resources and the desire to support one's kin in times of hardship. But the sharing of reservation land and its resources would also have been a means of affirming and sustaining a claim to Native lands that not only subverted colonially imposed cultural boundaries but also defied the colonial notion of private property, which legislators had attempted to impose on reservation communities via the 1717 measures.

Such cooperation between reservation communities might have been of little or no interest to the colonial government had there been no legally troublesome disputes over Native land rights in the eighteenth century. But when intercommunity alliances were mobilized for the purpose of conveying a political statement that contested colonial authority and asserted Native land rights, as was the case when Mohegans, Pequots, and Niantics rebuked Ben Uncas II in 1736, the legitimacy of the resisters was questioned. Just as Mahomet II had been labeled an "impostor," so too had Talcott cast Mohegans' Pequot and Niantic supporters as frauds. And in Talcott's 1730 report, cited above, the existence of any dissenting Native populations is wholly obscured.

Mohegans had been depicted as culturally illegitimate early in the eighteenth century, and the colonial notion of Pequot conquest had long before disparaged Pequots as a ruined people. But new ideas about Indian illegitimacy were fomenting by the 1730s, as Indian identity began to be treated as the necessary subject of government surveillance. As I argue, this emerged as a means of discrediting and silencing Native resistance to dispossession and of diverting attention from the illegality of colonial encroachment on reservation land. Ultimately, such ideas about Indian illegitimacy would come to be configured in terms of colonial racial categories that denied validity to particular Indian identities and further constrained Native rights to reservation land. Moreover, by the late eighteenth century, notions of race also began to incite debates about rights and legitimacy between members of reservation communities as well. The concluding chapter addresses the infusion of ideas about race into disputes over reservation land, revealing, I believe, an important connection between Native peoples' struggles to assert their rights in the past and those in the present.

# 6

# "Race" and the Denial of Local Histories

## *Waiting for "Extinction"*

In the diary of Joshua Hempstead, an elderly, well-to-do Anglo-American farmer and man of considerable political influence in the town of New London, an entry for Monday, July 13, 1752, opens as do most of the others – with a weather report. After a few words about his work that day Hempstead added: "An old Indian about 70 killed his Squaw with an ax yesterd[ay] at Stonington & Ran a little way & Hanged himself." The next day's entry immediately follows: "Tuesday 14 fair. I was about home all day haying" (*Diary of Joshua Hempstead* 1901:591).

The people Hempstead refers to were probably Eastern Pequots living on the Stonington reservation, which had been under siege by Anglo-American encroachers since the early eighteenth century. In May of 1749 Eastern Pequot leaders, among them their sachem Mary Momoho, had petitioned the General Assembly to explain that encroachers had "frequently in a great variety of Ways & Manners grievously Molested & interrupted them" in their use of the reservation land, and that as a result the reservation community was "gre[a]tly Distressed & become in great Measure Destitute of ye Common necessarys of life" (IND 1st, 2:40; see chapter 3). The committee appointed by the General Assembly to investigate the complaint reported in October 1749 that "the Indians [on the Stonington reservation] . . . are in Number about thirty eight of old & young, & the Greatest part Females." On the committee's recommendation that the encroachers be fined, and that "the Affairs of the sd Indians" be "inspected," another committee was appointed and thereupon met with Eastern Pequots in October 1750 (IND 1st, 2:41). Pequots explained to them that the encroachers' "unruly horses Cattle and Sheep . . . have Eat up & Destroyed good part of their Corn & beens," and while "ye

Indians have attempted to fence in some of their land for pasture, [they] have been beaten off from it and their fence thrown down" (2:44).

It is likely that Hempstead knew about the conditions of life at the Stonington reservation, and perhaps even of the individuals involved in the tragic event he mentions; in fact, he was knowledgeable of, and on occasion actively involved in, the local "Indian affairs" of his day. In addition to serving as a selectman and representative in the Connecticut General Assembly, he had been a member of a committee appointed by the Assembly in 1727 to inquire into Mashantucket Pequot complaints about encroachment on their reservation land in Groton (IND 1st, 1:134, 135). As a colonial official, then, as well as a land owner in both Stonington and New London, Hempstead would have been aware of ongoing Native resistance to dispossession; indeed, the attitudes and economic interests of such Anglo-American men shaped the colonial laws and policies that impacted reservation communities and their land rights.[1] Nonetheless, the Indian deaths at Stonington are reduced here to a journalistic aside, surrealistically suspended amid Hempstead's "average" day.

Hempstead's terse account of this event raises the question of how colonial officials who lived near reservation communities viewed their relationship to those communities, if indeed they acknowledged a relationship at all. By the mid-eighteenth century, when much of both the Mashantucket Pequot and Mohegan reservation lands were expropriated, and with their impending "extinction" having been declared several decades earlier, what was to be made of the existence of reservation communities? Hempstead's one-line remark on the murder-suicide in Stonington suggests the distance and indeed opposition the writer envisioned between his own life and that of the "old Indian" and "his Squaw." They are, for one thing, devoid of any identity other than that rendered by the categories "Indian" and "Squaw." Hempstead's diary is replete with the names of friends, relatives, and neighbors, yet the "old Indian" and "his Squaw" are unnamed, both as individuals and as members of a particular Native community. In a very basic sense, then, their humanity is muted, and the ineluctable connection between their tragedy and the history that conjoins their lives with Hempstead's is obscured.

Hempstead's comment on the tragedy at the Stonington reservation might be read as an eighteenth-century conquest anecdote, evoking a stark image of the presumed "degeneration" of Indian life: though geographically close to Hempstead's flourishing society, the world of the nameless "Indian" and his "Squaw" is wholly disconnected and dissolving into chaos. In a sense, their horrific fate offers absolution for conquest: for it is, on the surface, an act of self-destruction, beyond the realm of Euro-American complicity. Murdered by her own husband, the Squaw becomes the nullifier of violent European conquest, affirming the opposing colonial trajectories of "civilization" and "savagery."[2]

As noted in chapter 2, Daniel Gookin's account of "Indian origins" in 1674 depicted the Native peoples of New England as outcasts from their presumed "original" homeland and, in effect, aliens to the landscape they now lived upon. Gookin's theorizing about Indian origins not only rendered Native people culturally and historically detached from the world colonists had claimed as their homeland but also insisted that Natives' own knowledge of their beginnings – which Gookin denounced as "figments" and "fables" – was evidence of their alienation. Because they "lacked" written records of their past, they simply couldn't know who they really were, or how they came to be where they were.

In their efforts to protect their reservation lands in the eighteenth century, however, Native women and men evoked historical experiences and knowledges that were rooted in those very lands, and that propelled their struggles against dispossession. Their petitions to the Connecticut government, as well as the reports of investigatory committees and reservation overseers, documented their specific histories and the history of colonial policies and practices concerning reservation land. Natives' own accounts of the past and of the condition of their lives acknowledged the precise nature of their ongoing relationships with reservation overseers, missionaries, encroachers, and investigatory committees, as well as the colonial government itself. In their protests against encroachment, members of reservation communities did not deny that their lives were enmeshed in the colonial world. In important instances they clearly demonstrated the ways in which they sought to accommodate the demands of colonial society – as Mashantuckets had done, for instance, in submitting to Anglos' use of parts of their reserved lands and in arguing, in their 1735 petition, that although they and their children desired an "English" education and were willing to try to "live as the English," their impoverishment and the constant threat of encroachment had prevented them from making a viable place for their community within colonial society. In defending their land rights, then, reservation communities confronted colonists with the complexities of history and with the grim realities of colonial injustice.

Their local assessments of the colonial world – or views from the reservation – did not affirm the notion that Indians were prima facie alienated from the colonized landscape, nor did they validate the colonial historical vision that posited Indian "extinction" as a natural, benign, and socially isolated process, devoid of human responsibility. Yet, in their responses to Native complaints against encroachers, legislators and investigatory committees often masked the social and political realities of the colonial world that worked to undermine the land rights and livelihood of reservation communities. The 1717 "civilizing" measures are a classic example of how colonial law and Indian policy could be deployed to silence Native resistance and obfuscate the problem of illegal encroachment. Likewise, the colony's responses to the Mohegan land dispute embody a discourse of denial aimed at diverting attention from the problem of Mohegan dispossession and offering the purported "illegitimacy" of Mohegan resisters as the object of colonial concern.

William Samuel Johnson, who was appointed to represent Connecticut in the legal dispute over Mohegans' reservation land in 1766, stated the following in response to the Mohegan appeal to the 1743 decision of the imperial commission:

> It is Objected to the [1721] settlement [i.e., the reduction of the Mohegan reservation to one-fourth its initial size] that the Revers[i]on of these Lands is settled upon the Town of New London when the Indians shall be extinct, but it was Right it should be so . . . & *it was apparent the Indians were decreasing, & from their manner of life would probably in time be extinct.* (IND 1st, 2:277; emphasis added)

His statement, made on behalf of Connecticut as the Mohegan case was drawing to a close, indicates that it was the "apparent" condition of Indian existence – the postulated "extinction" that was to result from "their manner of life" – that validated the 1721 action and thus ensured that the remaining fourth of the Mohegan sequestration would ultimately belong to the town of New London. The "legality" of Mohegan dispossession in 1721 thus relied solely upon the colonial construction of Mohegans as a degenerating people. Governor Talcott's effort to undermine Mahomet's political authority in 1736 marks another important moment in the history of Connecticut's Indian policy, since it was in this context that Talcott introduced the idea that the only "proper" Mohegans were those who adhered to the colonially sanctioned sachem, and who thus ultimately obeyed colonial authority. Here then is a crucial example of how "legitimate" Indian identity was delimited and defined to meet the demands of government officials. The impact of such colonial manipulations on Mohegan community life were to be manifested later in the eighteenth century, as some Mohegans began to employ and elaborate colonial categories in the context of internal debates over what constituted "proper" or "legitimate" Mohegan identity.

I want to sketch briefly how official declarations of impending Indian extinction and government surveillance of reservation communities came to shape constructions of Indian identity and debates over rights to reservation land later in the century, as Mohegans and Mashantuckets continued to defend their remaining lands and as government officials, as well as reservation communities, contended with a colonial version of history that had demanded both Indian dispossession and the dissolution of reservation communities. As noted at the conclusion of chapter 4, the idea of Indian extinction introduced in the context of the Mohegan case implied an irrevocable cultural and historical separation between Indianness and colonial society. It was the idea of an "apparent" process of extinction that served as the crucial evidence of Mohegans' inherent cultural illegitimacy, and this notion rendered colonial supremacy over the landscape a "natural" historical phenomenon. And if Mohegans' purported degeneration had to be a "visible" or readily "recognizable" condition, so too would the presumed superiority of those whose flourishing "civilization" required complete dominion over Indian lands – whether they be colonial encroachers, reservation guardians, government officials, or simply any colonists who neighbored reservation lands.

In eighteenth-century Connecticut, colonial references to the relationship between reservation communities and the emergent category of "white" people offer insight into how ideas about colonial legitimacy continued to be fashioned as government officials contended with the presence of reservation communities that, while impoverished and increasingly threatened by encroachers, had not become "extinct." One of the first eighteenth-century documents relating to a dispute over reservation land in which the term "white" is used – and is opposed to the terms "Indian" and "tribe" – reveals that colonial ideas about "race" began to be employed to assert not simply the "naturalness" of Indian dispossession but also the beneficence of a "white" presence that had enveloped reservation communities. In their 1761 report to the General Assembly, the committee investigating the history of the dispute between Mashantuckets and the town of Groton indicated that the committee members "went in company with a Number of the Proprietors of Groton and with a Number of Pequot Indians . . . and thoroughly viewed the whole Tract of Land called the Masshantuxet Land." Referring to the General Assembly's 1732 decision to allow Groton proprietors the use of half of Mashantuckets' existing reservation land, the committee explained that "the proprietors of Groton Divided and laid out six hundred fifty six acres and one hundred rods in the west side of said Masshantuxet land to and among themselves some part of which land (as we are informed) has been sold and conveyed to strangers [i.e., 'white people'] who have settled upon it not knowing of any incumbrance" (IND 1st, 2:118). The "incumbrance" lay in the fact that the 1732 decision had not rendered that half of the Mashantucket land to Groton proprietors in fee simple; nonetheless, as Mashantuckets themselves had pointed out to the General Assembly on several occasions, the proprietors had long assumed a right to appropriate, divide, and sell parcels of Mashantuckets' land as they pleased. The committee's assessment of the matter, and the way in which its report obscures the illegality of the proprietors' actions, is telling:

> there is now standing on said divided part [the west side of the reservation] eight dwelling houses 2 barns and a shop most of them comfortable dwellings in which are dwelling 56 white people and they have made considerable improvements by fencing with Stonewall[s] &c. We also viewed the Indian Familys which seem to be flourishing their houses and wigwams fill'd with Children and youth but as there are Great Disputes Relating to their number we cannot Assertain the same with any Great Degree of Certainty some of them have made handsome improvements and have some cattle and seem to be desirous of Improving after the English Manner. (2:118)

This depiction of Mashantuckets' existence reflects a shifting perspective in colonial evaluations of the legitimacy of reservation communities. In fact, it stands in stark contrast to the 1766 report of the Reverend Jacob Johnson, in which he describes Mashantuckets as in a "miserable and suffering condition" (IND 1st, 2:237). Conspicuously absent in the committee's description is a tally of Mashantucket men: instead, the committee identifies the existence of "Indian Familys" that are not disappearing, nor suffering at all from the relentless processes of encroachment, but rather are "flourishing" and indeed benefiting from the proximity of "white people." But there is, as well, a distinct element of chaos implicit in this representation of Mashantuckets: the amorphous "Indian Familys" do not lend themselves to a body count, and "the great disputes" concerning the size of the Mashantucket population are clearly a problem for those attempting to monitor the reservation community. Such was the case in 1731 as well, when Groton proprietors contended that the men in the community were an amalgam of Pequots, Mohegans, and Narragansetts. Though beneficially impacted by impinging "civilization" and "desirous of Improving after the English Manner," the report suggests that the reservation population is something of an indeterminate entity as juxtaposed to the "56 white people" in their midst.

As explained in chapter 5, the 1761 committee determined that the long-running disputes over Mashantucket reservation land "very much Arise from the Unhappy tenure of their Lands which as it ever will have a tendency to Create Broils and Contentions so it ever will be a discouragement to Good Improvement in Husbandry" (IND 1st, 2:118). The Indian families were "flourishing," and the "56 white people," likewise, had made "comfortable" lives for themselves on the reservation upon which they had encroached, but there is no suggestion that the Mashantucket land base be unaltered or their land rights be affirmed. Instead, what is presumed to be at the heart of the "broils and contentions" over the reservation land was not illegal encroachment and the violation of Mashantucket land rights, but the "unhappy tenure of their lands." Despite the fact that the committee acknowledged that Mashantuckets had indeed "improved" the land, it was nonetheless the Mashantucket presence that served as a "discouragement" to "husbandry." The General Assembly approved the committee's report, and the reservation was accordingly reduced to 989 acres (2:123). Mashantuckets' existence was thus to be clearly delineated from that of the "white" people in their midst, and their rights to their reserved lands were, likewise, further constricted.

This suggests that, by midcentury, reservation communities and their land rights began to be assessed in terms of a problem of proximity between "whites" and the not yet readily manageable or definable Indian populations upon which they encroached. Reservation boundaries were constricted, as they had been so often before, in order to allow for the unimpeded expansion of "civilization" (e.g., good "husbandry"). But now the existence and exact number of "white people" on the reservation were emphasized, as if the presence of that "whiteness" was in itself an "improvement" as well as a physical marker of the proper hierarchy of land rights. The further reduction of the Mashantucket reservation was to contain "that Tribe" from the "white" presence. Might the colonial committee have conceived of potential problems for "white people" in "compounding too closely," to borrow John Eliot's seventeenth-century phrase, with reservation communities? How, and by whom, might colonial notions of racial difference be deployed to naturalize territorial boundaries and construct or manipulate rights to land?

The 1774 report of a colonial committee on the "Unsettled State & Difficultys and disputes" among Mohegans indicates that their protracted legal dispute with the colony, as well as the Connecticut government's continuous interference in matters of Mohegan leadership, had taken its toll on Mohegans. The committee noted that "the Long & unhappy Dispute between the Indians and the Colony is not wholly Rooted out but Subsists among them and Influences into all their Affairs" (IND 1st, 2:312).[3] Indeed, an internal political dispute over leadership among Mohegans had intensified since the time of Talcott's attack on the identity of Mahomet II in 1736, and the threat to Mohegans' remaining land endured as well.[4]

Colonial officials reported in 1774 that Mohegans' overseers continued to lease sections of the reservation to Euro-Americans, which, they claimed, was "to the Satisfaction of the Indians" (IND 1st, 2:312). But this was not what Mohegans told the committee appointed to establish a new sachem among them. Ben Uncas III, whom the General Assembly had installed as sachem, died in 1769 (CR 13:187–88; see also Fawcett 1995:40). By 1774 a committee was dispatched to "acquaint Isaiah Uncas, eldest son of Benjamin Uncas [III] . . . with the proceedings and doings of this Assembly from time to time" and with the history of the Mohegan case, and to "represent to [Mohegans] that Isaiah above named ought accordingly in convenient season to be installed their Sachem" (CR 13:188). The committee reported, however, that there were few Mohegans who had supported Ben Uncas III and who would now support his son Isaiah: "the greater part of the tribe" refused "to talk about an appointment of a sachem or to make distribution of their lands." The report also indicated that the majority of Mohegans at the time supported a rival of Isaiah Uncas, John Uncas (13:188n); but as Mohegan Tribal Historian Melissa Fawcett has explained, "fearful repercussions would have resulted had the Mohegans countered the colony's will" by naming John Uncas as their sachem (Fawcett 1995:40).

The General Assembly remained concerned that Mohegans were unwilling to let their legal case against the colony die and once again sought to cultivate a compliant sachem. Hence their committee was directed to "search after and procure any further papers that may be serviceable relative to [Mohegans'] suit" against the colony and was provided with "thirty pounds, money, to be used and improved for the benefit of said Sachem [i.e., Isaiah Uncas] and his Indians; and that some part thereof be now delivered into the hands of the said Sachem and his attendance, as a mark of the ancient friendship subsisting between the said tribe and his government" (CR 13:188–89). So charged, the committee was expected to do "what is needful to prevent any difficulties and disputes which have arisen or may be likely to arise among them concerning the improvements of their said lands" (13:187). New problems *had* arisen, or at least that was what Mohegans' overseers argued in a May 1774 petition, which they submitted to the General Assembly as a "memorial of [Mohegan] Zachery Johnson," supporter and adviser of Ben Uncas III (see note 4; see also DeForest 1852:459), and his followers (IND 1st, 2:310). The overseers' petition summarized the present state of affairs at Mohegan thus:

> Whereas your Hon[ors] have heretofore in Consideration of the ancient Amity & Friendship subsisting between sd Tribe and this Colony, extended your protecting Wing over us and whereas since the Death of their late Sachem Ben Uncas [III], who died about 4 Years agoe – sd Tribe have remained in an unsettld State and many difficulties & Disputes have arisen among them both with regard to that internal Policey & also with regard to the Possession & Improvement of their Lands & the Distribution of their Rents &c and many Interlopers from other Tribes & Straggling Indians & Molattoes have crouded themselves in upon said Lands whereby many Difficulties & Disputes have arisen. (2:310)

The petition, signed by the overseers only, requested a "judicious committee" to look into the matter.

The string of categories – "Straggling Indians," "Interlopers from other Tribes," and "Molattoes" – reflects the way in which notions of racial "illegitimacy" (i.e., "Molattoes") were merged with depictions of Indian "outsiders," those "Interlopers" or "Stragglers" from "other Tribes" whose presence is classed here as equally undesirable. Boundaries between identities and a hierarchy of rights were thus being assessed in interwoven cultural and racial terms, purportedly from within the Mohegan reservation community as well as without. The reference to the presence of "Molattoes" on the reservation is conspicuous, however, and should not necessarily be equated with the other categories of supposed "outsiders" from "other tribes." As Jack Forbes has explained, the term "mulatto," though borrowed from Spanish, has a long history in the English language, having first appeared in the 1590s. In its early usage in North America, during the colonial period, it was a designation regularly imposed upon people of combined African and Native American ancestry (Forbes 1993:192–93), but was also generally applied by English colonists to designate all mixed-ancestry people of color (90, 195, 211–15).[5] By the mid-eighteenth century, however, colonists began to classify those they deemed as having any African ancestry as "black" and "negro," as well as "mulatto" (85–88).[6] The terms "Indian" and "black" were used interchangeably in English as well: for example, Forbes cites a 1688 ad in the *London Gazette* for "A black boy, an Indian, about thirteen years old, run away . . . with a collar about his neck with this inscription: 'The Lady Bromfield's black.' " Likewise, the 1711 will of an English colonist in Connecticut distributed the members of a family of "Indian servants," also referring to them as "blacks." Even the famous Mohegan preacher Samson Occom, Forbes notes, was described in English newspapers in 1765 as " 'a Black' who could speak English very well" (85). Forbes observes that eighteenth-century uses of the term "mulatto" also included references to people of mixed Native American and Euro-American ancestry (214–15).

The colonial racial construct "mulatto" was thus enormously malleable – as were colonial and European applications of the term "black" – suggesting that it may have been used here as a "new" way to disparage and disinherit those Mohegans who might be perceived, from the perspective of colonial authority, to be troublemakers. The term had indeed been employed by English colonists since the late seventeenth century as a "catch-all," as Forbes puts it, not simply to refer to any person of color presumed to be of mixed ancestry but also to designate "limitations being placed on the civil and property rights of such people" (Forbes 1993:212–14).[7]

Was the term "molattoe" dictated by Zachary Johnson to the overseers? Perhaps. This and subsequent complaints from Johnson indicate that colonial racial categories began to be insinuated into the political struggle between Mohegans by the 1770s.[8] Although the May 1774 petition seeks to occlude it, the "difficulties & Disputes" plaguing Mohegans had been incited and fuelled by relentless colonial encroachment – abetted by the General Assembly – and by government intrusions into the internal matter of Mohegan leadership. Johnson, who was by 1778 identified as the "eldest Counsellor of the Mohegan Tribe" (IND 1st, 2:318), had opposed the legal case against the colony and looked to the Connecticut government as a "protecting wing" to sweep away those he identified in subsequent petitions as "foreign Indians" who "encroached" and committed "great Wastes and Trespasses" on the remaining reservation land(2:318 [Oct. 1778; signed "Zachry Johnson and others"]; 2:322 [May 1782; signed "Zachry Johnson and others"]).[9] In his October 1778 petition Johnson also identified himself and his followers as "the Original Owners" of the reservation and the "Rightful Indians" (2:318). Neither of these petitions refers to the presence of "molattoes," but the May 1782 petition does request that the General Assembly "remove" the "foreign Indians" as well as "whites and Blacks from said [Mohegan] Land, or at least make them pay something to keep them more in Subjection, for the benefit of the State and also for the true Mohegan tribe of Indians" (2:322).

Johnson's list of outsiders here is rather different from that offered in the 1774 petition submitted by the overseers. Encroaching colonists are included among the "interlopers," but they are now identified as "whites," and Johnson does not accept their presence either. But who are the "foreign Indians" and "Blacks"? Perhaps in this case the designation "black" is intended to mean the same as "mollatoe" in the 1774 petition and to suggest that "intruders" were to be identified by a particular (conceived) skin color. Would "true Mohegans" be likewise discernable by their own "color"? The 1782 petition also states that "most of these foreign Indians were the greatest Advocates for the Late Case Between this

Government and the Masons" (IND 1st, 2:322). Here the total erasure of the long history of Mohegans' struggle to protect their reserved lands is striking, and Talcott's campaign to cast all Mohegans who resisted dispossession and challenged colonial authority as "impostors" and puppets of the Mason family appears to have left its legacy: the "true" and "proper" Mohegans were beleaguered and disrupted not by encroachers and the Connecticut government, but by the "foreign Indians" within.

Zachary Johnson's sentiments, as indicated in the 1782 petition and possibly the 1774 petition as well, may reflect the way in which Mohegans who sought to consolidate power and influence – perhaps for the purpose of securing their own rights to the ever-diminishing reservation land – began to delineate their "enemies" by employing the most convenient and salient colonial designations of illegitimacy. And the particular categories of "outsiders" that the petitions list – "stragglers," "interlopers," "molattoes," "foreign Indians," "blacks," *and* encroaching "whites" – provides a register against which Johnson might not only position his own claim to an "authentic" (i.e., "true" or "rightful") Mohegan identity, but also, perhaps, to attempt to claim an *elite* status in a community in which *all* had been impoverished as a result of colonial domination and dispossession, and over whose fate the Connecticut government held sway. This may have been most keenly reflected in Johnson's attack on the highly educated and influential Samson Occum, who was described in an October 1774 petition signed by Johnson and five of his followers as having exacerbated Mohegans' "troublesome affairs" in 1774. They also charged that Occom was determined "to have the ordering of all the Indian Concerns Especially the Rent of our Lands and says let the Assembly do what they please he will Break it all to pieces in Spite of them (or something to that purpose)" (IND 1st, 2:314). Johnson apparently meant to thwart Occum's challenge to his own authority in the style of Governor Talcott: that is, Johnson and his council identified Occum as being among those "now living in Mohegan that are not Properly Mohegans." This list named the "heads of family" deemed "not properly Mohegans" – and thus listed the names of individual men. But the exclusionary list also included women: six widows, who were listed as such (e.g., "Widow Nanaboome") (2:315). This list was supplemented with the "list of Mohegan Indians Agreable to the Minds of Zachary [Johnson]" and four of his adherents. It named eleven *families* (e.g., "Late Sachem Ben Uncas Family," "Moses Mazeen and Family," etc.) and one individual man – "eijee Johan his son Eliphalet Johan": "This Person was Accepted as A Mohegan, On Condition that he took Care of & Buried the Dead in the Tribe Dureing his Life." The line at the bottom of this list reads: "Allowed to be proper Mohegians" (IND 1st, 2:316).

Though Zachary Johnson's 1782 petition wholly obscured the relevance of Mohegans' protracted land dispute to the conditions of life at Mohegan at that moment, the events of 1736 were alive in the Mohegan lists of 1774. The exclusion of widows from those "allowed to be proper Mohegans" recalls the disparaging commentary on Mohegans' "reckoning of families" in Bushnell's February 1736 report to Governor Talcott, in which Bushnell complained that Mohegans did indeed count widows as family. The widows on the 1774 list were perhaps not supporters of Johnson or "friends" to the Connecticut government; or, as women who were likely elderly, and who now had no male "head" to their households, were perhaps deemed – whether by Johnson and his men or perhaps by their colonial instigators – to be inconvenient and burdensome. If Johnson sought not only to secure the support and assistance of the Connecticut government but also to shore up what was left of Mohegans' resources for himself and his cohort, he may have been all too eager to remove these widows from the "official" list of "proper Mohegans."

And indeed Zachary Johnson did gain the favor of the Connecticut government: by 1783, the committee appointed to investigate his petition determined that Johnson was "almost the only inveterate opposer of the Mason Claim in all its Progress." Johnson, the committee explained, had "incurd ye Dislike of many of the Indians, who were most of them Masons Friends," because Johnson had claimed that they "ought to be cast off" (IND 1st, 2:326). They concluded that the "old Councillor" Johnson was "of pure Mohegan Blood, is & has been almost alone, a staunch Friend to the colony or State thro the Mason Quarrel." Since he was aged and "unable to labor," it was recommended that the government ensure that Johnson be supplied "out of the Profits of the Lands, with all the necessarys & Comforts of Life for himself & his Wife" (2:326). The General Assembly concurred (2:327).

While Johnson had apparently solved some of his own problems at the expense of other members of the reservation community, his effort to cast other Mohegans as impostors and thus deny their land rights incited similar attacks on his own followers. In 1789 Samson Occum, along with four of the Mohegan men on the 1774 list of "improper" Mohegans, charged that the grandson of Moses Mazzeen – one of Johnson's allies who had signed the October 1774 petition against Occum – was "blacker" than other Mohegans, and hence they declared that he should not have comparable rights.[10]

Given that Mohegans endured the history they did, with all the accompanying threats to their land rights and community life, it is not surprising that the internal political struggle at Mohegan became increasingly rancorous and tinged by the racism that structured eighteenth-century colonial society.[11] But did the efforts of some Mohegans to assert an "authentic" identity that would be acknowledged as such by the Connecticut government transform, in a politically significant fashion, colonial assessments of Mohegans *as a people* – a people who not only possessed rights to land but whose very presence and condition of life at the end of the eighteenth century reflected a long and arduous history of struggle in the colonial world? Indeed, precisely what government "recognition" was to be won from the claims of some Mohegans that their own identity was more "proper," *racially*, than other Mohegans? And what was the character of the racism of government authority – which had worked consistently to both obscure and legitimize its acts of oppression and dispossession – as it oversaw these internal dilemmas at Mohegan toward the end of the century? Could Johnson's colonially constructed status as a Mohegan of "pure blood" garner him a position of any privilege within the emergent Euro-American state?

Although the 1783 committee deigned to bestow upon Johnson the newly concocted status of "pure blooded Mohegan," this did not signal a significant change in how government officials viewed, or treated, the broader reservation community. In other words, there is no suggestion that government officials were eager to bestow this status on other members of the reservation community, or that they deemed "purity of blood" in Mohegans as something readily "recognizable" – or as a status that *Mohegans* were able to confer upon themselves. Government officials continued to treat Mohegans as an entity that required external surveillance, classification, and regulation. In fact, the 1783 committee reported that they found it "difficult precisely to distinguish" among members of the reservation community and recommended that Mohegans' "overseers [be] directed to keep for the future an exact Account of the Incrase or Decrase of the Tribe," the present number of which they determined to be 136 (IND 1st, 2:326). They declared as well that "many of ye present Indians" at Mohegan "*were not originally Mohegans*" – and these "many," it must be emphasized once again, were primarily those who were *not* considered "friends" of the Connecticut government but rather "Masons Friends" (2:326). But in a rather striking twist in the history of colonial politico-legal manipulations, the committee claimed that these individuals had nonetheless become "*naturalized*" by "*long Residence*, [and] *Consanguinity*" (2:326; emphasis added). Here, then, is an assessment of the reservation community that does not distinguish a group or "faction" of "elites" among Mohegans: no segments of "*royal* blood," for instance, the claimed absence of which was to have disqualified Mahomet II as both a sachem and a Mohegan in 1736. Nor does the committee acknowledge Johnson's 1774 list of "proper Mohegans" as a guide to determining the existence of a more privileged or "rightful" class of Mohegans as opposed to "interlopers" or "improper" Mohegans. The entire reservation community is in the same boat, as it were: Mohegan identity is cast now as being almost wholly composed of these "many" who are deemed "not originally Mohegans," and who are "indistinguishable" from one another, having become "naturalized" by *proximity* ("long residence" in the community) and by a *mixing of "blood"* ("consanguinity"). From the perspective of the government surveyors of Mohegan identity, Mohegans had become – to borrow James Clifford's apt phrase – a "muddle of lost origins" (Clifford 1988:5).

A similar assessment of Mohegan identity had been offered by the committee appointed in 1773 to investigate the "Unsettled State & Difficultys and disputes" among Mohegans (IND 1st, 2:312). That committee reported that the reservation community included "about 40 Families and Seem[s] to be Encreasing" since "the Children appear to be numerous":

> As to the Interlopers and Stragglers from other Tribes *it is very Difficult to find out who they are (If any) they having no Records to find out their Geneal[o]gy* and are very Differing in their Acc[oun]ts and we find none but what by Blood or Intermarriage Claim to belong to the Tribe and have been with them for a Long Space of Years and *It is very Difficult to Distinguish between the whole blood and the part blood. We cannot find they have any Internal Civil polity among them But Seem to be in a State of nature.* (2:312; emphasis added)

Without written accounts of their "genealogies," Mohegans are rendered incapable of accurately identifying themselves. Here then is a new criterion for "legitimacy" (the recorded "genealogy") imposed upon the reservation community – one they cannot meet. But this assessment of Mohegan "illegitimacy" also suggests a renewal of a much older means of constructing an irrevocable historical distance and political inequality between Indians and their presumed conquerors. A century earlier, Gookin's treatise on "Indian origins" dismissed New England Natives' oral accounts of their own beginnings in the land as "figments" and "fables," which, as he saw it, only proved their own historical "ignorance" as well as their cultural (and thereby "legal") detachment from the landscape. Depicted, in 1773, as lacking the key features of "civilization" – written records and "civil polity" – Mohegans are historically positioned in a time and way of life (i.e., a "state of nature") that are politically remote from and inferior to "civilized" society.

In the late eighteenth century, as some Mohegans employed colonial racial categories to jockey for internal political authority or an "improved" standing with the Connecticut government, government authorities also continued to refine the old colonial notion that Mohegans were no more than "inconsiderable Indians," and I would argue that these examples indicate – as did the 1761 depiction of Mashantuckets vis-à-vis "white people" – that by the last quarter of the eighteenth century the Connecticut government was edging toward a simplistically racialized (and, of course, wholly racist) assessment of reservation communities as uniformly "non-white" and thus as devoid of legal rights and social status comparable to that of their "white" neighbors. The above committee's final assessment of the Mohegan reservation community – that it is "difficult to distinguish" between "whole blood" and "part blood" Mohegans, and that they all "seem to be in a state of nature" – makes that point quite plainly. Indeed the constructed "racial" identity of Mohegans here – and the suggested inherent difference and inequality between the reservation community and the "white" society that surrounds and observes it – is underpinned by a timely evocation of "Indian savagery." Government officials surely imposed upon Mohegans the pernicious notions of "purity of blood" and "parts" of blood, but compared to the facts of power embodied in a sociopolitical hierarchy in which "white," and *only* "white," can be at the top, such constructs are fluff, ultimately politically ineffectual for those upon whom they have been imposed. Like other racial categories applied to "non-whites," they are part of an assembly of tools for the expedient manipulation and subjugation of those "others." Evoking a conceived *history*, as well as a conceived *way of life*, "white," as a racial designation, has an unequivocal bottom line: "they" are not, and *cannot* be, "us." Zachary Johnson may have relished, and to some minor degree benefited economically from, his government-conveyed, localized (that is, reservation-confined) status as a Mohegan of "pure blood," but the only real political relevance such a status would have in the context of the broader relations of domination that shaped the developing Euro-American state would be to provide government officials with a means of undermining Indian identities and Native rights with surgical precision, just as by the last quarter of the eighteenth century such notions worked to tear up the Mohegan body politic – the former unity of which, in 1736, had made a powerful statement of resistance to dispossession and to the colonial authorities who had abetted it.

For the officials reporting on the Mohegan reservation community in the late eighteenth century, the "evidence" of Mohegans' irrevocable otherness and inequality is not only their purportedly muddled identity, but also the presumed condition of their lives and their relationships with one another: Mohegans, whether "whole" or "part" blood, still exist in "a state of nature." Their legal case against Connecticut finally dismissed by the English Crown in 1773, Mohegans were, at this historical juncture, officially designated as detached from "civilization." Racialized assessments of Indian illegitimacy, then, were enmeshed with and dependent upon the "known" elements of "savagery," and it was, of course, the idea of savagery that had long been the consummate justification for colonial appropriation of indigenous lands. But racial categories and the idea of a "given" or readily "recognizable" racial hierarchy (bolstered by timeworn and reliable evocations of "Indian savagery") could be deployed and manipulated to do more than deflect attention from Natives' assertions of their rights and from the illegality of dispossession. Indeed, racial discourse could be deployed to supplant history altogether. The 1766 argument of Connecticut's representative William Samuel Johnson (*Wyllys Papers* 1924:440) is a case in point. In response to Mohegans' appeal to the 1743 decision, Johnson argued that Mohegans in no sense constituted *a people*:

> the Idea of the Mohegans being a separate or sovereign state [as suggested by the 1705 decision of the imperial commission] would, in America, where the State & Condition of the Indians is known to everybody, expose [his] Majesty & Sovereignty to Ridicule, might be of dangerous Consequence, & [ought] not to be suffered in a Court of Justice &c[.] When the English Treated with them it was not as with Independ[ent] States (for they had no such thing as a Civil Polity) . . . but as with savages, whom they were to quiet & manage as well as they could, sometimes by flattery, but oftener by force – Who would not treat a Company of Lyons Wolves or Bears (whom the Indians but too nearly resemble) if he saw himself surrounded by [them] ready to fall upon him, & even call them *Friends & Allies* too, if he tho[ugh]t it would for a Moment repress their Rage, & give him time to take measures for his security. (IND 1st, 2:277; emphasis in original)

While Johnson's argument builds on that articulated six decades earlier in Sir Henry Ashurst's appeal to the 1705 decision (see chapter 4), the Indian-hating expressed by Johnson appears far more extreme. As in Ashurst's account, Mohegans at the time of the English arrival were "inconsiderable Indians," or in Johnson's words, "Mohegans were neither free, Independant, nor numerous, but were only a small part of the Pequots from whom Uncas had revolted" (IND 1st, 2:227). However, in direct contradiction to that characterization, Mohegans, like all other Indians, were nonetheless like "a Company of Lyons Wolves or Bears" who had "surrounded" colonists. In turn, colonial officials were willing to "call [Mohegans] Friends & Allies" to protect colonial interests. This depiction, as Johnson well knew, did not reflect at all accurately upon the history of Connecticut's relationship to Mohegans, particularly with regard to the circumstances under which the 1640 "agreement" with Mohegan sachem Uncas was obtained – and through which Connecticut subsequently claimed ownership to the entirety of Mohegan lands.[12]

The differences between Connecticut's argument to the 1743 commission and Johnson's depiction of the colony's position several decades later are striking. For one thing, in the 1743 argument there is no such reference to Mohegans or other Indians in the region as a "Company of Lyons Wolves or Bears" – though the supremacy of colonial "civility" is stressed in references to colonists' treatment of Native peoples: as Connecticut's representatives then explained it, the colonial government always "behaved with great kindness and tenderness towards the said Indians," and any colonial acknowledgement of Mohegans' rights to their ancestral lands was a manifestation of the government's "extraordinary kindness towards the said Indians, over whom the government have had a general care and guardianship ever since" (*Proc.* 1769:80–81). Although Johnson denies that there was any genuine alliance with Mohegans, the colony's argument to the 1743 commission states instead that "the said English having gone through a war with the Pequots, and conquered them, in which Uncas (who was accounted a Pequot, and lived at Moheagan) had been friendly to the English, a friendship was cultivated between the English and said Uncas and his men; who, after the Pequot War, were accounted, and treated with, as a distinct people, and Uncas as the Sachem, and first Sachem, of that people" (77). Although such rhetoric obscures the fact that, after 1637, the threat of colonial violence lay at the root of subsequent alliances with Native people, it nonetheless acknowledges Mohegans' humanity: they are a "distinct people" with whom a "friendship was cultivated." In contrast, Johnson seeks not to glorify Pequot conquest but to deny it entirely, and thus to deny the intertwining of Mohegans' history with that of colonists: for Johnson there was not even a "Pequot War," but instead a "Treaty for settling the Country *was made with the Pequots*, & a right to all their Territories, which included the Mohegan Lands, was undoubtedly acquired by the Congress of the People [i.e., the colonial government]" (IND 1st, 2:277; emphasis added). This depiction – not of a conquest of Pequots but of a mutually agreed upon, orderly "acquisition" of Pequot lands – not only erases Mohegans' history but contradicts Johnson's own depiction of "the Indians" as "a Company of Lyons Wolves or Bears" who were then "surrounding" colonists. The question remains, then, how to explain this incongruity in Johnson's construction of Indianness and colonial history.

Johnson's suggestion that Mohegans, like other Indians, are to be seen not simply as savages but as *predators* lying in wait, is a colonial projection par excellence – indeed, who was "surrounding" and subsequently "fell upon" whom at Mystic in 1637?[13] But the introduction of this notion into the legal debate over the Mohegan case also suggests that the recycling of seventeenth-century colonial notions of savagery fueled a newly emerging imperative of Indian-hating, one that offered the "natural law" of racial hierarchy to trump historical realities. As Johnson's argument goes on to demonstrate, not only are Indians a threat to "white people," but their lifestyle is inherently destructive to private property, which is the very foundation of the expanding colonial "civilization." "The Indians," he contends

> have always had more Land than they knew what to do with. They Hunt, Fish, & Fowl where they please, & live the Indolent Life they love. To have more Land in their Power would be really a very great diservice to them, as they would Immediately sell it to the first Purchassor that offered, & whatever Money they get is Infallibly laid out in Strong drink which not only destroys them but in the mean time renders them terrible to all that are near them. *The experience of a Century & a half has demonstrated that Indians living among the English or white People, cannot, & will not have Property in Lands.* The only way to continue their Existence is to set lands apart for their use only, as has been done in this Instance. The Colony never have, nor never will suffer these Indians to want Land for Planting, & c . . . & all beyond that, is ruinous to them, & mischievous to the public. (IND 1st, 2:277; emphasis added)

For Johnson, the establishment of reservations is not an acknowledgment of Natives' land rights, as it had been in 1680 when the colony enacted its first reservation law, nor is it simply a means of controlling Native populations and segregating them from each other; rather, the reservation is to serve as the essential boundary distancing the degeneracy of Indianness from "the public" – that is, "white people." Here the irony of Johnson's construction of the predatory Indian finds its fullest expression: as "white people" more tightly surround Native populations, leaving them with only fragments of their ancestral lands and utterly devastated subsistence economies, so does colonial discourse come to produce a more virulent, and now overtly racialized, expression of Indian-hating.[14] But what such discourse betrays is not "white" fear of a confrontation with reservation communities in Connecticut – whose resistance to dispossession throughout the eighteenth century did not entail threats of violence against colonizers – but the refusal to acknowledge history itself, which Johnson's rhetoric so desperately seeks to obfuscate. Therein lies the totalizing power of Euro-American racial discourse, particularly as it has been articulated in the persistent fallacy of the innate "cultural" superiority of "white people." Johnson need not have historical facts, or even colonial law, on his side;[15] he need only evoke the claimed truth of white supremacy (as it is perhaps most accurately termed by this point). For Johnson, this truth is clearly evidenced in Indians' continuing resistance to the cultural and politico-legal hallmark of "white civilization": private property. As he put it, after "a Century & a half" of proximity to "the English or white People," Indians "cannot, & will not have Property in Lands" (IND 1st, 2:277). Ultimately, then, the racialized construction of Indian "illegitimacy" could be deployed to consolidate and "legalize" Euro-American authority over the landscape – wholly masking the inconvenient specificities of history – and casting that authority in terms of the inherent propensities of "white" society, the most important of which is an ever-expanding need for its own exclusive territory, or "living space."[16]

## *Native Identities Defying "Race"*

*Within a white supremacist culture, to be without documentation is to be without a legitimate history. In the culture of forgetfulness, memory alone has no meaning.*
— bell hooks, "Revolutionary 'Renegades': Native Americans, African Americans, and Black Indians"

I would like to close with a final gesture of linking past and present by looking briefly at a recent Euro-American attack on Indian identity in Connecticut, one in which notions of racial "illegitimacy" serve to obscure the complexity of Native histories, revealing that the old idea of the Indian "impostor," adeptly deployed by Governor Talcott in the 1730s, has been rejuvenated to deny validity to the federal acknowledgment petitions and land claims of Native communities in late-twentieth-century Connecticut.

In 1993, when Robert Englehart's cartoon ran in the *Hartford Courant*, a hearing on Golden Hill Paugussetts' land claims in southwestern Connecticut was soon to be underway in the town of Waterbury (*Golden Hill Paugussetts v. Town of Southbury* (Civ. Doc. No. 93–116486-S). As in the case of the now famous Mashpee land suit in the early 1970s (see Campisi 1991 and Clifford 1988), scrutiny of Paugussetts' identity was central to the Euro-American evaluation of their land claims. Golden Hill Paugussetts had long been acknowledged by the state of Connecticut as an Indian tribe, and their history – along with that of their existing one-quarter-acre reservation in Trumbull established in 1659 – had been documented by local historians and anthropologists. Nonetheless, Paugussetts' pur-

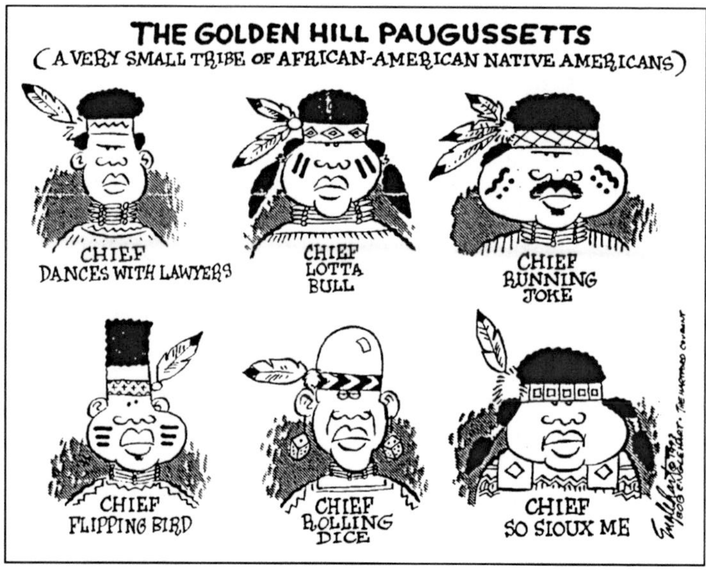


*The Hartford Courant*, July 21,1993. Reprinted with permission.

suit of federal acknowledgment and their claims to land were received with palpable hostility by Euro-Americans in the state.[17]

When Paugussett land claims were filed in 1992, their federal acknowledgment project had been ongoing for over a decade, and several Paugussett leaders – particularly their chief, Big Eagle (Aurelius Piper Sr.), and his son, Moon Face Bear (Kenny Piper) – had become rather well-known figures in the state of Connecticut. In the mid-1970s, Big Eagle had garnered considerable media attention when he led Paugussetts in challenging a neighbor who had encroached upon the Trumbull reservation, where Big Eagle then resided. Paugussetts were supported in this effort by the American Indian Movement, whose most prominent spokesperson at the time, Russell Means, spoke in defense of Paugussett protests. In a statement to local reporters, Means described Paugussetts' effort to defend their land rights as "a perfect example of the Indian people holding on by their fingernails to their being as a people" (*Bridgeport Post*, November 19, 1976). In this instance, the state acknowledged Paugussetts' land rights, the quarter-acre reservation was secured, and Paugussetts were subsequently awarded a federal grant to purchase land for another reservation. As of 1983, Paugussetts had acquired a second reservation, comprising eighty acres in Colchester, Connecticut.

If Paugussetts' Indian identity had not been a matter heavily debated in the Euro-American media in the mid-1970s – when it may have appeared to most Euro-Americans that this assertion of Paugussett land rights was but an isolated incident unlikely to be repeated (and not suggestive of any broader Native sovereignty movement fomenting in the region) – by the early 1990s, when multiple assertions of Native sovereignty had come to the fore more dramatically in Connecticut, Indian "racial" identity was subjected to intensifying scrutiny. With the enormous success of the Mashantucket Pequot Tribal Nation's casino inciting much public debate, and Mohegans' impending federal acknowledgment implying the possibility of another casino in southeastern Connecticut, it is perhaps not surprising that Paugussett land claims were perceived as "threatening." So, in 1992, when Moon Face Bear further defied Euro-American sensibilities and his own father's wishes (personal communication with Chief Big Eagle) by initiating a Paugussett-run business venture via the tax-free sale of cigarettes at the Colchester reservation, Euro-Americans responded with outrage, particularly when Moon Face Bear and those Paugussetts who supported him ultimately found themselves in an armed standoff with Connecticut state police. By July 1993, when Englehart's Paugussett cartoon appeared, and the standoff as well as the land claims were in progress, Paugussetts had come to be viewed, in archetypal fashion, as "hostiles," and the local media tended to depict Paugussett land claims as victimizing innocent (white) property owners, who were threatened with the loss of their yards and homes by the questionable land claims of an "unrecognized" Indian tribe. Paugussett land claims were referred to as "terrorism" in the editorial commentary of a local television news program; and residents of the town of Southbury, one of the towns in which Paugussetts had filed land claims, began to wear and distribute white T-shirts with bold black lettering that stated, "Paugussetts – Stay off our Land!" One Euro-American man asked by a local reporter to comment on Paugussett land claims summed up the prevailing Euro-American attitude of the moment when he remarked, "We fought the Indians 300 years ago. Do we have to fight them again?"

The presumptions underpinning the collective pronoun here are troubling, since the "we" rests upon a claimed history and position of power that, in the context of current debates over Native rights and Indian "racial" authenticity in southern New England, have not been openly interrogated. In pondering the historical significance of Englehart's "cartoon," it is important to consider that his representation of Paugussetts – here quite obviously cast as "racial impostors" – suggests that Englehart's intended Euro-American audience "observes" Paugussetts from a position of innocence, if not *self-defense*. This juxtaposition of the presumed "racial impostor" against the innocent (and victimized) white "observer" raises important questions about the precise means by which racial discourse is legitimized and its claims normalized. In a sociopolitical and historical context in which such racist representations are offered up as humorous public fare, and which indeed pose racism itself as good clean fun, can there be such a thing as an "innocent observer" among Englehart's Euro-American constituency? If Englehart's "cartoon" seeks to affirm the necessity (and the *right*) of white supervision over any claims to political, historical, and cultural legitimacy made by Native Americans, and to deploy notions of "race" in order to disparage such claims, then it is a representation that is linked to a particular history of strategic surveillance of subjugated populations, and it is not to be construed merely as a spontaneous, random, or "innocent" commentary on Paugussett identity.

Englehart's representation reflects what is, to be sure, a widely held racial conception of Indian identity in southern New England, one that insists that the "genuine" characteristics of Indianness, like those of imagined "blackness," are quite obvious physical manifestations and thus are readily "recognizable" (to Euro-Americans, that is). And it is important to emphasize that this depiction of Paugussett identity very much depends upon a virulently racist construction of "blackness" as uniformly exhibited and "apparent" in a particular configuration of (male) facial features, which are themselves intended to be markers of specific "traits" of character: thus Paugussetts' land claims and their bid for federal acknowledgment, as the cartoon conveys, are a sham as plain to see as the nose Englehart has drawn on these imagined Paugussett faces. The political salience of this rendering of "Indian impostors" is, of course, not to be underestimated, since Englehart's representation is enmeshed in the contemporary practice of racial profiling in the United States.

Here Paugussetts' racialized identity exists only in opposition to the unmarked, omni-presence of "whiteness" and its assumed thorough and implicit knowledge of "Indianness" as well as "blackness." The representation, and the racial discourse it evokes, demand the absolute silence of the "impostors," whose "true" identity is to be exposed and scandalized by the cartoon. In these mug shots Paugussetts are indeed mute, and Englehart's imagined and viciously rendered "blackness" bespeaks the claim to legitimate identity and to historical complexity that can only be made by unmarked, "*white*" authority. The visual impact of the multiple and only slightly varied heads, all mockingly labeled "Chief," not only serves to evoke the Euro-American racist truism about those classed as nonwhites ("you've seen one, you've seen 'em all"), but the conspicuously narrowed craniums hearken back to the late-nineteenth- and early-twentieth-century pseudoscience of "race" and its hallmark endeavor of head measuring as the means of "quantifying" presumed racial differences in intelligence and thus justifying white supremacy (Gould 1981). Englehart's representation thus situates Paugussetts among a host of racial grotesques that have been produced by European and Euro-American fantasies of "savage" inferiority, and the physiognomy it displays also links it to a colonial history of racial border patrol and to the familiar Western construction of the repugnant and ominous identity of the "interracial" other.

If it is "black looks," to borrow bell hooks's phrase (1992:192), that are offered by Euro-American imaginings as the unmistakable indicator of fraudulent Indian identity, then the claimed "racial truth" of the Englehart cartoon is all too evident and of no great surprise: and that is the preposterous notion that no legitimate Indian identity may be produced by historical, kin-based connections between Native Americans and African Americans.[18] And, indeed, the quintessential white supremacist notion of the "contaminating drop" of "black blood" hangs heavily over the Native peoples of southern New England, among whom – as among *all* populations in the Americas that have been distinguished according to colonially conceived racial categories – there are many individuals of multiple ancestry.

In spite of itself, Englehart's depiction of Paugussetts exposes the diversionary politics of racial scrutiny and the scandalizing of Indian identity in southern New England. This is a strategy that is diversionary on two levels: first, while Euro-Americans disparage local Indian identities as "racially" inauthentic, they also tend to claim that these are in no sense racist evaluations; second, and equally important, the apparent Euro-American obsession with what is conceived as "authentic" or "inauthentic" Indian identity is generally built upon a profound and far-reaching ignorance about the specific histories of the Native peoples of New England. Although many Euro-Americans know little about the pasts and the struggles of the Native communities in the region, they do have a thorough, implicit knowledge of *racial categories* and certainly of the standardized, Euro-American racial notion of what constitutes a "real Indian": these ideas are so deeply ingrained that (as many of my students over the years have noted) they are in play even in the most "routine" discussions about "the Indians." And so it is rather easy to understand why many Euro-Americans believe that they do indeed know a great deal about "the Indian," because, of course, they *do*: "the Indian" is, must be, a monolithic "racial" entity, such that when one has "seen one" (in a Hollywood film, for instance), one can claim to have seen them all. Likewise, it also tends to be very important that this real Indian be *dead*, faded into historical obscurity, or, at the very least, geographically very distant. Only then can popular racial icons of "Indian history" (such as the Indian names on road signs or the Indian mascots of local high schools) find their true diversionary meaning: for Indian identity to be "acknowledged" in a purportedly postcolonial world – one that yearns to be disengaged from the moral and legal dilemmas of conquest – Indians themselves must be absent (or *made* to be absent).

The particularity, complexity, and continuity of Native struggles – to preserve their legal rights to land, for instance – have long been effectively sidetracked if not utterly obfuscated by Euro-American racial imaginings of Indianness and assaults on Native identities. In charting these struggles, and investigating the startling moments of resistance to domination as well as the silences and accommodations to power that have made Native community life and a sense of historical continuity possible, one can also detect a contest of cultural inventions and historical imaginings. Mohegans who defied Governor Talcott and Connecticut Indian policy in September 1736 constructed and announced a local understanding of historical continuity, consciously rooting Mohegan identity and Mohegan political autonomy in a prohibited "black dance" – which was, at its most blatant, a Mohegan celebration of what was yet possible and hoped for: a future. Talcott's rhetoric, on the other hand, and his fashioning of Indian policy, claimed a colonial past and created an Indian "inauthenticity" that *had* to be, if the Connecticut government were to present itself as the legitimate and final authority over the lives and lands of local Native peoples.

Engelhart's cartoon likewise proclaims a history, and fashions an "Indian impostor," that must be: it tells us that there is no Paugussett history to acknowledge, but rather that there is only "race" to "recognize," which then allows his constituency to enter a familiar and comfortable world of racial fantasy. From that world, fallacious interpretations of conquest have been launched and passed off as history, as "the great awakening of the human mind . . . which swept over the Aryan races, impelling them to new explorations, new conquests of their mother earth" (Weeden 1963:2–3; see chapter 1).

Confronting us as it does with the ways in which appeals to racial "recognition" serve to divert questions of history, politics, and power, the Englehart cartoon must be placed in its proper historical context, one in which bodies of color – individual and collective – have been constructed and targeted as suspect. In eighteenth-century Connecticut, surveillance of reservation communities and Native identities emerged as a significant governmental strategy for controlling, silencing, and dispossessing Native peoples, particularly when they dared to resist colonial authority. I want to suggest, then, that Englehart's cartoon is linked to a history of struggle in which Indian identity was never simply "recognizable" or not to colonial, or white, "observers." Both official and routine assessments of Indian identity have been shaped by – and have likewise shaped – contests over rights (to land, for instance) and over the interpretation and production of history.

Governor Talcott, who ultimately cast as impostors all Mohegans and their Native supporters who opposed dispossession and challenged government authority, would have understood the political strategy embodied in the racist claims of the Paugussett cartoon. He might first have recognized its suggestion of "Indian conspiracy," a persistent colonial projection: here the implied "plot" is the cheating of whites via casinos and land claims. But Talcott would have been more than a little startled, no doubt, to find that debates over Native rights had not been quieted long ago. Although colonial efforts to quell Native resistance in the eighteenth century produced a lasting and ultimately racialized discourse of historical denial, the land struggles of reservation communities in eighteenth-century Connecticut left their own legacy. Natives' petitions and other documents that recount their efforts to protect their reservation lands and determine the course of their own futures suggest that the consciousness of a history of struggle – a history that was embedded in the landscape and inscribed in reservation borders – was a reason for remaining. Against the claims of conquest, the reservation became a place in which historical experiences, ancestral ties, and community identities were rooted. Like memory itself, reservations embodied possibility.

# Series Editors' Afterword

Amy Den Ouden's *Beyond Conquest* moves in two directions simultaneously, both of which are indicated in the title. The book, to begin, presents what happened to Native people in Connecticut beyond (i.e., after) conquest – continuing conquest, for it was not, and is not yet, a once-for-all-time event. After this incomplete conquest, *beyond* both chronologically and in terms of effects, lie not just the ever-renewed struggles to reverse this conquest but the efforts by both sides to make and remake culture and law – processes that remain close to the surface for both Connecticut and the Native peoples within its boundaries today. From the other direction Den Ouden examines the continuing struggles for history – for what history is, and for how it matters; how we write it, live it, harness it, resist it. History is in this sense only incidentally retrospective, and it is simultaneously here that culture and law come to life. For it is within this realm of the incomplete and mostly agonistic history-making that law and culture are made and remade. It is from such a perspective that we come to see history living around us.

The lessons of conquest are clear. Utter military supremacy – so total it can be given the aura of religious righteousness, so total it can be waved or draped, like a flag over toppled statues and shiny coffins, so total it can be turned indifferently into either journalism or theater – has little to do with the subjugation of the people who are its victims. Even totally destructive violence does not always subjugate its victims. That, of course, has been the first lesson of the Iraq disaster. Yet Den Ouden shows that this was also and already the case with comparatively small numbers of Native Americans in the Connecticut Colony, militarily beaten but far from subdued, and continually capable of conceptual surprises – surprises rooted seemingly paradoxically in the process of being made into the Janus-faced demonic/irrelevant other. Governor Talcott found this out in 1736, when he tried to muscle a Mohegan sachem aside to make room for his candidate – only to find out that when continuing conquest depends upon both creating *and* controlling a social, cultural, political and legal order for its victims, the exercise of that power far more readily creates chaos than an enduring social system.

In sum, what we have here is a brilliant case study of the far from benign innocence of power.

Far from benign because it is not the case that the victims could bathe in a reciprocal innocence of their own: in some instances they were bathed in blood – some of which they all-too-readily spilled themselves. Nor by any stretch of the imagination could it mean that the will to power that drove the conquest was innocent or pious (as was claimed by Talcott). It was, instead, exercising a kind of power that sought to remain apart from and blind to situations it created. Power that is utterly innocent of knowledge of its victims is capable of utter violence – violence that is at times as uninterested in its actual consequences as it is nonsensical. But the will to power that drove that blindness was far from vacuous, and even when it started in innocence it quickly filled the vacuum of its nonrecognition with its own fantasies of order and constitution. Unwilling or unable to see its own results, it dreamed its effects and found fault with a world that did not match its vision. When confronted with such a situation, we social scientists have noted that power constitutes its victims. Yet although it is clear that power is, in that sense, constructive, in the poststructural sense we can no longer escape with the simplification that it constitutes its victims only, as it would appear when other historians equate subjection with subjugation, and subjugation with subjectification. Rather, power that seeks the subjectification of its victims simultaneously seeks to make itself and does so not from the conditions of its execution but from the wellspring of its own fantasies.

And therein lies the crux of Den Ouden's analysis. What starts out as the systematic battering of Indians and their land rights turns out, by the time we reach her conclusions, to be the production of "race" – a notion that captures victim and victimizer, and far more. The vacuity supplied by the piety of the conquerors is filled not simply by this or that "Indian Tribe," nor simply by "Indians" in general, but by "race" as we use the term today – and more importantly, as it uses us. For as we see in Connecticut, or Mashpee, or Lumbee, it is frequently the victimizers, and not their victims, who are more conspicuously, more helplessly subject to notions of "race," more subject to their own fantasies than their victims ever were, and arguably, more than they ever could be. Then as now the security of the "homeland" meant violating both the homes of victims *and* victimizers, differently perhaps, but with equally devastating results. The core of the violation of life beyond conquest turned out to be the imposed, intrusive identities; identities made into membership passes to illusory – murderously illusory – collectivities; illusory collectivities that have their roots in horrifically efficient claims to innocence and unknowing.

*Beyond Conquest* is the fifth and final book in the *Fourth World Rising* series. As such, it presents a last opportunity for the editors to reflect on the issues and problems suggested by the books in the series as they have revealed the changing political, cultural, and economic situations of Native Peoples of the Americas. And so we will conclude the series with our suggestions for future research. Research along these lines is, in some cases, ongoing, though often at preliminary stages, the implications of which are just emerging; some of what is recommended below has yet to be pursued at all. All of what follows has its roots in the sorts of insights gained by going beyond the simple study of contemporary or past situations – no matter how nuanced or sympathetic – to the creation of those sorts of intellectual tools necessary to make changes in the situations in question. Three notions form the basis of what we see as a program for a new Native Studies:

1. That since the earliest colonial times, Native American societies have been formed in ways that ensure their fundamental social incompleteness – that is, that all Native groups were formed such that some critical element of their social reproduction could not be had or made locally. This is easiest to see when groups are dependent upon some locally unavailable material resource or technology, like firearms. It is more complex when what must be obtained elsewhere is not quite so obviously different – like slaves – or when it has no clear or obvious material component at all – like the boundary of a reservation.

2. That this incompleteness has meant that Native peoples are inescapably caught up in relationships with colonial regimes and, later, often as quasi-citizens in the surrounding settler society. This is true regardless of whether the social dependency that defines their incompleteness requires particular Native groups to deal directly with non-Native society or whether the dependency is only indirect. This is not to say that colonial or U.S. or some other society has ever had direct, hegemonic control. Far from it, and indeed the whole point of creating and

retaining the legal notion of "Indian Country," for example, has been the continuing necessity on the part of dominant groups to simultaneously create and maintain unique sorts of freedoms and maneuverings among Native groups that more direct control would foreclose.

3. That it is within this situation – of incomplete social reproduction and unavoidably necessary attempts to claim control over this same social reproduction – that Native struggles are waged. And to the extent that Native culture is a part of these struggles, it is within this context that Native culture (in its living and vibrant sense rather than archaic and romantic sense) is formed as well: as a product of and means to resist the incompleteness of their own social lives and to stake their own claims to both today and tomorrow.

It is thus – with a sense of Native culture as both rooted in a history of struggle and simultaneously unfinished, alive, and ongoing – that we conclude the Fourth World Rising series, simultaneously looking backward and forward. The editors would like to thank the University of Nebraska Press for their support of the series. And we look forward to seeing work that responds to and broadens our view of the new terrains, openings, and beginnings that the Fourth World Rising series has made.

*Kirk Dombrowski and Gerald Sider*

New York City, 2004

# Notes

## 1. DILEMMAS OF CONQUEST

1. In 1725, Connecticut governor Joseph Talcott reported that the Mohegan population included 351 persons (TP 2:397–402). By 1740, as Mohegans' legal dispute with the colony pressed on, Talcott claimed that among Mohegans there were only 41 adults (2:207). His accounting of the size of the Mohegan reservation community, however, was not detached from the struggle over rights to reservation land and must be viewed accordingly. In the early eighteenth century, the Connecticut government began to respond to Native resistance to dispossession by scrutinizing, and disparaging, Native populations. Colonial officials assessed the legitimacy of resisting reservation communities, and concomitantly their land rights, in terms of population size as well as their "improvements" of reservation land according to colonial cultural standards. As I explain in the following chapters, these assessments reflected colonial gender biases and patriarchal conceptions of land rights as well as the formation of a racialized notion of Indianness.
2. This is evident in the vehement opposition by the state of Connecticut and the towns of North Stonington, Ledyard, and Preston to the Bureau of Indian Affairs' proposed finding in favor of acknowledging the Eastern Pequot nation of North Stonington as a tribe. Having worked on Eastern Pequots' federal acknowledgment project as a researcher and consultant for a decade, I have read the arguments posed by the state and towns in southeastern Connecticut in their efforts to thwart Eastern Pequots' federal acknowledgment. A central theme of these arguments is that Pequots were long ago a conquered people, wholly subjected to colonial authority after the so-called Pequot War in 1637, and as such, they could not possibly continue to exist as a nation or "tribe." Conquest, it is suggested, thus precluded the possibility for historical continuity and the reproduction of Native identities, bonds of kinship, and political or cultural practices. For instance, in a report submitted to the Bureau of Indian Affairs by the towns of Ledyard, North Stonington, and Preston, it is argued that Eastern Pequots lacked "meaningful tribal existence" since

the beginning of the colonial period, and that since colonizers viewed Native peoples as "lesser beings over whom they could impose legal jurisdiction," the colonial claim to legal jurisdiction over the lives of indigenous people, and indeed the very existence of colonial "Indian law," serves as evidence that Native peoples *required* external authority and thus did not exist as tribes in the colonial period and beyond (see "Analysis of the Eastern Pequot and Paucatuck Eastern Pequot Tribal Acknowledgment Petitions and Comments on the Proposed Findings: A Report Submitted to the Bureau of Indian Affairs Branch of Acknowledgment and Research by the Towns of North Stonington, Ledyard, and Preston, Connecticut," August 2001, pp. 44–49). Such an argument is tantamount to writing Native history off of the claims of colonial law. As I argued in a response to the towns' report (written on behalf of the Eastern Pequot Tribal Nation, and submitted to the Bureau of Indian Affairs, Branch of Acknowledgment and Research), this is a dangerously ludicrous and racist logic, not unlike asserting that attitudes of slaveholders and laws regulating slavery in the southern United States during the nineteenth century constitute evidence that Africans needed to be enslaved.

3. By *community* I refer to Native women and men who share a land base and economic resources, and who are bound by kin ties and a shared history. Further, as I argue in subsequent chapters, kin ties and a shared struggle against dispossession also bound reservation communities to their lands and served as a foundation for political alliances between reservation communities. I want to emphasize as well that in using this term I do not imply that, by the eighteenth century, there were no longer Native sociopolitical entities that can be termed *nations*. Rather, what I mean to specify is that reservation communities did (and do) not necessarily constitute the entire nation or sociopolitical body of a people. The harsh economic realities of the eighteenth century meant that Native nations were dispersed, with adult men, for example, often working as wage laborers off the reservation (in the whaling industry, for instance), and with children sometimes indentured as servants in Anglo-American households (see discussion of eighteenth-century petitions of Eastern Pequot leader Mary Momoho in chapter 3).
4. Indigenous populations in Connecticut, as elsewhere in New England, were drastically diminished by European diseases and colonial violence in the seventeenth century (see Bragdon 1996:25–28 and Grumet 1995: 61–68). According to anthropologist Kathleen Bragdon, the Native pop-

ulation in southeastern New England in the early seventeenth century (prior to the epidemics of 1616 and 1633) included over 90,000 people (Bragdon 1996:25–26). By 1650, in the wake of epidemics as well as the Pequot massacre, the Native population of southern New England was "reduced to one-tenth of its former strength, with the highest concentrations on Marthas Vineyard and Nantucket, and in coastal Rhode Island and Connecticut" (28). The English population, however, "rose with rapidity in the decades following 1630": "In the 1620's there were few more than five hundred English settlers in southern New England, but by 1630 there were more than three times that many, and by 1640, close to 18,500 people of English descent populated the region" (28). By 1700, the "total English population in New England had grown to nearly ninety-one thousand" (Grumet 1995:64). According to Governor Talcott's report to the imperial Board of Trade in 1730, the total Anglo population of the colony of Connecticut at that time was 38,000; his report estimates the indigenous population to be 1,600 people, not including "about 700 Indian and negro slaves" (CR 7:584).

5. This will be discussed in further detail in chapters 3 through 5.
6. The Connecticut government produced documents to that effect between 1736 and 1738 (see, for instance, TP 1:354); but as I note in chapter 4, Ben Uncas II did not begin his sachemship with a show of compliance to colonial authority. Nevertheless, by the time a second imperial commission sat to review the Mohegan land case in 1738, the Connecticut government had in hand a declaration signed by Ben Uncas II which proclaimed that the colony had "hitherto duely & fully kept and performed their Covenant & Agreement with the Sachem and Nation of the Moheegin Indians" (IND 1st, 1:173; *Proc.* 1769:196–98).
7. See the concluding section of chapter 2 for further discussion of the relationship between Native communities in this region during the early eighteenth century. As I note, Experience Mayhew's account of his "visitations" to Mohegans and Pequots offers important insights into the enduring importance of kin and community ties at a time when reservation communities were contending with an intensified colonial land hunger, as well as the intrusions of missionaries.
8. Francis Jennings's important essay, "Virgin Land and Savage People," opens by making the point that "the most comprehensive of American conquest myths" ["that which presents European colonization and Indian subjection in terms of civilization (Good) overpowering and annihi-

lating savagery (Evil)"], "still powerfully sway[s] intellectuals as well as the multitude" in the United States (1971:519). Jennings's article further demonstrates the relationship between the discourse by which conquest was legitimized and the actual processes of dispossession in seventeenth-century New England; but he also points out ultimately that specific colonial tactics of dispossession in New England set "a precedent for such later American national ventures as Theodore Roosevelt's intervention in Panama and the current prolonged invasion of southeast Asia" (537). Jennings thus raises the thorny issue of the continuities between forms of domination in the colonial past and twentieth-century exertions of U.S. imperial power over the lives and lands of its designated "others." In the introductory chapter to his volume *Year 501: The Conquest Continues* (1993), entitled "The Great Work of Subjugation and Conquest," Noam Chomsky argues that the notion of a benign conquest of North America endures in the United States: "among the educated classes, fairy tales of righteous mission and benevolence have long risen to the level of doctrinal truths, and much of the general public seems to believe them as well" (Chomsky 1993:20).

9. The impact of colonial law on Natives' lives in the early eighteenth century is examined at length in chapter 4.

10. Examining Timothy Dwight's epic poem *Greenfield Hill* (1794), which celebrates Pequot conquest, historian Eve Kornfield has argued that in late colonial New England, Anglo-American intellectuals' "confidence in the future of American 'civilization' depended in large measure on the projection of a 'savage' Other" (Kornfield 1995:290). The recycling of the image of Pequots as the quintessential "savage Other" was a particularly expedient political and cultural maneuver in the context of eighteenth-century disputes over reservation land (see chapters 4 and 5 for further discussion).

11. Governor Joseph Talcott was informed by one of his advisers in February 1736, as Mahomet II made his way to London to deliver the Mohegans' second petition to the Crown, that the account of the 1637 massacre by its revered military leader, Major John Mason, had just come out as a "new book" (TP 1:350).

12. In his superb analysis of the ideological underpinnings of the Pequot massacre, historian Neal Salisbury maintains that, for English colonists, "the Pequots' most offensive traits were their 'pride' and their 'insolence' " (Salisbury 1982:224). Pequots thus "represented a world 'turned

upside down' with barbarians triumphing over civilization, Satan over Christ, anarchy over order" (224). The colonial assessment of Pequot identity should not be viewed as a "natural" outcome of a "clash" of cultures; for indeed this was colonial mythmaking at work, and as Salisbury notes, "the Pequot of the mid-1630's were anything but the ruthless conquerors of the Puritan-inspired legend that continues to enjoy historical currency" (210). What is obscured from the legendary image of Pequots as the "insolent" nemesis of "civilization" is the fact that colonial leaders did not simply demand alliances with Native peoples over which the colonies had control, but they also "required complete subjugation and humiliation in the form of an exorbitant tribute" (211).

13. This treaty was "a covenant and agreement" between English colonists, Mohegan sachem Uncas, and Narragansett sachem Miantinomo ("Articles of Agreement between the English in Connecticut and the Indian Sachems," in *Proc.* 1769:33–34). The two sachems had provided military support to the colonial forces that attacked the Pequot fort at Mystic in the spring of 1637, and the treaty stipulated that they were each to be rewarded with Pequot survivors – among whom, according to the treaty, there were "two hundred . . . that are men, besides squaws and papooses" (1769:34). The identity of Pequot survivors was to have been erased, and they were to become known as "Narragansets and Moheagans" (1769:34).

14. As historian John Frederick Martin has observed, "the ignoble connection between military conquest and land greed deserves a study by itself" (1991:20). And it is the *veiling* of that connection – in this case, the discursive transformation of violent military conquest into a "good deed" – that becomes important to the construction of colonial legitimacy and the maintenance of colonial authority; but it is also important to the production of history. The way in which conquest is depicted in history books, and "remembered" by subsequent generations, informs contemporary Native-Anglo relations and debates over Native rights.

15. This document is contained in *Hoadly Memorial: Early Letters and Documents Relating to Connecticut, 1643–1709* (Hoadly 1932:65–70). According to Hoadly, the 1693 "Narrative" was most likely written by William Pitkin, a member of the Connecticut General Assembly at the time.

16. Pequots have been depicted not only as the great "menace" to colonial "civilization" but as a threat to other Native peoples in the region as well. In such renderings, colonizers are transformed into "liberators."

As it was plainly put in one history of Connecticut published in the early twentieth century, "By the conquests of the Pequots, the colony acquired all the lands belonging to that nation, and reaped this additional benefit, that the territory controlled by other tribes was opened to them by their native owners, who were completely cowed by the English, but also deeply grateful for their deliverance from the domination of the Pequots" (Morgan 1904:275). This simplistic depiction of Pequots' precolonial relationships with other Native nations in southern New England has become a cliché, despite the fact that recent scholarship has shown that relations between indigenous polities and the nature of Native leaders' political authority in seventeenth-century southern New England were more complex than English colonists grasped (Salisbury 1982:48–49). As Salisbury has noted, the Native peoples of southern New England were "linked by a complex network of marriages," and it was a principle of reciprocity that regulated relationships between communities and between sachems and their constituencies (48). While seventeenth-century colonial accounts suggest that Pequots "exerted often-resented influence over other Indian people," as anthropologist Robert Grumet has phrased it (1995:140), it is nonetheless the case that kin ties, and their adherent relations of reciprocity and obligation, bound members of distinct Native nations in southern New England long after the so-called Pequot War (see concluding section of chapter 2 and also chapters 4 and 5). Had kin ties between Pequots, Mohegans, and Niantics, for instance, not had such local importance, and had the Native peoples of the region widely accepted the colonial notion that the Pequot nation was *their own* nemesis, post-1637 Pequot communities would not have been able to emerge and endure *as Pequots*. But the power of this colonial construction of Pequots as "dominators" or "destroyers" has had a lasting legacy. As I have learned, it is a notion that may pop up unexpectedly, as an expedient means of obscuring or diverting attention from the issue of Native land rights in the present. During a hearing on Golden Hill Paugussett land claims in 1994, for which I testified as a witness on behalf of Paugussett leaders Big Eagle and Quiet Hawk, the presiding judge, who occasionally interjected his own commentaries on Indianness, interrupted the attorney questioning me about the Paugussett case to say, "What about the Pequots? Weren't they a warlike people?" I suggested that it may well have been English colonists who would be better described by that term. He didn't have any "follow-up" questions on the matter, and I can only assume that he felt it was important to get his own statement about Pequots on the record.

17. See the concluding section of chapter 3, and chapters 4 and 5, for further discussion of reservations as Native homelands – land bases central to the production of community life – in eighteenth-century Connecticut. I should note that in Apartheid South Africa, the creation of artificial "homelands," or Bantustans, was a means of forging and reinforcing white supremacy and of attempting to incite acrimonious political divisions among subjugated Africans (Winant 2001:193–95). The term *homelands*, in the historical and political context of Apartheid South Africa, thus has a distinctly racist connotation; I am suggesting an altogether different meaning for the term *homeland* in the historical and political context of eighteenth-century Connecticut, one that is meant to challenge colonial and Euro-American assumptions about the nature of their own presumed "homeland" and to emphasize the historical importance of indigenous knowledges and the struggle to preserve reservation lands. It is, as I see it, a term that illuminates the local historical significance of reservation land, much in the same way anthropologist Patricia Rubertone has employed the term to describe Narragansett ancestral land in the seventeenth century: "homelands were not just territories that Narragansett people traveled through, settled on, and subsisted from; they were places steeped in long-term histories, enduring social relations, and sacred traditions. They were landscapes shaped by geography, history, beliefs, experience, and spirituality. As active and animated spaces, rather than simply static backdrops, homelands were important not only in sustaining the Narragansetts' daily lives but also in maintaining their social and historical identity as a people" (Rubertone 2001:103–4; see also Boissevain 1956).

18. Ortiz's words stayed with me throughout the writing of this book. Another important source that incited questions on the relationship between land, knowledge production, and community life is Keith Basso's *Wisdom Sits in Places: Landscape and Language among the Western Apache*. Basso notes that "the experience of place – or, as Ronnie Lupe [of the Western Apache community at Cibecue] said, how people 'know their country' – is, in anthropology and the social sciences generally, lightly charted territory" (Basso 1996:xvi). Basso goes on to illuminate the relationship between Western Apaches' knowledge of their ancestral lands and the production of both their history and community life. His book, and its

insights into Western Apache local knowledge, helped me to begin to explore the historical and cultural significance of reservation lands in eighteenth-century Connecticut.

19. It has been suggested that, given the increasingly oppressive economic and social conditions of the eighteenth century, Native peoples in southern New England "attempted to find isolation, and to continue a life as nearly as possible like that in former times," which purportedly "led to the rise of reservation cultures" (Brasser 1971:79). The disputes over rights to reservation land that ensued in post–"Indian War" Connecticut do not bear out such an assessment. Indeed, Pequot, Mohegan, and Niantic reservation communities in New London County, for instance, did not "find isolation" on their reservations; rather, life on reservation land kept them deeply immersed in colonial struggles over land, livelihood, and, as I am arguing, history itself.

20. An Eastern Pequot elder once reminded me that "the term 'reservation' was never our term," and that it does not reflect how Eastern Pequots today feel about their reservation land (field notes from unrecorded discussion with Eastern Pequot Elders' Group, April 2000). This is no minor point, of course, since the very concept of "reserved" or "sequestered" lands is an expression of the mundane way in which colonial cultural forms were deployed to render Native identities and indigenous relationships to the landscape *alien* and to obscure the relations of power that underlay that alienation.

21. In his introduction to *Apache Reservation: Indigenous Peoples and the American State*, anthropologist Richard Perry provides a very useful overview of "the concept of reservations," which "has become familiar to most Americans. But like many commonplace ideas, its familiarity masks contradictions" (Perry 1993:5). Perry notes that "the reservation was rationalized as a measure to protect Native American peoples from exploitation, but it became a device for the chronic and systematic divestment of their resources. It was touted as a means of promoting economic development, but reservations today are pockets of some of the most extreme poverty in North America. Reservations were part of the process of bringing Native Americans into the wider society as self-sufficient citizens, but their structure inhibited the people's capacity to exert control over their own affairs" (7). It becomes important to remember, then, that the U.S. reservation system continues to serve as a form of domination, and the economic and political exploitation that it has facilitated

has had a devastating impact on the lives of indigenous people in the twentieth century. Thus my analysis here does not intend to romanticize "the reservation," or to detach it from the realities of colonial, state, and U.S. federal government oppression of Native peoples. As Gerald Sider noted in his study of Lumbee history, Lumbees who had pressured the BIA for land in the 1930s did not make a request for "reservation" land (i.e., land that would be held "in trust" by the U.S. federal government), for, as one Lumbee leader told Sider in 1968, "that would have set us back 100 years" (Sider 1993:140). Lumbees "wanted Indian-owned land," not federal "trust" lands (147). Reservation land, then, is certainly not something that all Native nations or communities have deemed desirable. Indeed, in the film *Broken Treaty at Battle Mountain*, which details the ongoing struggle of Western Shoshones to retain their rights to their ancestral territory, a Western Shoshone leader refers to the Battle Mountain reservation in Nevada as "a concentration camp." As I write this note, the Narragansett Nation of Rhode Island prepares to bring suit against the state of Rhode Island, whose state police stormed a recently opened smoke shop on the Narragansett reservation and employed brutal tactics in their arrest of Narragansett women and men ("Narragansett Tribe's Smokeshop Closed" 2003). Reservations, once again, are not sanctuaries, but rather sites of continuing struggle.

22. The anthropology of colonialism has demonstrated that constructions of cultural difference and the policing of imposed cultural boundaries were crucial to the establishment and maintenance of colonialism as a system of domination. Indeed, colonial power confronted the reality that "the otherness of the colonized person was neither inherent nor stable," and thus that "his or her difference had to be defined and maintained" (Cooper and Stoler 1989:610). And as Ann Stoler has demonstrated, "the colonial politics of exclusion" (Stoler 1991:53) produced racial hierarchy and affirmed colonial claims to cultural "superiority." Racism became "the classic foil invoked to mitigate" imposed divisions between colonizers and colonized, while it also served as a means "of creating the sense of (colonial) community" that was necessary for the maintenance of "a particular set of relations of production and power" (Stoler 1989:73, 138).

23. As anthropologist Jonathan Hill has explained, "the categorical term 'Indian' " is "not only a European invention but one that was, and still is, part of a broader process of symbolically removing indigenous American

peoples from their histories and reducing them to stereotypic symbols of isolation and alienation from the colonial and independent state of the Americas" (Hill 1996:9).

24. For examples of the acculturation model in the ethnohistory of northeastern North America, see Axtell 1997:16; Van Lonkhuyzen 1990; Gadacz 1979; C. Martin 1974; Richter 1983.

25. The search for "original" Indian cultural forms goes on in ethnohistory, as demonstrated in a recent essay on ethnohistorical methodology by historian James Axtell. "It is not that ancient customs and cultural patterns do not endure," Axtell states, "they do. But they seldom survive in pure, timeless forms or in their original, defining contexts. They come encrusted with accretions and diminished by subtractions, so we must devise ways to peel off the later additions from, and restore the missing pieces to, the original" (Axtell 1997:17). The assumption of precolonial essential, static Indian cultural forms is evident here and elsewhere in the essay – as when Axtell refers to "the acculturated [Abenaki] reserve town of St. Francis" (17). For relevant critiques of the acculturation model, see, for example, Bee 1974; Caulfield 1969; Clemmer 1969; Cohn 1987:18–31; Colson 1986; Fabian 1991; Magubane 1971; Magubane and Faris 1985.

26. Eric Wolf offered a most useful definition of culture in his volume *Europe and the People without History* (1982): "Once we locate the reality of society in historically changing, imperfectly bounded, multiple and branching social alignments . . . the concept of a fixed, unitary, and bounded culture must give way to a sense of the fluidity and permeability of cultural sets. In the rough-and-tumble of social interaction, groups are known to exploit the ambiguities of inherited forms, to impart new evaluations or valences to them, to borrow forms more expressive of their interests, or to create wholly new forms to answer to changed circumstances. Furthermore, if we think of such interaction not as causative in its own terms but as responsive to larger economic and political forces, the explanation of cultural forms must take account of that larger context, that wider field of force. 'A culture' is thus better seen as a series of processes that construct, reconstruct, and dismantle cultural materials, in response to identifiable determinants" (Wolf 1982:387). Equally relevant here is Gerald Sider's analysis of culture as "a locus of struggle – necessary struggle – just as much as 'class' names a locus of struggle" (Sider 1994:116). As Sider argues, acknowledging culture as "an arena of conflict" requires

that we "address struggles that are simultaneously both against domination and amongst the dominated" (116).

27. Here I follow Gerald Sider's urging that ethnohistorians must examine how Native people, who have been "subject to intense and pervasive domination," nonetheless "continue to live, and continually form and reform their own agendas as Indians, as people, and as the continuing victims of and partial victors in continually changing, deeply interwoven forms of collaboration, opposition, and accommodation" (Sider 1994:117; see also Sider 1993).

28. Caussatuck (spelled variously as "Coassatuck," "Cossatuck," "Cowissat'tuck") refers to "a hill, and land about it" in what is now North Stonington (Trumbull 1881:11; Caulkins 1895:122). It lies north of the northeast corner of the present-day Eastern Pequot reservation. The Commissioners of the United Colonies ordered in 1663 that a reservation be created for Eastern Pequots at Caussatuck in Stonington, which was to have included 8,000 acres (CR 2:33). However colonists in Stonington "refused to assent to the settlement [of Eastern Pequots] as proposed by the Commissioners"; consequently, at a town meeting in June of 1664 the town ordered its own committee to "goe and warne the Indians from off the town's land . . . at Cowissatuck" (2:33n). As a result of the town's protests, it was determined that Eastern Pequots were to have a reservation outside of the town's boundaries, at Pachaug (2:56); however, "no lands were laid out for them at Pachog, nor in any other place . . . and wherever a portion was designated for them, it would be found intrenching upon some English grants" (Wheeler 1887:15). Eastern Pequots were compelled to pay rent to colonists for the lands they planted, as they continued to attempt to live within the realm of their ancestral territory in the Stonington area (15–16). By 1669, then, Masawmp purportedly told the son of a Stonington resident that Eastern Pequots "woulde have Causaltuck againe," and that "thay hated [the English] for living on causattuck Land" (IND 1st, 1:17). Colonist John Stanton testified at the time of the rumored "Indian conspiracy" of 1669 that another Eastern Pequot, Nesomet, "did say to mee, that they were now desperate, they did not now care where they now went to live or where they died – speaking about their being removed from Cowissattuck" (CR 2:551). Finally, in 1683 a 280-acre reservation was established for Eastern Pequots in Stonington (Wheeler 1887:17; see chapter 3 for further discussion).

29. The notion that colonial divide-and-rule policies and practices (most unabashedly expressed in English colonists' cultivation of alliances with Mohegan and Narragansett leaders for the purpose of carrying out the massacre of Pequots at Mystic in 1637) necessarily resulted in a permanent disaffection and disconnection between distinct Native peoples, such as Mohegans and Pequots, has been a powerful one, affecting even the way some Native Americans in New England today envision the history of relationships between neighboring Native nations in the region. Anthropologist Jack Campisi has stated that it is not uncommon for Mashantucket Pequots, when talking about their colonial history, to remark that Pequots and Mohegans "had not had much contact" since Mohegans "join[ed] the English in the massacre and enslavement" of Pequots in 1637 (Campisi 1990:117). But as I have already noted, Pequots and Mohegans, along with Niantics, did indeed interact after the Pequot massacre, and not just as kin but as political allies. In the early eighteenth century, the Connecticut government was aware of the fact that Mohegans held leadership ceremonies that were attended by Pequots and Niantics, and sent officials to monitor these gatherings (see chapter 4). Such alliances between reservation communities suggest that kin ties and the common historical experience of struggle against dispossession bound Native peoples to each other long after military conquest.
30. As Carolyn Merchant explains, "women's horticulture was the major source of food, [with] corn alone providing the Indians of southeastern New England with about 65 percent of their caloric intake" (Merchant 1989:76; see also Cronon 1983:44–45).
31. Trudie Lamb Richmond has researched and written on the history of the Green Corn Ceremony in southern New England and has pointed out that preparation for the ceremony incited suspicions in colonists, who "often interpreted this flurry of activity as being a preparation for war because the warriors always carried a pouch of yokeg (traveling corn) to feed themselves" (Richmond 1989:24). According to Richmond, "Green corn is the high point of the summer cycle, epitomizing native people's relationship to all living and growing things." In turn, the wigwam symbolizes more than living space, it shelters and strengthens those spiritual ties as it embraces Mother Earth. The women with their mortars and pestles continually grinding corn also sustain that connection between the people and the spirit world" (25). It occurred "usually five days after

the full moon during the month of the ripening corn – when it is still green but edible (late August or early September)" and lasted for at least four days (Richmond 1991:13).

32. The Green Corn Ceremony also highlighted the importance of Native women's role as the primary agriculturalists in Native societies of southern New England (see Richmond 1989:25 and Merchant 1989:72–74). As Richmond observes, the "great preparation of corn" entailed in the Green Corn Ceremony was carried out by women: "their mortars and pestles continually grinding corn," Richmond explains, "sustain [the] connection between the people and the spirit world" (1989:25). As I discuss in chapter 4, the distinctly gendered aspect of Mohegans' resistance in the context of the 1736 ceremony was not lost on colonial officials. Connecticuts governor Talcott warned Mohegans that "if they would set up a queen or impostor, and not own Ben Uncas [II] for their Sachem or King," then the colonial government "would protect only Ben and his family, with those that adhered to him" (*Proc.* 1769:237). The colonial government ultimately sought to quell Mohegan resistance and silence Anne, named as a leader by Mohegans at the 1736 ceremony, by imposing a marriage between Anne and the son of Ben Uncas II (IND 1st, 1:236; TP 2:198).

33. This reference to the 1680 meeting and the subsequent reservation law is cited as an exhibit in the legal proceedings of the Mohegan land dispute with Connecticut. *The Book of Proceedings* also includes the report of "the committee appointed to hear the Indians" (*Proc.* 1769:x, 215–17). The Niantic people of Connecticut are often referred to in the historiography of the region as Western Niantics (or Western Nehantics [DeForest 1852:57; Caulkins 1895:20]) and were distinguished from the Eastern Niantics of Rhode Island (many of whom began to identify themselves as Narragansetts after King Philip's War; see Grumet 1995:69). In the eighteenth-century colonial records of Connecticut, the term *Western* is not used to identify the Niantics who lived on their reserved land in the town of Lyme; in addition, there are various spellings of Niantic that appear in the colonial records (e.g., Nahantick, Niantecutt, Nayantaquit; see Caulkins 1895:4, 24).

34. According to English law, petitioning was a right of all the monarchs "subjects," and as such even petitions from members of colonized populations required a response from colonial governments (Higginson 1986:2). The practice of petitioning thus allowed Native women and men

not only to articulate the dilemmas that shaped their daily lives but also to engage the colonial government and its laws directly.

35. This was made apparent in Governor Talcott's attack on the identity and political authority of Mahomet II (see chapter 4).
36. *Sunksquaw* is an Algonquian term for woman sachem. In the seventeenth century, colonist Roger Williams "translated the [Algonquian] term *saunks* as 'the Queen, or Sachims Wife,' with the plural 'Queenes' translating out as *sauncksquuaog*" (Grumet 1980:49). Grumet explains that while Williams did not acknowledge sunksquaws as "anything more than wives . . . the ethnographic record has indicated otherwise," establishing that "women were able to inherit chiefly office" (49). Native women in southern New England were engaged in other politically and economically significant activities before and during the colonial period, among the most important of which was their role as agriculturalists and sustainers of kin ties and community life (see Fawcett-Sayet 1988; Merchant 1989; O'Brien 1997; Richmond 1988; Richmond and Den Ouden 2003).
37. I draw this conclusion from comments made by Euro-Americans in college classrooms and at powwows, for instance, and in the news media. Jimmie Durham offers an important critique of Euro-American denials of the indigenous presence in the twentieth century, linking such denials to a history of genocide (Durham 1992:423–38). Euro-American anthropology and historiography have provided support for the notion that no "real Indians" exist in New England (see Baron, Hood, and Izard 1996:561; O'Connell 1992:xiii–lxxvii; Hauptman 1995:93).
38. Barbara Jean Fields's excellent essay "Ideology and Race in American History" is an extremely useful overview of the sociopolitical construction of race, revealing the absurdity of assumptions about "biological" or "innate" characteristics that are claimed to constitute distinct human groups. As she makes clear, the notion of race has a particular history: it is "neither the reflex of primordial attitudes nor a tragically recurring central theme." Rather, race is "constructed within the context of particular struggles in a particular historical moment" (Fields 1982:168–69). In U.S. history, "race became the ideological medium through which people posed and apprehended basic questions of power and dominance, sovereignty and citizenship, justice and right" (162). In a more recent study, sociologist Howard Winant traces the formation of white supremacy, and resistance to it, from the period of European colonial ex-

pansion to the twentieth century (Winant 2001:1–129). He explains that notions of race and racial hierarchy emerged out of and were reinvented in multiple contexts of struggle as European imperial states sought out wealth, resources, and labor in colonized territories (37–50). "By the early eighteenth century," Winant explains, "the existence of a divided, racialized world, a world system distinguishing systematically between persons and slaves, between Europeans and 'others,' between white and non-white, was a generally acknowledged, comprehensive phenomenon" (49). The racial categories that have been employed in the service of white supremacy served "to interpret and enforce developing inequalities within the laboring classes"; but "racial regimes," as Winant refers to them, have also worked to restrict "the political terrain upon which colonized and enslaved people, subaltern groups, could mobilize within civil society. It thus constituted these groups as outside what civil society there was" (93, 112). But Winant is also very concerned to show that racialized systems of rule have been formed against sustained resistance by those that have been categorized and exploited as racial "others" (51–129).

39. As is the case with all nations and peoples of the world, the Native peoples of the Americas are not, and never were, uniform in physical appearance (just as "whites," for instance, are not and never were uniform in physical appearance). Even a quick glance through Edward Curtis's famous photographs of the Native peoples of southwestern and western North America in the early twentieth century makes it quite plain that among Native Americans, as among Euro-Americans, African Americans, Asian Americans, and Latinos, there has always been a great diversity in, for example, facial features (see, for instance, Curtis's photographs in *Portraits from North American Indian Life* [1972]). The idea of the "pure Indian type" is a Euro-American racial fantasy. Nevertheless, it is a fantasy that continues to hold sway over Euro-American assessments of contemporary Native identities and concomitantly Native rights.

40. I have put the term "Indian tribes" in quotes here to stress that it is the federal government's definition of "tribe" that members of Native nations involved in the federal acknowledgment process must adhere to, which does not allow them to define themselves in terms of their own understandings of who they are. At a meeting with Eastern Pequot elders on the reservation in the early 1990s, an attorney working on the Eastern Pequots' federal acknowledgment project passed out a genealogy

chart to each elder, at the top of which were the words "pedigree chart." It was explained to the elders that documentation of their genealogies was required for the project, at which point many of them expressed resentment at the intrusiveness of the federal acknowledgment process and the suggestion – implied in the term "pedigree chart" – that they were being treated as animals rather than people (Den Ouden 1991–94: field notes). In my work as a researcher and consultant for the federal acknowledgment projects of the Golden Hill Paugussetts and Eastern Pequots, I have often heard such feelings of anger and resentment expressed about the invasive and indeed at times dehumanizing nature of the federal acknowledgement process. One Eastern Pequot man may have best summed up these responses to the process of having to prove one's identity according to objectifying, externally imposed standards when he remarked, "I'm tired of people trying to tell me that my grandmother lied to me" (Den Ouden 1991–94: field notes).

41. James Clifford, in his essay "Identity in Mashpee" (1988), discusses the problematic and destructive notion of cultural "authenticity" as it is imposed on Native Americans. As he points out, for Native people today, to be simply engaged in the modern world is to be "inauthentic" (from the perspective of Euro-Americans, that is). I want to emphasize here that my analysis of Native resistance in the eighteenth century neither assumes nor seeks a single authentic or "pure indigenous" Native voice, culture, or historical experience. Rather, it acknowledges that the Native people of Connecticut, like indigenous people throughout the Americas, did not uniformly experience or respond to colonial domination. Moreover, it acknowledges that all cultural identities embody multiple and often inharmonious understandings and expressions. The Euro-American racialized notion of "the Indian" does not, and never will, explain what it means to be Paugussett, for instance, in the eighteenth century or in the twentieth. Ultimately, I hope that an examination of reservation communities' resistance to dispossession in the eighteenth century will shed light on the connections between current and past discourses on Indianness and on the colonial roots of ideas about "racial purity" that have been deployed as weapons against Native people in their struggles to defend their land and sovereignty.

42. I have begun a detailed analysis of the production of racial discourse on Indianness in twentieth-century southern New England and presented preliminary findings in a paper given at the annual meeting of the Amer-

ican Anthropological Association in November 2002 (Den Ouden 2002). This essay is currently being expanded for publication under the working title "Scandalous Genealogies: 'Race' and 'Recognition' in Southern New England."

43. Den Ouden 2000–2002: oral history interview, April 2001; discussions of this event with the same elder were also recorded in a 1993 interview. In my most recent discussion with this elder about these events, he remembered that he had talked about the cross burnings with his mother, who told him that she and other Eastern Pequots knew who some of these men were, and that they were in fact local people, residents of Stonington and Mystic – in effect, "neighbors" of Eastern Pequots. A special feature section of the *Norwich Bulletin* entitled "Tillie's Past Times" noted recently that the Knights of the Ku Klux Klan's women held their "Old Home Day" Meeting on September 29, 1924, on "an open lot" at the Wheeler farm in Stonington, Connecticut: "more than 1,000 automobiles brought members of the order to the field" (September 29, 1999). The article also mentioned that "those preparing for 'Old Home Day' were in charge of the Mystic division of the Klan," thus indicating that the Klan was alive and well in southeastern Connecticut at the time. Indeed, a *Hartford Courant* feature section entitled "A Page from History" also pointed out recently that the Klan, in Connecticut as well as other parts of the United States, "was on its second wind in the 1920's," and that "the Republican Party's failure to denounce [the Klan] became a major 1924 political issue" in the state (*Hartford Courant*, May 13, 1998:F10).

44. For example, a committee appointed in 1774 by the General Assembly to investigate the "unsettled state" of "the Tribe of the Mohegan Indians" and determine whether there were among them "interlopers from other Tribes and Stragling Indians and Mollattoes," reported that "it is very Difficult to Distinguish between the whole blood and the part blood" (IND 1st, 2:312; see chapter 6).

45. This may reflect, as well, a Euro-American fear of "racial contamination" – that is, that an expanding reservation population might impinge upon and "infect" white society. Robert Young has pointed out that this notion of "racial contamination," rooted in European history, "can be traced all the way back to [Roman historian] Tacitus [ca. AD 55–117] and . . . was reinvoked in the United States by Confederate propagandists in the 1860's" (Young 1995:150). Young cites Edward Long's 1774 *History of Jamaica* as an important articulation of English colonizers' fear

of miscegenation, in this case between English and Africans. Long wrote that "in the course of a few generations more, the English blood will become so contaminated . . . till the whole nation resembles the Portuguese and the Moriscos in complexion of skin and baseness of mind. This is a venomous and dangerous ulcer, that threatens to disperse its malignancy far and wide, until every family catches infection from it" (cited in Young 1995:150). Young adds, however, that such racial thought also embodied colonial sexual fantasies, and "Long's comments reveal the extent to which his racism constantly teeters into what has now become the familiar structure of sexual attraction and repulsion" (150). By the late nineteenth century, Euro-American and European notions of racial contamination "fused with . . . increasing cultural pessimism" and with "the claim that not only the population of cities but the world itself, that is the West, was degenerating. Each new racial ramification of miscegenation traced an historical trajectory that betrayed a narrative of conquest, absorption and inevitable decline" (75).

46. In an article on the history of the Narragansett nation, historian Ruth Wallis Herndon and Narragansett elder and tribal historian Ella Wilcox Sekatau point out that "between 1750 and 1800 'Indians' disappeared from [town] records" in Rhode Island (Herndon and Sekatau 1997:445). As their research demonstrates, Euro-American racial categories served to obscure Narragansett identity, so that "by 1800 the town records contain only scattered references to 'Indians'; instead, 'Negroes' and 'blacks' fill the pages" (445).

47. According to Barry O'Connell, "the racial assignments in the federal census [in the nineteenth century] are rightly notorious for their inaccuracy and arbitrariness" (O'Connell 1992:xxvii n. 17), having no categories available for people who would have identified themselves as Pequot, for instance, since "one could only be 'white,' 'colored,' or 'mulatto' " (lxiii; see also Forbes 1993:199). Likewise, sociologist Sharon M. Lee explains that by 1890 the U.S. census categorized the U.S. population based on a dichotomy between "white" and "non-white" (Lee 1993:81). In the nineteenth century, individuals could not self-identify: enumerators designated a person's "race" based on "observation" – according to the "fundamental rule of measurement," which held that "the categories be mutually exclusive" (83).

48. Anthropologist Verena Stolcke explains that the idea of race as denoting biological, and therefore inherent and immutable (i.e., "natural")

inequalities, is rooted in mid-fifteenth-century Spain, when "converted Jews and Moriscos [converted Muslims], together with their ancestors and descendants . . . became objects of discrimination based on the doctrine of 'purity of blood'" (Stolcke 1991:24). Although this notion of "purity of blood" was "initially a Spanish product for domestic consumption," it "became most important in the [Latin American] colonies by the early eighteenth century," where it "lost any religious connotation, becoming a clearly racial notion" (25–27). As Stolcke argues, racial categories were employed in Latin American colonies to establish and enforce the sociopolitical hierarchy of colonial society. Likewise, the emergence of the idea of "Indian blood" in late-eighteenth-century Connecticut was linked to tactics of social control and dispossession.

49. In his discussion of history making as a form of domination created by European conquest states, anthropologist Edward Spicer argues that "each nation-state saw itself in the center of the stage of history, and chronicles were written accordingly. As dominant peoples continued to write from this viewpoint, they became less and less able to discern the presence, even in their immediate theater of history, of any other peoples besides themselves, except as temporary obstacles to their own dominance, as disappearing remnants, or as persisting, backward peoples unworthy to be regarded as in the same category with the dominant nation. The standardization of history was a destructive process, eliminating from the sphere of historical knowledge hundreds of peoples who, equally with the dominant peoples, had histories" (Spicer 1992:43–44; see also Hill 1996:16; Schmidt and Patterson 1995:5–14; Sider 1994:3–16; Silverblatt 1987:xix–xxv).

## 2. MANUFACTURING COLONIAL LEGITIMACY

1. There have been a number of important analyses of English colonial notions of "Indian savagery" during the early period of colonization in North America (e.g., Jennings 1971, 1975; Liggio 1976; Pearce 1952, 1988:1–35; Salisbury 1972). Francis Jennings argues that English conquest in New England entailed an ideological campaign that created the "myth of the Indian Menace," which depicts "the Indian as a ferocious wild creature, possessed of an alternately demonic and bestial nature, that had to be exterminated to make humanity safe" (Jennings 1975:213). Likewise, legal scholar Robert Williams explains that English notions about "the savage Indians' lack of rational capacity" and their "deficient

use of the 'unmanned wild country' of America" formed the crux of early-seventeenth-century conquest discourse, which was "a most potent instrument of empire" (Williams 1990:220; see also Waswo 1996).

2. The work of Edward Said has made perhaps the most important contribution to our understanding of the power of colonial discourse and its pervasive and grossly distorted, if not utterly fabricated, constructions of the non-Western "other" (Said 1979). Moreover, Said's emphasis on the connections between cultural production and the establishment, expansion, and legitimizing of empire reveals that imperial authority over non-Western territories and peoples is necessarily underpinned by non-military forms of control: the "persuasive means" that he refers to as "the quotidian processes of hegemony – very often creative, inventive, interesting, and above all executive" (Said 1993:109). Said demonstrates that imperialism yields its own art forms, while it also produces administrative and educational imperatives (108–10). Anthropology has been the classic example of the persuasive and creative articulation of Western imperialism, serving both the administrative and educational intentions of empire (see Asad 1973; Fabian 1983; and Said 1989).
3. Peter Hulme offers a definition of colonial discourse that highlights its administrative intent as well as its pervasiveness: it is "an ensemble of linguistically-based practices unified by their common deployment in the management of colonial relationships, an ensemble that could combine the most formulaic and bureaucratic of official documents . . . with the most non-functional, unprepossessing of romantic novels" (Hulme 1986:2).
4. In an important study, *The Rhetoric of Empire: Colonial Discourse in Journalism, Travel Writing, and Imperial Administration*, David Spurr contends that colonial discourse reflects a "constant uncertainty . . . a simultaneous avowal and disavowal of its own authority." This is apparent, he argues, in the Western obsession with scrutinizing, representing, and controlling the "savage other": "we assert authority over the savage both within us and abroad, but the very energy devoted to such an assertion acknowledges its own incompleteness *as* authority" (Spurr 1993:7).
5. In the context of seventeenth-century English imperial law, Indians were categorized as "aliens to the imperial dominion, or to the laws of England," as were all those who were not, by "natural or native birth," English subjects (Hurd 1968:316 n. 2; 320). As John Codman Hurd has explained, a legal distinction was made between two types of "aliens to

the empire." First, there were those "of white or European race," who were "native or domiciled subject[s] of some Christian nationality, or of such a state as was a recognized participant in the jurisdiction of public international law"; when "aliens" of this category became domiciled inhabitants of a colony, they became subject to the charters and laws of "naturalization" applied to any "inhabitant of English birth or descent" and thus were under the protection of public international law when in that colony or any other within the English empire (320–21). However, Native American and African peoples, as well as "every alien of a barbarian or heathen race" existing within the geographic territory of the English empire, were subject primarily to local colonial law, even if they were to be acknowledged by the imperial sovereign as "domiciled inhabitants" themselves (321–22). Thus "while the legal condition of the African or Indian inhabitant, in any particular jurisdiction, might vary therein, from chattel slavery – the negation of all legal rights – to the possession of all individual and relative rights of a private person known to the common law of England, that condition rested, apparently, only on the local law of that jurisdiction, and was not supported therein by a law of the national power, having national extent and recognition as a law of the national or imperial jurisdiction" (322). The point here is that while colonizers may have built from imperial legal theory and English notions of "savagery" in imposing a system of domination in New England, they also created their own strategies of rule and their own cultural forms of control.

6. See Roy Harvey Pearce's *Savagism and Civilization: A Study of the Indian and the Puritan Mind*, for an analysis of colonial constructions of Indianness and their implications for Euro-American identity and history. In his discussion of seventeenth-century colonial ruminations on Indianness in New England, Pearce explains that "precisely because the Puritan was so deeply concerned with the meaning of the Indian for the whole of his culture, he hardly could conceive of describing that Indian disinterestedly" (Pearce 1988:26). For Euro-Americans in the following centuries, "the Indian" was to be "understood as one who had not and somehow could not progress into the civilized, who would inevitably be destroyed by the civilized"; for "the Indian" had come to be cast as a "*remnant*" of "a savage past": "To study him was to study the past. To civilize him was to triumph over the past. History would thus be the key to the moral worth of cultures; the history of American civilization would thus be conceived

of as three-dimensional, progressing from past to present, from east to west, from lower to higher" (49).

Enmeshed notions of Indianness and "inevitable" historical process (even the notion of a divinely preordained destiny to conquer and control "others") remain alive in Euro-American society. How and when such notions were asserted or manipulated in the context of Native-Anglo struggles over land rights and political authority in the late seventeenth and eighteenth century reveal much about the nature of nonmilitary processes of conquest and point to important connections between past and present strategies of domination. Native peoples in 1990s Connecticut who have petitioned for federal acknowledgment or brought land claims to court have been cast as "remnants" and impostors, and government officials who have opposed federal acknowledgment have evoked colonial law and colonial notions of the "right of conquest" in an effort to invalidate Native assertions of sovereignty (or "tribal existence," as government terminology has wrought it). Euro-American ideas about the right and necessity of conquest and domination, as I have noted in chapter 1, underpin popular Euro-American opposition to federal acknowledgment in Connecticut and are often cast in overtly racist terms (see chapter 6).

7. Historian Louis B. Wright, in his volume *The Atlantic Frontier: Colonial American Civilization, 1607–1763*, argues that while Indians were considered by seventeenth-century colonists to be a "problem" to be pondered, there was ultimately only one solution: "The Indians within the colonies were a disturbing problem to the peace and consciences of Europeans. Pious folk earnestly debated whether the redskins were children of God or the devil. If of the devil, they might be destroyed in good conscience and their land appropriated to Christian use. This view had much in its favor. A few charitable souls, like gentle John Eliot, the missionary, believed that Christ in his mercy meant to save even Indian souls, and to reserve at least a portion of land for their sustenance . . . but in general, the good Indian in the seventeenth century, as in the nineteenth, was a dead Indian" (Wright 1963:9).

How colonial hostility toward Indianness, linked always to the desire for Native lands, was reproduced, justified, and *masked as something else*, in the context of nonmilitary struggles or confrontations (e.g., "converting" the Indians, a project that was not detached from the process of dispossession) remains a crucial historical problem to explore and analyze. The discourse of the "gentle" missionaries, as I am arguing here, is telling on this point and sheds light on the means by which a racial notion of Indianness was formulated and deployed to explain, and obscure, history.

8. According to William Kellaway, the "extreme claim that God had expressly reserved for English use the land of North America was widely advanced in England by the beginning of the seventeenth century," along with "its corollary – that the Indians had no right to the land" (Kellaway 1975:2).

9. S. L. Mershon's *English Crown Grants* summarizes the connection between "Indian savagery" and the justification of imperial land claims thus: "Impressions formed and conclusions arrived at by European authorities based upon such erroneous information [i.e., that Indians were "better classed among the wild animals of the forest than to be considered a part of the human family"] developed the doctrine which became woven into international law, that the American Indians were nomads or wanderers; that they were pagans and had no real vested or true title to the soil they occupied, and that they were unworthy of or in fact did not possess any real national life or substantial political existence" (Mershon 1918:93).

10. Roger Williams, for instance, wrote with admiration about the efficiency and cooperative nature of Narragansetts' agricultural practices in 1643, concluding that Narragansetts demonstrated that "by concord little things grow great" (Williams 1810:221). William Cronon's *Changes in the Land: Indians, Colonists, and the Ecology of New England* (1983:19–53) offers an excellent discussion of Native economies in seventeenth-century New England. Historian Neal Salisbury explains that agriculture "had replaced hunting as the principal source of food for Indians in southern New England by the seventeenth century" (Salisbury 1982:31). See also Nabokov and Snow, who observe that, by the time of Columbus's invasion of the Americas, "techniques for growing and storing vegetables had been developing in the Northeast for four or five centuries" (1992:126).

11. According to English international law, the "right of discovery" was to have given the monarch "the sole right of acquiring the soil from the natives as against all other European powers" (Kent 1896:597); yet this right was not in itself considered to serve as the extinguishment of Native land rights, understood by Europeans at the time as a "right of occupancy" (597). The notion that the monarch was the sole source of

legal title to colonized land was challenged by some seventeenth- and eighteenth-century colonists in Connecticut, who claimed title to particular lands by their own individual purchases from Native people (referred to as the "purchase of Native right"), which were unapproved by the General Assembly (see chapter 3). It should also be noted that royal charters did not clearly define the nature of Native land rights and were, according to Kent, "blank paper so far as the rights of the natives were concerned" (Kent 1896:384). In the colony of Connecticut, how this "blank paper" on Native rights was to be inscribed was not finally decided by the military conquests of the seventeenth century but remained a matter of debate into and beyond the eighteenth century.

12. Such acts of "taking possession" were also a means by which Native land was rendered a commodity; and indeed the commodification of land lay at the core of the colonial politico-economic system in New England. John Frederick Martin, in his book *Profits in the Wilderness: Entrepreneurship and the Founding of New England Towns in the Seventeenth Century*, explains that, for New England colonists, "the need for commerce in land . . . was greater than it had ever been in England": "Although in England their wealth had consisted of many things, now it lay largely in land. In New England there were little money, capital, and labor; but land and its products abounded. By default land was the principal capital of seventeenth-century America" (Martin 1991:123).

13. As Jennings notes, English colonists believed that Indians had "only a 'natural' and not a 'civil' right" to the land – a right that "need not be respected in the same way as civil right; only the latter imposed the obligations of true legal property" (Jennings 1975:82; see also Seed 1995:39). In English law, as well as subsequent colonial and Euro-American law in North America, the term *property* does not refer to things but to "rights in or to things" (MacPherson 1978:2; see also Harris 1953:1–3). As such, property is "an enforceable claim" that implies "a political relation between persons": "That property is political is evident. The idea of an enforceable claim implies that there be some body to enforce it . . . so property is a political phenomenon" (MacPherson 1978:4). Eric Cheyfitz aptly observes, however, that "property" is also an English cultural notion that should not be applied to indigenous relationships to land and notions of land rights in the colonial period. Cheyfitz explains that "the use of the English terms property, possession, and ownership to refer to the Algonquians' land usages in seventeenth-century New Eng-

land risks collapsing the cultures and histories of these peoples into . . . English histories . . . *which was precisely the prime mode of expropriation that the colonists used in their 'legal' dealings with the Indians*" (Cheyfitz 1991:48; emphasis added). Cheyfitz contends that investigating "the politics of cultural translation" (xv) is essential to understanding the colonial appropriation of the "New World": "the process of translation, initiated by Columbus and perpetuated by the European voyagers who followed him, prepares the way for and is forever involved in the dispossession by which Native American land was translated (the term is used in English common law to refer to transfers of real estate) into the European identity of property" (43).

14. There were, of course, other crucial cultural forms through which the indigenous landscape was officially overwritten. Colonial maps are an important example. J. B. Harley investigates colonial cartography as "a classic form of power knowledge" and explains that mapmaking was integral to the process of establishing control over indigenous populations while also serving as a means of obfuscating Native histories and identities (Harley 1994:287).
15. Benjamin Bissell points out that by the eighteenth century, European interest in "the question of the Indian's origins provoked the wildest speculations, and an amazing bulk of pseudo-scientific theorizing" (Bissell 1925:8). This was the period during which the idea of "the noble savage" emerged and was popularized by Rousseau. Bissell explains that Rousseau's praising of "the Indian" as existing in a "state of nature" was intended to encourage envy, but that "keeping Indians in a 'state of nature' was a very practical means of legitimizing their dispossession" (44). A "noble savage," like any other "savage" in European imaginations, was ultimately devoid of land rights.
16. In his brilliant examination of the formation and literary and "scientific" articulation of European and Euro-American racial thought in the context of imperial expansion and domination, Robert Young argues that notions about "culture and race developed together, imbricated within each other" (Young 1995:28). As it was produced and manipulated in the realm of imperial power relations, the idea of culture "has always been comparative" and focused upon "producing the other"; thus "racism has always been an integral part of it: the two are inextricably clustered together, feeding off and generating each other. Race has always been culturally constructed. Culture has always been racially constructed" (54).

17. The question of the density of Native populations of the Americas during the sixteenth and seventeenth centuries (the initial colonial invasion periods) remains an important aspect of *contemporary* Euro-American conquest mythology (see Campbell 1994). The reason is rather obvious: the more "thinly" populated the continents, the more justifiable the conquests.
18. I should note that Gookin's text must be viewed in the context of what was, by the late seventeenth century, an established European tradition of anthropological and political writings on the indigenous peoples of the Americas, of which the "authoritative canon," as Anthony Pagden explains, demanded that writers establish textual authority via the claim to eyewitness experience. The lauded early historians of Spanish America – such as Oviedo and Las Casas – explicitly and repeatedly asserted the authenticity of their accounts of Indians (and, in Las Casas's case in particular, of the nature of conquest) through autobiographical references and the assertion of firsthand observations (see Pagden 1993:51–87). Pagden points out that "the appeal to the authority of the eye witness, to the privileged understanding which those present at an event have over all those who have only read or been told about it" – which is "in ancient rhetoric called 'autopsy' " – "was to dominate the long and bitter struggle over the nature, representation and status of the New World and its inhabitants. The ability to 'bear witness' . . . was also to sharpen the boundary which divided the Old World from the New, and the 'them' from the 'us' " (51–52).
19. The *Oxford English Dictionary* indicates that the term *compound* had, at the time, a particular cultural usage. It cites this phrase from Hobbes's *Leviathan* (1651) as an example: "When a man compoundeth the image of his own person with the image of the actions of another man." It seems clear that Eliot asserted a similar notion of a purported cultural "merging" with Indians in his use of the term here, one intended to emphasize the beneficence of the colonial presence in New England.
20. As I explain later in the chapter, missionaries Eleazar Wheelock and Experience Mayhew, for instance, reported that New England Natives' rejection of Christianity was tied to their resentment of Christians who stole their land; indeed Mayhew, during his "visitations" to Mohegans, Pequots, and Narragansetts in 1713 and 1714, was chastised on this point by Narragansett sachem Ninigret. Eliot, as well, knew that "increasing colonial land hunger" was "one of the most difficult problems con-

fronting the missionaries of New England – to which no satisfactory solution was ever found" (Kellaway 1975:85–87).

21. Thus the extraction of the body itself from the site of cultural and "racial" production is deemed necessary to attempt to effect the transformation from "savagery" to "civilization." Here it is instructive to consider Michel Foucault's discussion of the historical development, in seventeenth- and eighteenth-century Europe, of a form of state power that was focused on control of both the *individual body* and of *populations*. The very idea of populations, as a focus of scientific study and state surveillance, was itself a new idea in the eighteenth century (Foucault 1980:25). What Foucault calls "biopower" is rooted in a sovereign's claim to "a right of seizure" (of "things, time, bodies, and ultimately life itself") and poses "the biological existence of a population" as a main concern or problem with which the state must contend (136–37). The state thus "endeavors to administer, optimize, and multiply [life], subjecting it to precise controls and comprehensive regulations" (137). Foucault's discussion in this instance does not examine biopower as it took shape in colonial settings, but it is nonetheless directly relevant to colonial projects of domination and particularly the colonial construction and policing of racial hierarchy (see Stoler 2002:140–61). Biopower deploys particular techniques of control that are focused on "the species body," the regulation of which was preeminently a political matter (Foucault 1980:139–43). Thus this form of power that claims to "take charge of life" requires "continuous regulatory and corrective mechanisms. . . . Such a power has to qualify, measure, appraise, and hierarchize" (144). As I suggest here, the colonial construction and policing of "racial" hierarchy in eighteenth-century southern New England – evidenced in the discourse and proposed strategies of the "civilizing" mission (e.g., Wheelock's call for systematic "removals") – identified individual Indian bodies, as well as "the Indian" as a body politic, as the targets of necessary governmental manipulation and control.

22. From Experience Mayhew, "A brief Journal of my visitation of the Pequot & Mohegin Indians, at the desire of the Honorable Commissioners for the Propogation of the Gospel among the Indians in New England &c. 1713," pp. 97–127, in *Some Correspondence Between the Governors and Treasurers of the New England Company in London and the Commissioners of the United Colonies of America, the Missionaries of the Company, and Others Between the Years 1657 and 1712* (1896).

23. Skuttaub, or Scattup, as he is also referred to (see McBride 1996 and Campisi 1990), may have been recognized by colonial officials at the time as the "chief" sachem among Mashantuckets, but there was another important Mashantucket leader at the time, Robin Cassacinamon II, who had petitioned the General Assembly along with Scattup in May of 1713 to complain against colonial encroachment at Noank and to request that the General Assembly secure Mashantuckets' rights there (IND 1st, 1:75; see chapter 5). Following the General Assembly's abolishment of the Noank reservation in 1714, Scattup appears to have decided to accommodate the demands of Grotons town proprietors, while Cassacinamon II, as his 1721 petition to the General Assembly indicates, refused to acquiesce to colonial demands for Mashantucket land.

24. Joseph was the son of Cattapassett, who had been a sachem among the Eastern Pequots at the Stonington reservation (CR 4:86). Mayhew notes that Joseph was at the time a sachem of the Niantics at the Lyme reservation, which suggests that colonially imposed reservation boundaries had not undermined kinship ties nor prevented possibilities for political cooperation between neighboring reservation communities.

25. As scholars have noted, Native women in seventeenth-century southern New England had an important role in yielding the end product of subsistence hunting. Indeed, the gendered division of labor in coastal Algonquian societies did not prevent cooperative or complementary participation by men and women in most subsistence activities (see Merchant 1989:82 and Nabokov and Snow 1992:126–27). While women were the primary agriculturalists in southern New England Native societies (see Salisbury 1982:30; Cronon 1983:44–46; Merchant 1989:80–82), "both men and women participated in fishing and seafood gathering" (Merchant 1989:82). And in the fall and winter, when men hunted bear or deer, women "hauled dead game back to camp," where they "butchered and processed it, preparing the hides for clothing, cooking the meat, and smoking some of it for use later in the winter" (Cronon 1983:46–47).

26. In Connecticut, particularly between 1723 and 1725, such transgressions could have deadly consequences, since, as I explain in the following chapter, laws intended to restrict the mobility of local Native populations during the imperial border wars served to classify Native men who moved beyond the bounds of reservations and into "restricted" areas, for whatever reason, as "enemy Indians." Colonists who took the scalps

of "enemy Indians" were offered a hefty bounty by the Connecticut government.

27. Mohegans' hunting grounds, for instance, did not lie within the lands that had been officially designated by the colony as their "sequestered" land in the late seventeenth century; yet Mohegans in the early eighteenth century continued to argue for their right to hunt on those lands and contested the Connecticut General Assembly's bestowal of these lands to the town of Colchester in 1699 (see Mohegan petition, October 1703 [IND 1st, 1:52], cited in chapter 3).

28. As historian Colin Calloway has noted, there is an important irony to acknowledge here: although "European missionaries and other groups intent on 'civilizing' Indians urged them to give up hunting and concentrate on farming . . . many European settlers who lived in the backcountry were becoming more dependent on hunting and less tied to agriculture" (Calloway 1997:55). Calloway explains that while "seventeenth-century Puritans had feared the wilderness; by the mid-eighteenth century, backcountry settlers were living and hunting on it, much as the Indians did" (55–56). And thus colonists' "Indian-style" hunting was a means of laying claim to Natives' own hunting lands.

## 3. COLONIAL LAW AND NATIVE LIVES

1. The "common and undivided lands" of colonial towns were controlled by town proprietors, who were "the original grantees or purchasers of a tract of land, usually a township" (Akagi 1963:3). Town proprietors not only owned and controlled the lands that were granted to them, but they were also town developers: that is, they "were responsible for inducing and enlisting settlers and newcomers, for locating home lots and dwelling houses, for building highways and streets, for subdividing the adjacent arable land, and subjecting the meadow and forest . . . to a common management" (3).

2. See chapter 4 for further discussion of the details of this petition.

3. As I explain in this and subsequent chapters, Natives' petitions against encroachment and the reports of overseers or General Assembly committees detail the destruction to crops and fences by Anglos' livestock and the instances of the theft of timber and threats of physical violence to reservation communities (e.g., IND 1st, 1:52, 1:101, 1:132, 2:44, 2:147, 2:149).

4. The General Assembly was not, nor did it act as, a monolithic political

entity. The colonial government in eighteenth-century Connecticut was embroiled in its own internal power struggles, which were evidenced, for example, in some cases of dissension between the upper and lower house, the two branches of the General Assembly. The upper house consisted of "Magistrates or Assistants elected by the freemen at large; and the lower . . . of Deputies or representatives chosen by the several towns" (Riley 1896:128). Both houses of the assembly "occupied the same chamber, and were presided over by the Governor or Deputy Governor" (128). The assembly met for a fall and a spring session, the former for making laws and the latter for electing officers; and as Riley explains, "the legislative power of this court extended over the whole colony and was practically unrestricted" (128). While "the election of local officers and the management of local affairs were left entirely to the towns," the General Court (known by the eighteenth century as the General Assembly) held "an indefinite power of supervision" (Johnston 1883:16). The extent of the English Crown's control over colonial governments was a source of internal contention as well, and in the eighteenth century the lower houses of New England's colonial governments "engaged in a successful quest for power as they set about to restrict the authority of the executive [the colonial governors], undermine the system of colonial administration laid down by imperial and proprietary authorities, and make themselves paramount in the affairs of their respective colonies"(Greene 1967:426). Greene's summation of the precise means by which the lower houses gained their power is important to an understanding of how colonial law impacted Natives struggles against dispossession: "in the course of routine business" throughout the eighteenth century, lower houses were "quietly and simply extending and consolidating their authority by passing laws and establishing practices, the implications of which escaped both colonial executives and imperial authorities" (431–32). In eighteenth-century Connecticut the General Assembly's attempt to throw off the yoke of imperial authority was demonstrated in the context of the Mohegan land controversy, ultimately to the detriment of Mohegans seeking the Crown's protection of their remaining lands (see chapter 4).

5. William Wheeler was the son of Isaac Wheeler, a resident of Stonington, Connecticut. In 1683 the Connecticut government purchased land from Isaac Wheeler for the purpose of creating a 280-acre reservation for Eastern Pequots, who would be commonly referred to in the eigh-

teenth century as the Pequots at Stonington. Upon a 1683 order of the General Assembly, colonists James Avery and Thomas Leffingwell were appointed a committee to purchase the land for Eastern Pequots, then known by the colonial government as "Pequots under Momoho." In the 1660s this Pequot community had attempted to live and plant at a place called Cossatuck, near Stonington, but colonists there objected to their presence, so the General Assembly decided to "remove" them to Stonington. Thus in 1683 Leffingwell and Avery purchased the 280 acres from Isaac Wheeler to reserve for Eastern Pequots (IND 1st, 2:41). The committee looking into the complaint made by Mary Momoho and other Eastern Pequots in 1749 does not cite the precise wording of the deed with regard to the nature of Eastern Pequots' legal rights to that land, but it did indicate that Wheeler's deed retained rights for himself to the 280-acre reservation, by which Wheeler claimed a right to "the whole benefit of Their fields for my Cattle Horses." "The Indians" were to "Secure Themselves by Fencing" (2:41). The General Assembly approved the deed in October 1683. Exactly where within this 280-acre tract Eastern Pequots were to be able to plant and harvest crops without the continual risk of their destruction by livestock was not made clear.

6. Neither this petition nor the General Assembly's response to it is recorded with a date. Three other petitions from the Eastern Pequot reservation community to the General Assembly in the first half of the eighteenth century, in 1723, 1749, and 1750, indicate that Mary Momoho held a position of leadership in her community for at least twenty-five years. It seems likely that Mary Momoho became a leader in the early eighteenth century, and that this petition was submitted before the 1723 petition. Both petitions begin with a reminder to the colonial government of Momoho's previous service to the colony during King Philip's War in 1675. This petition also refers to Isaac Wheeler as "now being dead" (IND 1st, 1:73). Since he died in 1712 (see Wheeler 1887), it seems likely that this petition was submitted not long after his death. The way in which the petition is concluded – "These from the sunks squaw which was the wife of Momoho and her men" – suggests that this was Mary Momoho's first formal introduction of herself as a leader and petitioner.

7. Over a hundred Mohegans and Pequots were recruited in 1675 to serve the colony during King Philip's War (*Wyllys Papers* 1924:228). In 1676 James Fitch reported that Mohegan and Pequot soldiers were "so wearie . . . that they are not willing to move" and that they were "not sat-

isfied with the conditions propounded" (*Wyllys Papers* 1924:246). Colonial accounts indicate that Native men in Connecticut were reluctant to be recruited as English colonizers' "allies" in border wars with France. In July 1700, during King William's War, John Tracy wrote to Fitz John Winthrop that "our English soldiers wait and loose their time for want of Indians not knowing the woods nor manners of that work, & Indians we can git none. I have taken all the pains & care I can in goeing & sending to the Indians but attain nothing . . . I would humbly offer my thoughts concerning the matter that it be [thoroughly] prosecuted . . . if prosecuted the Indians must be engaged to have their men ready before hand & some of them to take it as their work" (Hoadly 1932:163–64). In 1704, during Queen Anne's War, Connecticut officials wrote that they "doe not fully concur to send out [100] Indians against the Enemy . . . Our Indians are but few in number and are scattered some a hunting & the people are suspitious that some have been with the enemy in the late mischief at Deefield [the French raid of February 29, 1704], and we are doubtful whether any will be prevailed with to undertake the service, the late calamity flushing of them in opinion of themselves" (172–73).

8. In 1675 the Momoho referred to here was designated by colonial officials as a "chief counselor" to another Eastern Pequot leader, Herman Garret, who had been appointed as "principle officer" of Pequots (CR 2:574–76).
9. Historian Francis Jennings discusses the "deed game" as a tactic employed by colonists in seventeenth-century New England to "seize Indian property with some show of legality" (Jennings 1975:144). See chapters 4 and 5 for further discussion of how colonial committees operated in the context of Mohegans' and Mashantuckets' efforts to resist dispossession.
10. Native people in Connecticut began to be taken as slaves by colonizers after the Pequot massacre; in the eighteenth century they were taken as indentured servants in significant numbers. English colonists did not consider Indians to be adequate servants, however, since they frequently escaped (Lauber 1913) and were perceived as a general threat to the social order (Kawashima 1978; Weld 1933).
11. Warner explains that by the early eighteenth century, laws directed at controlling Native American and African "servants and slaves" took "a race classification form and tended to become discriminatory" (Warner 1935:328). But "free" persons of color were also subjected to the racialized system of social control. In the 1720s, when "Negroes" were pre-

sumed to be responsible for a number of fires in Boston, and "a slave revolt was feared," "strict repressive regulations were enacted" and were directed at enslaved Indians and Africans as well as "free 'Indians, Negroes, or Mulattos' " (328). Warner explains as well that by the beginning of the eighteenth century the practice of "rating" enslaved Africans and Indians as chattel in tax assessments – comparable, as Sewall noted, to "horses and hogs" – had become "custom" (329 n. 3).

12. "Indian treachery" was evidenced, for instance, in this comment of Robert Treat to Fitz John Winthrop in 1700 regarding the Native peoples who inhabited the western "frontier" of the colony: "Ye Scattacook Indians alwayes since ye warr [i.e., King Philip's War] have been ready to vent their mallice if they durst. . . . I have been also apt to think if there be such a designe against ye English [that] ye Podatuck & Oweantinuck Indians may know of it and therefore have sent to Capt. Minor of Woodberry to . . . pump some of their Indians if they know of anie designe on foot against the English" (Hoadly 1932:165).

    Historian Harold Selesky contends that the famous French raid on Deerfield, Massachusetts, in 1704 "grabbed Connecticut's attention by showing how unexpected, devastating and uncomfortably close a raid could be" (Selesky 1990:49). Consequently, Connecticut "ordered towns to fortify to reduce their vulnerability to surprise attack," "established a system of scouts, reinforced the more western towns, paid residents to guard themselves (which it had refused to do during King Philip's War), and even restricted the movements of Indians within the colony" (49).

13. Legislators indicate that this was to apply primarily to "the Western Indians, living in the County of Fairfield and New Haven" (IND 1st, 1:117). Presumably, they were referring to Paugussett people, since they list the location of the "Western Indians" as New Milford, Potatuck, Pequannuck, and Lonetown, all within the territory of the Paugussett nation (see Wojciechowski 1985). As the legislators explained it, "Western Indians" were suspected of many "notorious villanys" and so had been "confined below the Country Road in sd County" (1:117).

14. The final wording of the law made it clear that if any Natives throughout Connecticut should "paint their faces . . . as is usual for them," they would be "taken for Enemies and dealt with accordingly" (IND 1st, 1:117).

15. In October 1744 it was ordered that "the Indians that live within our frontier towns" were to be given not only limits within which they must be confined but also a "badge by which they shall be known" (CR 6:76).

16. The town of Colchester (adjacent to Hebron) encompasses Mohegan hunting lands and was established by the General Assembly in 1699 under questionable circumstances; Colchester was subsequently among the lands in dispute during the course of the Mohegan case in the eighteenth century. See chapter 4 for further discussion.
17. In her book *Women and the Law of Property in Early America*, Marilyn Salmon points out that Puritan lawmakers in seventeenth-century Connecticut and Massachusetts "changed English law on conveyancing, dower, and marriage settlements to reduce the possibility of separate marital interests," and thus "they increased mens power to control their wives estates, eliminating or changing [English] procedures designed to protect women from coercion," such as the English law requiring that a husband retain his wife's signature before attempting to sell land his wife brought to the marriage (Salmon 1986:7–8). As she explains, requiring a wife's signature on a land deed, for instance, not only made "conveyancing more expensive and time-consuming, it also contradicted a central tenet of Puritanism: the wife's submission to her husband's will" (8). She notes, as well, that "Connecticut, even more than Massachusetts, tended to restrict the independent property rights of wives" (9). The 1717 measures may reflect colonial officials' concern to impose similar restrictions on Native women, which would thus further undermine Native communities' collective land rights and potentially serve to justify the abolishment of reservation lands altogether.
18. Although some scholars have debated the question of whether seventeenth-century Native societies in southern New England were matrilineal (see O'Brien 1997), others assert that they were indeed (Grumet 1980:46; Herndon and Sekatau 1997), and that rights to agricultural lands passed through women (Nabokov and Snow 1992). It is clear that Native women in seventeenth- and eighteenth-century southern New England engaged in activities of immense political, cultural, and economic importance to their communities (see Plane 1996; Grumet 1980; Richmond and Den Ouden 2003). It is important to note here that women were particularly important to alliance making between Native communities, and to community formation itself, after the Pequot massacre, as efforts made by Niantic and Mohegan male leaders to marry Pequot women in the aftermath of the massacre suggest. Roger Williams reported to colonial officials that the Eastern Niantic sachem Wequashcook had married the mother of the dead Pequot sachem Sassacus and

was harboring a number of Pequot refugees after the massacre (Roger Williams 1988:117). LaFantasie, editor of Williams's correspondence, explains that the marriage "strengthened Wequashcook's rights to lands that overlapped into the Pequot Country, gave him added rights to incorporate Pequot survivors into his band, and allowed him, at the very least, to demand hunting rights in the Pequot territory" (121). Roger Williams reported, as well, that the Mohegan sachem Uncas, in marrying the sister of Sassacus, "hath drawn all the scattered Pequts to himselfe and drawne much wealth from them" (146). At least part of the "wealth" men like Uncas and Wequashcook had acquired through their marriages to these Pequot women, in addition to the economic benefit of access to Pequot lands and the political benefit of strengthening the numbers within their own communities, was cultural capital. Native women were not simply tokens of kinship or producers of offspring; they were purveyors of both cultural identities and ties to land. There is also the overlooked likelihood that these women were sought after by Wequashcook and Uncas because they had considerable political savvy and influence themselves. As anthropologist Eleanor Leacock observes, anthropologists, often too readily assuming male power, have failed to adequately examine "the very nature of 'politics' and 'power' themselves" in Native societies in northeastern North America (Leacock 1983:17–18; see also Klein and Ackerman 1995:8). "It is not enough to repeat that in such societies the 'political' sphere is scarcely separable from the social"; rather, Leacock contends, there are "two basic sociopolitical principles that govern decision making" in these societies: "first, the parties who are responsible for carrying a decision out or who are directly affected by it must have a share in making it commensurate with their experience and wisdom; and, second, those who do not agree to a decision are not bound by it" (Leacock 1983:20). This becomes particularly important with respect to an investigation of colonial "purchases" of Native lands and the colonial notion that (male) sachems had the right, unilaterally, to "sell" land. It seems highly unlikely that in communities where sachems were facilitators of decision making rather than autocratic rulers, Native women, as the agriculturalists and primary food producers, would have readily accepted such a practice.

19. It might be argued that colonial legislators were simply attempting to impose on Native communities the same patriarchal social order that existed within their own communities, in order to better incorporate

Indians into colonial society. But eighteenth-century Indian policy in Connecticut, particularly as it was expressed in the laws regarding slavery and limitations on the movement of Native populations, indicates that the colonial government had little interest in incorporating Native women and men into Anglo communities as citizens with comparable rights. As the 1717 measures state, the proposed "Native village" was to be just that: a village set apart from Anglo communities, not integrated with them.

20. Francis Jennings explains that although colonists in New England frequently made individual purchases of Native lands, eventually "all colonial governments outlawed the purchase of Indian land by private persons, because the practice had led to circumvention of laws regarding the distribution of property. Privately purchased 'Indian titles' frequently conflicted with governmental intentions and also led to endless litigation over purchase of fraudulent titles. At certain times and places private purchases of the same land were made by persons subject to different colonial governments, whereupon their property claims became the basis for competition over jurisdiction" (Jennings 1975:130; see also Bushman 1967:84–103).

21. According to Connecticut governor Joseph Talcott's population figures for 1725, the Mohegan population totaled 351 individuals, making theirs the largest Native community in the colony, followed by the Pequot communities at the Mashantucket reservation in Groton (321) and at the reservation in Stonington (218), and Niantics at their reservation in Lyme (163). All within the county of New London, these four reservation communities comprised approximately three quarters of the entire indigenous population of the colony at the time: Talcott's figures put the total indigenous population in Connecticut in 1725 at 1,390, with 1,053 Native people in New London county alone (TP 2:99–402).

22. Jennings notes that seventeenth-century colonial leaders "were very ready to abandon their early theses about Indian land being free for the taking when the takers were people other than themselves" (Jennings 1975:143–44). More important, he adds that the various means by which colonizers established interprovincial boundaries, for instance, "requires attention to its own circumstances, because official acceptance of Indian property right did not guarantee ethical practices in Englishmen's acquisition of those rights" (144).

## 4. "ONLY AN INDIAN'S STORY"

1. Legal scholar Mark D. Walters (1995) gives an excellent overview of the legal case, but his analysis is focused more on illuminating colonial and imperial perspectives on the dispute, while I am interested in examining Mohegans' strategies of resistance during the dispute and their local political and historical significance.
2. The Connecticut government enlisted Mohegan men to serve in King Philip's War in 1675 and subsequently in the imperial border wars of the early eighteenth century. In 1675, for instance, Connecticut authorities recruited "above an hundred Moheages and Pequots" (*Wyllys Papers* 1924:228). Mohegans and other Native men in Connecticut did not necessarily serve willingly in these wars, however. In 1676 James Fitch reported that Mohegan and Pequot soldiers were "so wearie . . . that they are not willing to move," and that they were "not satisfied with the conditions propounded" (246). John Tracy, complaining to Connecticut governor Fitz-John Winthrop in 1700 about the inadequacies of English border scouts, stated that he had "taken all the pains & care I can in goeing & sending to the Indians but attain nothing" (Hoadly 1932:163). He advised the governor that "the matter . . . be throwly [thoroughly] prosecuted . . . if prosecuted the Indians must be ingaged to have their men ready" (163–64). The account of a Captain Williams, who "command[ed] a company of Mohegan Indians" in Deerfield, Massachusetts, in 1724 indicates that the demands placed on Native men by the colonial government during the border wars drew them away, unwillingly, from matters important to their reservation community, namely their participation in subsistence activities. Williams reported that Mohegan men were "impatient to return and be at home, to gather their corn" and that they "will not be perswaded to stay there till the leaves fall from the trees" (CR 6:61).
3. According to Smith, Connecticut officials held that Owaneco's initial complaint to the queen was groundless and had been "originated in attempts of Nicholas Hallam [an attorney for Mohegans], Joseph Dudley [governor of Massachusetts and head of the 1705 commission], and other foes to discredit the colony in the eyes of the imperial authorities" (Smith 1950:424).
4. Captain John Mason inherited his role as Mohegans' guardian and adviser from his grandfather, Major John Mason, in the late seventeenth century. In 1711 he resigned but was subsequently entreated by Mohegan

sachem Ben Uncas I to take up the position again in 1723. The General Assembly granted Ben Uncas's request and allowed Captain Mason to live on Mohegan reserved land (see TP 1:9).

5. I draw these designations for Mohegan sachems (e.g., Ben Uncas "II") from Mohegan sources: namely, Mohegans' Federal Acknowledgement Petition (vol. 1, 1984) and Mohegan tribal historian Melissa Fawcett's *The Lasting of the Mohegans* (1995).

6. As it was later summarized by the 1743 commission of review, Owaneco's petition to the queen made the following complaint: "That in several treaties between the said Moheagans and the said English subjects of Connecticut, it had been agreed that the said Indians should be protected in the possession of their said reserved lands. That contrary to the said treaties and to common justice, the government of Connecticut had passed an act or order in their general court or assembly, by which they had taken from the said Indians that small tract of land which those Indians had reserved to themselves, and were possessed of as aforesaid" (*Proc.* 1769:4). In the early stages of the proceedings of the 1743 commission of review (intended to hear Mohegans' appeal of the judgment of the 1738 commission, which had overturned the 1705 decision), it was ordered by the commissioners that "the judgement pronounced by the commissioners in the year 1705, in favour of Owaneco . . . and the Mohegan Indians, against the governor and company of the colony of Connecticut . . . be laid before this court" (14). The Mohegans' attorney insisted that it was the responsibility of the colony – which had never fulfilled the order of the 1705 commission (22) – to produce the judgment; attorneys for the colony "denied that it was their duty to produce the same" (14). The Mohegans' attorney then offered to "produce authentic copies of the said judgement," but the colony refused to acknowledge what Mohegans had submitted as a legitimate copy of the proceedings and judgment of the 1705 commission because it was not an "original" and did not contain Owaneco's petition to the Crown (14, 20–21). The documents submitted by the Mohegans' attorney were admitted as an exhibit in the case, but the whereabouts of Owaneco's petition became an issue in the proceedings of the 1743 commission of review. The Mohegans' attorney asserted that although the petition had been searched for, it could not be found, and the colony's attorney claimed that the governor and company had never seen it (21–22). From the perspective of the colony's attorney, the absence of Owaneco's petition from the 1743

proceedings discredited the Mohegans' case, since "the said complaint of Owaneco . . . is supposed to be the foundation of the [1705] decree" (21).

7. Ethnohistorian Eric Johnson maintains that Uncas "was the political leader, or sachem, of the Mohegan community of southeastern Connecticut from at least the 1630's until his death in 1683" (E. Johnson 1996:29). With regard to the nature of Mohegan-Pequot relations, Johnson points out that "although the Mohegans and Pequots were closely allied up to the Pequot War in 1636, and although their subsequent histories are also closely linked, they were separate communities, albeit closely tied through kinship and political alliance. As early as 1614 the two groups were described as distinct entities by their first Dutch chroniclers" (30–31; see also Speck 1928:254). On the distinction between Mohegan and Pequot territories in the seventeenth century, Johnson states that "the Mohegan homeland is the Thames River Valley" and that "the Pequot homeland comprises the lower Mystic River Valley and adjacent parts of the Connecticut coast" (E. Johnson 1996:29–30). Mohegans' and Pequots' shifting political relationships with other Native communities in the area, both east and west of Mohegan and Pequot homelands, meant that both nations at times "exercised their political influence and power beyond the river valleys, estuaries, and shorelines of their homelands" (30; see also Grumet 1995:139–41 and Weinstein-Farson 1989).
8. Colonists who claimed title by virtue of their purchases from sachems "came to be known as the 'native right' men" (Bushman 1967:97). As Bushman observes, they had taken this designation "from a legal doctrine familiar in New England since Roger Williams dramatized it. They asserted that royal charters granted jurisdiction, the right to govern, but not ownership, which only the Indians could bestow. The rulers of the colony insisted that the Assembly must confirm Indian purchases, which allowed the government to nullify inconvenient claims" (97).
9. A Connecticut law of 1663 held that "no person in this Colony shall buy, hire or receive as a gift or mortgage, any parcel of land or lands of any Indian or Indians, for the future, except he doe buy or receive the same for the use of the Colony or the benefitt of some Towne, with the allowance of the Court" (CR 1:402).
10. The colonial government had failed to adequately oversee such individual grants or purchases from sachems, which resulted in conflicts among colonists who claimed ownership of the same or overlapping

tracts of land (IND 1st, 1:84; see also Bushman 1967:83–89). When, in 1717, the General Assembly's "Committee About the Indian Claimes" set about the task of putting an end to the "varyous Law Sutes, troubles and confusions which have happened Respecting the Title of sd [Mohegan] Lands, which is still growing and Increasing," colonists claiming "the Lands at Coventry" through a grant from Attawanhood, a son of Uncas, reminded the committee that "the practis of the c[o]untry was to purchass the lands of sachems," and that since Attawanhood, called Joshua by colonists, "was acknowledged in [16]72 by the Ge[neral] Court to be a Sachem," their titles were valid. The committee subsequently found that the General Assembly had acknowledged "Joshua's Right to sd Lands" and "did [in 1679] Establish and Allow" Joshua's will as a legal conveyance of title (IND 1st, 1:84).

11. Mohegan people continue to live within and around the area they know as Mohegan, which is situated, according to contemporary land marks, "on the east side of the Norwich–New London Road, about 4 miles from Norwich" (Mohegan Federal Acknowledgment Petition, vol. 1, 1984:74).
12. The validity of the 1640 "agreement" later became an important legal issue in *Mohegan Indians v. Connecticut*, since the colony claimed that it constituted the legal conveyance of the entirety of Mohegan lands to the colony, while Mohegan attorneys argued both that the document produced as the 1640 "deed" was not legitimate, and that even if Uncas had signed it, it was only to grant English colonists the right to acquire Mohegan lands by purchase.
13. The General Assembly's enlargement of the town of New London did not "grant" the Mohegan sequestration to the town, but neither did it state what its boundaries were. Mohegans' 1703 petition, as well as their subsequent complaints against encroachment, indicate that the Connecticut government had offered little disincentive to those colonists who coveted Mohegan lands.
14. Ben Uncas I is referred to in the colonial records as Major Ben Uncas and Ben Uncas. The Mohegan federal acknowledgement petition states that there was a hierarchy of leadership among Mohegans at this time, consisting of a "sachem, lesser chiefs, [and] council" (Mohegan Federal Acknowledgment Petition vol. 1, 1984:127).
15. Likewise, at a meeting with Connecticut officials in December 1703, both Owaneco and Ben Uncas I protested when it was demanded that Mohegans "give in their names," and as the record of the meeting states,

Owaneco remarked that "they had not done and would not do it. They have not shed any English blood nor were ever captivated, but have always been true to the English. Ben Uncas said, if he were furnisht with arms and going forth in the country's service he would give in his name, but to require them to give in their names while they remain at home seems a mean business. But upon further consideration they consented to give in their names" (CR 15:550–51).

16. As explained in chapter 3, the Connecticut General Assembly passed laws ostensibly intended to protect the colony from attacks by "enemy Indians" (for instance, Mohawks who were allied with French forces), but these laws nonetheless put all Native communities under scrutiny and rendered all Indians potential "enemies" and targets.

17. Following Connecticut's appeal of the 1705 decision, an imperial commission of review was granted in 1706, but no commission of review actually met until 1737 (Walters 1995:805–10; Smith 1950:424–27). In 1738 this commission overturned the 1705 judgment, allowing that Mohegans had rights only to "one field, called the Moheagan Field," which they described as the remaining fourth of the sequestration that existed after the 1721 reduction (*Proc.* 1769:6).

18. Morgan's history of Connecticut refers to this document as an "agreement" rather than a "sale," pointing out that it was "ambiguous" (F. Morgan 1904:279). Smith's discussion of Uncas's purported "grant" of Mohegan lands indicates that it was not recorded by the colonial government until 1736, and that the legitimacy of the colony's claim to Mohegan lands, as based on the 1640 agreement, continued to be a central issue throughout the Mohegan case (1950:439). Near the end of the case, in 1771, Mohegans' attorney argued that "it was either a spurious or a deserted title. Even admitting that the 1640 grant might have weight, it was designed only to give pre-emptive rights to the colony, not to surrender the property in the lands" (439).

19. While Connecticut representatives argued before the commission of review in 1743 that the 1640 "instrument" was a "deed" to the entirety of Mohegan lands (*Proc.* 1769:77), Mohegans' attorneys held that the "supposed deed was never executed by Uncas," and that if it had been, "it was made with the intent to keep off the Dutch, who were then endeavouring to get footing in these parts, or with some such view, and not with the intent to pass away the said Mohegan lands from them" (90). Whether Connecticut's intentions in this "agreement" were actually explained to

Uncas and how he himself may have understood its meaning are perhaps impossible to finally determine. But the fact that Uncas continued to engage in land transactions with individual colonists after 1640 suggests, as Conroy points out, that he "continued to believe that he owned or possessed rights to the use of the land" (Conroy 1994:400). In addition, the colonial government's approval of such individual "purchases" from Uncas – "many of them without monetary consideration, but naming as acknowledgments love and affection" (F. Morgan 1904:279) – indicates that Connecticut officials themselves continued to acknowledge Mohegan land rights. This argument against the 1640 agreement as a deed of sale was made by Mohegans' attorney in 1743 as well (Proc. 1769:91).

20. As noted previously, it was not only Mohegans' complaints against encroachers and against the colony's granting of the sequestered lands to New London that prevented the "quiet settlement" of the area: colonists' competing claims to the same or overlapping lands also constituted a considerable portion of the "varyous Law Sutes, troubles and confu[s]ions . . . respecting the Title of [said] Lands," as it was put by "the Committee About the Indian Claimes" in September of 1717 (IND 1st, 1:84). Following Owaneco's death in 1715, the next Mohegan sachem, Cesar, may have agreed, or may have been coerced, to assist the town of New London and the General Assembly in the matter of "confused" titles to Mohegan lands (1:90; Fawcett 1995:40). A May 1715 document referred to as "Caesar's deed to New London" was intended to nullify individual purchases from Owaneco that were "fraudulent and contrary to the English laws of the colony," and which Cesar purportedly deemed to have "wrongfully abus[ed] the town of New London" (Proc. 1769:185). According to the 1715 "deed," "I [Cesar] finding the just right of purchase of the said lands doth belong to the town of New London, and no other, and that I might live in good friendship with my neighbours, nor to have a hand in the said former fraud, who have by animating the Indians against said town, to hinder them of their rightful purchase, and having special confidence and no scruple of said town of New London, will take care to secure sufficient lands for the use of me and my people" (185). Cesar was paid a "consideration of one hundred pounds" by the town. It is possible that Cesar may have construed this as a means of gaining protection from the town against individual encroachers who sought to expand the lands they had acquired through previous "purchases" from

Owaneco. Nonetheless, it is clear that this "deed" was designed to benefit the town, and not Mohegans.

21. For a brief discussion of the Connecticut government's interference in Mohegans' internal political affairs, and the colony's "outlawing [of] the Mohegan Sachemship" in 1769, see Fawcett 1995:17–18, 40. Connecticut had cultivated the allegiance of Ben Uncas II, named as sachem in 1726, but his legitimacy was openly contested by many Mohegans, who in September 1736 formally announced their own allegiance to two other Mohegan leaders, Mahomet II and Anne. Nonetheless, Ben Uncas II has been referred to by some twentieth-century Euro-American historians as "the last of the Mohegan sachems" (e.g., Spiess 1933:14).

22. Mohegans also attended the ceremonies hosted by other Native communities in the colony. Missionary Richard Treat's account of "a Great dance" held by Wangunks in Middletown in late summer of 1735 indicates that Mohegans as well as Niantics attended this event (TP 2:479–84). Treat explains that he had been directed by Governor Talcott and the commissioners of the Society for the Propagation of the Gospel to "get an account of their number." He went to the dance since he "supposed they [Wangunks] would be together" at the event, thus facilitating his task of counting them (2:482). Wangunks had "come together to take off their mourning cloths for one that was dead," and Treat "found them in a most forlorn Condition, Singing, dancing, yelling, huming, &c, the like to which I had never before seen" (2:483). Treat was not well received at the event, however, and reported that he was told by some of the participants that "I had no business there, and [they] bid me begone"; but Treat persisted, having hoped his presence "might be a means to prevent no little wickedness which they are commonly Guilty of at Such times" (2:482). His presence so upset some of the Wangunks that he claimed to have been threatened, at which point, according to Treat, Mohegans interjected in an effort to prevent any violence and asked Treat to leave the ceremony (2:483–84). In his 1725 account of the Native populations of Connecticut, Talcott included the Indians "at Middletown" among those he classified as the "small persels scattered though out ye plantations in this Colony" and reported that their community included only forty-nine persons (2:399–402).

23. Narragansetts of Rhode Island also consulted members of neighboring Native communities regarding matters of leadership in the early eighteenth century: in 1733, according to Ezra Stiles, Narragansetts met with

Mohegans and Niantics, in a meeting of about three hundred individuals, to address a Narragansett leadership dispute (Stiles 1901:130).

24. The General Assembly ordered that officials should be present at the 1723 ceremony "who understand well the language and manner of the Indians . . . to signify the concurrence of this government to the said installment, and to keep order among the Indians on this occasion" (CR 6:408–9). The report of the two observers who attended – Captain John Mason and William Whiting – details the means by which the colonial government sought to control the ceremony: first, Mason and Whiting read "the order of the governor and council" at the opening of the ceremony, which relayed the colony's official approval of the event and of the sachemship of Ben Uncas I, with the provision that "the government would justly expect from them that their love and friendship to the English should hereafter be manifested on all occasions" (*Proc.* 1769:201). Mason and Whiting remained for the entirety of the ceremony and reported that it included members of other Native communities – among them Pequots and Niantics – and that Ben Uncas I had included Niantics on his council. While the Connecticut government clearly acknowledged that it was customary for such events to include "Indians from divers parts of this colony," the observers were required to follow "instructions from the governor . . . to discover any strange Indians that might be invited thither upon this festival" (202). Mason and Whiting explained that they "found none," thus indicating that it was expected, and accepted, by the Connecticut officials that Pequots and Niantics would participate in the celebration of the new sachem – provided, of course, that it was a sachem who had been approved by the colonial government.

25. The "Hartford Indians" referred to here were probably Podunks, whose villages were located on the east side of the Connecticut River (see DeForest 1852:55 and Grumet 1995:153–55). Trumbull states that "the 'Showtucket Indians' occupied the crotch of the Quinebaug and Shetucket Rivers" in Norwich (Trumbull 1881:67). He identifies the term itself as Mohegan, spelled variously by colonists – Shetucket, Shootucket, Shawtucket (67). A colonist testifying on the matter of Mohegan leadership during the proceedings of the 1738 commission stated that Mahomet I died "at Shoutuckott" (*Proc.* 1769:206).

26. Thomas Stanton of Preston also testified before the commission in 1738, claiming that "upwards of fifty years ago Uncas Grand Sachem of Moheegan & his son Owaneco . . . came to my Fathers House at Stonington

in Order to get my Father to write his Will," during which encounter the younger Stanton claimed that he "heard the Chief Sachem Uncas Discourse Concerning his Sons . . . [and] as for Ben who was his Youngest Son the sd Sachem Uncas said He was Poquiem (that is half Dog) because he said he begat Him in a Frolick of a poor Beggarly Squa not his Wife" (IND 1st, 1:173). Again, there may have been some accuracy to Stanton's account here, or it may have been a fabrication. At the very least, one has to be aware that the colonial depiction of the "poor Beggarly Squa" also has a history rooted in the legitimizing of colonial domination (see Smits 1982 and Green 1975) – and thus, in this instance, the derogation of "the Squa" may have been a construct imposed or assumed in the colonial interpretation of both Uncas's and Owaneco's purported assessment of Ben Uncas I.

27. Reverend Barber was appointed as minister to Mohegans in 1733 by the Society for the Propagation of the Gospel in New England and was dismissed in 1738 (Love 1899:29; TP 1:290n).

28. Love states that Ben Uncas II was "the most prominent friend of the Christian religion during this period." He had sent his son, Ben Uncas III, to be educated with the Reverend Eliphalet Adams in 1729 (Love 1899:30).

29. See, for instance, Talcott's letter of February 1736 to Francis Wilks, a merchant and member of the East India Company who lived in London (TP 1:335–38). Talcott sought Wilks's assistance in providing information on the complaint Mason and Mahomet were to make to the Crown and to forward his "evidences and answers to it" (1:337). In addition, see Talcott's letter of February 17, 1736, to Colonel Adam Winthrop, a commissioner for the Society for the Propagation of the Gospel in New England (1:338–44).

30. According to Talcott, later in 1736 the Mohegan reservation community consisted of "47 men 12 and up" and "48 women 12 and up" (TP 1:377).

31. As I have already noted, colonists whose 1738 testimony questioned the validity of the sachemship of Ben Uncas II proffered the notion that *he* was the product of "a poor beggarly Squa." These assessments undoubtedly reflected the salient colonial categories that had been infused into the dispute over Mohegan land and leadership. As Bushnell's report indicates, colonial disparagements of the Mohegan reservation community emphasized both impoverishment and a preponderance of women in the population to suggest that they were unworthy of government pro-

tection. But it should be remembered that neither Mohegan leaders nor leaders of other reservation communities asked the colonial government for special or "private" land rights for themselves based on any claim to an elite status. According to Governor Saltonstall's 1720 report, for instance, Mohegan leaders Cesar and Ben Uncas I defended the rights of Mohegan people and their children and did not claim that they or any other Mohegans were "royality" who deserved greater rights or protection from the government than other Mohegans.

32. According to historian Colin Calloway, English colonists "often lumped Abenakis and Passamaquoddies [of Vermont and Maine] together – along with Micmacs and Maliseets [of northern Maine and eastern Canada] – as 'Eastern Indians' " (Calloway 1991:5).

33. Neither is Anne mentioned by nineteenth-century historians Frances Caulkins and John DeForest, who are noted chroniclers of Indian histories in Connecticut and who address the Mohegan case (Caulkins 1895; DeForest 1852).

34. In a genealogical chart (the "Uncas Geneaology") in the unnumbered pages at the opening of volume 2 of *The Talcott Papers*, Anne is shown as married to Ben Uncas II, but obviously this is an error.

### 5. "NOW THEY MAKE US AS GOATS"

1. Native men played an important role in the colony's defense during King Philip's War as well as the imperial border wars. In 1675, for instance, Connecticut authorities ordered "above an hundred Moheages and Pequots" to serve in King Philip's War (*Wyllys Papers*, 1924:228). As one historian has pointed out, in 1689, during King William's War, "Connecticut had great difficulty finding soldiers, and instead relied on Indian allies, whose importance increased as the war dragged on" (Selesky 1990:44). And in 1704, during Queen Anne's War, the Connecticut General Assembly ordered "that as many of our friend Indians as are fitt for warre and can be prevailed with, and furnished with all things suitable, shall goe with our forces against the common enemy" (CR 4:463). The colonial government thereby "imploy[ed] suitable persons to acquaint the Indians in the counties of Newhaven and Fairfield of this conclusion concerning them. . . . The like to be done with respect to raising Indians in the countie of New London [which thus included Pequots]" (4:464). McBride has explained that Mashantucket and Eastern Pequot men served "in every major conflict during the colonial era" (McBride

1996:86). Though "never able to field collectively more than two hundred men at any one time, the Pequots nevertheless provided important service. The Pequot warriors fighting alongside Connecticut soldiers helped ensure that the Connecticut militias suffered the lowest casualty rate of any new England force in King Philip's War" (86; see also Selesky 1990:10–32).

2. Talcott was obviously not forthcoming about the colony's "labour of love" with respect to the "lesser tribes." He failed to inform Winthrop that, since he began his governorship in 1725, Niantics, for instance, had indeed complained against encroachment on their reserved lands (IND 1st, 1:168, 132). The report of the committee assigned to address Niantics' complaint in 1734 reveals the extent to which the colonial government had failed to monitor and prevent encroachment on the Niantics' reservation, and that the absence of official records regarding the reservation's boundaries had proved an encouragement to encroachers and a distinct problem for Niantics' efforts at resistance. After stating that they had spoken with both "the owners of the Lands adjoyning" the reservation and "the Indians," the committee then explained what they had determined to be the boundaries of the reservation (1:168). Whether or not Niantics were consulted as a part of the process of establishing these boundaries is not made clear in the report; significantly, however, the committee concludes that "the Indians did compl[ain] they had been wronged by the English peoples cattle, brea[k]ing into theire fields, and that they were wronged under the pretence of the english haveing the herbage on theire Land, and that the English had Incroached by fenceing on theire Lands[.] as to the first, we hope that complaint will not be any more mentioned for the Indians have now got a pound, as to the second we could not so well look into that matter, for want of the Records, which were not to be had at this place, but we feare the Indians have beene wronged, and as to the third complaint, in refereance to the Incroachment, we supose now the line is settled that the fences will be set in the proper place, and that greivance come to an end" (1:168).

The service done for Niantics by the committee was tenuous at best; and, indeed, Niantics petitioned the General Assembly again in 1743 to explain that "we meet with Much Difficulty in Respect of the Improvement of our Lands," since "our English Neighbors claime the Grass that G[r]ows uppon two Hundred [acres] of it and ye fall feed of ye rest and in

Taking the Grass they Almost render the land unprofitable to us" (IND 1st, 1:251).

3. As McBride explains, a group of Pequots who had been consigned, according to the 1638 Treaty of Hartford, to the authority of Mohegan sachem Uncas, began to establish villages on the west side of the Thames River at a place called Nameag, within what is now New London, and lived there between 1638 and 1650 (McBride 1990:105, 1996:79). In 1646 John Winthrop Jr. established "Pequot Plantation" at Nameag, where, according to McBride, relations between Pequots and colonists were "very good": evidenced, for instance, in the fact that "Pequots sheltered some of the settlers during the first year and hunted for them" (McBride 1990:105). Furthermore, McBride explains that it was due to the leadership of Mashantucket sachem Cassacinamon I – particularly his opposition to the colonial order that his community remain under the authority of Uncas – and his relationship with Winthrop that the Noank reservation was finally established in 1651 with the assistance of Winthrop himself (McBride 1996:79–86).
4. This is perhaps a reference to Winthrop's support of Pequots at Nameag who opposed the authority of Uncas (see McBride 1996: 79–86). As McBride explains, Winthrop's friendship with Pequots was not motivated entirely by altruism. He had established his plantation at Nameag because of "the presence of a deepwater port and access to interior areas where he was prospecting for minerals." In describing Pequots at Nameag, Winthrop referred to them as people who "do wholly adhere to [the English], and are apt to fall into English employment" (81).
5. As Caulkins and Trumbull explain, there are various spellings of the term in the colonial records (eg., "Naiwayonk" and "Nowayunk"), and "Noank" is a Euro-American abbreviation of the term (Caulkins 1895:4, 123; Trumbull 1881:34). Trumbull states that it is a Mohegan-Pequot term for "a point" (34).
6. Archaeologist Kevin McBride, who has researched Mashantucket Pequot precolonial and colonial history for several decades, explains that "the principal residences and occupation sites of the Pequots are believed to have been located between Niantic Bay on the west and the Pawcatuck River on the east. The northern boundary of Pequot settlements is less clear, but probably does not extend much farther north than Pachaug Pond in the present town of Griswold, Connecticut" (McBride 1990:97). Ethnohistorian Eric Johnson, whose research has focused on Mohegan

history, explains that "the Pequot homeland comprised the lower Mystic River Valley and adjacent parts of the Connecticut coast," while "the Mohegan homeland is the Thames River Valley" (E. Johnson 1996:29–30).

7. This is the population estimate that McBride gives for the time of the emergence of the Mashantucket community, when they resided at Nameag, within what is now New London, between 1638 and 1650 (McBride 1996:79). In 1725 Governor Talcott reported that "ye Number of Pequots in Groton is three hundred twenty and two" (TP 2:397). By the early 1730s, colonial officials reported "66 men" at the Mashantucket reservation (IND 1st, 1:143), which suggests that the entire reservation population may have included several hundred people.
8. The island, according to Caulkins, was "called by the Indians Chippachaug" until the grant to Mason, after which it was "known as Mason's Island" (Caulkins 1895:78).
9. Cassacinamon's leadership, and his name, came to be associated with Pequot resistance in the eighteenth century. According to McBride, there had been an internal dispute among Pequots regarding leadership beginning in 1692, with the death of Robin Cassacinamon I. Scattup's position of authority had been contested in the early years of the eighteenth century by Mashantucket elders and councilors who desired Kutchamaquan, the son of the Eastern Pequot sachem Momoho, to be their leader. McBride thus contends that "Scattup's refusal to step down from his position of leadership" resulted in "a bitter controversy within the tribe over leadership and the nature of succession" during the eighteenth century. In addition, he explains that "contesting political groups invoked Cassacinamon's name and other symbols of his leadership in their struggles for power. Scattup, for example, used Cassacinamon's distinctive mark when signing documents as the community's leader. Other documents indicate that Kutchamaquan or his successor adopted Robin Cassacinamon's name," thus accounting for the emergence of Robin Cassacinamon II (McBride 1996:88–89). While both Scattup and Robin Cassacinamon II signed the 1713 petition, Scattup later came to oppose further resistance to dispossession (see McBride 1993:67–69).
10. Colonial accounts offer no estimate for the size of the population at Noank in 1713; curiously, while the General Assembly ordered a committee to count Pequots there, the 1714 ruling does not indicate whether such a count was ever made or reported to them. In fact, years later,

during the course of Mashantucket Pequots' struggle to protect their reservation at Mashantucket, a committee investigating their complaints against encroachment by the town of Groton claimed in their 1761 report to the General Assembly that that they "could find no return [i.e., report]" from the committee appointed in 1713 (IND 1st, 1:118).

11. Wheeler also contends that when Cassacinamon I requested that the colonial government secure additional land for his people after the Noank reservation was established, he "had wanted their lands laid out at the head of the Mystic River, nearer to their fishing places; but the committee appointed to locate it [the additional reserved land] thought otherwise, and established their lands at Mashantuxet, and the Court ratified their doings in 1666.". He adds that Cassacinamon I remained dissatisfied with the committee's decision and thus chose not to make his residence at Mashantucket (Wheeler 1887:19).
12. See Carolyn Merchant (1989:76–77) on Native agriculture and use of hoes in colonial New England.
13. Robin Cassacinamon I, who died in 1692, was a leader in the period after the 1637 massacre when, as anthropologist Kevin McBride has explained, Pequots worked to "reestablish themselves as a self-governing people in their old territory" (McBride 1996:74). The second Cassacinamon, discussed in this chapter, emerged as a leader in the early eighteenth century (1996:88; 1993:66–68).
14. This is likely a reference to the survey ordered by the General Assembly in October 1713, subsequent to Mashantuckets' petition in May of that year (IND 1st, 1:71).
15. This is a reference to Nehemiah Smith Jr., whose father, Caulkins notes, was one of the "early settlers of New London" (Caulkins 1895:323). According to Caulkins, Nehemiah Smith Jr. was "for many years in the commission of the peace [in New London], an honorable and venerated man; usually styled on the records, Mr. Justice Smith. He died in 1727, and was buried at Pequonuck, in Groton, where the latter years of his life were spent" (Caulkins 1895:323). He and his father are listed in Mashantuckets' 1713 petition as among those colonists who had "bought up" the majority of the "shares" of the Noank reservation land after the town of Groton decided in May 1712 to "voat away [Mashantucket] land at Newayonk to all their Inhabitants" (IND 1st, 1:75). Judging from Cassacinamon's remark in the petition, it seems possible that Nehemiah Smith Jr. – "old Justice Smith" – may have attempted to "quiet" Mashantuckets' dispute

with the town by promising that "they would never move us from . . . Mashuntuxit, nor lott it out as they had Nawayonk" (1:95).

16. McBride explains that at the time of its establishment, in 1666, the Mashantucket reservation included approximately three thousand acres, and that Mashantuckets had been planting in the area as early as 1658 (McBride 1990:106).

17. According to DeForest, in 1653 "John Winthrop of New London had received from the colony a grant of a considerable tract, which he never made use of, and which seems to have been covered afterwards by the Pequot reservation at Mashantuxet." In the early eighteenth century the claim was "revived by one of his descendants" (DeForest 1852:425).

18. The west side of the reservation, which includes what is here referred to as Walnut Hill, was used by Mashantuckets for planting and for the extraction of wood for burning. Mashantuckets' dwelling sites were at that time located within the remaining 1,000 acres of the reservation (see McBride 1990:106–7; 110–11).

19. It is important to note here that, through this action in 1720, the town essentially usurped the authority of the General Assembly, denying the existence of the reservation that had been previously established by government authority and then "creating" one itself, on its own terms – terms that were clearly intended to limit Mashantuckets' land rights. This evident power struggle between the town and the General Assembly subsequently impacted the Assembly's response to Cassacinamon's petition, since the upper and lower houses had considerable difficulty reaching an agreement on the matter. In May 1722 the upper house determined that Mashantuckets were "setled on the sd land by the Authority of this Court," and that "No consent of any of ye sd Indians, with the Town of Groton or any other Persons, can give Rights to any Persons whatsoever to have any part of the sd Mashuntuxet Lands, without the Actual consent and Order of this Assembly" (IND 1st, 1:105). The lower house dissented, perhaps supporting the town proprietors' desire to control the entirety of the town's common lands (it was agreed at a Groton town meeting in May 1722 that the town should petition the General Assembly "to Enable ye proprietors of undivided land . . . to dispose of ye Comon or undivided lands as they shall judge to be most fit and right" [1:103]). It was not until May 1723 that the two houses of the General Assembly managed to reach agreement on Cassacinamon's complaint of May 1721, ordering that Captain James Avery was to "prosecute" those who by

any "pretence whatsoever enter upon the sd [Mashantucket reservation] land" (1:110).

20. McBride reports that throughout the late seventeenth and early eighteenth centuries Mashantuckets moved between Noank and the inland reservation at Mashantucket, and that "through at least the early part of the eighteenth century, the Pequots were engaged in traditional subsistence practices involving cultivation of maize, hunting, and seasonal movements to coastal areas to procure resources" (McBride 1990:108–9; see also McBride 1993). According to McBride's analysis of archaeological sites on the Mashantucket reservation between 1650 and 1750, most are "short-term occupations, such as hunting camps or sites of other seasonal activities such as planting. This interpretation is generally consistent with the documentary evidence, which indicates that before 1720 there were few, if any, permanent occupations in the area of the reservation. . . . Small groups apparently lived in the area seasonally to hunt and tend orchards and cornfields; then they returned to Noank" (McBride 1990:110).

21. As McBride points out, "throughout the eighteenth century the population of the reservation declined steadily. The mortality rate among Pequot males was high because of their participation in colonial wars, and many Pequot males also moved off the reservation to find work as laborers on nearby farms or as whalers" (McBride 1990:107). In 1725 Governor Talcott reported that the "Pequots in Groaton" numbered 321 (TP 2:401); in 1732, a colonial committee assessing the reservation population at Mashantucket stated that "the male persons of the Indians, from fourteen years and upwards, are sixty six, most of which live with the English" (CR 7:412). It must be pointed out that this committee – which proved ultimately to sympathize with Groton residents who sought to appropriate the reservation land – may have underestimated or inaccurately reported the size of the resident adult male population on the reservation. The committee members recommended, in this report, that "one half of the [existing reservation] is fully sufficient for the Indians to dwell on and cut firewood," and the General Assembly accepted their recommendation in October 1732 (7:412).

22. Historian Carolyn Merchant observes that "for most of the tribes of the eastern American woodlands . . . corn was the gift of the Corn Mother, a mythical female from whose body had come the corn plant, maize" (Merchant 1989:72). The Native peoples of southern New England, she

explains, "produced their subsistence primarily though the planting of corn, beans, and squash by women, supplemented by male hunting and mixed-gender fishing" (74). As the primary agriculturalists, Algonquian women of southern New England provided their communities with approximately "65 percent of their caloric intake" through the production of corn (76). Likewise, historian William Cronon points out, with regard to Native agriculture in seventeenth-century southern New England, that "except for tobacco [a crop tended by men only], crops were primarily the responsibility of women": "A single Indian woman could raise anywhere from twenty-five to sixty bushels of corn by working an acre or two, enough to provide half or more of the annual caloric requirements for a family of five. When corn was combined with the other foods for which they were responsible, women may have contributed as much as three-fourths of a family's total subsistence needs" (Cronon 1983:44).

23. According to Jennings, colonists in seventeenth-century New England were able to "seize Indian property with some show of legality" by "allow[ing] livestock to roam into an Indian's crops until he despaired and removed. Even when the Indian uncharacteristically fenced his cropland, he found that there was something nocturnally mysterious that did not love an Indian's wall. The Indian who dared to kill an Englishman's marauding animals was promptly hauled into a hostile court" (Jennings 1975:144). The 1651 "covenant" regarding the Noank reservation required that Mashantuckets tolerate the destruction wrought by their colonial neighbors' livestock, at their own cost (IND 1st, 1:2). Native people sometimes took action against colonists' unruly livestock, however. Caulkins notes that in the seventeenth century Narragansetts "killed two hundred of Mr. Winthrop's goats" that had intruded upon their lands (Caulkins 1895:80).

24. This is John Plumbe Jr., whose father, of the same name, died in 1696 (Caulkins 1895:785). He was the "County Surveyor" for New London (IND 1st, 1:135). In addition, he was among the New London residents who had "settled on the [Mohegan] fields" – that is, on Mohegan sequestered land between New London and Norwich – and whose encroachment was protested by Mohegans (see Caulkins 1895:428). His claim to Mohegan land was subsequently secured by the actions of the 1721 committee, which radically reduced the Mohegan sequestration (*Proc.* 1769:193).

25. Among the names, however, is "Robin onneson," who may be Robin

Cassacinamon II; there is also a "Charl" who may be the same Charls who is the main signatory, identified as sachem, on a 1741 petition, upon which the name of Robin also appears (IND 1st, 1:231).

26. Captain Avery's son James was appointed as overseer after the father's death; John Morgan was still an overseer for Mashantuckets at this time as well (DeForest 1852:428). It does not appear that James Avery Jr. was sympathetic to the plight of Mashantuckets, as his father had been. Indeed, he petitioned the General Assembly to counter the charges made in Mashantuckets' September 1735 petition, stating that he "can't find that there has been any Real Damage done them" (IND 1st, 1:228).

27. By 1855 "all but 204 acres of [the Mashantucket reservation] was auctioned off by the state of Connecticut" (McBride 1990:107). This action was taken against the protests of Mashantuckets (see Campisi 1990:132) and, equally important, was in violation of federal law – namely, the 1790 Trade and Intercourse Act that prohibited the sale of Indian lands without the approval of Congress (see Campisi 1990:180–81 and Bee 1990:194–96).

28. It should be noted that the categorization of a reservation community's identity as one of mixed ancestry could be used against that community. This is clearly articulated today, often in distinctly racialized terms, in Euro-American opposition to federal acknowledgment in Connecticut. As I note in chapter 1 and address further in the concluding chapter, Native people with any "degree" of African American ancestry are those most commonly targeted by racist attacks on their "authenticity."

## 6. "RACE" AND THE DENIAL OF LOCAL HISTORIES

1. Historian Richard Brown explains that in his lifetime Hempstead became "the farmers' champion" and in general an adviser to New London residents (1989:135). He points out that "Hempstead's diary marked the achievements and failures of Hempstead's neighbors and kin, their virtues and vices, God's blessings and His admonitions. For Hempstead they constituted a record and a guide to the shifting pattern of relationships – familial and communal, economic and political – of the people with whom he lived. To be ignorant of these matters in an interdependent community assured one's exclusion from community decision-making and risked the failure of one's agricultural endeavors and the well-being of one's family" (136). Brown does not mention Native women and men as among those "people with whom [Hempstead] lived" (neither is there

a heading for "Indians," "Native Americans," "Pequots," "Mohegans," etc., in the index of his volume cited here, entitled *Knowledge Is Power: The Diffusion of Information in Early America, 1700–1865*).

2. Colonial notions of the "Squaw" have varied strategically when deployed as a justification for conquest. While the "squaw drudge" was a slave to her indolent Indian husband but mercifully rescued by her European conquerors, the "squaw" has also been constructed as a valiant protector – and temptress – of European "explorers," inviting conquest and smoothing its path. For some detailed analysis of Euro-American myths of the "Squaw," see, for example, Green (1975) and Smits (1982); see also Montrose (1991) and McClintock (1995:21–36) on the relationship between conquering land and conquering women in the "New World."

3. Government officials had been informed before of the intensifying internal conflicts among Mohegans. In 1758, for instance, Ben Uncas III (see note 4, below) and his council petitioned the General Assembly to explain that although Mohegans had "Sufferid much by some of our Tenants [colonists who 'leased,' or claimed to have leases to, acreage on Mohegan reservation land], on Account of their bad fences, our Tribe now beings [begins] To tast the Sweets of Agreculture & our Stocks increase but As there is Devision Subsisting amongst us, Numbers hav No regard to the Secham & his Council but does what is Right in their own Eyes." Ben Uncas III thus requested that legislators appoint a guardian who "has leasure time to Visit us frequently" in order "to promote industry peace & order amongst us" (IND 1st, 2:99). The General Assembly appointed the requested overseer. It is interesting to note that the term "our Stocks" is used to refer to the reservation community, here described as "increasing"; "stock" was first used to refer to the Mohegan reservation community (i.e., as "the stock of said Indians) in the 1721 legislative action that declared their imminent extinction.

4. Ben Uncas III was formally named as sachem in a petition of June 19, 1749, which was signed by 41 Mohegan men, among them Zachary Johnson and Samson Occom (IND 1st, 2:34). The May 1745 will of Ben Uncas II named his son, known as Ben Uncas Jr., as "my successor," but allowed that this required the approval of the Connecticut General Assembly. The will also stipulated that his son would be sachem "on condition also that he Submit and Subject himselfe to the directions and Instructions of the General Assembly," and that he must "maintain unspoiled" his father's "friendship" with Connecticut, "upon paine of being dis-

posed of the Sachemship of sd Tribe" (2:38). Ben Uncas II also named his "loving friends and overseers" Samuel Lynde and John Richards as his executors. Ben Uncas II may have demanded that his son "subject himself" to the Connecticut government, or he may have been advised by his executors to make such a statement. Indeed, colonial officials may have learned that Ben Uncas Jr. (or Ben Uncas III) was perhaps not to be readily cowed by the Connecticut government, as indicated in his own petition to the General Assembly – dated the same day as his father's will. Joined by Samson Occum, Ben Uncas Jr. submitted his May 8, 1745, complaint to the General Assembly to protest the acts of colonial encroachers (among them James Harris, a "witness" to the execution of his father's will [2:38]) who claimed to have leases to Mohegan land for which Mohegans received little, if any, compensation; instead, Mohegans were subjected to the threats and abuses of the encroachers. One of them, James Harris, "threatens to Send us to prison or Sell us to Sea if we Do not Intirly Submitt to his Government which we think is tiranicle if Not Diabolical." Ben Uncas Jr. and Occom also declare in this petition that "Ben our Sacham [Ben Uncas II]" had "no Right to Leas our Lands without our Leave," and that the pillaging of the reservation by the colonial encroachers in question has left Mohegans "exceedingly Distressed impoverished and almost undone" (1:255). Ben Uncas III and Zachary Johnson, who was also among the signatories of this petition, remained allied and eventually came to oppose Samson Occom (see 2:258).

5. Forbes explains that the term "mulatto" was also intended to reference a certain skin color and was used "to designate a certain type of land or soil, sometimes described as 'a black mould and red earth' (1789) or 'the red or mulatto lands' (1883)" (Forbes 1993:194). When applied to human beings, it was clearly meant as a disparagement: for instance, Forbes cites a 1657 English definition of "mulatto" as "one that is of a mongrel complexion" (194).
6. Forbes observes that it is unclear whether the term "negro," in its early English usage, was used to refer to "an African, a 'black' person, or any dark-skinned individual"; but by the nineteenth century, " 'negro' and 'black' both became synonymous with enslavement"(Forbes 1993:84).
7. For an excellent discussion of the colonial legal construction and enforcement of a racial hierarchy of rights and the significance of the category "mulatto" in that context, see Higginbotham and Kopytoff's "Racial Purity and Interracial Sex in the Law of Colonial and Antebel-

lum Virginia" (1989). They explain that colonial law in early-eighteenth-century Virginia indicated that it was presumed by colonists to be easier for the descendants of mixed Indian-"white" ancestry (also classed as "mulatto" in Virginia) to "wash out the taint" of "Indian blood" than it was for those descendants of a "mulatto" classed as bearing "Negro blood" to likewise "wash out the taint" of that "blood." "Mulattos" of any presumed ancestry, however, did not by law have rights in any way comparable to those of "white" colonists: a 1705 law, for instance, "barred mulattoes, along with Negroes, Indians, and criminals, form holding 'any office, ecclesiasticall, civill or military, or be[ing] in any place of public trust or power' " (Higginbotham and Kopytoff 1989: 1977).

8. A May 1760 petition of Ben Uncas III identifies "outsiders" on the reservation as those who are "not Mohegan's but by marriage," and who, the petition claims, had been "instigated by persons call'd the Masen [Mason] party" to "sett up another Sechem, and *with drawn their allegiance from Ben Uncas* [III]" (IND 1st, 2:103; emphasis added). What this suggests, of course, is that these individuals who are now classified essentially as "impostors" were *not* considered as such when they had paid their allegiance to Ben Uncas III. Thus ideas and conflicts concerning the nature of kin ties – which perhaps included a gendered debate about one's rights and status as a Mohegan (the petition doesn't indicate whether there were more women or men among these now undesirable "in-laws") – figured into this particular construction of illegitimacy. It will be recalled that Bushnell's 1736 report on the reservation community indicated that, to Mohegans, all those living on the reservation were "reckoned as families," including "widows" – which Bushnell obviously found objectionable.

9. Zachary Johnson had been identified as belonging to the Mohegan council since the early 1740s (see IND 1st, 1:248, 249) and is listed as such on the July 1742 petition of Ben Uncas II, renouncing Samuel Mason's appeal to the 1738 judgment in the Mohegans' legal case against the colony, which overturned the 1705 decision. In addition to asserting that Mohegans had no "grievances" against the colony, the petition lists Ben Uncas's "choice of [twelve] Councellors," as approved by John Richards, "Guardian or Agent to the Moheagan Indians."

10. Mohegan Indians to Richard Law (trustee for the Mohegans), Dec. 5, 1789; (Ernest Law Papers, Connecticut Historical Society, Hartford).

11. For a most useful and relevant examination of the formation of colonial and Euro-American racial thought in North America see Reginald Horsman's *Race and Manifest Destiny: The Origins of American Racial Anglo-Saxonism* (1981:1–61). Another invaluable source on this topic is, of course, Edmund S. Morgan's discussion of the colonial beginnings of Indian-hating and the institutionalization of particular racist practices in Virginia in his classic work *American Slavery, American Freedom* (1975). He argues that by 1682 Virginia law had established slavery "on a squarely racial foundation." By the late seventeenth-century, "white" Virginians "treated black, red, and intermediate shades of brown as interchangeable" because they were, at base, "unwhite" (329).
12. Nor, of course, does the depiction reflect the circumstances under which the colony's 1680 reservation law was established.
13. "In times of trouble," Richard Drinnon observes, "natives were always wild animals that had to be rooted out of their dens, swamps, jungles." He notes that even seventeenth-century colonist Roger Williams, who has been known as the great friend of Narragansetts, commented in July 1637 that he would "deale with [Narragansetts] wisely as with wolves endewed with mens braines." Wolves, Drinnon adds, were defined by Williams in his *Key to the Language of America* (1643) as "an emblem of a fierce, blood-sucking persecutor" (Drinnon 1980:53). Regarding Pequots who had survived the 1637 massacre, Williams commented, "The generall speech is, all must be rooted out etc. The body of Pequin men yet live, and are onely removed from their dens" (Drinnon 1980:53).
14. Robert Young argues that "culture and race developed together, imbricated within each other": "culture has always marked cultural difference by producing the other; it has always been comparative, and racism has always been an integral part of it: the two are inextricably clustered together, feeding off and generating each other" (Young 1995:28, 54). As he explains, the early English notion of "culture as cultivation" eventually "extended to the process of human development," and by the eighteenth century "it came to represent also the intellectual side of civilization," and thus the notion of "culture as cultivation" subsequently "took on a class-fix" – such that "cultured," by the mid-eighteenth century, was used to refer to "refined" behavior (31). But the importance of the idea of cultivation as focused on "proper" use of land did not lose significance in English usage, for it "operated within the terms of the later ideological polarity of the country and the city": "the city people became the culti-

vated ones," while "the savages outside" were "defined by their lack of culture – agricultural, civil and intellectual" (Young 1995:31). Johnson seems to be making a similar distinction here between the world of the reservation and the "white" public surrounding it.

15. Johnson incorrectly argues that the 1680 reservation law "had no relation to the Mohegan Lands, which were not allow'd nor set apart, nor Rewarded to them, in the sense of that Order, till the sequestration of the Mohegan Fields in 1721" (IND 1st, 2:277). The Mohegan "sequestration" was first established as such in 1671. At the 1680 meeting between colonial officials and Native leaders, which resulted in the establishment of the 1680 reservation law, Uncas had requested that the boundaries of the Mohegan Fields be secured (IND 1st, 1:39). In March of 1684 Uncas's son Owaneco deeded "to his peapol . . . all the Lands called the Sequestration," and the deed was acknowledged and recorded by colonial officials (*Proc.* 1769:217; TP 1:348). The General Assembly's 1703 "Act for the englargement of New London," by which the Mohegan sequestration was incorporated within the bounds of the town, indicated that "whatsoever proprieties, whether of English or Indians, that are within the said tract of land so granted and added, shall be and are hereby reserved and saved, for the respective possession, use, and improvement of the several proprietors of the same" (*Proc.* 1769:177, 180). The 1703 Act also specifically indicated that Mohegans' reserved land "shall be and remain good and free to them, to all intents and purposes in the law . . . as if it had not been included in the bounds of the aforesaid New London" (180). As I have argued, such declarations did not serve to protect reservation lands from encroachment, but nonetheless, they indicated the colonial government's official acknowledgment of Natives' land rights and, in this case, of the existence of Mohegans' reservation as defined by the 1680 law. That acknowledgment was reiterated in 1720, when in response to the complaints against encroachers made by Mohegan sachems Cesar and Ben Uncas II, the General Assembly indicated that "according to the former promises covenants and Contracts with the said Indians of Mohegan . . . It is the duty and Honour of this Court to Take Care that the Indians within this Government should not be ejected out of the Lands reserved to them or put out of their Rights and Improvements upon them (*Wyllys Papers* 1924:396–97). It is also important to note that in 1726 the General Assembly clearly stated that reservations were defined as "tracts of land which they have reserved for themselves or by ye Care

of this Govt hath been for themselves . . . set apart and sequestered for the use of them and their posterity" (IND 1st, 1:130). In no sense, then, did Johnson have a valid legal argument that Mohegans did not have a reservation, acknowledged by colonial law, until the 1721 reduction of the sequestration.

16. The nineteenth-century notion of Euro-American "manifest destiny" had its roots in the colonial period (see Stephanson 1995:3–27). "Manifest destiny" relied upon and reaffirmed colonial notions about "Indian savagery," against which it pitted the necessary "progress" of an "advanced" ("white") "civilization" (see Patterson 1997:108–12). Like the European program of "discovery" in the sixteenth and seventeenth centuries, Euro-American "progress" in the nineteenth century required ever-increasing amounts of "living space" for "settlers" or "pioneers" (see Churchill 1994:28–36).

17. While a graduate student in anthropology at the University of Connecticut in the 1990s, I worked as a researcher and consultant for the Golden Hill Paugussetts' federal acknowledgment project. As part of that work, I wrote an early draft of the historical narrative that was to be part of the federal acknowledgment petition presented by Paugussetts to the Bureau of Indian Affairs (BIA) Branch of Acknowledgment and Research (BAR). Among the local historians and other scholars whose work has documented the history of the Golden Hill Paugussetts are DeForest (1852), Orcutt (1882), Stiles (1916), Speiss (1933), and Wojciechowski (1985).

18. The Euro-American demand for "racial purity" in Indianness – which disqualifies as "Indian" those Native people who also have African American ancestry – is, as I have already indicated, not new. In the nineteenth and twentieth centuries Euro-American government officials deployed notions of "racial purity" to disparage kin ties between African Americans and Native Americans in southern New England and deny Indian identity to Native communities whose members include people of mixed Native and African American ancestry (see Herndon and Sekatau 1997 and O'Connell 1991). As noted in chapter 1, I gave a preliminary assessment of the twentieth-century production and proliferation of Euro-American discourse on "racial purity," as applied to Native communities in southern New England, in a paper titled " 'Race,' Reservations, and 'Recognition': A Cursory Genealogy of Racial Discourse on Indian-

ness in Southern New England." This research is ongoing and is concerned with tracing both racial discourse and racist practices of those who sought to monitor, define, and control Indianness for varied reasons – including government officials as well as self-identified "friends" of Indians.

# References

Akagi, Roy Hidemichi. 1963. *The Town Proprietors of the New England Colonies: A Study of Their Development, Organization, Activities, and Controversies, 1620–1770*. Gloucester MA: Peter Smith.

Alexander, Sir William. 1873 [1624]. "Encouragement to Colonies." Pamphlet. Boston: Prince Society.

Alexie, Sherman. 1995. *Reservation Blues*. New York: Atlantic Monthly Press.

Asad, Talal, ed. 1973. *Anthropology and the Colonial Encounter*. Atlantic Heights NJ: Humanities Press.

Axtell, James. 1997. "The Ethnohistory of Native America." In *Rethinking American Indian History*, Donald Fixico, ed. Albuquerque: University of New Mexico Press.

Baron, Donna Keith, J. Edward Hood, and Holly V. Izard. 1996. "They Were Here All Along: The Native American Presence in Lower-Central New England in the Eighteenth and Nineteenth Centuries." *William and Mary Quarterly*, 3rd ser., 53(3): 561–86.

Basso, Keith. 1996. *Wisdom Sits in Places: Landscape and Language among the Western Apache*. Albuquerque: University of New Mexico Press.

Beardsley, E. Edwards. 1882. "The Mohegan Land Controversy." In *Papers of the New Haven Colony Historical Society*, vol. 3: 205–25. New Haven CT: New Haven Colony Historical Society.

Bee, Robert L. 1974. *Patterns and Processes: An Introduction to Anthropological Strategies for the Study of Sociocultural Change*. New York: Free Press.

———. 1990. "Connecticut's Indian Policy: From Testy Arrogance to Benign Bemusement." In *The Pequots in Southern New England: The Fall and Rise of an American Indian Nation*, Laurence M. Hauptman and James D. Wherry, eds. Norman: University of Oklahoma Press.

Bissell, Benjamin. 1925. *The American Indian in English Literature of the 18th Century*. New Haven: Yale University Press.

Boissevain, Ethel. 1956. "The Detribalization of the Narragansett Indians: A Case Study." *Ethnohistory* 3(3): 225–45.

Bowen, Clarence Winthrop. 1882. *Boundary Disputes of Connecticut*. Boston: James R. Osgood.

Bradshaw, Harold Clayton. 1935. *The Indians of Connecticut: The Effect of English Colonization and of Missionary Activity on Indian Life in Connecticut*. Deep River CT: New Era Press.

Bragdon, Kathleen J. 1996. *Native People of Southern New England, 1500–1650*. Norman: University of Oklahoma Press.

Brasser, T. J. C. 1971. "Coastal Algonkians: People of the First Frontiers." In *North American Indians in Historical Perspective*, Eleanor Burke Leacock and Nancy Oestreich Lurie, eds. New York: Random House.

Brown, Richard. 1989. *Knowledge Is Power: The Diffusion of Information in Early America, 1700–1865*. New York: Oxford University Press.

Bushman, Richard L. 1967. *From Puritan to Yankee: Character and the Social Order in Connecticut, 1690–1765*. Cambridge MA: Harvard University Press.

Calloway, Colin. 1991. *Dawnland Encounters: Indian and Europeans in Northern New England*. Hanover NH: University Press of New England.

———. 1996. "Introduction: Surviving the Dark Ages." In *After King Philip's War: Presence and Persistence in Indian New England*, Colin Calloway, ed. Hanover NH: University Press of New England.

———. 1997. *New Worlds for All: Indians, Europeans, and the Remaking of Early America*. Baltimore: Johns Hopkins University Press.

Campbell, Gregory R. 1994. "The Politics of Counting: Critical Reflections on the Depopulation Question of Native North America." In *The Unheard Voices: American Indian Responses to the Columbian Quincentenary, 1492–1992*, Carole M. Gentry and Donald A. Grinde Jr., eds. Los Angeles: American Indian Studies Center.

Campisi, Jack. 1990. "The Emergence of the Mashantucket Pequot Tribe, 1637–1975." In *The Pequots of Southern New England: The Fall and Rise of an American Indian Nation*, Laurence Hauptman and James Wherry, eds. Norman: University of Oklahoma Press.

———. 1991. *The Mashpee Indians: Tribe on Trial*. Syracuse: Syracuse University Press.

Caulfield, Mina Davis. 1969. "Culture and Imperialism: Proposing a New Dialectic." In *Reinventing Anthropology*, Dell Hymes, ed. New York: Pantheon.

Caulkins, Frances M. 1895. *History of New London, Connecticut*. New London CT: H. D. Utley.

Cheyfitz, Eric. 1991. *The Poetics of Imperialism: Translation and Colonization from The Tempest to Tarzan*. New York: Oxford University Press.

Chomsky, Noam. 1993. *Year 501: The Conquest Continues*. Boston: South End.

Churchill, Ward. 1994. *Indians Are Us? Culture and Genocide in Native North America*. Monroe ME: Common Courage.

———. 1998. "The Crucible of American Indian Identity." *Z Magazine*, January, 47–51.

Clemmer, Richard. 1969. "Resistance and Revitalization of Anthropologists: A New Perspective on Cultural Change and Resistance." In *Reinventing Anthropology*, Dell Hymes, ed. New York: Pantheon.

Clifford, James. 1986. "Introduction: Partial Truths." In *Writing Culture: The Poetics and Politics of Ethnography*, James Clifford and George Marcus, eds. Berkeley: University of California Press.

———. 1988. "Identity in Mashpee." *The Predicament of Culture: Twentieth-Century Ethnography, Literature, and Art*. Cambridge MA: Harvard University Press.

Clinton, Robert N. 1993. "Redressing the Legacy of Conquest: A Vision Quest for a Decolonized Federal Indian Law." *Arkansas Law Review* 46(77): 77–159.

Cohn, Bernard S. 1987. *An Anthropologist among the Historians and Other Essays*. Delhi: Oxford University Press.

———. 1996. *Colonialism and Its Forms of Knowledge: The British in India*. Princeton NJ: Princeton University Press.

Colson, Elizabeth. 1986. "Political Organization in Tribal Societies." *American Indian Quarterly* 10 (Winter): 5–19.

Conkey, L., E. Boissevain, and I. Goddard. 1978. "Indians of Southern New England and Long Island: Late Period." In *Handbook of North American Indians, vol. 15: Northeast*. Washington DC: Smithsonian Institution Press.

Conroy, David W. 1994. "The Defense of Indian Land Rights: William Bollan and the Mohegan Case in 1743." In *Proceedings of the American Antiquarian Society*, vol. 103, pt. 2. Worcester MA: American Antiquarian Society.

Cooper, Frederick, and Ann L. Stoler. 1989. "Introduction. Tensions of Empire: Colonial Control and Visions of Rule." *American Ethnologist* 16(4): 609–21.

Crane, Ellery. 1904. "The Treatment of the Indians by the Colonists." *Proceedings of the Worcester Society of Antiquity* 20: 220–48.

Cronon, William. 1983. *Changes in the Land: Indians, Colonists, and the Ecology of New England*. New York: Hill and Wang.

Curtis, Edward S. 1972. *Portraits from North American Indian Life*. New York: Promontory.

DeForest, John W. 1852. *History of the Indians of Connecticut*. Hartford: Wm. Jas. Hamersley.

Deloria, Vine, Jr. 1969. *Custer Died for Your Sins*. Norman: University of Oklahoma Press.

———. 1992. "Comfortable Fictions and the Struggle for Turf: An Essay Review of *The Invented Indian: Cultural Fictions and Government Policies*." *American Indian Quarterly* 16(3): 397–410.

Den Ouden, Amy E. 1991–94. Field notes and oral history interviews. Eastern Pequot federal acknowledgment project.

———. 2000–2002. Field notes and oral history interviews. Eastern Pequot federal acknowledgment project.

———. 2002. " 'Race,' Reservations, and 'Recognition': A Cursory Genealogy of Racial Discourse on Indianness in Southern New England." Paper presented at the annual meeting of the American Anthropological Association, New Orleans, November.

*Diary of Joshua Hempstead of New London, Connecticut, 1711–1858*. 1901. Collections of the New London County Historical Society. Providence RI.

Drinnon, Richard. 1980. *Facing West: The Metaphysics of Indian Hating and Empire Building*. New York: Schocken.

Durham, Jimmie. 1992. "Cowboys and . . . Notes on Art, Literature, and American Indians in the Modern American Mind." In *The State of Native America: Genocide, Colonization and Resistance*, M. Annette Jaimes, ed. Boston: South End.

Eastern Pequot Indians of Connecticut. 1998. Petition for Federal Acknowledgment as an American Indian Tribe.

Eliot, John. 1643. *New England's First Fruits*. London: Henry Overton. American Culture Series, Smithsonian Library Collections. Ann Arbor MI: University Microfilms.

Fabian, Johannes. 1983. *Time and the Other: How Anthropology Makes Its Object*. New York: Columbia University Press.

———. 1991. *Time and the Work of Anthropology: Critical Essays 1971–1991*. Chur, Switzerland: Harwood Academic Publishers.

Fawcett, Melissa Jayne. 1995. *The Lasting of the Mohegans: The Story of the Wolf People*. Ledyard CT: Pequot.

Fawcett-Sayet, Melissa. 1988. "Sociocultural Authority in Mohegan Society." *Artifacts* 16(3–4): 28–29.

Fields, Barbara J. 1982. "Ideology and Race in American History." In *Region, Race and Reconstruction*, J. Morgan Kousser and James M. McPherson, eds. New York: Oxford University Press.

Forbes, Jack D. 1993. *Africans and Native Americans: The Language of Race and the Evolution of Red-Black Peoples*, 2nd ed. Urbana: University of Illinois Press.

Ford, Amelia Clewly. 1976. *Colonial Precedents of Our National Land System as It Existed in 1800*. Philadelphia: Porcupine.

Foucault, Michel. 1980. *History of Sexuality*, vol. 1. New York: Vintage Books.

Friedman, L. M. 1985. *A History of American Law*. New York: Simon and Schuster.

Gadacz, Rene R. 1979. "Acculturation as Paradigm in Historical Ethnology: The Montagnais Example." *Ethnohistory* 26(3): 265–75.

Gookin, Daniel. 1972 [1674]. *Historical Collections of the Indians in New England*. New York: Arno.

Gould, Stephen Jay. 1981. *The Mismeasure of Man*. New York: W. W. Norton.

*Governor and Company of Connecticut, and Moheagan Indians, by their Guardians. Certified Copy of Book of Proceedings before Commissioners of Review*, 1743, 1769. London: W. and J. Richardson. (Cited as *Proc.*)

Grant, Charles S. 1967. "Land Speculation and the Settlement of Kent, 1738-1760." In *Essays in American Colonial History*, Paul Goodman, ed. New York: Holt, Rinehart and Winston.

Green, Rayna. 1975. "The Pocahontas Perplex: The Image of Indian Women in American Culture." *Massachusetts Review* 16(4): 698–714.

Greene, Jack P. 1967. "The Role of the Lower Houses of Assembly in Eighteenth-Century Politics." In *Essays in American Colonial History*, Paul Goodman, ed. New York: Holt, Rinehart and Winston.

Grumet, Robert S. 1980. "Sunksquaws, Shamans and Tradeswomen: Middle Atlantic Coastal Algonkian Women during the 17th and 18th Centuries." In *Women and Colonization: Anthropological Perspectives*, Mona Etienne and Eleanor Leacock, eds. New York: Praeger.

———. 1995. *Historic Contact: Indian People and Colonists in Today's Northeastern United States in the Sixteenth through Eighteenth Centuries*. Norman: University of Oklahoma Press.

Hallowell, Irving. 1957. "The Backwash of the Frontier: The Impact of the Indian on American Culture." In *The Frontier in Perspective*, Walker D. Wyman and Clifton B. Kroeber, eds. Madison: University of Wisconsin Press.

Handsman, Russell G., and Trudie Lamb Richmond. 1995. "The Mahican and Schaghticoke Peoples and Us." In *Making Alternative Histories: The Practice of Archaeology and History in Non-Western Settings*, Peter R. Schmidt and Thomas C. Patterson, eds. Santa Fe: School of American Research.

Harley, J. B. 1994. "New England Cartography and the Native Americans." In *American Beginnings: Exploration, Culture, and Cartography in the Land of Nurembega*, Emerson W. Baker et al., eds. Lincoln: University of Nebraska Press.

Harris, Marshall D. 1953. *Origin of the Land Tenure System in the United States*. Ames: Iowa State College Press.

Hauptman, Laurence M. 1995. *Tribes and Tribulations: Misconceptions about American Indians and Their Histories*. Albuquerque: University of New Mexico Press.

Herndon, Ruth Wallis. and Ella Wilcox Sekatau. 1997. "The Right to a Name: The Narragansett People and Rhode Island Officials in the Revolutionary Era." *Ethnohistory* 44(3): 433–62.

Higginbotham, A. Leon, Jr., and Barbara K. Kopytoff. 1989. "Racial Purity and Interracial Sex in the Law of Colonial and Antebellum Virginia." *Georgetown Law Journal* 77: 1967–2029.

Higginson, Stephen A. 1986. "A Short History of the Right to Petition Government for the Redress of Grievances." *Yale Law Journal* 96 (142).

Hill, Jonathan D. 1996. "Introduction: Ethnogenesis in the Americas, 1492–1992." In *History, Identity, Power: Ethnogenesis in the Americas, 1492–1992*, Jonathan D. Hill, ed. Iowa City: University of Iowa Press.

Hoadly, Charles J., ed. 1932 [1643–1709]. *Hoadly Memorial: Early Letters and Documents Relating to Connecticut*. In *Collections of the Connecticut Historical Society*, vol. 24. Hartford: Connecticut Historical Society.

hooks, bell. 1992. "Revolutionary 'Renegades': Native Americans, African Americans, and Black Indians." *Black Looks: Race and Representation*. Boston: South End.

Horsman, Reginald. 1981. *Race and Manifest Destiny: The Origins of American Racial Anglo-Saxonism*. Cambridge MA: Harvard University Press.

Hulme, Peter. 1985. "Polytropic Man: Tropes of Sexuality and Mobility in Early Colonial Discourse." In *Europe and Its Others: Proceedings of the Essex Conference on the Sociology of Literature, July 1984*, 2 vols., Francis Barker, Peter Hulme, Margaret Iverson, and Diana Loxley, eds. Colchester: University of Essex.

———. 1986. *Colonial Encounters: Europe and the Native Caribbean, 1492–1797*. London: Routledge.

Hurd, John Codman. 1968 [1851]. *The Law of Freedom and Bondage in the U.S.* New York: Negro University Press.

"Indian Papers." Connecticut State Archives Collection, 1st ser. (1647–1789) and 2nd ser. (1666–1820). Early General Records of Connecticut: Papers and Correspondence of the General Assembly, the Governor and Counsel, and other Colony or State Officials. Connecticut State Archives, Hartford. (Cited as IND 1st.)

Jaimes, M. Annette. 1992. "Federal Indian Identification Policy: A Usurpation of Indigenous Sovereignty in North America." In *The State of Native America: Genocide, Colonization and Resistance*, M. Annette Jaimes, ed. Boston: South End.

———. 1994. "American Racism: The Impact on American Indian Identity and Survival." In *Race*, Steven Gregory and Roger Sanjek, eds. New Brunswick NJ: Rutgers University Press.

Jennings, Francis. 1971. "Virgin Land and Savage People." *American Quarterly* 23(4): 519–41.

———. 1975. *The Invasion of America: Indians, Colonialism and the Cant of Conquest*. New York: W. W. Norton.

Jensen, Joan. M. 1994. "Native American Women and Agriculture: A Seneca Case Study." In *Unequal Sisters: A Multicultural Reader in U.S. Women's History*, V. L. Ruiz and E. C. DuBois, eds. New York: Rutledge.

Johnson, Eric S. 1996. "Uncas and the Politics of Contact." In *Northeastern Indian Lives, 1632–1816*. Robert S. Grumet, ed. Amherst: University of Massachusetts Press.

Johnson, Robert. 1968 [1609]. *Nova Brittania*. In *English Colonization of North America*, ed. Louis B. Wright and Elaine W. Fowler. New York: St. Martin's Press.

Johnston, Alexander. 1883. "The Genesis of a New England State (Connecticut)." In *Johns Hopkins University Studies in Historical and Political Science*, vol. 2, Herbert B. Adams, ed. Baltimore: Johns Hopkins University.

Kawashima, Yasuhide. 1978. "Indian Servitude in the Northeast." In *Handbook of North American Indians*, vol. 15: *Northeast*, William C. Sturtevant, gen. ed. Washington DC: Smithsonian Institution Press.

Kellaway, William. 1975. *The New England Company, 1649–1776: Missionary Society to the American Indians*. Westport CT: Greenwood Press.

Kent, James. 1896. *Commentaries on American Law*, vol. 3. Boston: Little, Brown.

Klein, Laura F., and Lillian A. Ackerman. 1995. Introduction. In *Women and*

*Power in Native North America*, Laura F. Klein and Lillian A. Ackerman, eds. Norman: University of Oklahoma Press.

Koehler, Lyle. 1979. "Red-White Power Relations and Justice in the Courts of Seventeenth-Century New England." *American Indian Culture and Research Journal* 3(4): 1–32.

Kornfield, Eve. 1995. "Encountering 'the Other': American Intellectuals and Indians in the 1790's." *William and Mary Quarterly*, 3rd ser., 52(2): 287–314.

Lauber, Almon Wheeler. 1913. "Indian Slavery in Colonial Times within the Present Limits of the United States." In *Columbia University Studies in History, Economics and Public Law*, vol. 54(3). New York.

Leacock, Eleanor. 1983. "Ethnohistorical Investigation of Egalitarian Politics in Eastern North America." In *The Development of Political Organization in Native North America*, Elisabeth Tooker, ed. Washington DC: American Ethnological Society.

Learned, Maj. Bela Peck. 1902. "The Distribution of the Pequot Lands." *Papers and Addresses of the Society of Colonial Wars in the State of Connecticut*, vol. 1: 51–60.

Lee, Sharon M. 1993. "Racial Classifications in the U.S. Census: 1890–1990." *Ethnic and Racial Studies* 16(1): 75–94.

Liggio, L. P. 1976. "English Origins of Early American Racism." *Radical History Review* 3: 1–36.

Lloyd, Peter. 1975. "The Emergence of Racial Prejudice towards the Indians in Seventeenth-Century New England: Some Notes on an Explanation." Ph.D. dissertation, Ohio State University.

Love, W. DeLoss. 1899. *Samson Occom and The Christian Indians of New England*. Boston: Pilgrim.

Lovell, W. George. 1988. "Surviving Conquest: The Maya of Guatemala in Historical Perspective." *Latin American Research Review* 23(2): 25–57.

MacPherson, C. B. 1978. *Property: Mainstream and Critical Positions*. Toronto: University of Toronto Press.

Magubane, Bernard. 1971. "A Critical Look at Indices Used in the Study of Social Change in Colonial Africa." *Current Anthropology* 12(4–5): 419–45.

Magubane, Bernard, and James C. Faris. 1985. "On the Political Relevance of Anthropology." *Dialectical Anthropology* 9(1): 91–104.

Martin, Calvin. 1974. "The European Impact on the Culture of a Northeastern Algonkian Tribe: An Ecological Interpretation." *William and Mary Quarterly*, 3rd ser., 31(1): 3–26.

Martin, John Frederick. 1991. *Profits in the Wilderness: Entrepreneurship and the Founding of New England Towns in the Seventeenth Century*. Chapel Hill: University of North Carolina Press.

Mather, Cotton. 1912 [1711]. "Diary of Cotton Mather." *Massachusetts Historical Society Collections*, 7th ser., vol. 7. Boston: Massachusetts Historical Society.

Mayhew, Experience. 1896 [1713–1714]. "Journals of the Rev. Experience Mayhew." In *Some Correspondence Between the Governors and Treasurers of the New England Company in London and the Commissioners of the United Colonies in America (1657–1712)*. London: Spottiswoode.

McBride, Kevin. 1990. "The Historical Archaeology of the Mashantucket Pequots." In *The Pequots of Southern New England*, Laurence Hauptman and James Wherry, eds. Norman: University of Oklahoma Press.

———. 1993. " 'Ancient and Crazie': Pequot Lifeways during the Historic Period." In *Algonkians of New England: Past and Present*, Peter Benes, ed. Annual Proceedings of the Dublin Seminar. Boston: Boston University Press.

———. 1996. "The Legacy of Robin Cassacinamon: Mashantucket Pequot Leadership in the Historic Period." In *Northeastern Indian Lives*, Robert S. Grumet, ed. Amherst: University of Massachusetts Press.

McClintock, Anne. 1995. *Imperial Leather: Race, Gender and Sexuality in the Colonial Contest*. New York: Routledge.

McCusker, John J., and Russell R. Menard. 1985. *The Economy of British America, 1607–1789*. Chapel Hill: University of North Carolina Press.

Merchant, Carolyn. 1989. *Ecological Revolutions: Nature, Gender, and Science in New England*. Chapel Hill: University of North Carolina Press.

Mershon, S. L. 1918. "The Indian and Crown Grants." *English Crown Grants*. New York: Law and History Club.

Miles, Lion. 1994. "The Red Man Dispossessed: The Williams Family and the Alienation of Indian Land in Stockbridge, Massachusetts, 1736–1818." *New England Quarterly* 67(1): 46–76.

Montrose, Louis. 1991. "The Work of Gender in the Discourse of Discovery." *Representations* 33 (Winter): 1–41.

Mohegan Tribe. 1984. Petition for Federal Recognition, vol. 1.

Morgan, Edmund S. 1975. *American Slavery, American Freedom: The Ordeal of Colonial Virginia*. New York: W. W. Norton.

Morgan, Forrest, ed. 1904. *Connecticut as a Colony and as a State; or, One of the Original Thirteen*, vol. 1. Hartford: Publishing Society of Connecticut.

Morison, Samuel Eliot. 1958. Introduction to *Flintlock and Tomahawk* by Douglas Edward Leach. Hyannis MA: Parnassus.

Morris, R. B. 1974. *Studies in the History of American Law*. New York: Octagon Books.

Nabokov, Peter, and Dean Snow. 1992. "Farmers of the Woodlands." In *America in 1492: The World of the Indian Peoples before the Arrival of Columbus*, Alvin M. Josephy ed. New York: Alfred A. Knopf.

"Narragansett Tribe's Smokeshop Closed." 2003. *Pequot Times*, August.

Nash, Gary. 1992. *Red, White and Black: The Peoples of Early North America*. Englewood Cliffs NJ: Prentice Hall.

Neal, Daniel. 1720. *The History of New England, Containing an Impartial Account of the Civil and Ecclesiastical Affairs of the Country to the Year of Our Lord, 1700*. London: J. Clark. American Culture Series, Smithsonian Library Collections. Reprint, Ann Arbor MI: University Microfilms.

Neuwirth, Steven Douglas. 1982. "The Imagined Savage: The American Indian and the New England Mind, 1620–1675." Ph.D. dissertation. Reprint, Ann Arbor MI: University Microfilms International.

O'Brien, Jean M. 1997. " 'Divorced' from the Land: Resistance and Survival of Indian Women in Eighteenth-Century New England." In *After King Philip's War: Presence and Persistence in Indian New England*, Colin G. Calloway, ed. Hanover NH: University Press of New England.

O'Connell, Barry. 1991. "William Apess and the Survival of the Pequot People." In *Algonkians of New England: Past and Present*, Proceedings of the Dublin Seminar for New England Folk Life. Boston: Boston University Press.

———. 1992. "Introduction." In *On Our Own Ground: The Complete Writings of William Apess, a Pequot*, Barry O'Connell, ed. Amherst: University of Massachusetts Press.

Orcutt, Samuel. 1882. *The Indians of the Housatonic and Naugatuck Valleys*. Hartford CT: Case, Lockwood and Brainard.

Ortiz, Alfonso. 1977. "Some Concerns Central to the Writing of 'Indian' History." *Indian Historian* 10 (Winter): 17–22.

———. 1994. "The Dynamics of Pueblo Cultural Survival." In *North American Indian Anthropology*, Raymond DeMallie and Alfonso Ortiz, eds. Norman: University of Oklahoma Press.

Pagden, Anthony. 1993. "The Autoptic Imagination." In *European Encounters with the New World*. New Haven CT: Yale University Press.

Patterson, Thomas C. 1997. *Inventing Western Civilization*. New York: Monthly Review.

Pearce, Roy Harvey. 1952. "The 'Ruines of Mankind': The Indian and the Puritan Mind." *Journal of the History of Ideas* 13: 200–17.

———. 1957. "The Metaphysics of Indian-Hating." *Ethnohistory* 4(1): 27–40.

———. 1988. *Savagism and Civilization: A Study of the Indian and the American Mind*. Berkeley: University of California Press.

Perry, Richard J. 1993. *Apache Reservation: Indigenous Peoples and the American State*. Austin: University of Texas Press.

Plane, Anne Marie. 1996. "Putting a Face on Colonization: Factionalism and Gender Politics in the Life History of Awashunkes, the 'Squaw Sachem' of Saconet." In *Northeastern Indian Lives, 1632–1816*, Robert S. Grumet, ed. Amherst: University of Massachusetts Press.

Prakash, Gyan. 1992. "Can the Subaltern Ride? A Reply to O'Hanlon and Washbrook." *Comparative Studies in Society and History* 34(2): 168–84.

Price, Edward T. 1995. *Dividing the Land: Early American Beginnings of Our Private Property Mosaic*. Chicago: University of Chicago Press.

*Public Records of the Colony of Connecticut*. 1850–1890 [1636–1776]. 15 vols. J. H. Trumbull, ed., vols. 1–3; C. J. Hoadley, ed., vols. 4–15. Hartford: Press of Case, Lockwood & Brainard. (Cited as CR)

Richmond, Trudie Lamb. 1988. "Native Women as Leaders in Algonkian Society." *Artifacts* 16(3–4): 7–10.

———. 1989. "'Put Your Ear to the Ground and Listen': The Wigwam Festival Is the Green Corn Ceremony." *Artifacts* 17(4): 24–27.

———. 1991. "Out of the Earth I Sing: The Story of Corn." *Artifacts* 19(2): 12–13.

Richmond, Trudie Lamb, and Amy E. Den Ouden. 2003. "Recovering Gendered Political Histories: Local Struggles and Native Women's Resistance in Colonial Southern New England." In *Reinterpreting New England Indians and the Colonial Experience*, Colin G. Calloway and Neal Salisbury, eds. Boston: Colonial Society of Massachusetts.

Richter, Daniel K. 1983. "War and Culture: The Iroquois Experience." *William and Mary Quarterly*, 3rd ser., 40: 528–59.

Riley, F. L. 1896. "Colonial Origins of New England Senates." In *Johns Hopkins University Studies in Historical and Political Science*, 14th ser., vol. 3, Herbert B. Adams, ed. Baltimore: Johns Hopkins University Press.

Roseberry, William. 1982. "Balinese Cockfights and the Seduction of Anthropology." *Social Research* 49(4): 1013–27.

Rubertone, Patricia E. 2001. *Grave Undertakings: An Archaeology of Roger Williams and the Narragansett Indians*. Washington DC: Smithsonian Institution Press.

Said, Edward. 1979. *Orientalism*. New York: Random House.

———. 1989. "Representing the Colonized: Anthropology's Interlocutors." *Critical Inquiry* 15(2): 205–25.

———. 1993. *Culture and Imperialism*. New York: Vintage Books.

Salisbury, Neal. 1972. "Conquest of the 'Savage': Puritans, Puritan Missions, and Indians, 1620–1680." Ph.D. dissertation, University of California, Los Angeles.

———. 1982. *Manitou and Providence: Indians, Europeans and the Making of New England, 1500–1643*. New York: Oxford University Press.

———. 1985. "The Colonizing of Indian New England." *Massachusetts Review* 26 (Summer/Fall): 447–60.

Salmon, Marylynn. 1986. *Women and the Law of Property in Early America*. Chapel Hill: University of North Carolina Press.

Sanford, Victoria. 2003. *Buried Secrets: Truth and Human Rights in Guatemala*. New York: Palgrave Macmillan.

Schmidt, Peter R., and Thomas C. Patterson. 1995. "Introduction: From Constructing to Making Alternative Histories." In *Making Alternative Histories: The Practice of Archaeology and History in Non-Western Settings*, Peter R. Schmidt and Thomas C. Patterson, eds. Santa Fe NM: School of American Research Press.

Scott, James C. 1990. *Domination and the Arts of Resistance: Hidden Transcripts*. New Haven CT: Yale University Press.

Seed, Patricia. 1995. *Ceremonies of Possession in Europe's Conquest of the New World, 1492–1640*. Cambridge: Cambridge University Press.

Selesky, Harold. 1990. *War and Society in Colonial Connecticut*. New Haven CT: Yale University Press.

Sewall, Samuel. 1973. *The Diary of Samuel Sewall, 1674–1729*, vol. 2. M. Halsey Thomas, ed. New York: Farrar, Straus and Giroux.

Sider, Gerald. 1987. "When Parrots Learn to Talk, and Why They Can't: Domination, Deception, and Self-Deception in Indian-White Relations." *Comparative Studies in Society and History* 29(1): 3–23.

———. 1993. *Lumbee Indian Histories: Race, Ethnicity, and Indian Identity in the Southeastern United States*. Cambridge: Cambridge University Press.

———. 1994. "Identity as History: Ethnohistory, Ethnogenesis and Ethnocide in the Southeastern United States." *Identities: Global Studies in Culture and Power* 1(1): 109–22.

Silverblatt, Irene. 1987. *Moon, Sun and Witches: Gender Ideologies and Class in Inca and Colonial Peru.* Princeton NJ: Princeton University Press.

———. 1995. "Becoming Indian in the Central Andes of Seventeenth-Century Peru." In *After Colonialism: Imperial Histories and Postcolonial Displacements*, Gyan Prakash, ed. Princeton NJ: Princeton University Press.

Smith, Joseph Henry. 1950. *Appeals to the Privy Council form the American Plantations.* New York: Columbia University Press.

Smits, David D. 1982. "The Squaw Drudge: A Prime Index of Savagism." *Ethnohistory* 29(2): 281–306.

Snyderman, George S. 1951. "Concepts of Land Ownership among the Iroquois and Their Neighbors." Symposium on Local Diversity in Iroquois Culture. *Bulletin of the Bureau of American Ethnology* 149: 15–34.

Speck, Frank. 1928. "Native Tribes and Dialects of Connecticut: A Mohegan-Pequot Diary." *Annual Report of the Bureau of American Ethnology*, no. 43.

Spicer, Edward H. 1992. "The Nations of a State." *Boundary 2* 19(3): 26–48.

Spiess, Mathias. 1933. *The Indians of Connecticut.* Tercentenary Commission of the State of Connecticut. Committee of Historical Publications. Pamphlet no. 19. New Haven CT: Yale University Press.

Spurr, David. 1993. *The Rhetoric of Empire: Colonial Discourse in Journalism, Travel Writing, and Imperial Administration.* Durham NC: Duke University Press.

Starna, William A. 1989. "Aboriginal Title and Traditional Iroquois Land Use: An Anthropological Perspective." In *Iroquois Land Claims*, Christopher Vecsey and William A. Starna, eds. Syracuse: Syracuse University Press.

Steiner, Bernard C. 1893. "The History of Slavery in Connecticut." *Johns Hopkins University Studies in Historical and Political Science*, 11th ser., Herbert B. Adams, ed. Baltimore: Johns Hopkins University Press.

Stephanson, Anders. 1995. *Manifest Destiny: American Expansion and the Empire of Right.* New York: Hill and Wang.

Stiles, Ezra. 1901. *The Literary Diary of Ezra Stiles (1769–1776).* New York: Charles Scribner's Sons.

———. 1916. *Extracts from Itineraries and Other Miscellanies of Ezra Stiles, 1755–794.* F. B. Dexter, ed. New Haven CT: Yale University Press.

Stock, Leo Francis, ed. 1930. *Proceedings and Debates of the British Parliaments*

*Respecting North America*, vol. 3 (1702–1727). Washington DC: Carnegie Institution.

Stoddard, Solomon. [1723]. *Question: Whether GOD Is Not Angry with the Country for Doing So Little Towards the Conversion of the Indians?* Boston: B. Green. American Culture Series, Smithsonian Library Collections. Ann Arbor MI: University Microfilms.

Stolcke, Verena. 1991. "Conquered Women." NACLA *Report on the Americas: Reinventing America 1492–1992* 24(5): 23–28.

Stoler, Ann Laura. 1989. "Rethinking Colonial Categories: European Communities and the Boundaries of Rule." *Comparative Studies in Society and History* 31(1): 134–61.

———. 1991. "Carnal Knowledge and Imperial Power: Gender, Race and Morality in Colonial Asia." In *Gender at the Crossroads of Knowledge: Feminist Anthropology in the Postmodern Era*, Micaela di Leonardo, ed. Berkeley: University of California Press.

———. 2002. *Carnal Knowledge and Imperial Power: Race and the Intimate in Colonial Rule*. Berkeley, University of California Press.

Strong, John. 1985. "Tribal Systems and Land Alienation: A Case Study." *Papers of the Sixteenth Algonquian Conference*. William Cowen, ed. Ottawa: Carleton University Press.

Strong, Pauline Turner, and Barrik Van Winkle. 1996. " 'Indian Blood': Reflections on the Reckoning and Refiguring of Native North American Identity." *Cultural Anthropology* 11(4): 547–76.

Sylvester, Herbert Milton. 1910. *Indian Wars of New England*, vol. 1. Boston: W. B. Clark.

Talcott, Joseph. 1892–1896. *The Talcott Papers: Correspondence and Documents during Joseph Talcott's Governorship, 1724–1741*. Vol. 1 (1724–1736); vol. 2 (1737–1741). Collections of the Connecticut Historical Society, vols. 4 and 5. Hartford: Connecticut Historical Society. (Cited as TP)

Thomas, G. E. 1975. "Puritans, Indians and the Concept of Race." *New England Quarterly* 47(1): 3–27.

Trouillot, Michel-Rolph. 1995. *Silencing the Past: Power and the Production of History*. Boston: Beacon.

Trumbull, J. Hammond. 1881. *Indian Names of Places etc., in and on the Borders of Connecticut*. Hartford CT: Brown & Gross.

Van Lonkhuyzen, Harold W. 1990. "A Reappraisal of the Praying Indians: Acculturation, Conversion, and Identity at Natick, Massachusetts, 1646–1730." *New England Quarterly* 63: 396–428.

Walters, Mark D. 1995. "*Mohegan Indians v. Connecticut* (1705–1773) and the Legal Status of Aboriginal Customary Laws and Government in British North America." *Osgoode Hall Law Journal* 33(4): 785–829.

Warner, Robert Austin. 1935. "The Southern New England Indians to 1725: A Study in Culture Contact." Ph.D. dissertation, Yale University. Reprint, Ann Arbor: University Microfilms, 1970.

Waswo, Richard. 1996. "The Formation of Natural Law to Justify Colonialism." *New Literary History* 27: 743–59.

Weeden, William B. 1884. "Indian Money as a Factor in New England Civilization." In *Johns Hopkins University Studies in Historical and Political Science*, Herbert B. Adams, ed. Baltimore: Johns Hopkins University Press.

———. 1963 [1890]. *Economic and Social History of New England, 1620- 1789*, vol. 1. New York: Hillary House.

Weinstein, Laurie Lee. 1983. "Indian vs. Colonist: Competition for Land in 17th Century Plymouth Colony." Ph.D. dissertation, Southern Methodist University.

Weinstein-Farson, Laurie. 1989. "Land, Politics and Power: The Mohegan Indians in the 17th and 18th Centuries." Paper presented at the Annual Meeting of the American Society for Ethnohistory, Chicago.

Weld, Ralph Foster. 1933. "Slavery in Connecticut." Tercentenary Commission of the State of Connecticut, Committee on Historical Publications. New Haven CT: Yale University Press.

Wheeler, Richard A. 1887. "The Pequot Indians. An Historical Sketch." Westerly: G. B. and J. H. Utter.

Wheelock, Eleazar. 1763. *A Plain and Faithful Narrative of the Original Design, Rise, Progress and Present State of the Indian Charity-School at Lebanon, in Connecticut*. Boston: Richard and Samuel Draper, American Culture Series; reprint, Ann Arbor MI: University Microfilms.

Williams, Robert A. 1990. *The American Indian in Western Legal Thought: The Discourses of Conquest*. New York: Oxford University Press.

Williams, Roger. 1819 [1643]. "A Key into the Language of America." In *Collections of the Massachusetts Historical Society*, vol. 3. Boston: Massachusetts Historical Society.

———. 1988. *The Correspondence of Roger Williams*. Glenn LaFantasie, ed. 2 vols. Hanover NH: University Press of New England.

Winant, Howard. 2001. *The World Is a Ghetto: Race and Democracy since World War II*. New York: Basic.

Wojciechowski, Franz L. 1985. *The Paugussett Tribes: An Ethnohistorical Study of the Tribal Interrelationships of the Indians in the Lower Housatonic River Area.* Nijmegen, Netherlands: Catholic University of Nijmegen.

Wolcott, Roger. 1895 [1759]. "A Memoir for the History of Connecticut." In *Collections of the Connecticut Historical Society*, vol. 3. Hartford.

Wolf, Eric. 1982. *Europe and the People without History.* Berkeley: University of California Press.

Wright, Louis B. 1963. *The Atlantic Frontier: Colonial American Civilization, 1607–1763.* Ithaca NY: Great Seal Books.

Wright, Louis B., and Elaine W. Fowler. 1968. *English Colonization of North America.* New York: St. Martin's Press.

*Wyllys Papers: Correspondence and Documents Chiefly of the Descendants of Governor George Wyllys, 1590–1796.* 1924. Hartford: Connecticut Historical Society.

Young, Robert. 1995. *Colonial Desire: Hybridity in Theory, Culture and Race.* London: Routledge.

# Index

*Fourth World Rising series*

**Beyond Conquest**
*Native Peoples and the Struggle for History in New England*
Amy E. Den Ouden

**Against Culture**
*Development, Politics, and Religion in Indian Alaska*
Kirk Dombrowski

**Alejandro Tsakimp**
*The Many Lives of a Shuar Healer*
Steven Rubenstein

**The Problem of Justice**
*Tradition and Law in the Coast Salish World*
Bruce G. Miller

**Grave Injustice**
*The American Indian Repatriation Movement and* NAGPRA
Kathleen S. Fine-Dare

CPSIA information can be obtained at www.ICGtesting.com
Printed in the USA
BVOW04s0431200614

356880BV00015B/66/P